The Global Citizenship Nexus

In the spirit of Ivan Illich's 1968 speech 'To hell with good intentions', the book takes aim at a ubiquitous form of contemporary ideology, namely the concept of global citizenship.

Its characteristic discourse can be found inhabiting a nexus of four complexes of 'ruling' institutions, namely universities with their international service learning, the United Nations and allied international institutions bent on global citizenship education, international non-governmental organizations and foundations promoting social entrepreneurship, and global corporations and their mouthpieces pitching corporate social responsibility and sustainable development. The question is: in the context of Northern or Western imperialism and US-led, neoliberal, global, corporate capitalism, and the planetary Armageddon they are wringing, what is the concept of global citizenship doing for these institutions? The studies in the book put this question to each of these four institutional complexes from broadly political-economic and post-colonial premises, focusing on the concept's discursive use, against the background of the mounting production of the global *non-citizen* as the global citizen's 'other'.

Addressed to all users of the concept of global citizen(ship) from university students and faculty in global studies to social entrepreneurs and United Nations bureaucrats, the book's studies ultimately ask whether the idea helps or hinders the global quest for social and economic justice.

Debra D. Chapman is a professor teaching in Global Studies, Political Science and North American Studies at Wilfrid Laurier University. She has authored *The struggle for Mexico: state corporatism and popular opposition* (2012).

Tania Ruiz-Chapman is a PhD candidate in Social Justice Education at the Ontario Institute for Studies in Education of the University of Toronto.

Peter Eglin is Emeritus Professor of Sociology, Wilfrid Laurier University. His publications include *The Montreal massacre: a story of membership categorization analysis* (2003) and *A sociology of crime* (2nd edn, 2017), both with Stephen Hester.

Routledge Advances in Sociology

275 Impoverishment and Asylum
Social Policy as Slow Violence
Lucy Mayblin

276 Later Life
Exploring Aging through Literature
Barbara A. Misztal

277 On the Genealogy of Critique
Or How We Have Become Decadently Indignant
Diana Stypinska

278 Nostalgia Now
Cross-Disciplinary Perspectives on the Past in the Present
Edited by Michael Hviid Jacobsen

279 Magical Realist Sociologies of Belonging and Becoming
The Explorer
Rodanthi Tzanelli

280 Queer Campus Climate
An Ethnographic Fantasia
Benjamin Arnberg

281 Children in Social Movements
Rethinking Agency, Mobilization and Rights
Diane M. Rodgers

282 The Global Citizenship Nexus
Critical Studies
Edited by Debra D. Chapman, Tania Ruiz-Chapman and Peter Eglin

For more information about this series, please visit: www.routledge.com/Routledge-Advances-in-Sociology/book-series/SE0511

The Global Citizenship Nexus

Critical Studies

Edited by Debra D. Chapman,
Tania Ruiz-Chapman
and Peter Eglin

LONDON AND NEW YORK

First published 2020 by Routledge

2 Park Square, Milton Park, Abingdon, Oxon OX14 4RN

605 Third Avenue, New York, NY 10017

Routledge is an imprint of the Taylor & Francis Group, an informa business

First issued in paperback 2021

Copyright © 2020 selection and editorial matter, Debra D. Chapman, Tania Ruiz-Chapman and Peter Eglin; individual chapters, the contributors

The right of Debra D. Chapman, Tania Ruiz-Chapman and Peter Eglin to be identified as the authors of the editorial material, and of the authors for their individual chapters, has been asserted in accordance with sections 77 and 78 of the Copyright, Designs and Patents Act 1988.

All rights reserved. No part of this book may be reprinted or reproduced or utilized in any form or by any electronic, mechanical, or other means, now known or hereafter invented, including photocopying and recording, or in any information storage or retrieval system, without permission in writing from the publishers.

Notice:
Product or corporate names may be trademarks or registered trademarks, and are used only for identification and explanation without intent to infringe.

Publisher's Note

The publisher has gone to great lengths to ensure the quality of this reprint but points out that some imperfections in the original copies may be apparent.

British Library Cataloguing-in-Publication Data
A catalogue record for this book is available from the British Library

Library of Congress Cataloging-in-Publication Data
A catalog record for this book has been requested

ISBN: 978-0-367-33581-6 (hbk)
ISBN: 978-1-03-217267-5 (pbk)
DOI: 10.4324/9780429320668

Typeset in Times New Roman
by Wearset Ltd, Boldon, Tyne and Wear

For Leo, beloved grandson and nephew,
to help you keep your feet on the ground
in the coming whirlwind.

Contents

List of figures   x
Notes on contributors   xi
Acknowledgements   xv

PART I
Stance and origin   1

1 Introduction   3
　PETER EGLIN

2 Global citizenship education and the making
　of America's neoliberal empire   22
　TALYA ZEMACH-BERSIN

PART II
Borders and global non-citizenship   43

3 The Cartesian subject as global citizen, the
　migrant as non-human: humanity, subjectivity
　and citizenship at the US–Mexican border   45
　TANIA RUIZ-CHAPMAN

4 Global capitalism, immanent borders,
　and corporeal citizenship   63
　CHARLES T. LEE

PART III
Global citizenship and the universities   81

5   Global citizenship in the neoliberal Canadian university   83
DEBRA D. CHAPMAN

6   Global citizenship education and its discontents, from the global North to the global South   105
POLINA GOLOVÁTINA-MORA, SUSAN HARPER, JESSICA SMARTT GULLION, ATHINA KARATZOGIANNI AND TRACY SIMMONS

PART IV
Global citizenship and the international institutions   127

7   Global citizenship and neo-republicanism? Problematising the 'neoliberal subjectivities' critique   129
APRIL BICCUM

8   International policy influencers and their agendas on global citizenship: a critical analysis of OECD and UNESCO discourses   153
FRANCISCA COSTA AND PEDRO PONTE E SOUSA

PART V
Global citizenship and the benevolent actors   173

9   Benevolence, global citizenship, and post-racial politics   175
DAVID JEFFERESS

10   The social entrepreneur as global citizen: a critical appraisal of a theory of social change   194
JOHN ABRAHAM

PART VI
Global citizenship and the multi/trans-national corporations   209

11   Constructing 'progressive neoliberal' citizens: the political economy of corporate global imaginaries   211
KEVIN FUNK

12   The empire of 'global civil society': corporations, NGOs, and international development   241
KYLE BAILEY

Index   260

Figures

11.1	Emirates tagline 1	211
11.2	Emirates tagline 2	212
11.3	Emirates tagline 3	213
11.4	Emirates tagline 4	214
11.5	Emirates, the airline of the 'global ruling class'	220
11.6	Children skateboarding in Emirates ad	221
11.7	HSBC on 'emerging markets'	224
11.8	HSBC's lemonade stand	225
11.9	HSBC's UK 'Global Citizen' print ad	227
11.10	Itaú 'global Latin American' ad 1	229
11.11	Itaú 'global Latin American' ad 2	230
11.12	Itaú 'world powers' ad	232

Contributors

John Abraham is a Continuing Lecturer in the International Development programme at St. Paul's University College and the School of Environment, Enterprise and Development (SEED) at the University of Waterloo.

Kyle Bailey is a PhD candidate in the Department of Politics at York University in Toronto. He holds a Bachelor's degree from the University of Essex and Master's degrees from the Universities of Essex and Helsinki. His research interests include comparative and international political economy, critical international relations theory, international historical sociology, materialist state theory, and the study of labour and social movements.

April Biccum is Senior Lecturer in Postcolonial International Relations at Australian National University. Her research focuses on global governance and education, political communication and political mobilization in the study of Empire and Global Citizenship, looking specifically at the conceptualization and theorization of empire and imperialism and the politics of knowledge embedded in Global Citizenship Education. She is author of *Global citizenship and the legacy of empire: marketing development* (Routledge, 2013).

Debra D. Chapman, PhD, teaches Global Studies, Political Science and North American Studies at Wilfrid Laurier University. She is the author of *The struggle for Mexico: state corporatism and popular opposition* (McFarland, 2012), 'The ethics of International Service Learning as a pedagogical development practice' in *Third World Quarterly* (2016), and other articles and chapters on non-governmental organizations and Mexican politics, plus a 2014 article on voting in municipal elections (with Peter Eglin). With Tania Ruiz-Chapman and Peter Eglin she is co-author of 'Global citizenship as neoliberal propaganda' (*Alternate Routes*, 2018). She currently serves as Councillor for Ward 9 in the City of Kitchener, Ontario.

Francisca Costa holds an MA in History, International Relations and Cooperation, and a BA in Education Sciences, both at the University of Porto. She currently studies Psychology at the Faculty of Psychology and Education Sciences of the University of Porto, and is a researcher.

Peter Eglin is Emeritus Professor of Sociology, Wilfrid Laurier University, located on the Haldimand Tract and on the traditional territory of the Attawandaron, Anishnawbe and Haudenosaunee peoples. His publications include *The Montreal massacre: a story of membership categorization analysis* (Wilfrid Laurier University Press, 2003) and *A sociology of crime* (Routledge, 2nd edn, 2017), both with Stephen Hester, *Intellectual citizenship and the problem of incarnation* (University Press of America, 2013), 'Language, culture and interaction' in the *Routledge handbook of language and culture* (Routledge, 2015) and 'Ethnomethodology and conversation analysis' in *Handbook of sociology and human rights* (Paradigm, 2013).

Kevin Funk is Assistant Professor of Political Science at the University of the District of Columbia. He specializes in global political economy, the politics of Latin America and the Southern Cone, and qualitative and interpretive methods. His current research analyses the socio-spatial changes generated by neoliberal urban mega-projects in Rio de Janeiro, Santiago de Chile and beyond. His writing has appeared in such venues as *Journal of Cultural Economy*, *International Studies Perspectives*, *New Political Science*, and *PS: Political Science & Politics*. He received his PhD in 2016 from the Department of Political Science and the Center for Latin American Studies at the University of Florida.

Polina Golovátina-Mora, PhD, is Professor at the Social Communication-Journalism Department of Universidad Pontificia Bolivariana, Medellin, Colombia. She teaches courses in research methodology and introduction to critical discourse analysis. She is the author of a number of peer-reviewed journal articles and book chapters on monstrous theory, inner emigration, social activism, art theory and critical reading of the urban space. She favours transdisciplinary and art-based research.

Jessica Smartt Gullion, PhD, is Associate Dean of Research for the College of Arts and Sciences and Associate Professor of Sociology at Texas Woman's University. She has published more than 30 peer-reviewed journal articles and book chapters. Her most recent books include *Diffractive ethnography: social sciences and the ontological turn* (Routledge, 2018); *Writing ethnography* (Sense, 2016); and the forthcoming *Researching with: a decolonizing approach to community-based action research* (Sense).

Susan Harper, PhD, is a US-based feminist writer, educator, activist and advocate. She is engaged in a number of broad community-based, public and academic projects. She speaks widely about topics such as LGBTQ rights and representation; creating LGBTQ-competent care in sexual violence advocacy, response and prevention; employment issues and LGBTQ workers; religious diversity in the United States; and women's empowerment. She currently serves as Student Services Associate in Student Affairs at the University of North Texas at Dallas, where she oversees multicultural programming and student activities.

David Jefferess is an Associate Professor of Cultural Studies and English at UBC Okanagan, located in the traditional and unceded territories of the syilx/Okanagan peoples. His publications include *Postcolonial resistance: culture, liberation, and transformation* (University of Toronto Press, 2008), *Globalizing Afghanistan: terrorism, war, and the rhetoric of nation-building* (Duke University Press, 2011; co-edited) and numerous articles/chapters on humanitarian discourse and global citizenship. He also edited a special issue of the journal *Critical Race and Whiteness Studies*, 'The white man's burden "after race"' (March 2015).

Charles T. Lee is Associate Professor of Justice and Social Inquiry in the School of Social Transformation at Arizona State University. Working at the intersections of political theory, cultural theory and critical citizenship studies, his research is broadly concerned with the questions of abjection, agency and resistance in the global circuits of neoliberal capitalism. He is the author of *Ingenious citizenship: recrafting democracy for social change* (Duke University Press, 2016).

Athina Karatzogianni, PhD is Associate Professor in Media and Communication at the University of Leicester, UK. She has an extensive record of publications and citations in disciplinary, field-specific and cross-disciplinary research outlets, and has demonstrated sustained success in securing research income from Research Councils UK and the European Commission. Her most recent book is *Platform economics: rhetoric and reality in the "sharing economy"* (Emerald Publishing, 2019).

Pedro Ponte e Sousa is currently a PhD candidate in Global Studies in the Department of Political Studies, Faculty of Social Sciences and Humanities, New University of Lisbon (FCSH-UNL). He is a researcher at the Portuguese Institute of International Relations (IPRI).

Tania Ruiz-Chapman is currently a PhD candidate in Social Justice Education at the Ontario Institute for Studies in Education of the University of Toronto. In 2017 she received a Merit Award Certificate as one of six finalists of the International Sociological Association Seventh Worldwide Competition for Junior Sociologists engaged in social research. With Debra Chapman and Peter Eglin she is co-author of 'Global citizenship as neoliberal propaganda' (*Alternate Routes*, 2018).

Tracy Simmons, PhD, is Lecturer in the School of Media Communication and Sociology at the University of Leicester. Her research interests include the field of sexualities, specifically focused on sexual citizenship and immigration, theoretical work on queer and feminist perspectives, uses of digital resources by international students during their postgraduate studies in the UK with a particular focus on digital literacy, and critical reading skills among the second language students.

Talya Zemach-Bersin received her PhD in American Studies from Yale University, where she is currently an instructor in the interdisciplinary Education Studies Program. Over the past decade, she has published numerous articles and book chapters on the politics of study abroad and works with institutions of higher education to improve their approach to international education. Her first book, *Education and the making of American globalism: 1898–1950*, is forthcoming from Harvard University Press and explores the historical relationship between international education and US foreign relations.

Acknowledgements

The editors wish to acknowledge with thanks the following: Dr Carlo Fanelli, editor of *Alternate Routes: A Journal of Critical Social Research*, for permission to adapt or otherwise use in Chapters 1, 3 and 5 of this volume passages from Debra D. Chapman, Tania Ruiz-Chapman and Peter Eglin (2018), 'Global citizenship as neoliberal propaganda: a political-economic and postcolonial critique', *Alternate Routes*, vol. 29, pp. 142–66; Martin Llewellyn, Editorial Co-ordinator, Journals at University of Toronto Press, for permission to publish as Chapter 9 in this volume a revised version of David Jefferess (2011), 'Benevolence, global citizenship and post-racial politics', *Topia: Canadian Journal of Cultural Studies*, vol. 25, pp. 77–95; Taylor & Francis Ltd, for permission to publish as Chapter 11 in this volume a revised version of Kevin Funk (2018), 'Between freedom and futility: on the political uses of corporate globalizing discourses', *Journal of Cultural Economy*, vol. 11, no. 6, pp. 565–90, DOI: 10.1080/17530350.2018.1477687, www.tandfonline.com; Bob Anderson for helpful editorial guidance; the anonymous reviewers of the book proposal; at Routledge, Gerhard Boomgarden and Emily Briggs for their faith in the project, and Lakshita Joshi for her thorough assistance; at Wearset, Claire Toal and her team, notably Sally Quinn for rigorous copyediting.

Part I

Stance and origin

Chapter 1

Introduction[1]

Peter Eglin

Why this book?

The motivation critically to examine contemporary uses of the concept of global citizenship arose from Chapman's teaching experience of the jarring disconnect between the life circumstances of students from the global North, setting out as would-be global citizens, over six weeks or so, to serve and learn from (a village of) people in the global South, and the life circumstance of such people for whom the possibility of global citizenship was, and is, an idle dream or cruel joke (Chapman 2016). Like much enquiry in the social studies the urge to enquire further derived, then, less from a disinterested inquisitiveness about a puzzling topic and far more from a sense of pedagogical, political and moral/ethical disquiet, if not outrage, that she should be engaging in this 'postcolonial sentimentalism' (see Golovátina-Mora et al., this volume, Chapter 6; Krabill 2012; see also Illich 2012 [1968]) with its 'euphoric aspirations' (Lee, this volume, Chapter 4). An attitude towards the topic was formed, then, early on. It has not been dispelled by further enquiry into it (see Chapman, this volume, Chapter 5). Rather, as Ruiz-Chapman and Eglin were brought into the project and its scope broadened beyond global studies departments in universities, it became evident both how widespread the use of the concept of global citizenship is across a range of ruling institutions, and how embedded it is in these institutions. We quickly collected readily available data such as the following:

> Global Citizenship: [Our] mission is: to responsibly provide financial services that enable growth and progress ... global institutions like ours are uniquely positioned to help society address global problems on a global scale.
> (Michael Corbat, CEO, Citigroup n.d.)

> It takes a global outlook and a global approach to solve problems. In a word, it takes global citizenship – citizenship that acknowledges that each and every one of us has a responsibility to be part of the solution.
> (UN Secretary-General Ban Ki-moon 2012)

Education for global citizenship helps enable young people to develop the core competencies which allow them to actively engage with the world, and help to make it a more just and sustainable place.

(Oxfam n.d.)

The Thoughtful Citizen. The Start-Up Citizen. The Dream Big Citizen. The Hands-On Citizen. What kind of Global Citizen Are You? Take the Global Citizen Quiz. Click Here To Find Out.

(Aga Khan Foundation Canada n.d.)

Our mission is to build a movement of 100M action-taking Global Citizens to help achieve our vision of ending extreme poverty by 2030.

(Global Citizen n.d.)

To all members of the Antarctic Marine Conservation Convention (CCAMLR):
    As global citizens, we urge you to build on the amazing success creating the Ross Sea Reserve and agree now to designate the full network of sanctuaries – including the waters around the East Antarctic, the Weddell Sea and the Antarctic Peninsula – to save these pristine habitats for penguins, whales and other precious species.

(Avaaz 2018)

Take off with York International. Broaden your horizons. Experience new cultures. Become a global citizen.

(York University n.d.)

To be truly global citizens, we cannot just focus on recruitment of international students, but must also support the development of strong local educational institutions in partner countries. Working together, universities can be at the forefront of achieving the UN's Sustainable Development Goal #4 for Quality Education around the world.

(Academica Forum 2015)[2]

2019 Global Citizen Award in partnership with RBC and the WE Organization.
    The Royal Bank launched the Global Citizen award in 2016 that supports RBC's purpose of helping communities prosper. This award recognizes top performing employees in their roles who have also displayed incredible commitment to giving their time and expertise to their communities by volunteering and leading charitable initiatives. These employees show what can be accomplished by their acts of giving.
    'Just do it! Don't even think twice! It is the most amazing experience you will ever have giving back to your community and students of all ages. There is no thinking about this.'

(Carleton University 2019)

These observations then invited the obvious question: what is the concept of global citizenship doing in them? A first formulation of the problem and an attempt to address it in both political-economic and post-colonial terms appeared as Chapman, Ruiz-Chapman and Eglin (2018). The paper proposed a programme of enquiry into the subject, resulting in this collection of studies. We hope it will stimulate others to take up further enquiry into the subject, for we believe there is much to say about it.

Not that much has not already been said about the subject (see especially Schattle 2008a). Some international development *scholarship* has indeed developed a radical understanding of global citizenship as the practice of interrogating Northerners' own participation in the imperialist subjection of the people of the global South. But it has been largely confined to the topic of global citizenship *education* (GCE), with the focus on universities (Abdi and Shultz 2008; Shultz, Abdi and Richardson 2011; Schattle 2008a, pp. 93–116; 2008b). Vanessa de Oliveira Andreotti has been notable for her contributions to the field of 'critical GCE' in the form of both her own writings (for example, Andreotti 2006) and assembling the writings of others under the headings of political-economic (Andreotti 2014) and post-colonial (Andreotti and de Souza 2012) critique. In this volume we have sought to extend such analyses from universities to the institutions of global governance, global philanthropy and global economy so as to invite consideration of the uses to which the concept of global citizenship is being put across what we are conceptualizing as a *nexus* of such institutions.[3]

The foregoing is a capsule account of how we came to take up the critical examination of the concept of global citizenship. To understand what sustains our desire to subject it to further critical scrutiny, however, requires reflection on the global consequences of neoliberal, global, corporate capitalism's (NGCC's) hegemony over these past forty-odd years of 'globalization' and 'the Washington consensus'.[4] In a truly remarkable essay in the February 2019 issue of *Monthly Review* John Bellamy Foster depicts these consequences in all their devastating detail (see Zolo 2017 for a similarly chilling, 'realist' account). What follows is an attempt to capture the heart of his description, along with some additional observations. He begins (Foster 2019a, p. 1),

> Less than two decades into the twenty-first century, it is evident that capitalism has failed as a social system. The world is mired in economic stagnation, financialization, and the most extreme inequality in human history, accompanied by mass unemployment and underemployment, precariousness, poverty, hunger, wasted output and lives, and what at this point can only be called a planetary ecological 'death spiral'.

He starts to fill out this picture as follows:

> Indications of this failure of capitalism are everywhere. Stagnation of investment punctuated by bubbles of financial expansion, which then inevitably burst,

now characterizes the so-called free market. Soaring inequality in income and wealth has its counterpart in the declining material circumstances of a majority of the population ... Unemployment data has become more and more meaningless due to a new institutionalized underemployment in the form of contract labour in the gig economy.

(ibid.)

Workers work harder in less safe conditions and more precarious employment, and increasingly without the benefit and protection of unions. European-style social democracy withers.

The capture of the surplus value produced by overexploited populations in the poorest regions of the world, via the global labour arbitrage instituted by multinational corporations, is leading to an unprecedented amassing of financial wealth at the centre of the world economy and relative poverty in the periphery. Around $21 trillion of offshore funds are currently lodged in tax havens on islands mostly in the Caribbean ... Forty-two billionaires now enjoy as much wealth as half the world's population ... More than 60 percent of the world's employed population, some two billion people, now work in the impoverished informal sector ... The global reserve army of labour is some 70 percent larger than the active labour army of formally employed workers.

(ibid., pp. 1–2)

The rights to adequate health care, education and housing that were enshrined in the Universal Declaration of Human Rights (UDHR) of 1948 and subsequently incorporated into the International Covenant of Economic, Social and Cultural Rights that came into force in 1976 are still not enjoyed by large parts of the global population.

In the United States and other high-income countries, life expectancy is in decline, with a remarkable resurgence of Victorian illnesses related to poverty and exploitation. In Britain, gout, scarlet fever, whooping cough, and even scurvy, are now resurgent, along with tuberculosis.

(ibid., p. 2)

In 2019 a study at the University of Liverpool reported a sustained and unprecedented rise in infant mortality in England from 2014 to 2017, one that was linked to a rise in child poverty (University of Liverpool 2019). The World Health Organization declared a 'global health emergency' resulting from the overuse of antibiotics (Foster 2019a, p. 2).

More than three-quarters of a billion people, over 10 percent of the world population, are chronically malnourished ... Subsistence farmers are being

> pushed off their lands by agribusiness, private capital, and sovereign wealth funds in a global depeasantization process that constitutes the greatest movement of people in history. Urban overcrowding and poverty across much of the globe is so severe that one can now reasonably refer to a 'planet of slums' [Davis 2006]. Meanwhile, the world housing market is estimated to be worth up to $163 trillion.
>
> (ibid., pp. 4–5)

And then there's the climate crisis and its associated ecological crises.

> Science tells us that a new and dangerous stage in planetary evolution has begun, the Anthropocene, a time of rising temperatures, extreme weather, rising oceans, and mass species extinctions. Humanity faces not just more pollution or warmer weather, but a crisis of the Earth System. If business as usual continues, this century will be marked by rapid deterioration of our physical, social, and economic environment. Large parts of Earth will become uninhabitable, and civilization itself will be threatened ... capitalism's inexorable drive for growth, powered by the rapid burning of fossil fuels that took millions of years to form, has driven our world to the brink of disaster.
>
> (Angus 2016)

Responsibility lies with NGCC. 'Just 100 companies have been the source of more than 70% of the world's greenhouse gas emissions since 1988' (*CDP Carbon majors report 2017*, cited in Riley 2017). 'The world's wealthiest 10% are responsible for half of all harmful emissions, whereas the poorest half create just 10%' (Gore, *Extreme carbon inequality* 2015, cited in Corry 2019).

The world is facing major threats to the survival of human civilization, not just from the environmental consequences of global warming, but also from nuclear re-armament and the consequent renewed threat of nuclear war, from a more and more permanent-looking, US-led, Orwellian, terrorist 'War on Terror' (Cohn 2016) and the aforementioned staggering levels of economic inequality. Actually existing wars, notably the catastrophe of Syria, but also the disasters in Afghanistan, Central African Republic, Democratic Republic of the Congo, Gaza, Iraq, Libya, Mali, Somalia, South Sudan, Sudan, Ukraine, Yemen (Deutsch 2019) and elsewhere have produced the highest number of refugees and displaced persons since the Second World War. Globalization's deleterious effects are generating huge movements of people from South to North, not just of refugees but of economic migrants and migrant labour, against which we have been witnessing the building of walls and other disgraceful means of closing borders, together with the rise of fascist or anti-immigrant parties and the execrable Donald Trump:

> some 60 million refugees and internally displaced peoples flee devastated environments. Migrant populations worldwide have risen to 250 million, with those residing in high-income countries constituting more than 14 percent

of the populations of those countries, up from less than 10 percent in 2000. Meanwhile, ruling circles and wealthy countries seek to wall off islands of power and privilege from the mass of humanity, who are to be left to their fate.

(Foster 2019a, p. 4)

Sherene Razack writes:

the abandonment of populations, an abandonment configured as emergency is accomplished as a racial project ... today's empire is most distinguished by the proliferation of camps and by the culture of exception that underpins the eviction of increasing numbers of people from political community.

(2008, pp. 6–7)

A subset of those to whom Razack refers is

[s]tateless persons [who] have no citizenship to any country. They are among the most vulnerable and are subject to exploitation, abuse, indefinite detention and the inability to access housing, education, health care and legal protections. The United Nations High Commissioner for Refugees ... estimates that there are more than 10 million stateless persons worldwide.

(Liew and Esteves Domingues 2019)

As I write, the press (for example, Doherty 2019) is reporting the story of Kurdish Iranian refugee Behrouz Boochani (2019), who, over the course of six years, was forcibly held by Australia's 'offshore processing regime' in Papua New Guinea, where he was the voice of those incarcerated in the hellish Manus Island detention centre. It is a testament to the dreadful consequences of NGCC's denial of the 'right to have rights' – Arendt's (1968, p. 296) definition of citizenship – to so many people.

The US empire continues to flex its muscles both militarily and economically in support of the very global capitalist system that is now increasingly seen as wrecking the planet. Russia and China respond in kind. And in response to the turmoil and worldwide resistance generated by its own military and economic policies and practices the United States and its North Atlantic Treaty Organization (NATO) allies fortify their bastions with global co-operation and co-ordination in intelligence, surveillance, armed forces, military bases and militarization of policing at all levels.[5]

What links these things together – the climate crisis, obstruction of effective measures to combat it, the ongoing destruction of the earth's environment and the pillaging of its resources, the threat posed by nuclear weapons and conventional warfare, the global assault on workers, the creation of a huge mass of 'surplus humanity', their massive migrations and the huge resources being put into their pacification and control on a global scale – is US imperialism, given its

800+ military sites or bases world-wide and its self-appointed role as guardian of global corporate capitalism (Panitch and Gindin 2012). US corporations own close to 50 per cent of the global economy (Chomsky, in Polychroniou 2017), and, as of 2014, control more than 50 per cent of the global weaponry market (Nicks 2015).

Foster concludes his essay saying,

> As a direct result of capitalist social relations, the material challenges now facing humanity are greater than anything ever seen before, pointing to an accumulation of catastrophe along with the accumulation of capital. Hundreds of millions of people under these circumstances are already being drawn into struggles with the system.
>
> (2019a, p. 18)

'The signs of popular revolt are everywhere' (Harvey 2005, p. 163), from the UK miners' strike of 1984–85 to the so-called 'anti-globalization movement' of the late 1980s through the early 2000s, including the Zapatista uprising of 1994, to the 'worldwide upsurge of labor unrest and class-based mobilizations taking place since' the great financial collapse of 2007–08 (Silver 2016, n.p.), especially in the global South (Ness 2015), including major anti-war, anti-austerity and anti-capitalist movements (Makwana 2016). These include the Arab Spring of 2010, Occupy in 2011, the 'March for the Planet' on 29 November 2015, the Global Climate Strikes of September 2019 and the dizzying number of revolts in 2018–19 including in Algeria, Bolivia, Catalonia, Chile, Colombia, Ecuador, France, Haiti, Hong Kong, Iraq, Iran, Lebanon, Sudan … (see Sale 2019).

> In the Anthropocene, the planetary ecological emergency overlaps with the overaccumulation of capital and an intensified imperialist expropriation, creating an epochal economic and ecological crisis. It is the overaccumulation of capital that accelerates the global ecological crisis by propelling capital to find new ways to stimulate consumption to keep the profits flowing. *The result is a state of planetary Armageddon, threatening not just socioeconomic stability, but the survival of human civilization and the human species itself.*
>
> (Foster 2019c, p. 15; emphasis added; see also Klein 2015; Angus 2016)[6]

The question then poses itself: in the face of US-led, imperialist NGCC, the 'planetary Armageddon' it has wrought and continues to effect, and the global resistance it has occasioned, how shall we understand the widespread promotion of a discourse of global citizenship by institutions ranging from universities to global corporations? It might be said, reasonably enough, that given the global scale of the horrors and struggles we are witnessing, a programme to advance the idea of global citizenship is just what is required. The people of the world need to lift their sights from narrower loyalties to self, family, clan and nation so as to see not only what they have in common with the rest of the world's people but that in a crucial sense 'we' are all in it together. Surely no one can object to that. And, indeed, we have no objection to that. The question we are raising, rather, is how anyone can think that global citizenship in the form of education and/or entrepreneurial philanthropy (see, for example, Jefferess 2012a; Nash 2008) and/or international sustainable development goals and/or corporate social responsibility is any kind of adequate answer to the global existential crisis we face in all its ecological, political, economic and social dimensions, including in particular both the restriction of the possibility of being a global citizen to a privileged few and the active proliferation of global non-citizens.[7] The problem is not new. Writing of the United States in the 1930s Zemach-Bersin (this volume, Chapter 2, p. 34) says, 'Indeed, like much of today's global citizenship education landscape, interwar initiatives claiming to promote "world-mindedness" tended to sidestep controversial questions of racism, imperialism, economic exploitation, and inequality while upholding depoliticized and abstracted ideals of "international understanding"'.

More specifically, just what are global citizenship *education*, global *philanthropy*, global *policy-making* and global *corporate capitalism* doing with the concept of global citizenship in the context of said crisis?

Theoretical perspective(s)

The book's conceptual framework, theoretical affiliations and methodological approach to the critical study of the concept of global citizenship are drawn from three strands of social thought. These are Marxist political economy and its attendant critical discourse analysis, Foucault's post-structuralism and its attendant post-colonial theory, and Wittgenstein's ideas about the meaning and use of concepts. These strands are set out here in the Introduction that, together with a historical chapter on the origins of the use of the concept of global citizenship in US imperial planning, form Part I of the book.

First, the whole idea of the book is grounded in the Marxist concept of ideology in which the ideas current in a society are said to reflect and serve the material interests of the 'ruling class' in a given mode of production (Marx and Engels 1970 [1845/46], p. 64). For the last forty-odd years the prevailing mode of production has been and continues to be *neoliberal* GCC (see Foster 2019b; Harvey 2005). The particular *idea* the book explores is, of course, the concept of global citizenship. The first theoretical question the book raises, then, is the extent to which the concept of global citizenship is ideological insofar as it serves the interests of NGCC.

But, second, the Marxist analysis of class-based domination, both material and ideological, only goes so far in accounting for the character of political-economic exploitation and its ideological legitimation in the world. Race is clearly of major importance. The colonial and neo-colonial history of the world since 1492 has produced largely race-based divisions between the dominant 'West' or 'North' and the subordinate 'East' or 'South' (not to mention between settlers and indigenous *within* the global West or North). Since it is post-colonial theory after Edward

Said (1978, 1994), with its roots in Foucault's post-structuralism (see Cuff et al. 2016, pp. 221–65), that seeks to account for the particular character of race-based exploitation and its accompanying ideology, we add its insights to the Marxist theoretical framework. A second question the book addresses is, then, the extent to which the concept of global citizenship comes to reflect and express the relations between the largely white, 'developed' North and the largely non-white, underdeveloped South. Following Foucault's idea of binary opposition, as applied by Said to the us/them opposition of colonialism, we consider how the same structural arrangements that give rise to the idea of the 'global citizen' may also produce its binary opposite, namely the 'global non-citizen' (see Rygiel 2010, esp. chaps 3, 4, 5 and 6; Johnson 2014). This is the subject matter of Part II of the book in the form of studies of citizenship at the US–Mexico border (see Ruiz-Chapman, this volume, Chapter 3), and in the Asian restaurant industry in Southern California (see Lee, this volume, Chapter 4).

Third, however, our methodological approach to the study of the concept of global citizenship is informed by Wittgenstein's (1972, 1, para. 43) dictum, 'the meaning of a word is its use in the language'. Thus, each of the book's contributors to Parts III–VI of the book was enjoined to examine how the concept of global citizenship is used in the particular institutional context they are examining. This entails critical analytic attention to the discourse in which the concept is embedded. We elaborate the plan of the book and the contents of each chapter below.

The theoretical argument: global citizenship as neoliberal capitalist subjectivity

The concept of citizen implies the liberal state. The concept of global citizen implies the neoliberal state (cf. Rygiel 2010, p. 1). In the liberal state the citizen is the locus of the rights and responsibilities that define citizenship. In this conception the state is a nation-state, one among a population of such states, with ad hoc international bodies like the United Nations (UN) dependent on their will; this is liberal internationalism. But in a political economy of 'global monopoly-finance capitalism' (Foster 2015) – what Harvey (2003, p. 158) calls 'accumulation by dispossession' via privatization and market liberalization, a new 'enclosure of the commons' – neoliberalism extols the primacy of private property rights and thus the commodification, privatization and deregulation of everything except state protection of these very rights (Teeple 1995, pp. 75–127; George 2000; Harvey 2005, pp. 64–7; Teeple and McBride 2011). Via the concept of globalization the neoliberal state claims[8] that it seeks to remove the boundaries of nation-states for the purpose of conducting global economic transactions in the name of free trade. These transactions are then to be regulated by corresponding global institutions, like the World Trade Organization, that define the rights and responsibilities of the relevant actors. These actors are de-nationalized entities that, thanks to 135 years of US corporate law, are primarily corporations defined as persons

(Noble 2005, p. 117). They are, in effect, the actual global citizens of the neoliberal world order, corporate citizens conceived as investors whose rights are paramount.[9] They seek to re-make the world after their own image by postulating such a 'global citizen' as the fitting identity for any fully integrated member of that order (cf. Marx and Engels 1987 [1848], p. 25; see also Shultz 2007, p. 249, as cited in DeCaro 2014, p. 6). Citigroup is such a corporate global citizen (see Funk, and Bailey, this volume, Chapters 11 and 12 respectively, for further candidates).

The neoliberal capitalist corporation does not, however, own the concept of global citizen. Like citizenship itself (Rygiel 2010, p. 23) it is a 'contested concept' (DeCaro 2014, p. 5) with ancient antecedents (Carter 2001, p. 1; Schattle 2008a, pp. 1–2). Previous formulations include international citizen, cosmopolitan citizen (see, for example, Hutchings and Dannreuther 1999) and world citizen. They reached a sort of culmination in the kind of citizen postulated in the UDHR of 1948. Though still defined in relation to the nation-state to which they belong, the rights-bearing individual of the Declaration is 'born free and equal in dignity and rights' and is thereby nominally a member of a single, universal 'human family', a noble ideal. But when translated from the national to the global scale, and in the context of the long history of Western imperialism, the idea of universal human rights has itself been understood in terms of other, longstanding notions of how to think about the foreign 'other'. Thus, the good global citizen is constructed as a 'helper' motivated by a 'saviour complex' to deliver a 'gift' to the 'other' who, being 'in poverty', is thereby 'in need' (Jefferess 2014; cf. Boltanski 1999, as cited in Martin 2003, p. 79; see also Jefferess 2012b; Jefferess, this volume, Chapter 9; Bryan 2013). This is the benevolent image promoted in the rhetoric of the UN, international non-governmental organizations (INGOs) and universities; see, for examples, Benham Rennick and Desjardins (2013). It has its roots in the secular humanism, liberal possessive individualism, Christian evangelism and obligation of self-realization that have formed the modern self in Western thought (cf. Delanty 2000, pp. 68–73).

Following Foucault's discussion in his lectures of 1978–79 of how 'liberalism was transformed into neoliberalism' (Hammer 2011, p. 87) with its particular technologies of governance, including of the self, we may say that under the *neoliberal* dispensation both the corporate capitalist global citizen and the benevolent global citizen come to embrace the idea of 'one's life as the enterprise of oneself' (Gordon 1991, p. 44, as quoted in Hammer 2011, p. 87; see Brady and Lippert 2016) where the market is a 'regime of truth' (Hammer 2011, p. 87). This motivational idea is evident in the proliferation of social entrepreneurship programmes at universities and in the corresponding growth of individually run NGOs (Chapman 2017, 2020; see Abraham, this volume, Chapter 10), alongside the rhapsodic embrace of 'corporate social responsibility' in business organizations, business schools and businesses themselves (see Bailey, this volume, Chapter 12). What is missing from this picture, however, is a fuller account of the socio-political-economic context in which these concepts of the global citizen are formulated and applied.

Historically, liberalism came to political prominence in societies that were already capitalist, imperialist, racist, patriarchal, heteronormative and ableist. Its attendant rights were understood to be those of the white, heterosexual, male, colonizing, able-bodied, property owner (cf. Rygiel 2010, pp. 22–5). The task of extending these rights to non-property owning, female (and now trans), gay, non-white, colonized and disabled persons has been taking centuries of struggle and remains far from completion. While the contemporary idea of the global citizen may be thought to represent the culmination of the liberal dream of universal citizenship, our position is that the dream, in theory and practice, is fatally compromised. It is compromised by the restriction of the possibility of its realization to a small minority of the world's mostly rich, mostly male, mostly white, mostly straight, mostly Northern and mostly able-bodied people. It is also itself a means by which that subjection is actually exercised. That is, it has an ideological affordance in itself. Capitalism, imperialism, racism, patriarchy, heteronormativity and ableism work to ensure that a designated few realize the dream while the rest of us, in being seduced by it, are thereby mystified (Potter 2010). Given that we are talking about *global* citizenship then it is capitalist imperialism that is of particular significance (see Hardt and Negri's 'imperial citizenship', as cited in Zolo 2017, p. 82). As DeCaro (2014, p. 5) puts it,

> Imperialism is thus advanced through a concept of global citizenship in which Northerners impose their own values, and political and economic systems on the South. The global citizen becomes representative of the North through embracing a neoliberal approach to economic globalization.

Furthermore, although we do not develop the point here, part of our argument is that the concept of global citizenship is particularly focused on the young people who will become what Michael Albert (2009) calls the 'co-ordinator class', the technocrats, professionals and managers who will run the neoliberal world order for the party of Davos, including taking on the task of international social work required to manage the global poor who are permanently re-produced as the inevitable outcome of the workings of global capital (for the racial dimension of international social work see Thomas and Chandrasekera 2014). Since the managers are found in both the global North and South this distinction is better articulated as one between the rich of the North and the South and their respective poor.

The empirical argument and structure of the book

Following this introduction and an historical account of the origins of the concept of global citizenship in twentieth-century US imperial planning around 'international education' (see Zemach-Bersin, this volume, Chapter 2) that together form Part I, the production of the global non-citizen is examined in Part II, which sets the context for the critical examination of the uses of the concept of global citizenship itself across a range of institutional contexts in Parts III–VI. We will now turn to explaining how we come to select the particular institutional contexts that comprise Parts III–VI and thus the chapters that fill these parts. We would like to think that this is a principal part of the book's contribution to the field of global citizenship studies.

It is the book's principal empirical claim that the dominant users of the concept of global citizenship are to be found in a relatively small, if wide-ranging, set of social locations that together form a nexus of interrelated, 'ruling' institutions. This claim is not entirely original with us – 'educational institutions, multinational corporations, advocacy groups, community service organizations, and even some national governments are embracing the idea of global citizenship' (Schattle 2008a, p. 3; 2008b, p. 75) – and it is, in any case, readily observable if one takes the time to look. Whereas Schattle's study is based on the discursive findings of *interviews* with users of the concept, the present compilation focuses on the discursive findings of *documentary* uses of the concept across the institutions concerned. The institutions are universities (see Part III), the UN (see Part IV), INGOs (see Part V), and multi/trans-national corporations (see Part VI). We think of these four classes of institution as themselves complexes embracing allied institutions. Thus the corporations are linked to business forums, lobbies and think tanks (see Funk, and Bailey, this volume, Chapters 11 and 12 respectively). The UN is itself a range of bodies, like UNESCO (see Biccum, this volume, Chapter 7) that are themselves related to others such as the international financial institutions and the OECD (see Costa and Ponte e Sousa, this volume, Chapter 8). The INGOs are related to national and local NGOs and to foundations and other philanthropic organizations (see Jefferess, this volume, Chapter 9 and Abraham, this volume, Chapter 10). Finally, universities (see Chapman, this volume, Chapter 5 and Golovátina-Mora et al., this volume, Chapter 6), colleges and schools are linked to national and international bodies that represent their interests.[10]

We use the word 'nexus' for these four institutional complexes because it is also readily observable that the complexes are themselves inter-connected. Thus, since the so-called Global Compact was established in 1999 transnational corporations have had a prominent 'seat' at the UN (Teeple 2004, pp. 153–9; Bailey, this volume, Chapter 12). The various councils and committees of the UN are linked in various ways to the INGOs, notably those involved with human rights, the environment, emergency aid and 'development' in general. In pursuit of 'internationalization' strategies universities (and to some extent, schools) link themselves to INGOs, UN agencies and the corporate sector (Eglin 2013). *The empirical argument sustaining the book's thesis, organization and chapter selection is, then, that it is in this web or nexus of institutions that the concept of global citizenship finds its home.* Our objective in the book is to explore critically how it operates, how it is used and what it is used to do across the various settings in which it is characteristically found. That the whole nexus is very much focused on global citizenship *education*, albeit with the *neo*liberal twist argued above, is hardly surprising as education is liberalism's panacea for all social ills.

The foregoing is the framework contributors were invited to adopt when the call for submissions was sent out. Because citizenship studies was not a primary field of expertise for any one of the editors – despite considerable experience researching and teaching in such closely related fields as global governance, NGOs and international service learning (Chapman 2016, 2017, 2020; Chapman, Ruiz-Chapman and Eglin 2018), the bio-politics of citizenship (Ruiz-Chapman 2018) and the political economy of human rights and intellectual citizenship (Eglin 1999, 2013) – we were not sure what to expect in response to the call for submissions. As it turned out, all our contributors found our proffered approach congenial while, nevertheless, adding to it, qualifying it or pushing it in deconstructionist directions (if that is not an oxymoron!). The result, we would like to think, has been to enrich what we initially envisaged.

Notes

1 Parts of this chapter are adapted, with the permission of *Alternate Routes: A Journal of Critical Social Research*, from a section of Chapman, DD, Ruiz-Chapman, T and Eglin, P 2018, 'Global citizenship as neoliberal propaganda: a political-economic and postcolonial critique', *Alternate Routes*, vol. 29, pp. 142–66.

2

> Students Offering Support (SOS) [is] a student-powered organization that works to create accessible, holistic, and inspiring learning environments to help students realize their full potential as community leaders, innovators, and thought leaders. Started at Wilfrid Laurier University in 2004, SOS began as a registered student club that offered peer tutoring support. But quickly, the group began applying the philosophy of 'students helping students' on a global scale, raising funds through its on-campus sessions to support third-party organizations focused on international access to education. Today, SOS is a registered national charity that issues grants and recruits an incredible 1,000+ student volunteers every year.
>
> (Academica Forum 2015)

3 It is important to note that although we approach our subject through the theoretical lenses of primarily political-economic and post-colonial critique we are not ourselves advancing, theorizing or debating any particular definition of citizenship, whether global or otherwise, but attempting to describe and analyse a concept to be found in use across a range of contemporary institutions. And that includes not theorizing actions that traverse frontiers such as, for example, those of would-be global activists (see Isin 2012). Accordingly, we don't engage, beyond perfunctory citations and a cursory statement of our theoretical argument later in this chapter, the large literature on citizenship in professional political science, global studies and sociology devoted to distinguishing liberal, communitarian, radical and cosmopolitan theories of citizenship (Delanty 2000), or legal, social and other forms of the concept (see, for example, Dower 2003; Dower and Williams 2002; Hudson and Slaughter 2007). Similarly, we don't engage other critiques of global citizenship that are developed under different auspices, such as Miller's (1999) argument that when stacked up against the weighty demands of republican citizenship the global type comes off as thin in substance. Or, as Soguk (2014, p. 49) puts it,

> Like the buzzwords 'global' and 'citizenship' from which it is formed, 'global citizenship,' both as concept and praxis, is often simply announced rather than exemplified or substantiated ... [D]espite considerable advances in theory, global citizenship as a practical ordering ideal and political agency is yet to establish strong roots ... It remains resilient as an aspiration but is unable to shake off doubts about its materiality.

Consistent with Soguk's point is the rather remarkable fact that his is one of only two contributions to the 600-page *Routledge handbook of global citizenship studies* (Isin and Nyers 2014), the other being Lee's (2014) consideration of decolonizing global citizenship, that actually addresses the concept of global citizenship. The book otherwise surveys citizenship by continental regions of the globe, a different matter entirely.

4 But see Biccum (this volume, Chapter 7) for a partial critique of this perspective based on the notions of a '*post*-Washington consensus' and a Polanyian 'double movement'.
5 A recent example is the revelation that the Mexican government is using spyware from Israel's NSO corporation to spy on Mexican journalists, lawyers and human rights activists (Real News Network 2017; see Halper 2015; Klein 2007, p. 532; Deutsch 2019). As of this writing, NSO is being sued by WhatsApp (Hopkins and Kirchgaessner 2019).
6 The inimitable John McMurtry (2019) puts it like this:

> The ultimate imperative of evolved planetary life is to prevent our cumulative ruin by competitively life-blind money-sequencing set up to amass ever more wealth as an end-in-itself. This borderless fanaticism of instituted avarice without limit or regulation has cumulatively destabilized and collapsed organic, social, and ecological life support systems across the planet, with the beneficiaries, once again, touting it as 'freedom'. Life security at all levels is now in more extreme systemic danger than at any time before in history, or indeed, throughout mammalian evolution.

7 For a more positive, encouraging view of what we might call the 'movement of global citizens' see the conclusion to the study by Schattle (2008a, pp. 163–4). For a 'more somber picture' of the 'new spaces and opportunities for citizen engagement' globally (Gaventa and Tandon 2010a, p. 4) see the studies collected in Gaventa and Tandon (2010b).
8 As Chomsky, in many places (for example, 2014, pp. 139–40), and Mirowski (2013) have stated, neoliberals neither believe nor practise their own free-market doctrines when it doesn't suit them.
9 Richard Falk recounts a conversation on a plane with a Danish business leader who declared he was a 'global citizen' (rather than a European):

> what he meant was that his friends, his networks, his travels were global, that he slept in the same kind of hotels whether he was in Tokyo or London or New York, that he talked English everywhere, that there was a global culture of experience, symbols and infrastructure that was supporting his way of life.
>
> (Falk 1994, p. 134)

10 Also, although we do not deal with them specifically in this book, national governments are related in various ways to all the aforementioned institutional complexes and may themselves, or as nation-states, sometimes lay claim to, or have attributed to them, the status of global citizen (Schattle 2008a, pp. 138–54).

References

Academica Forum 2015, 'Students reach beyond their institutions to spread education around the globe', viewed 24 October 2019, https://forum.academica.ca/forum/students-reach-beyond-their-institutions-to-spread-education-around-the-globe.

Abdi, AA and Shultz, L (eds) 2008, *Educating for human rights and global citizenship*, State University of New York Press, Albany, NY.

Aga Khan Foundation Canada n.d., 'Together: take the global citizen quiz', viewed 30 October 2019, http://together.akfc.ca/exhibit/en/.

Albert, M 2009, 'Taking up the task: responding to the *Nation* Ehrenreich/Fletcher Symposium', *ZNet*, 9 March, viewed 25 March 2009, www.zmag.org/znet/viewArticle/20826.

Andreotti, V de O 2006, 'Soft versus critical global citizenship education', *Policy & Practice: A Development Education Review*, vol. 3, autumn, pp. 40–51.

Andreotti, V de O (ed.) 2014, *The political economy of global citizenship education*, Routledge, New York.

Andreotti, V de O and de Souza, LMTM (eds) 2012, *Postcolonial perspectives on global citizenship education*, Routledge, New York.

Angus, I 2016, *Facing the anthropocene: fossil capitalism and the crisis of the earth system*, Monthly Review Press, New York.

Arendt, H 1968, *The origins of totalitarianism, new edition with added prefaces*, Harcourt, San Diego, CA.

Avaaz, 2018, 'Save Antarctica's ocean wilderness', viewed 20 November 2019, https://secure.avaaz.org/campaign/en/antarctic_ocean_151/.

Benham Rennick, J and Desjardins, M (eds) 2013, *The world is my classroom: international learning and Canadian higher education*, University of Toronto Press, Toronto.

Boltanski, L 1999, *Distant suffering: morality, media and politics*, trans. G Burchell, Cambridge University Press, Cambridge, UK.

Boochani, B 2019, *No friend but the mountains: writing from Manus Prison*, trans. O Tofighian, House of Anansi Press, Toronto.

Brady, M and Lippert, RK (eds) 2016, *Governing practices: neoliberalism, governmentality, and the ethnographic imaginary*, University of Toronto Press, Toronto.

Bryan, A 2013, '"The impulse to help." (Post)humanitarianism in an era of the "new" development advocacy', *International Journal of Development Education & Global Learning*, vol. 5, no. 2, pp. 5–29.

Carleton University 2019, 'Global citizen award ...', viewed 20 November 2019, https://carleton.ca/creww/wp-content/uploads/Maria-Artuso.pdf.

Carter, A 2001, *The political theory of global citizenship*, Routledge, New York and London.

Chapman, DD 2016, 'The ethics of international service learning as a pedagogical development practice: a Canadian study', *Third World Quarterly*, doi:10.1080/01436597.2016.1175935.

Chapman, DD 2017, 'Emprendimiento social y las ciencias sociales: Evaluacion de una practica de desarrollo pedaggico neoliberal' ['Social entrepreneurship and the social sciences: Assessing a neoliberal pedagogical development practice'], *Revista Observatorio del Desarrollo: Investigación, Reflexión y Análisis*, vol. 6, no. 16, pp. 31–8.

Chapman, DD 2020, '¿Facilitando la desposesión? Complejidades de la industria de las ong' ['Facilitating dispossession? The complexities of the NGO industry'], in D Tetreault and M Chavez Elorza (eds), *Los rostros del desarrollo neoliberal en México*, 309–33, Universidad Autónoma de Zacatecas, Zacatecas, Mexico.

Chapman, DD, Ruiz-Chapman, T and Eglin, P 2018, 'Global citizenship as neoliberal propaganda: a political-economic and postcolonial critique', *Alternate Routes*, vol. 29, pp. 142–66.

Chomsky, N 2014, *Masters of mankind: essays and lectures, 1969–2013*, Haymarket Books, Chicago, IL.

Cohn, M 2016, 'Fifteen years after 9/11, perpetual "war on terror" continues unabated', *truthout.org*, 11 September, viewed 17 November 2019, https://truthout.org/articles/fifteen-years-after-9-11-perpetual-war-on-terror-continues-unabated/.

Corbat, ML n.d., 'Global citizenship, CEO message, Citigroup', viewed 15 April 2017, www.citigroup.com/citi/about/citizenship/ceo-statement.html.

Corry, S 2019, 'Diversity rules environment, OK?' *counterpunch.org*, 20 December, viewed 30 December 2019, www.counterpunch.org/2019/12/20/diversity-rules-environment-ok/.

Cuff, EC, Dennis, AJ, Francis, DW and Sharrock, WW 2016, *Perspectives in sociology*, 6th edn, Routledge, London.

Davis, M 2006, *Planet of slums*, Verso, London.

DeCaro, L 2014, 'Who is a global citizen?' *Citizenship Education Research Journal*, vol. 4, no. 1, pp. 3–12.

Delanty, G 2000, *Citizenship in a global age: society, culture, politics*, Open University Press, Buckingham, UK.

Deutsch, J 2019, 'Global Israel: securocratic war, securocratic borders, securocratic emissions', *Bullet*, 1 November, viewed 1 November, https://socialistproject.ca/2019/11/global-israel/#more.

Doherty, B 2019, 'Behrouz Boochani, voice of Manus Island refugees, is free in New Zealand', *Guardian*, 14 November.

Dower, N 2003, *An introduction to global citizenship*, Edinburgh University Press, Edinburgh, UK.

Dower, N and Williams, J (eds) 2002, *Global citizenship: a critical introduction*, Routledge, New York.

Eglin, PA 1999, 'The sociologist as global citizen: re-specifying intellectual responsibility in the political economy of global corporate capitalism', in E Ortiz and A Cabello (eds), *Proceedings of the Fifth International Congress of the International Society for Intercommunication of New Ideas, Volume 1 – Economic issues and globalization: theory and evidence*, 11–19, Universidad Nacional Autónoma de Mexico, Mexico City.

Eglin, PA 2013, *Intellectual citizenship and the problem of incarnation*, University Press of America, Lanham, MD.

Falk, R 1994, 'The making of global citizenship', in B van Steenbergen (ed.), *The condition of citizenship*, 127–40, Sage, London.

Foster, JB 2015, 'The new imperialism of globalized monopoly finance capital: an introduction', *Monthly Review*, vol. 67, no. 3, pp. 1–22.

Foster, JB 2019a, 'Capitalism has failed: what next?' *Monthly Review*, vol. 70, no. 9, pp. 1–24.

Foster, JB 2019b, 'Absolute capitalism', *Monthly Review*, vol. 71, no. 1, pp. 1–13.

Foster, JB 2019c, 'On fire this time', *Monthly Review*, vol. 71, no. 6, pp. 1–17.

Gaventa, J and Tandon R 2010a, 'Citizen engagements in a globalizing world', in J Gaventa and R Tandon (eds), *Globalizing citizens: new dynamics of inclusion and exclusion*, 3–30, Zed Books, London and New York.

Gaventa, J and Tandon R (eds) 2010b, *Globalizing citizens: new dynamics of inclusion and exclusion*, Zed Books, London and New York.

George, S 2000, 'A short history of neoliberalism: twenty years of elite economics and emerging opportunities for structural change', in W Bello, N Bullard and K Malhotra (eds), *Global finance: new thinking on regulating speculative capital markets*, 27–35, Zed Books, London.

Global Citizen n.d., viewed 28 November 2019, www.globalcitizen.org/en/about/who-we-are/.

Gordon, C 1991, 'Government rationality: an introduction', in G Burchell, C Gordon and P Miller (eds), *The Foucault effect: studies in governmentality*, 1–51, University of Chicago Press, Chicago, IL.

Halper, J 2015, *War against the people: Israel, the Palestinians and global pacification*, Pluto Press, London.

Hammer, S 2011, 'Governing by indicators and outcomes: a neoliberal governmentality?' in AR Saetnan, HM Lomell and S Hammer (eds), *The mutual construction of statistics and society*, 79–95, Routledge, New York.

Harvey, D 2003, *The new imperialism*, Oxford University Press, Oxford, UK.

Harvey, D 2005, *A brief history of neoliberalism*, Oxford University Press, Oxford, UK.

Hopkins, N and Kirchgaessner, S 2019, 'WhatsApp sues Israeli firm, accusing it of hacking activists' phones', *Guardian*, 29 October.

Hudson, W and Slaughter, S (eds) 2017, *Globalisation and citizenship: the transnational challenge*, Routledge, London and New York.

Hutchings, K and Dannreuther, R (eds) 1999, *Cosmopolitan citizenship*, Macmillan, Basingstoke, UK.

Illich, I 2012, 'To hell with good intentions', in A Gilvin, GM Roberts and C Martin (eds), *Collaborative futures: critical reflections on publicly active graduate education*, 314–20, Graduate School Press, Syracuse University, Syracuse, NY, originally given as a speech to the Conference on Inter-American Student Projects in Cuernavaca, Mexico in 1968.

Isin, EF 2012, *Citizens without frontiers*, Bloomsbury Academic, New York and London.

Isin, EF and Nyers, P (eds) 2014, *Routledge handbook of global citizenship studies*, Routledge, New York and London.

Jefferess, D 2012a, 'The "Me to We" social enterprise: global education as lifestyle brand', *Critical Literacy: Theories and Practices*, vol. 6, no. 1, pp. 18–30.

Jefferess, D 2012b, 'Unsettling cosmopolitanism: global citizenship and the cultural politics of benevolence', in V de O Andreotti and LMTM de Souza (eds), *Postcolonial perspectives on global citizenship education*, 27–46, Routledge, New York and London.

Jefferess, D (ed.) 2014, *What does it mean to be a global citizen? A study of the Global Citizen Kelowna Initiative*, Licensed under a Creative Commons Attribution-Åã″-NonCommercial 4.0 International License.

Johnson, V 2014, *Borders, asylum and global non-citizenship: the other side of the fence*, Cambridge University Press, Cambridge, UK.

Ki-moon, B 2012, 'Secretary-general, addressing Drake University students on "global citizenship", says no issue can be seen in isolation as world changes', United Nations, Meetings Coverage and Press Releases, SG/SM/14595, 19 October, viewed 15 April 2017, www.un.org/press/en/2012/sgsm14595.doc.htm.

Klein, N 2007, *The shock doctrine: the rise of disaster capitalism*, Alfred A. Knopf Canada, Toronto.

Klein, N 2015, *This changes everything: capitalism vs. the climate*, Alfred A. Knopf Canada, Toronto.

Krabill, R 2012, 'American sentimentalism and the production of global citizens', *Contexts*, vol. 11, no. 4, pp. 52–4.

Lee, CT 2014, 'Decolonizing global citizenship', in EF Isin and P Nyers (eds), *Routledge handbook of global citizenship studies*, 75–85, Routledge, New York and London.

Liew, J and Esteves Domingues, S 2019, 'New government needs a new look at citizenship and statelessness', *Waterloo Region Record*, 13 November, A11.

McMurtry, J 2019, 'From Canada's election to public action', *Bullet*, 19 November, viewed 19 November, https://socialistproject.ca/2019/11/from-canadas-election-to-public-action/#more.

Makwana, R 2016, 'A new era of global protest begins', *truthout.org*, 6 February, viewed 17 November 2019, https://truthout.org/articles/a-new-era-of-global-protest-begins/.

Martin, F 2003, 'The changing configurations of inequality in postindustrial society: volunteering as a case study', *Alternate Routes*, vol. 19, pp. 79–108.

Marx, K and Engels, F 1970, *The German ideology: part one*, International Publishers, New York, originally written in German in 1845/46.

Marx, K and Engels, F 1987, *The communist manifesto*, trans. J Wayne, Canadian Scholars' Press, Toronto, original work published 1848.

Miller, D 1999, 'Bounded citizenship', in K Hutchings and R Dannreuther (eds), *Cosmopolitan citizenship*, 60–80, Macmillan, Basingstoke, UK.

Mirowski, P 2013, *Never let a serious crisis go to waste: how neoliberalism survived the financial meltdown*, Verso, London.

Nash, K 2008, 'Global citizenship as showbusiness: the cultural politics of Make Poverty History', *Media, Culture and Society*, vol. 30, no. 2, pp. 167–81.

Ness, I 2015, *Southern insurgency: the coming of the global working class*, Pluto Press, London.

Nicks, D 2015, 'The U.S. is still no. 1 at selling arms to the world', *Time*, 26 December, viewed 25 June 2017, http://time.com/4161613/us-arms-sales-exports-weapons/.

Noble, DF 2005, *Beyond the promised land: the movement and the myth*, Between the Lines, Toronto.

Oxfam n.d., 'Global citizenship, Oxfam Education', viewed 16 April 2017, www.oxfam.org.uk/education/global-citizenship.

Panitch, L and Gindin, S 2012, *The making of global capitalism: the political economy of American empire*, Verso, London and New York.

Polychroniou, CJ 2017, 'Myths of globalization: Noam Chomsky and Ha-Joon Chang in conversation', *truthout.org*, 22 June, viewed 25 June 2017, www.truth-out.org/opinion/item/41037-myths-of-globalization-noam-chomsky-and-ha-joon-chang-in-conversation.

Potter, G 2010, 'Structural mystification and the failures of critical understanding', in G Potter, *Dystopia: what is to be done?* 255–94, New Revolution Press in association with CreateSpace, self-published.

Razack, S 2008, *Casting out: the eviction of Muslims from western law and politics*, University of Toronto Press, Toronto.

Real News Network 2017, 'Mexico uses Israeli spyware to target lawyers, journalists and activists', *Real News Network*, 24 June, viewed 25 June 2017, http://therealnews.com/t2/story:19392:Mexico-Uses-Israeli-Spyware-to-Target-Lawyers%2C-Journalists-and-Activists.

Riley, T 2017, 'Just 100 companies responsible for 71% of global emissions, study says', *Guardian*, 10 July, viewed 30 December 2019, www.theguardian.com/sustainable-business/2017/jul/10/100-fossil-fuel-companies-investors-responsible-71-global-emissions-cdp-study-climate-change.

Ruiz-Chapman, T 2018, 'The bare life of undocumented migration: maintaining the Cartesian subject through the "illegal Mexican"', 11 July, Seventh International Sociological Association Worldwide Competition for Junior Sociologists, Seminar, World Congress of Sociology, Toronto.

Rygiel, K 2010, *Globalizing citizenship*, University of British Columbia Press, Vancouver, BC.

Rygiel, K 2014, 'In life through death: transgressive citizenship at the border', in EF Isin and P Nyers (eds), *Routledge handbook of global citizenship studies*, 62–72, Routledge, New York and London.

Said, EW 1978, *Orientalism*, Pantheon, New York.

Said, EW 1994, *Culture and imperialism*, Vintage, New York.

Sale, K 2019, 'Political collapse: the center cannot hold', *counterpunch*, 9 December, viewed 9 December, www.counterpunch.org/2019/12/09/political-collapse-the-center-cannot-hold/.

Schattle, H 2008a, *The practices of global citizenship*, Rowman & Littlefield, Lanham, MD.

Schattle, H 2008b, 'Education for global citizenship: illustrations of ideological pluralism and adaptation', *Journal of Political Ideologies*, vol. 13, no. 1, pp. 73–94.

Shultz, L 2007, 'Educating for global citizenship: conflicting agendas and understandings', *Alberta Journal of Educational Research*, vol. 53, no. 3, pp. 248–58.

Shultz, L, Abdi, AA and Richardson, GH (eds) 2011, *Global citizenship education in post-secondary institutions: theories, practices, policies*, Peter Lang, New York.

Silver, B 2016, 'The remaking of the global working class', *Roar Magazine*, 2, viewed 17 November 2019, https://roarmag.org/magazine/the-remaking-of-the-global-working-class/.

Soguk, N 2014, 'Global citizenship in an insurrectional era', in EF Isin and P Nyers (eds), *Routledge handbook of global citizenship studies*, 49–61, Routledge, New York and London.

Teeple, G 1995, *Globalization and the decline of social reform*, Garamond, Toronto, 2nd edition published in 2000.

Teeple, G 2004, *The riddle of human rights*, Garamond, Toronto.

Teeple, G and McBride, S (eds) 2011, *Relations of global power: neoliberal order and disorder*, University of Toronto Press, Toronto.

Thomas, L and Chandrasekera, U 2014, 'Uncovering what lies beneath: an examination of power, privilege, and racialization in international social work', in R Tiessen and R Huish (eds), *Globetrotting or global citizenship: perils and potential of international experiential learning*, 90–111, University of Toronto Press, Toronto.

University of Liverpool 2019, 'An "unprecedented" rise in infant mortality in England linked to poverty', *Science Daily*, viewed 24 October, www.sciencedaily.com/releases/2019/10/191005134007.htm.

Wittgenstein, L 1972, *Philosophical investigations*, trans. GEM Anscombe, Basil Blackwell, Oxford.

York University n.d., 'This is impact: go global. York International', viewed 15 April 2017, http://yorkinternational.yorku.ca/go-global/this-is-impact/.

Zolo, D 2017, 'Global citizenship: a realist critique', in W Hudson and S Slaughter (eds), *Globalisation and citizenship: the transnational challenge*, 78–84, Routledge, London and New York.

Chapter 2

Global citizenship education and the making of America's neoliberal empire

Talya Zemach-Bersin

The present

In 2018, the U.S. Department of Education released "Succeeding Globally Through International Education and Engagement," an international strategy report asserting "the Department's commitment to preparing today's students, and our country more broadly, for a hyper-connected world." To succeed in such a world, the report explained, U.S. students would need to develop "global and cultural competence," defined as "understanding and appreciating other parts of the world, different religions, cultures, and points of view."[1] Doing so would have distinct benefits, not just for young citizens seeking "meaningful employment" in a globalized economy, but for the nation-state. "Global and cultural competence," the report asserted, will "enhance the country's economic competitiveness," "strengthen our national security and diplomacy," and "support relationships with peers around the world."[2] As Secretary of Education Betsy DeVos put it, American students who develop "cultural intelligence" by learning foreign languages and studying other cultures "keep America safe."[3] President Trump's Secretary of State Mike Pompeo agreed, explaining similarly that international education is "among the most important tools in our diplomatic arsenal," enabling students to help "maintain America's leadership role in the world."[4]

Such a valorization of international understanding, when coming from the administration of Donald Trump, reads as ironic, if not outright insincere. Indeed, observers would be right to argue that the Trump administration seems, more accurately, to detest multiculturalist and internationalist values, doing all it can to foster the flames of white supremacist resentment and xenophobic nationalism, including its decision to empower the Department of Homeland Security to obsessively hunt down and deport immigrant residents, who, it could be convincingly argued, represent a vast well of "globally and culturally competent" human capital. In this sense, the Department of Education's report represents a return of the repressed, a concession that the administration's own cultural zeitgeist and political agenda, while insisting on national greatness, actually represents a vast threat to U.S. global power and "economic viability."[5] But, at the same time, the 2018 report recovers its own coherence by detailing the psychosocial process through which global competency must be homegrown, cultivated as an asset of the native-born American, and gained in specific schooling contexts. This is to be a decidedly American brand of "global competency."

The task, as outlined by the Department of Education, would require attending to more than straightforward language acquisition or academic training in global issues. This would be an enterprise in character and personality development from the ground up, the educational engineering of a particular kind of normative capitalist subject fit for success in an economic system that prioritizes employees "who can work effectively with customers, clients, and businesses from other countries and cultures."[6] Beginning in early childhood and elementary education, the report details, American students would need to develop a key set of "socio-emotional skills" like empathy, sensitivity, cooperation, and conflict management. By secondary and postsecondary education, those same socio-emotional skills could be deployed as "leadership skills," namely the ability to "effectively collaborate and communicate with people in cross-cultural settings."[7] When it comes to economic competitiveness, the report reveals, "global competency" takes more than an expected cognitive mastery of information about other people, culture, and languages – it requires mastering the self: disciplining emotions, conditioning personalities, cultivating the marketable viability of one's own "disposition." What the Trump administration's Department of Education is calling for, in short, is not a structural or social change – but an achievement of self-making, a status-marker of American cosmopolitan ability, designed for the explicit purpose of ensuring that the nation-state will continue to benefit from, and maintain control over, a capitalist world system, even – or especially – at a time when the nation's most powerful elected officials encourage white nationalism and cast liberal internationalism as an elite conspiracy seeking to undermine the sovereignty of the nation-state.

Jodi Melamed has charged rhetoric such as that spouted in the Department of Education's report with reflecting a spirit of "neoliberal multiculturalism" that seizes on progressive ideals to cast "the wealth, mobility, and political power of neoliberalism's beneficiaries to be the just desserts of 'multicultural world citizens.'" Neoliberal multiculturalism, she argues, establishes the innocence and "moral legitimacy of U.S. global leadership" while "obscuring the racial antagonisms and inequalities on which the neoliberal project depends." Wrapped in the rhetoric of multiculturalism, neoliberalism appears "just," and global capitalist relations become a "multicultural imperative."[8] Scholars have argued that this inclusive and "abstract valorization" of global and cultural diversity has been a key global management technique of U.S. Empire since World War II. As Roderick A. Ferguson has so convincingly argued, America's "modern idea of empire" emerged alongside an affirming "modern idea of difference," in which "the management of the international would coextend with the management of diversity."[9] This "mode of power," required a new type of "white racial formation" that could renew and revitalize white privilege in an era of decolonization by way of racial liberalism.[10] Rather than exerting power through repression or divisiveness, the white American agent of Empire would need to cultivate status and legitimacy – for the individual and the nation-state – through a mastery of the foreign characterized by affirmation, inclusion, and understanding; a warm embrace of "global citizenship." If such managerial subjects did not yet exist, they would need to be made.

Today, enthusiastic calls for international education tend to posit the need to rear a native battalion of global citizens as a straightforward response to pre-existing conditions of globalization. Articulating claims to innocence and even victimhood, such rhetoric exaggerates the "neoliberal logic that the state itself has given way to the forces of globalization," casting global capitalism "as an indefatigable power that apparently no nation-state has the means to resist or oppose."[11] As the American Council on Education put it in 2002, global education has become necessary because "like it or not, Americans are connected with people the world over," but are "unready" and lack the required "global competence" to cope successfully with such conditions.[12] But long before the current neoliberal moment, before proclamations of globalization, and even before the postwar "American Century," educators, politicians, social scientists, and philanthropists were hard at work seeking to develop the very same "economically viable" American citizens that the Trump administration called for in 2018. In fact, the roots of the educational enterprise stretch back to America's imperial planning in the early twentieth century. This chapter offers a genealogy of global citizenship education in the first half of the twentieth century and argues that the making – not just the management – of U.S. global power has long required educational efforts to engineer a native-born citizenry capable of profiting from cosmopolitan dispositions.

From the opening decade of the twentieth century, this movement insisted that managing human emotion was central to controlling human behavior, and that controlling human behavior was central to building America's global power. As Sarah Ahmed has argued, feelings often become naturalized, like the commodity fetish, "through an erasure of the history of their production and circulation."[13] In an effort to return the capacity to *feel* "globally and culturally competent" to the conditions of its making, this history of global citizenship education is also a political and economic history of emotion. It is not just that politics are felt intimately, but that intimate feelings – like the socio-emotional skills called for by Trump's Department of Education – tell political stories and have material consequences. I spin this history of affect, education, and empire less out of a concern for descriptively correcting a common historical blind-spot, and more out of an interest in expanding our critique of today's neoliberal global citizens into an understanding of how educated performances of multiculturalism and white racial liberalism have long underpinned the making of U.S. Empire. Efforts to master the world by enumerating, ordering, and identifying differences are already well known as an enterprise of power-knowledge that fuels the economic and administrative apparatus of imperialism. But what the Trump administration's international strategy report lays bare is the way that attaining competency over those differences is also a biopolitical project that is as much concerned with the management of human emotion and personality as it is driven by an imperial will to know.[14]

Pre-World War I

At the dawn of the twentieth century, two advancements in America's relationship to the world had become clear. First, the United States had proven that it was an ambitious nation steeped in grandiose visions of cultural, political, and economic expansion, with an imperialist will that had failed to be satiated by 300 preceding years of settler colonialism. Not only would America retain control of overseas territories after the Spanish–American and Philippine–American Wars and continue to develop the foreign policy of a world power in Latin America and Asia, but the industrial revolution had so transformed the landscape that by 1909 the United States was the lead exporter of both capital and goods to the rest of the world. The second thing that was clear to many early twentieth-century observers was that they were living in a revolutionary epoch defined by the rise of "an interdependent human society."[15] International trade, immigration, technological advancements in travel, media, and communication, along with the undeniable impact of both European and American imperialism, had indeed brought the world into closer, faster, and easier contact than ever before. These advancements were so profound to many Americans that it is easy to confuse exclamations of their wonderment with those from the lips of contemporary globalization enthusiasts. International trade, one man remarked, had become as "easy today between New York and Calcutta or between London and Hong Kong as it once was between two neighboring shops in the bazaars of Damascus."[16] Declaring that "modern science has made the whole world a veritable whispering gallery," one student happily declared the arrival of "worldism."[17] "The time has passed," concluded another excited observer, "when any nation can call itself strictly sovereign or independent."[18]

What this new era of "worldism" would mean for America remained up for debate. While isolationists and imperialists rehearsed their well-known debate, some religious peace activists heralded the coming of the millennium – a harmonious world brotherhood living in plenty and peace. American socialists and leftists, on the other hand, scoffed at the elitist fantasy of universal brotherhood, and identified instead a single worldwide system of economic and racial exploitation. Black American leaders like W.E.B. Du Bois saw in the new interconnected world the potential to join black Americans together with the "brown and yellow myriads elsewhere" in a shared global fight against colonialism, slavery, and oppression.[19] Other Americans responded with a reactionary embrace of nativism and anti-immigrant fears of "balkanization." But a powerful contingent of Anglo-Saxon American elites – statesmen, university presidents, philanthropists, and wealthy leaders of business, law, and industry, along with a cadre of patriotic teachers and reformers – called themselves "internationalists," and insisted that the time had at last come for the United States to extend its glory to the world. Progressive female social reformers like Mead and Jane Addams, imperialist statesmen like

President Theodore Roosevelt's Secretary of State Elihu Root, business tycoons like Andrew Carnegie, conservative academics like Columbia University President Nicholas Murray Butler, anti-war eugenicists like David Starr Jordan, and social Darwinists like Herbert Spencer all identified as internationalists. What they shared in common was the belief that U.S. global power could be forged by an alluring form of legal, political, cultural, and economic leadership that was powerful, yet executed under an umbrella of benevolence. "The weary nations," one Boston internationalist wrote, were awaiting America to become "a leader to guide them out of bondage."[20]

The enthusiasm America's elite internationalists held for the prospect of an interconnected world order cultivated under the tutelage of the United States can be attributed to a great many ideals – not least of which would be the promise of internationally enforced private property rights and the expansion of capitalism's reach – but the political and intellectual lineage that helps us to best understand the centrality of education to the project of U.S. Empire is, perhaps unexpectedly, Social Darwinism. In the late nineteenth century, English philosopher Herbert Spencer had popularized the application of evolutionary biology to social life when he declared that the principles of the survival of the fittest and natural selection were inevitable and necessary for the advancement of civilization. While Spencer did indeed call for a ruthless embrace of individualism and laissez-faire governance, he had also predicted that the ultimate achievement of human evolution would be a cooperative and unified world society. The creation of larger and larger social units forged by the modern industrial order was rapidly careening toward the establishment of a new environment in which the fittest character types – through a process of mental evolution – would be those most adapted to life in a world community. According to the internationalists, tribalism, pugilism, and "the inveterate hatred or contempt for what is Alien" had become markers of inferiority – befitting "only the early, the elementary, and low stages of civilization."[21] Rather than resorting to antagonism or violence when confronted with people unlike oneself, truly civilized peoples would have the ability to communicate and cooperate with all of mankind, and would solve conflicts through altruism, sympathy, and peaceful arbitration.

Like so much of Darwinian thinking, Spencer's foresight had imbedded within it a racial hierarchy that positioned Anglo-Saxons and Western civilization at the forefront of evolutionary progress. But, more specifically, it contained within it a specific faith in U.S. global supremacy. Spencer believed that in America a new variety of the Aryan race would develop "more powerful," "more plastic, more adaptable," and finer than any "type of man that has hitherto existed," destined to produce a "civilization grander than any the world has known."[22] The progress of civilization would be, in essence, a process of Americanization, in which white native-born Americans reigned supreme not through violence, but through particular feats of character and personality development translatable into both benevolence and economic gain. Columbia University President Nicholas Murray Butler proudly titled this achievement the "International Mind," which he defined as a "habit of thinking of foreign relations and business" dedicated to "aiding the progress of civilization, in developing commerce and industry, and in spreading enlightenment and culture throughout the world."[23] For Butler and his peers, internationalism was almost indecipherable from capitalism, U.S. global power, and racial supremacy – and, importantly, its success depended on civilized "habits of thinking" more so than military might.

The great irony of this internationalist prophecy, of course, was that according to Spencer's understanding of evolutionary advancement, a great majority of Anglo-Americans appeared to be savages themselves. Their tendency toward pugilism, isolationism, nationalism, racism, prejudice, xenophobia, and provincial values appeared to signal a catastrophic failure in the natural process of "mental evolution" that Spencer called "non-adaptation" or "behindness."[24] When behaviors and opinions that had once aided in survival were "carried by the force of habit" into more advanced evolutionary moments in which they were no longer conducive to survival, people could become "maladapted" to their surroundings, no longer fit to survive.[25] America's internationalist elites, who celebrated Spencer's prophecy of racial and national supremacy and stood so much to gain from its actualization, had begun to fear that their less-than civilized racial brethren, so plagued by their mental behindness, threatened to undermine their own country's rise to power. Even the American elite, internationalists bemoaned, might be "able to discuss the merits of Monet and Brahms," but often appeared ignorant of "the first principles of civilization" and had yet to "bound the ape and tiger within."[26] Domestically, maladaptation primed the American public to reject the internationalist agenda of world leadership. Not only could public opinion drive the tide of foreign policy decision making in undesirable ways, but men incapable of understanding other cultures or men likely to resort to pugilism, could hardly make successful international businessmen or diplomats. To make matters worse, America's nativist and white supremacist reputation posed nothing less than a geopolitical liability in the intensely interconnected world, such as when the San Francisco school board's decision to segregate Japanese students in 1905 became a diplomatic crisis between Tokyo and Washington.[27]

Perhaps most damning of all, social Darwinism taught that maladapted groups – whether they be finches or people – would meet their end at the hand of natural selection. By adhering to outdated social patterns and political limitations, Anglo-Americans risked being displaced; an evolutionary death knell to white supremacy. In fact, as internationalist and peace activist Jane Addams observed, it was actually America's immigrant population that had most clearly attained the status of "kindly citizens of the world." Addams argued in 1907 that in the pressure-cooker of poor and urban immigrant neighborhoods, immigrants had found "the opportunity and necessity for breaking through the tribal bond," and had already attained the types of "cosmopolitan relations" and "cosmopolitan affection" that Spencer identified as traits of "the ideal man." Though recent immigrants were perhaps unfamiliar with the legal frameworks for international arbitration or Kant's arguments against war, Addams concluded that they nevertheless exhibited an evolutionarily advanced "gravitation toward the universal" that was found lacking in the privileged yet parochial classes.[28] Surely Addams was romanticizing life in immigrant neighborhoods, but nonetheless it would have been difficult for even a casual observer to deny that a great many native-born citizens appeared decidedly provincial by comparison; less equipped than their immigrant counterparts to thrive in an interconnected global society.

Fearing the consequences of this maladaptation among the ruling class of white native-born citizens, internationalists sought to seize control of the evolutionary process by creating "a different psychology in the citizen of the future" fit for cultivating international power well into the new century.[29] Concurrent, therefore, with civilizing missions that targeted the subjects of U.S. Empire, was a lesser known civilizing mission focused on the potential agents of U.S. Empire. Concluding that it was time for America to show "the courage to rely upon the teacher more than on machine guns for national defense," they set out to lay the foundation that underpins today's international education landscape.[30] Educators did sometimes preach that students ought to "think of themselves first of all as citizens of the world," but the label of global citizenship education as we know it was yet to enter the popular lexicon.[31] Instead, early efforts to prepare students for an interdependent world were promoted under the banner of peace education, which, like today's education for global citizenship, typically obscured the underlying interests.

Leading the effort was the American School Peace League, founded in 1907 by two Boston women active in the peace movement who believed that "the civilization of tomorrow" depended on "the highest development of the human race."[32] With forty-five state chapters throughout the country and the support of the Carnegie Endowment for International Peace, the National Education Association, and a collection of America's leading intellectuals, the American School Peace League initiated ambitious curricular reforms dedicated to teaching primary and secondary students to internationalize their understanding of American citizenship.[33] The League was even hired by the U.S. Bureau of Education to design a national program for "Peace Day" school assemblies.[34] Openly inspired by the British Empire's "Empire Day," the American School Peace League's "Peace Day" program sought to "emotionalize" the notion that, as President William Taft asserted in his contribution to the program, the United States was "specially qualified to set a pace for the rest of the world."[35]

The crowning achievement of the American School Peace League, however, was a far-reaching multi-year civics curriculum, titled simply *A Course in Citizenship*. Drawing from child psychology, the curriculum was designed to encourage the "evolution of social consciousness," such that the American student would come to understand that "his nation has duties and privileges and responsibilities in the family of nations." Just like the Department of Education's 2018 strategy report, *A Course in Citizenship* pinned the fate of America's world leadership on childhood emotional conditioning. In order to "drill out of the American youth all anti-social predilections" that might hold the United States back from its global destiny, the course insisted that young citizens must be taught appropriate emotional behaviors, like self-control, helpfulness, cooperation, sympathy, kindness, a spirit of goodwill, and obedience to rules. Intergroup hostility was frowned upon, and students were taught to "recognize the rights and feelings of the Chinese Laundryman, the Italian fruit-dealer, the Jewish tailor," and to "treat kindly any foreigners they meet." "The highest development of the world," the authors argued, required eliminating savage psychological habits like xenophobia and anti-social isolationism before they could persist into adulthood.[36]

Yet the curriculum also conflated interpersonal social and moral virtues with American imperialism and obedience to white supremacy. Certainly "American life is made rich and fruitful by the gifts and services of many nationalities," the *Course* noted, but Anglo-Saxons were an especially gifted people, endowed with "great mental and physical power," who drew on their kindly dispositions to bring "vigor" to the Orient and Africa. An internationalist enthusiasm for cultural diversity was taught as consistent with imperial longings and capitalist expansion, drawing students into a sense of responsibility toward "all the children whose schoolhouses fly the American flag" in Puerto Rico, Hawaii, and the Philippines. Lessons taught students that the United States had shared the "wonders of Western progress" with Japan, civilized the Indians, "maintained the attitude of older brother toward China," and cultivated the adoration of Greeks by bringing industry and commerce to their country. Thus America's expansionist economic interests took shape as the noble extension of appropriate socio-emotional virtues. "World brotherhood," students learned, "is but the expansion of American faith." Rather than allowing for the possibility that international sympathy, kindness, and goodwill might be "psychological habits" that could logically draw one into dis-alignment with imperialism, the textbook's assurance that "the ideals of the United States [are] becoming the ideals of the world," established interpersonal virtues and a celebration of diversity *as* obedience to the interests of the nation-state.[37]

In institutions of higher education, educators attempted to similarly link the promotion of international friendship and understanding to America's geopolitical positioning. But rather than relying only on textbook reforms to internationalize curricular offerings, colleges and universities had the benefit of being host to a growing number of foreign students. Enthusiastic observers declared this a development "of tremendous import for the future of amicable international relations," transforming institutions of higher education into "melting pots of nations" where students become "transfused with the spirit of internationalism."[38] Beginning in 1903, American colleges and universities established Cosmopolitan Clubs where cross-national friendships amongst elite international students and their American peers could be fostered such that students might come to see themselves as "citizens of the world – members of the brotherhood of man."[39] But this enthusiastic rhetoric neglected to reflect the nationalist goals lurking behind enthusiasm for transnational friendships amongst the world's young elites. Indeed, international students studying in the United States in the first decades of the century were already identified as valuable tools for the advancement of U.S. global interests.

In 1909, at the behest of President Theodore Roosevelt, the United States arranged fellowships for Chinese students to study in America based on the presumption that by creating an elite cadre of future Chinese leaders with sympathetic ties to the United States, the United States would be able to "reap the largest possible returns in moral, intellectual, and commercial influence." America, the Roosevelt administration calculated, would be able to control China "in that most satisfactory and subtle of all ways, – through the intellectual and spiritual domination of its leaders."[40] Soon, this vision extended to include all students of non-Western nations studying in the United States, and when educators realized that international students often had negative experiences in the United States due to facing rampant racial and religious discrimination, in 1911 the Committee to Promote Friendly Relations Among Foreign Students was established to promote "sympathetic and helpful relations between Americans and the foreign students," "influence the character, spirit, and attitude of future leaders," and to "bring the educated men and young women of these different lands under the best influences of the Western nations."[41] Once again, the interpersonal skills of cross-cultural friendship and understanding was harnessed unilaterally to the expansion of U.S. influence, while antagonism toward foreign others was a national liability. "If we are to instruct the world's intelligence and to accomplish the direction of the world's intelligence," wrote Butler, "we must first reach the world's heart."[42]

Many elite American students did partake in the tradition of studying in Western Europe, an aristocratic rite of passage, but U.S. colleges would not establish student travel programs for academic credit until after World War I. Nor would the U.S. government formally embrace the diplomatic possibilities of educational travel for American students, as they had already done with regards to international students, until the build-up to World War II. In fact, some international educators warned against undergraduate travel for American students, warning that because young people were not yet "thoroughly grounded in their own civilization and culture," they might "become denaturalized or expatriate." Worse yet, they might become dangerously critical of the United States by "comparing the best in the foreign system to the worst in our own."[43] Vulnerabilities that for international students studying in the United States signified a geopolitical opportunity for America were considered national risks when it came to America's own. Making clear that the international mind was to be defined by certain nationalist ideologies and not actually foreign influence, some educators felt that it was best for native-born students to first learn about the interdependent world from a safe distance and under the watchful guidance of U.S. institutions.

The interwar years

The optimism of those who believed that the world was progressing toward a peaceful global society was dealt a heavy blow in 1914 with the outbreak of

World War I. But the war actually did less to illustrate the futility of international education than to prove its necessity. Despite the masterful way in which President Wilson had framed U.S. military intervention as an acceptance of global responsibility and moral leadership, by the end of the war Americans appeared to turn their back on internationalism – signified by the Senate's rejection of the League of Nations followed by Warren G. Harding's landslide victory in November 1920. "America's present needs," Harding had asserted on the campaign trail, is "not submergence in internationality, but sustainment in triumphant nationality." "There is nothing wrong with world civilization," he assured Americans, and there was no need to "revise human nature."[44] Alongside Harding, the 1920s ushered in an onslaught of anti-immigrant sentiment, the large-scale revival of the Ku Klux Klan, and a revitalized conservative movement that eagerly cast internationalism as a dangerous leftist effort to weaken national sovereignty. For those who longed for an era of U.S. global supremacy defined by progressive internationalism, the nation's retreat into isolationism, racism, and nationalism offered the ultimate evidence that fulfilling America's global destiny would require important changes to the ways in which young Americans were educated to understand their nation's relationship to the world. Without the "international mind," U.S. moral and political leadership would continue to be out of reach.

Underpinning America's failure to embrace both the mantle of world leadership and life in an interconnected society more generally, many progressives and intellectuals concluded, was a collective mental health crisis known as "maladjustment." Rapid modernization and technological advancement had left people in a state of "social confusion," explained sociologist Lawrence Frank, causing their behavior to become "naturally conflicting, confused, neurotic, and anti-social."[45] "There is a profound maladjustment," the *New Republic* warned, "between the condition of the world today and the mental equipment of the American nation for dealing with it."[46] People psychologically "maladjusted" to their surroundings suffered from "pathological reactions," like introversion, inflexibility, antagonism, closed-mindedness, and aggression. This same clinical language of maladjustment was used to rationalize immigration restriction, and to pathologize any social group from nonconforming women to labor activists who refused to comply with existing systems of power, but it was the psychopathologies of the normative American citizen, the native-born white citizen who was expected to inhabit positions of power, that worried many internationalists the most.

Studies revealed that white children in particular had taken on maladjusted attitudes of prejudice and feelings of superiority, causing them to become "domineering," "egotistic and self-centered," and resulting in "stunted" emotional growth and antisocial personality development. Not only could this condition hinder "the progress of the race," it could lead to "cataclysmic ruptures" – including economic precarity, social disintegration, and isolationist views that worked against the nation's best interest.[47] The prejudice and antagonistic attitudes held by white native-born populations, which rendered them unable to get along cooperatively and peacefully with other people, was considered a symptom of "anti-social" or "introverted" behavior.[48] Coined by Carl Jung, the concept of introverted and extroverted personality types was quickly gaining popularity in the 1920s. While the gregarious extroverted personality type was idealized for enhancing American economic, social, and political life, introversion was denounced as not just a social disability, but an economic liability.[49]

Social scientists and psychiatrists noted that maladjusted personalities and attitudes were generally not biologically innate conditions, but rather were reflections of cultural conditioning – signaling societal dysfunction more so than an individual pathology, but in the period of postwar political conservativism, making Americans embrace global responsibilities through political reforms seemed impossible. Instead, it was the socialization of young people, understood as nascent social beings still in the formative stages of personality development, that offered the possibility of recuperating the promises of U.S. global power – if and only if they could be taught "the proper spirit and attitudes" of "world mindedness."[50] Educators concerned with improving America's global standing thus set out to ensure that each young citizen was "equipped to perform his part in a social structure which has a world basis."[51]

Some of these initiatives followed the conventional formula of transmitting academic knowledge in traditional classroom settings. Institutions of higher education across the country, for example, founded pioneering schools and programs in international relations. But, to a large degree, educators focused on developing new pedagogies capable of "training" and "conditioning" emotions through the "educational management of experience."[52] "Anti-social" or "introverted" behaviors were to be replaced with extroverted personality types who could thrive in a complex world. In that spirit, Boy Scouts of America initiated "World Jamborees" and offered Scouts membership in the "World Brotherhood of Boys." Girl Scouts established March of each year as "International Month," during which Scouts would "take imaginary trips around the world," cook food from around the world, and play games in which members would gather household items produced outside the United States.[53] The Junior Red Cross coordinated an international school correspondence program, and public-school children formed World Friendship Clubs and performed in world friendship pageants. Rockefeller's new International House Movement on college campuses enabled American students to live under a shared roof with their foreign counterparts – a project in no small part underwritten by economic ideals. Church groups orchestrated the international exchange of toy dolls, and *Parents* magazine offered tips on how to rear young citizens of the world. One book published in 1925 titled *Education for World-Citizenship* even argued that American children could develop the "qualities useful in creating a basis for world-citizenship" on the playgrounds of their own "cosmopolitan country."[54]

A great many of the formal international education programs that emerged in the 1920s and 1930s prioritized the socialization of elite students who were expected to eventually take on powerful positions as adults in the world of business and government. To facilitate student travel in the name of the "world-wide expansion of American cultural influence," Nicholas Murray Butler and Elihu Root, the statesman considered the legal architect of U.S. imperialism, helped found the Institute of International Education (IIE) in 1919.[55] IIE supported institutions like Smith College, Marymount College, and the University of Delaware as they formalized junior year abroad programs for their American students. Affluent students able to afford the cost of overseas travel were able to gain academic credit while developing an understanding of "a foreign culture and foreign ways of thinking and feeling." Student travel, as the president of Smith College put it, was the best and most effective thing that educational institutions could do "for the fitting of our students for the life of a citizen in the post-war world."[56]

One self-proclaimed "emotional education" and "attitude training" program that emerged in the late 1930s, the Experiment in International Living, brought small groups of American preparatory school students – "the finest America has to send" with "minds and bodies above the average" – to Western European countries, where each student spent their summer living with a host family.[57] Having undergone the emotional experience of becoming the child of a foreign family, the young privileged Americans could be socialized into something new – true citizens of the world conditioned to embrace global responsibility and to seek peace as an extension of familial duty. When one young critic from Camden, New Jersey, accused the Experiment in International Living for embracing an "undemocratic plan," insisting that instead of forging an internationally minded aristocracy, the program might consider sending "a delegation of the John Does, the Mary Browns, the office workers, the factory workers, the farmers," and "youths from the masses regardless of whether he is of Italian parentage, Polish, Jewish, Chinese, Negro, Russian or what have you," the program's founder quickly accused her of harboring "class bitterness."[58] Certainly, the young critic was on to something more than a class critique, for though the program insisted it was "working for world peace" and "international understanding," it prioritized its trips to Nazi Germany, where students attended Nazi rallies and parades and joined in the activities of Nazi youth groups.[59] Sargent Shriver, who attended one such program before his freshman year at Yale, reported upon his return that "the German truly wanted us to be their friends because they saw in America, more than in almost any other nation of the world, people whom they believed were their kind."[60] Stripped of any concern for social justice or even moral commitment, the Experiment in International Living proved just how easy it was to embrace an internationalist spirit of brotherhood and understanding that upheld a privileged global white supremacist alliance.

The racist, classist, and political presumptions of many of the interwar international education initiatives were not lost on America's more radical critics. Sociologist Bruno Lasker, an expert on the formation of racial prejudice in children, disapproved of what he considered "an appalling amount of vague sentimentalism" pervading international education. Moreover, he argued, "methods adopted in the belief that they will teach 'world-mindedness' will be found on closer examination to implant in children attitudes of snobbishness and condescension toward the members of other races."[61] An even more cutting critique was embraced by the Communist Party USA's youth group, the Young Pioneers. In 1935, when President Franklin Roosevelt hosted an international Boy Scout Jamboree in the nation's capital, the Young Pioneers accused Roosevelt of strategically fostering international brotherhood between young Americans and "just those countries which everyone knows are controlled by American interests." Moreover, the Pioneers pointed out, the Jamboree was to be a segregated affair, teaching youth that "contempt or hatred for their brothers of another race is part of the 'right attitude of mind.'" "The scouts who pledge international brotherhood today will be set at each other's throats like mad dogs tomorrow," the Pioneers presciently observed, for though they celebrated "goodwill" they had yet to free themselves from the grips of capitalist control and thus remained subordinate to "those who profit by destruction."[62]

Indeed, like much of today's global citizenship education landscape, interwar initiatives claiming to promote "world-mindedness" tended to sidestep controversial questions of racism, imperialism, economic exploitation, and inequality while upholding depoliticized and abstracted ideals of "international understanding." Even the more progressive programs that sought to link world-mindedness to intercultural education at home were likely to teach a depoliticized and essentialized appreciation for cultural difference stripped of any recognition of power or inequality. Yet, in so doing, as the Young Pioneers argued so clearly, such programs were in no way taking an apolitical stance. Toddlers studying picture books about their foreign "cousins," Boy Scouts writing letters to their foreign friends, Sunday school children sending gifts to partner congregations in other countries, and school groups performing colorful peace pageants fostered a very particular kind of world consciousness or "international mindedness" that functioned to facilitate, rather than disrupt, the expansion of U.S. influence. In a setting where a privileged American student could celebrate membership in a world brotherhood without fighting for racial justice, without challenging economic inequality or reflecting critically on one's own positionality, education for world-mindedness typically obscured geopolitical realities while instead socializing citizens' fit to maximize their own standing in a world society. By drawing the world close in an imagined community of abstract goodwill, international education helped to translate America's preferred economic relationships and arrangements of power into personally felt emotions – forming what Raymond Williams calls "structures of feeling."[63] Youth who *felt* themselves to be members of a world family were well prepared to embrace the economic and political integration of the world under U.S. leadership.

By the late 1930s, educators were not the only ones interested in the benefits of facilitating opportunities for American students to travel abroad. At the behest of President Roosevelt's Good Neighbor Policy – a broad campaign aimed at shifting U.S. power in Latin America from interventionist military and territorial domination to economic and cultural hegemony – the State Department had begun to experiment with new forms of educational diplomacy. Sometimes referred to as the "chosen-instrument approach," this new foreign policy formula required that the government merely "assist and coordinate" the international activities of private agencies, as any cultural initiative interpreted as government propaganda would be rendered ineffective.[64] As private citizens, American students appeared capable of gaining the friendship, "confidence," "cooperation and respect of South Americans" in a way that official government representatives could not. In 1940, for example, the Department of State and the Council of National Defense provided the Experiment in International Living with financial backing to launch a series of new student travel programs in Latin America with the requirement that the program take the appearance of "a spontaneous expression of the friendliness of the people in the United States."[65] Such programs, one prescient government official noted, had the added benefit of training the young Americans to accept the "coming role of world leadership."[66] By the time the U.S. entered World War II, international education was well on its way to becoming a calculated vehicle for achieving foreign policy aims both specific and general through a state–private sector alliance.

Post-World War II

When the United States emerged from World War II wielding more geopolitical power than ever before, the longstanding sense that young Americans would need to learn how to "carry their responsibilities as world citizens" took on an even more urgent cast.[67] America had emerged from the war "in a position of overwhelming influence" and therefore faced an unprecedented opportunity to "lead the rest of mankind," State Department officials warned, but could fall as quickly as it had risen if the public did not accept the "responsibilities, the obligations, the self-sacrifices of world leadership."[68] Anxious that Americans might again turn their backs on international engagement as they did after World War I, educators, government officials, foundations, leaders of public thought, and psychiatrists and social scientists all launched full-throated efforts to make world citizenship education a standard national practice. Defined as malleable and innocent, young people were once again the prime targets of efforts to engineer this new global consciousness.

In 1945, over 2,000 American psychologists signed a public statement asserting that young people needed to be taught "an international way of thinking," and in 1948 an international committee of social scientists went so far as to assert that "world citizenship" was a required dimension of mental health.[69] Even a special Presidential Commission on education called for by President Truman demanded that America's students be educated "directly and explicitly" to develop "a global vision" and "the international mind."[70] "Young people must be taught to recognize and think constructively about the major social, economic and political problems which confront them as citizens of One World," pronounced U.S. Commissioner of Education J.W. Studebaker.[71] The task facing educators only intensified as the contours of the Cold War came into focus in the immediate postwar years. Not only did young Americans need to understand their duties as citizens of a global superpower; they were now sutured into foreign policy as key players in a bilateral power struggle between the United States and the Soviet Union that increasingly blurred the boundaries between civil society and the state. As international education entered the sphere of Federal influence and even control after World War II, "global citizenship" and "international understanding" became carefully controlled political concepts, tied at once to expansive white racial liberalism and the personnel needs of Empire.

One such public–private partnership, an alliance between the State Department and private sector international education groups, shuttled American students across the Atlantic for three summers aboard decommissioned World War II troopships in hopes that the student diplomats would cultivate a "legacy of friendship" in postwar Europe that would "have an important bearing on the security of the world."[72] Constricting the political possibilities generated by international friendships, student groups deemed too leftist – such as those who openly agitated against "the poison of white supremacy," or who advocated "the right of labor to organize," and "civil liberties for colored people" – were denied passage, and those who were approved to travel were trained in how to appropriately discuss U.S. race relations and economic inequality in a way that secured U.S. innocence and the virtues of democratic progress.[73] Participation in the program, known as "Operation Understanding," came alongside a demand to "exhibit only what is best of America," which, the State Department made clear, would require taking on an air of practiced patriotic racial liberalism (while traveling to Europe, students were to read Ruth Benedict's wartime tract against biological racism *The Races of Mankind* along with *The Negro in America*, a summary of Gunnar Myrdal's *An American Dilemma*).[74] This strategic marriage between international education, multiculturalism, and the state was further formalized with the increase of Federal funding to higher education programs in language and area studies, and the formation of the Fulbright Program and the Peace Corps – the latter of which, it should be noted, was presided over by Sargent Shriver, one notable alumnus of the Experiment in International Living. After his summer in Nazi Germany with the Experiment, but before becoming the first director of the Peace Corps, Shriver had been a founding member of the America First Committee.[75]

The Cold War is best known as a time of conservative suspicion of internationalism and ever-escalating violence, but it is also true that as the United States sought to profit from the fruits of Empire while gaining the allegiance of the decolonizing world, the American ideals of education for world-mindedness, now half a century in the making, became the federal government's windfall. It offered the precise answer to how America might rule the world while maintaining the appearance of a non-imperial, non-coercive superpower. After World War II, Americans in both civil society and the state would seek to advance U.S. global power through the very same discourses of cross-national empathy, friendship, and brotherhood that the American School Peace League promoted in the first decade of the century. As a strategic "anti-conquest narrative," this chosen framework for making sense of U.S. power legitimated U.S. expansion while denying its coercive or imperial nature.[76] Christina Klein describes the same phenomenon as a "global imaginary of integration," forging the emotional pathways along which American hard power and economic interests flowed.[77] International understanding, appreciation for depoliticized cultural differences, sentimental cross-national friendships, and expressions of brotherly concern for foreign others became just as important a vector of postwar American Empire as was military intervention. Indeed, the making of U.S. power throughout the twentieth century and into the twenty-first has been characterized by insistent and calculated attempts to rear American global citizens whose ability to celebrate interdependence and cultural difference will translate into profit; never racial and economic justice.

The present again

Today, some observers have pronounced the death of U.S. Empire, warning that China or Russia may fill the void left in the wake of America's retreat. Educators have wondered if the resurgence of nationalist fervor might diminish enrollment interest in international education. Trump administration policies have certainly reduced the number of international students willing to subject themselves to an education in the United States, but thus far the rhetoric of "America First" has not had the same chilling effect for American college students eager to become world citizens through privileged educational opportunities like study abroad. As Inderpal Grewal has argued, it appears that in keeping with the forces of neoliberalism, the U.S. nation state's exceptionalism, and its power, has shifted to its citizens. America's exceptional citizens, Grewal explains, see themselves as both separate from the state and superior to it – more efficient, virtuous, caring, and authentic than the state. By perceiving their activities as private and virtuous, exceptional citizens are able to dis-identify with the violence enacted by U.S. Empire, and to instead view themselves as the solutions – capable of succeeding where the state has failed.[78] Global citizenship education has always been tied to the interests of U.S. power and capitalist expansion, but it has never required a government that truly embraces internationalist or multiculturalist ideals. In fact, from the opening years of the twentieth century, young and privileged Americans were trained to possess an inclusive and affirming orientation to the world such that they might be able to achieve what the government has not, cannot, or simply will not do itself – all the while confusing the nation's imperial desires for their own personal capacity to virtuously connect with, and understand, people unlike themselves.

But, for just as long, the mystifying enterprise has been critiqued and laid bare, whether by the likes of the Young Pioneers, W.E.B. DuBois and his brand of anti-colonial internationalism, the youth groups turned away from "Operation Understanding" for their desire to eliminate "all traces of fascism from the earth," or Mildred Yemmens, the young woman in Camden, New Jersey, who dared the Experiment in International Living to send a more accurate "cross-section" of the country "on errands of friendship."[79] What these critics from our past help remind us is that the mystification of relations of power is never complete and the extent to which it is successfully obscuring is a political choice. To a large degree, it is only those who benefit from global inequalities who are vulnerable to such confusion in the first place, who even have the capacity to believe that the American School Peace League, the Experiment in International Living, Operation Understanding, or the U.S. Department of Education are concerned with anything other than expanding U.S. global power, preserving racial and class privilege, and unfettered access to markets. As Marx once scoffed, "to call cosmopolitan exploitation universal brotherhood is an idea that could only be engendered in the brain of the bourgeoisie."[80] One need only to listen to the voices of those denied access to the freedoms of "global citizenship," the objects of knowledge and subjects of one's precious "global and cultural competency," to see that this is so.

Notes

1 International Affairs Office, U.S. Department of Education, "Global and Cultural Competency," 2018, https://sites.ed.gov/international/global-and-cultural-competency/.
2 International Affairs Office, U.S. Department of Education, "International Strategy," 2018, https://sites.ed.gov/international/international-strategy-2/.
3 U.S. Department of Education, "Secretary's Message on International Education Week," October 23, 2017, www.youtube.com/watch?v=FsOKR_qpjbY.
4 Bureau of Educational and Cultural Affairs, "U.S. Secretary of State Mike Pompeo kicks off International Education Week 2018," December 7, 2018, https://eca.state.gov/video/us-secretary-state-mike-pompeo-kicks-international-education-week-2018.
5 International Affairs Office, U.S. Department of Education, "International Strategy," 2018, https://sites.ed.gov/international/international-strategy-2/.
6 International Affairs Office, U.S. Department of Education, "Objective 1: Increase Global and Cultural Competencies of All U.S. Students," 2018, https://sites.ed.gov/international/objective-1-increase-global-and-cultural-competencies-of-all-u-s-students/.
7 International Affairs Office, U.S. Department of Education, "Global and Cultural Competency," 2018, https://sites.ed.gov/international/global-and-cultural-competency/.
8 Jodi Melamed, "The Spirit of Neoliberalism: From Racial Liberalism to Neoliberal Multiculturalism," *Social Text* 89, Vol. 24, No. 4 (Winter 2006), 1.
9 Roderick A. Ferguson, *The Reorder of Things: The University and its Pedagogies of Minority Difference* (Minneapolis, MN: University of Minnesota Press, 2012), 24.
10 Melamed, "The Spirit of Neoliberalism," 7.
11 Sandy Grande, *Red Pedagogy: Native American Social and Political Thought* (Lanham, MD: Rowman & Littlefield Publishers, 2004), 50; Peter McLaren and Ramin Farahmandpur, "The Globalization of Capitalism and the New Imperialism: Notes Toward a Revolutionary Pedagogy," *Review of Education, Pedagogy, Cultural Studies*, Vol. 23 (2001), 271–313.
12 American Council on Education, *Beyond September 11: A Comprehensive National Policy on International Education* (Washington, DC, 2002), 7.
13 Sara Ahmed, *The Cultural Politics of Emotion* (New York: Routledge, 2004), 11.
14 Foucault develops the concept of biopolitics in *The History of Sexuality, Vol 1: An Introduction* (New York: Vintage, 1978), 133–160 and Michel Foucault, "Lecture:

17 March 1976," in M. Mertani and A. Fontana, eds., *Society Must Be Defended* (London: Allen & Lane, 2003).
15 Ruby Smith, "Race Problems of World Contact," in Lucia Ames Mead, ed., *Overthrow of the War System* (Boston, MA: Massachusetts Branch of the Woman's Peace Party, 1917), 87–88.
16 Nicholas Murray Butler, Opening Address of the Sixteenth Annual Meeting of the Lake Mohonk Conference on International Arbitration (Published by the Lake Mohonk Conference on International Arbitration, 1910), 22.
17 Marcus Lehman, "Worldism versus Nationalism," *Advocate of Peace*, Vol. 70, No. 2 (February 1908), 43–45.
18 Lucia Ames Mead, *Patriotism and the New Internationalism* (Boston, MA: Ginn & Company, 1906), 65.
19 W.E.B. Du Bois, "To the Nations of the World, 1900," in Alexander Walters, ed., *My Life and My Work* (New York: Fleming H. Revell, 1917), 157–264.
20 Lucia Ames Mead, *Patriotism and the New Internationalism*, 75.
21 Lucia Ames Mead, *Patriotism and the New Internationalism*, 15–16, 78.
22 Josiah Strong, *Our Country: Its Possible Future and Its Present Crisis* (New York: Baker & Tayor Co., 1885), 172.
23 Nicholas Murray Butler "The International Mind: How to Develop It," *Academy of Political Science* (1917), 209; Nicholas Murray Butler, "The International Mind," in *The International Mind: An Argument for Judicial Settlement of International Disputes* (New York: Charles Scribner's Sons, 1912), 101–102.
24 Herbert Spencer, *Social Statics: or the Conditions Essential to Human Happiness Specified, and the First of them Developed* (New York: Robert Schalkenbach Foundation, 1995, 1951), 54–55.
25 E.B. Tylor, *Primitive Culture* (New York: Harper & Row, 1871, 1958), 16.
26 Lucia Ames Mead, "Address of Miss Lucia T. Ames," *Report of the Third Annual Meeting of the Lake Mohonk Conference on International Arbitration* (Lake Mohonk Arbitration Conference, 1897), 97; Lucia Ames Mead, *To Whom Much is Given* (Boston, MA and New York: Thomas Y. Crowell & Company, 1898), 27–28.
27 Mae M. Ngai, *Impossible Subjects: Illegal Aliens and the Making of Modern America* (Princeton, NJ: Princeton University Press, 2004), 39.
28 Jane Addams, *Newer Ideals of Peace* (New York: Macmillan & Co., 1907), 8–18.
29 Lucia Ames Mead, "Educational Organizations Promoting International Friendship," World Peace Foundation Pamphlet Series, No. 6, Part IV (July 1912), 3.
30 Lucia Ames Mead, *Swords and Ploughshares: The Supplanting of the System of War by the System of Law* (New York and London: G.P. Putnam's Sons, 1912), 168.
31 Mead, "Educational Organizations Promoting International Friendship," 10–12.
32 *Third Annual Report of the American School Peace League* (Boston, MA, American School Peace League, 1911), 42.
33 Prominent philanthropists including Rose Forbes and Grace Dodge provided financial support for the organization along with the newly formed Carnegie Endowment for International Peace. The League's Vice-Presidents included Stanford's eugenicist president David Starr Jordan, Harvard professor of education Paul Hanus, and Jane Addams.
34 Wilbur F. Gordy, *Teaching Peace in the Schools Through Instruction in American History* (Boston, MA: American School Peace League, 1909), 4.
35 Fannie Fern Andrews, ed., *Peace Day Suggestions and Materials for its Observance in the Schools* (Washington, DC: Government Printing Office, 1912), 5–6, 14.

36 Ella Lyman Cabot, ed., *A Course in Citizenship* (Boston, MA: Houghton Mifflin Company, 1914), 375, 169, 327.
37 Cabot, ed., *A Course in Citizenship*, 330, 307–309, 325.
38 Louis P. Lochner, *Internationalism Among Universities* (Boston, MA: World Peace Foundation, July 1913), 7.
39 Mead, "Educational Organizations Promoting International Friendship," 10, 12.
40 Arthur H. Smith, *China and America To-day: A Study of Conditions and Relations* (New York: Fleming H. Revell Company, 1907), 215.
41 Liping Bu, *Making the World Like Us: Education, Cultural Expansion, and the American Century* (Westport, CT: Praeger, 2003), 23.
42 Nicholas Murray Butler, *Across the Busy Years: Recollections and Reflections II* (New York: Charles Scribner's Sons, 1935), 97.
43 Stephen Duggan, *A Professor at Large* (New York: Macmillan, 1943), 49.
44 Warren G. Harding, "Return to Normalcy," Boston, MA, May 14, 1920.
45 Laurence Frank, "Society as the Patient," *American Journal of Sociology*, Vol. 42, No. 3 (1936), 340.
46 "America as the Promised Land," *New Republic* (October 4, 1922), 134–136.
47 Bruno Lasker and The Inquiry, *Race Attitudes in Children* (New York: Henry Holt & Company, 1929), 253; Lucy Freeman, "War Cause Traced to Childhood Ills: Mass Expression of Neurotic Disturbances," *New York Times* (August 31, 1948), 25; Lt Colonel John R. Lord and Clifford Beers, "The Human Factor in International Relations," *Mental Hygiene*, Vol. XVIII, No. 2 (April 1934), 177–188.
48 Rachel Davis DuBois, "The Cost in Mental Health," in "The Development of World Mindedness as a Major Educational Objective," Rachel Davis DuBois papers, Immigration History Research Center, University of Minnesota, Box 17 Folder 4.
49 Warren Susman, "'Personality' and the Making of Twentieth-Century Culture," in *Culture as History: The Transformation of American Society in the Twentieth Century* (New York: Pantheon Books, 1983).
50 William Heard Kilpatrick, "Schools and War," *Educational Review* (March 1921), 212.
51 "Report of the First Conference on the Cause and Cure of War," *Progressive Education*, 2 (April-May-June 1925), 105.
52 E.C. Carter and The Inquiry, *What Makes Up my Mind on International Questions* (New York: Association Press and The Womans Press, 1926), 87; Goodwin Watson, "Emotional Conditioning," in *Educational Problems for Psychological Study* (New York: Macmillan Company, 1927), 222–255.
53 See *The American Girl: For All Girls*, "International Issues," archived at Girl Scouts National Historic Preservation Center, New York.
54 William Carr, *Education for World Citizenship* (Stanford, CA: Stanford University Press, 1928), 111.
55 Stephen Duggan, *A Professor at Large* (New York: Macmillan, 1943), 17, xvii.
56 William Hoffa, *A History of US Study Abroad: Beginnings to 1965* (Lancaster, PA: Frontiers, 2007), 76, 82.
57 Donald Watt, "Dear Friend," 1942. World Learning Institutional Archives, Filing Cabinet 2B, Folder: Dear Friend 3.13.
58 Mildred Yemmens to Mr. Kenneth W. Payne, January 27, 1942. World Learning Institutional Archive, Filing Cabinet 1.1–1.4, Folder: Reader's Digest Correspondence 1.12; Donald Watt "Dear Friend," 1942.

59 "Student Group Home, Pleased with Reich," *New York Times*, September 8, 1934, 17; Donald Watt, *Intelligence is Not Enough* (Putney, VT: Experiment Press, 1967), 116–117.
60 Sargent Shriver, "Freshman Who Spent Summer in Germany Describes Reactions of People to Hitlerism: Germans Determined to Achieve National Individualism at Expense of Personal Individualism Believes Student; Thinks Nazis May Not Be Altogether Crazy; Lived in Backnang," *Yale Daily News*, No. 50, November 20, 1934.
61 Bruno Lasker and The Inquiry, *Race Attitudes in Children*, 375.
62 *Scouting and the Boy Scout Jamboree* (New York: New Pioneer Publishing Co., August 1935), 9, 20. Beinecke Rare Book and Manuscript Library, Yale University.
63 Raymond Williams, *Marxism and Literature* (Oxford: Oxford University Press, 1977), 132–133.
64 Ben Mark Cherrington, "The Mission of Rotary in a Troubled World," *Proceedings: Thirtieth Annual Convention of Rotary International* (Cleveland, OH, June 19–23, 1939), 121.
65 Donald Watt to Dr. Robert G. Caldwell, January 8, 1941, 3. World Learning Institutional Archives, Cabinet File: 2.33–2.54, Folder: Co-Ordinator of Inter-American Affairs, 2.43.
66 "Americas Warned on Post-War Role," *New York Times*, March 2, 1941, 33.
67 G.B. Chisolm, "The Reestablishment of Peacetime Society," William Alanson White Memorial Lecture, published in *Psychiatry: Journal of the Biology and the Pathology of Interpersonal Relations*, Vol. 9, No. 1 (February 1946), 1, 10.
68 William Benton, "Operation Understanding: An Address by Assistant Secretary Benton on the Occasion of the Sailing of the Special Ship for Students and Teachers, June 21, 1947," 1–5. National Archives, RG 59 General Records of Department of State. Records of Division of Exchange of Persons. Records of Sylvia Miller and Mary French. Box 2, Lot 52–86. Folder: Transportation.
69 *Mental Health and World Citizenship: A Statement Prepared for the International Congress on Mental Health* (London: World Federation for Mental Health, Summer 1948), 16.
70 President's Commission on Higher Education, *Higher Education for American Democracy: A Report of the President's Commission on Higher Education, Volume 1: Establishing the Goals* (New York: Harper & Brother Publishers, 1947), 16.
71 Address by John W. Studebaker, *Social Education*, Vol. 11 (1947), 127.
72 Benton, "Operation Understanding," 1–5.
73 House Committee on Un-American Activities, "Testimony of Walter S. Steele Regarding Communist Activities in the United States" (Washington: U.S. Govt. Printing Office, 1947), 80; Talya Zemach-Bersin, *Imperial Pedagogies: Education and the Making of U.S. Global Power*, PhD Dissertation, Yale University, 2015.
74 American Friends Service Committee letter on Operation Understanding (June 3, 1948),1. RG 59 General Records of Department of State. Records of Division of Exchange of Persons. Records of Sylvia Miller and Mary French. Box 2, Lot 52–86. Folder: Transportation.
75 Scott Stossel, *Sarge: The Life and Times of Sargent Shriver* (New York: Other Press, 2004), 2011.
76 Mary Louise Pratt, *Imperial Eyes: Travel Writing and Transculturation* (New York: Routledge, 1992), 7.
77 Christina Klein, *Cold War Orientalism: Asia in the Middlebrow Imagination, 1945–1961* (Berkeley, Los Angeles and London: University of California Press, 2003), 13.

78 Inderpal Grewal, "American Humanitarian Citizenship: The 'Soft' Power of Empire," in *Saving the Security State: Exceptional Citizens in Twenty-First-Century America* (Durham, NC: Duke University Press, 2017), 59–86.
79 Mildred Yemmens to Mr. Kenneth W. Payne, January 27, 1942. World Learning Institutional Archive, Filing Cabinet 1.1–1.4, Folder: Reader's Digest Correspondence 1.12.
80 Karl Marx, "Address on Free Trade," in *The Poverty of Philosophy* (London: Martin Lawrence, 1936), 207.

Part II

Borders and global non-citizenship

Chapter 3

The Cartesian subject as global citizen, the migrant as non-human
Humanity, subjectivity and citizenship at the US–Mexican border[1]

Tania Ruiz-Chapman

'Global citizenship' is an ideological expression taken up by many organizations, including the United Nations (UN), to end a multitude of global inequities, with a specific focus on global poverty. The UN defines global citizenship as

> an umbrella term for social, political, environmental, and economic actions of globally minded individuals and communities on a worldwide scale. The term can refer to the belief that individuals are members of multiple, diverse, local and non-local networks rather than single actors affecting isolated societies. Promoting global citizenship in sustainable development, according to the UN, will allow individuals to embrace their social responsibility to act for the benefit of all societies, not just their own.
>
> (UN n.d., para. 1)

Global citizenship calls for individuals to unite across borders in the name of humanity. I will show how this rhetoric is problematic, as it does not attend to the modes of production that create inequities in the first place. The concept of global citizenship is rooted in the assumption that since we are all human, we share a commonality of values and rights. However, materially, we are not born equal. Neoliberal global corporate capitalism would not function if we were.

In what follows I describe the existential situation of the undocumented migrant at the US–Mexican border in terms of a Foucauldian, postcolonial analysis of the mutual constituting of the Cartesian subject-citizen and the non-human non-citizen.[2] The purpose of this is to show not just that global citizenship, actually rather than ideally, implicates a global non-citizen, but who it is that fills that slot. I intend to show how global citizenship ultimately aids in the re-staging of some bodies, specifically Latinx ones (though not confined to them), as non-human or less than human, which in turn borders them out of any form of citizenship, including global citizenship. I will interrogate how crossing borders is a privilege of the Cartesian subject while migrants face 'death zones' in the search for work, subjectivity and humanity. The global citizen is always already embodied by the Cartesian subject. The celebration of global citizenship rhetoric reduces citizenship to a metaphor, one that erases the material inequities of access to legal and social citizenship. Global citizenship is a celebrated concept that has primarily targeted young people as consumers of the ideology. It intends to inspire young people to join the global fight against poverty.

An example of the political-economic problem

Consider the case of the organization 'Global Citizen' which holds annual 'Global Goal Live' music festivals worldwide. For a fee young people are encouraged to join Global Citizen's fight against poverty by attending a concert near them. Global Citizen writes

> the end of poverty is in sight, if an additional $350 billion is secured each year for the world's poorest countries ... But to do that, we ... [need] ... governments, corporations, philanthropists, and, *most importantly, you*, to take action now for people and for the planet.
> (Global Citizen 2012–2019, emphasis added)

The proposed solution to the problem of poverty amounts to little more than the re-staging of the problem, while erasing the culpability corporations and governments have in perpetuating the problem. Working in partnership with Johnson & Johnson, Verizon, Procter & Gamble, the National Broadcasting Company, the World Bank Group, and others, Global Citizen still has the audacity to put the weight of the responsibility on individual actors to take action 'for people and the planet'. In this seemingly positive call to action, Global Citizen completely erases the material conditions of inequality that these corporations profit from and perpetually reproduce. For example, as recently as October 2018, Verizon workers in Memphis lodged complaints against the company citing issues of poor working conditions, and discrimination. In particular, multiple women experienced miscarriages when they were denied the request to work with lighter cargo (Silver-Greenberg and Kitroeff 2018). Verizon valued productivity and the corporate bottom line over their already underpaid workers' health and wellbeing.

Still, if we take Global Citizen's call to action at face value we would be made to believe and accept that they work only with 'good corporate citizens', those who are thereby legitimate citizens and trustworthy actors in the 'fight against poverty'. But then consider their partnership with the World Bank, surely a leading promoter of the neoliberal agenda. For example, as is well known, privatization is a leading cause of poverty. Privatization is

> the transfer of productive public assets from the state to private companies. Productive assets include natural resources. Earth, forest, water, air. These

are the assets that the state holds in trust for the people it represents ... To snatch these away and sell them as stock to private companies is a process of barbaric [*sic*] dispossession.

(Roy, quoted in Harvey 2003, p. 161)

The World Bank has had a leading role in mandating privatization in Mexico and throughout the world. To align global citizenship with the World Bank Group is demonstrative of the lack of critique of the neoliberal global corporate capitalist world order. Without this critique the fight against poverty is lost from the outset.

Borders

The current formulation of the division of the world into nation-states is a legacy of colonialism. This legacy is one that is founded on the perpetual legitimization of borders both physical-geographic and social-relational. As Mignolo and Walsh note,

> borders are everywhere and they are not only geographic; they are racial and sexual, epistemic and ontological, religious and aesthetic, linguistic and national. Borders are the interior routes to modernity/coloniality and the consequences of international law and global linear thinking.
>
> (2018, p. 112)

Mignolo and Walsh do not differentiate between modernity and coloniality as modernity is an ongoing colonial project or, as they put it, 'coloniality is constitutive, not derivative, of modernity' (ibid., p. 4). In my analysis the Cartesian subject is the modern subject and the legal citizen of the imperial US power. This does not include indigenous bodies that have been colonized. Furthermore, while it is true that 'for many people of color, becoming a subordinate settler is an option even when becoming white is not' (Tuck and Yang 2012, p. 18), not all settlers come to embody Cartesian subjectivity. So although minoritized and oppressed groups can and have become settlers within the imperial state, they can never embody the ideality of whiteness. I will demonstrate how the perpetual bordering out of undocumented migrants legitimizes imperial rule and the imperial space as ideally imagined as white, thereby demonstrating the fallacy of global citizenship.

Descartes put forward the dualism of body and nonbody discourse, wherein there was a 'radical separation between reason/subject and body' (Quijano 2000, p. 555). Descartes' move was a secularization of the Judeo-Christian concept of the soul. According to Descartes, the body was incapable of reason; it was rather the reason/subject that was capable of rational thought. Descartes' dualism is rooted in Eurocentric logics of colonization and imperialism, which construct racialized bodies as closer to nature,[3] lacking reason and/or subjectivity and understood as pure body. This in turn validates the exploitation and domination of colonized groups. The Cartesian subject, hence, is the colonizing subject under Mignolo and Walsh's colonial matrix of power. The Cartesian subject is one that embodies coherent, consistent, rational space, demarcated by exclusionary borders. It is through the development of the science and logics of cartography, a consequence of colonialism and the European scramble to claim control over territory across the globe, that the Cartesian subject was further fortified. 'Cartography ... is both an expression of the new form of subjectivity and a technology allowing (or causing) the new subjectivity to coalesce' (Kirby 1998, p. 25). Cartography is the science of mapping borders corresponding to the territorialization of power and control. The Cartesian subject can only be formed through an identification and subsequent bordering out of the 'Other'. 'Otherized' bodies can never embody Western/Eurocentric superiority and are part of an exploitable class, one that represents, and is only ever approached as, cheap labour or as an excessive burden. This in turn keeps the 'Other' in a state of non-humanity reduced to pure body lacking reason/subjectivity.

The Cartesian subject is the legal citizen of the imperial state. However, citizenship does not grant Cartesian subjectivity as not all who hold citizenship have access to the same type of claims to reason/subjectivity because of racist and misogynist logics of Descartes' dualism. The undocumented migrant is perpetually excluded from enlightened subjectivity, which in today's world order requires legal citizenship according to the white imaginary of the Cartesian subject. This

> white spatial imaginary [is] based on exclusivity ... [and] functions as a central mechanism for skewing opportunities and life chances in the United States along racial lines. Whiteness as used here, is an analytic category that refers to the structured advantages that accrue to whites because of past and present discrimination.
>
> (Lipsitz 2007, p. 13)

The presence of racialized settlers within the imagined white space, however, upholds the power of white settlement on indigenous land, through their complicity in imperial settlement. The undocumented migrant, though seeking to engage in this system, is always already excluded because of the processes of racialization that understand the Latinx – as the relevant case here – as degenerate, but also because of their illegal status and inability to hold legal citizenship.

I use Loomba's definition of imperialism where 'the imperial country is the "metropole" from which power flows, and the colony or neo-colony is the place which it penetrates and controls' (1998, p. 12). The US state is a modern colonial metropole. Though not a formal colony of the United States, Mexico acts as its periphery: it is a site to be exploited and controlled in order for the United States to gain access to labour and resources. The maintenance of this unbalanced relationship (through unequal international relations) upholds the superiority of the Cartesian subject within the United States.

Merleau-Ponty points to the importance of marking boundaries as a way to organize, categorize and establish hierarchies. The 'marking of boundaries is necessary to give a sense of organization to the world, thus building "into geographical setting a behavioural one"' (Merleau-Ponty, quoted in Mohanram 1999, p. 17). Mapping the physical boundaries of the nation-state identifies who belongs where, which bodies belong on which side of specific borders. Through their undocumented status, and 'taking up' of imagined white space, the undocumented migrant suggests a weak imperial control of the border. The policies and institutions that target the capture, containment and/or death of undocumented migrants attempt to re-establish imperial rule and the superiority of the valid Cartesian subject.

Mohanram writes, 'bodies are specifically linked with nations' (ibid., p. 4). The white subject is the truest embodiment of the American nation-state and the Cartesian subject, while the undocumented migrant gets locked into a 'zone of illegality' (Da Silva 2001). Through a re-articulation and reproduction of these hierarchies the legitimacy and power of the Cartesian subject and the imperial/neo-colonial state, under which the Cartesian subject exists, is fortified. Boundaries (both physical border boundaries and categorical boundaries) are constructed in order to exclude some bodies from fully enlightened subjectivity.

Teune acknowledges that 'the linkage of citizenship to territory attained maturity with the emergence of the modern territorial state, where land is decisive as a component of wealth and hence of political power' (2008, p. 239). Global citizenship calls for the deterritorialization of citizenship (ibid.). Global citizenship embraces the idea that we can identify with a global community as an entry point for resistance and/or socio-political change. It understands identity to transcend geographic borders and calls for a unity amongst people. It celebrates that we are, at our core, all humans. The idealism of unity and underlying humanism is easy to accept as wholly beneficial. However, there are issues in accepting this take on resistance and change as it overlooks material conditions which create the inequities faced by marginalized groups, specifically by migrants who are perpetually deported to the site of non-humanity and global non-citizenship. A non-critical embracing of global citizenship reduces the concept to a metaphor at best, a restaging of the Cartesian subject as all-powerful at worst. This is especially true when global citizenship is an ideal propagated by corporations and banks.

Subjectivity and the US–Mexican border

The barriers along the Mexican–US border are an overwhelming exemplification of the US imperial state's vested interest in securing the exclusionary power of the border. They also mark the boundaries of Cartesian subjectivity and global citizenship. I refer to the so-called border wall as 'barriers' to denote that Trump's promised wall is not yet built, as well as to remind the reader that investment into border barriers (fences, walls and traffic checkpoints) long predates Trump. Regardless of whether we refer to the fences, the walls or the natural barriers along the US–Mexico border, 'the border is physical and ideological; it constitutes identity as well as exclusion' (Cisneros 2014, p. 5). The barriers along the Mexico–US border are physical manifestation (both constructed and natural) of the boundaries of US citizenship. These barriers act as territorial reaffirmations of US power against the threat of the non-citizen. The border is a physical display of the celebrated image of US strength and control, as well as a supposed barrier against the entrance of degeneracy. Constructed barriers mark a physical representation of the celebrated and notorious image of US strength and control.

The first state-funded, low-tech border fencing was contracted in 1990 and has expanded much since then. Indeed in 2005 the US Congress passed the Real ID Act (Maril 2011), which made it possible to waive any and all laws that may hamper border fence construction. 'As of April, 2009, $3.1 billion had been allocated by Congress for border wall construction' (Sierra Club 2019), without any evidence that the fence was accomplishing what it was meant to do, namely to keep the Latinx body out of the nation. In 2018 Congress approved $1.57 billion in funding for Trump's border wall project. To date it remains unclear where exactly this money is being spent, but Trump claims it is being used to replace or fix sections of the existing barriers, as well as being used to construct new border barriers. This figure does not include funding granted to US Customs and Border Protection (CBP) for services rendered beyond border wall construction. For example, according to CBP's latest available financial report, in 2016 they had net total assets of $16.2 billion. The fence does not stand alone, but rather is geared with militarized equipment and people: 'customs and border protection is now the largest law enforcement agency in the US employing almost 60,000 agents and employees' (*The Real Death Valley* 2014). These forces are the first line of defence against the undocumented migrant. The fence renders the journey into the United States more dangerous for undocumented migrants but does not deter them from crossing. The fence and the institutions of border protection create the illusion of control and a recognizable representation of government promises to keep Latinx migrants outside the United States. However, the logics that the fence embodies are built on the myth of deterrence.

Deterrence theory asserts that 'the greater the perception of punishment [and] ... the swifter the punishment is likely to be, the less likely the criminal will choose to commit the crime' (Maril 2011, p. 91). This logic coupled with the severity of the punishment the 'criminal' (read 'undocumented migrant') could face, is said to deter migrants from attempting to cross the border illegally. Deterrence theory informs the investment into patrolling the border and 'serves as the fundamental rationalization for the work engaged in by all CBP agents' (ibid.). Border barriers, both natural and constructed, deter by reproducing the threat of injury, disablement, death, detention and deportation. Border barriers, and the armed guards along the fence, act as a warning to those considering crossing illegally. The border and its guards are meant to exhibit the liberal value of upholding the law against the inherent criminality of the undocumented subject. The law and its enforcement are tightly bound with American patriotism and enlightened subjectivity, that is Cartesian subjectivity. The rationality of the Cartesian subject relies on the maintenance of order and exclusion. Upholding the law is part of the perpetuation of this order. The undocumented migrant is then always already a criminal and a threat to the true imperial Cartesian subject when they come up against or cross this border.

However, barriers along the border do more than physically propagate deterrence theory. They do something very real in terms of reifying imperial dominance beyond the maintenance and representation of the law. They create a boundary of humanity. Those who attempt to cross the border illegally are inevitably dehumanized because they are exposed to death. This exposure and the accompanying investment into the death of undocumented migrants are validated and legitimized by deterrence theory and the policies/procedures enacted in the name of deterrence. Razack (2010) writes, in regards to the wall constructed under Israeli apartheid, that 'openings in the wall, parts somehow left unfinished, or parts of the wall that can be scaled produce Palestinians as pre-modern, animal like in their movements, clandestine and illegitimate' (p. 97). Similarly, barriers at the US–Mexico border require migrants to scale, scramble, swim, duck and hide. The presence of border barriers and the increased enforcement pushes the desperate undocumented migrant into more dangerous conditions of travel. The quest to reach the 'American Dream' coupled with the imperial state's investment in blocking their entry create a dehumanizing ordeal for the undocumented migrant. This dehumanization borders the migrant out of global citizenship. They are not imagined as actors who can take up the fight against poverty, just as they are not imagined, or even politically and socially approached, as actors (other than criminals) at all.

As previously noted, there are natural barriers that act as natural 'fences' to the undocumented migrant. Crossing at these routes can be deadly. However, the chance of being captured at these natural barriers is lessened, as these areas are not as heavily patrolled. For example, fences, walls and checkpoints push migrants to attempt to swim across the Rio Grande, the danger of which is said to act as its own figure of deterrence for illegal crossing in general. While 'the "man of consciousness" has to separate himself from the bestial body' (Mohanram 1999, p. 35), the undocumented migrant is reduced to that body during their trek across the border. When attempting to cross these barriers, whether natural or constructed, the undocumented migrant is in a constant state of restlessness. To rest is to expose oneself to capture and subsequent deportation. Survival and reaching 'safety' (in the imperial metropole) require the undocumented migrant to continue to climb, hide, swim, walk and so on, that is to keep moving forward. This in turn borders undocumented migrants out of reason/subjectivity and locks them into their bodies; they cannot access Cartesian subjectivity.

Razack (2010), again in her analysis of occupied Palestine, writes

> the wall has the important psychological advantage of enabling those on the Israeli side to imagine what lies beyond the wall ... if seeing holds out the possibility of understanding, Marton and Baum wryly comment, then the wall blocks the possibility of 'insight' into the conditions of the lives of Palestinians.
>
> (p. 100)

The US–Mexican border is not opaque. There are areas that act as barriers to vehicle crossing rather than human crossing, and are relatively open. Those Mexican border areas that have townships adjacent to the United States are where the highest and least porous walls exist. While this is certainly because of a high concentration of 'threatening' Latinxs in these areas, this shielding of visibility also blocks the American view of the degeneracy on the Mexican side of the border. From the American side the border is protective, while from the Mexican side imperial domination and exclusion from the metropole loom over the migrant.

The Mexican side of the border: the site of imagined degeneracy, criminality and non-subjectivity

Constructed border barriers along the US–Mexico border are a wholly American initiative. The Mexican side of the border tells a very different story. Juárez, Chihuahua, for example, is often cited as a dangerous, deadly city. Juárez is directly across from El Paso, Texas. Juárez is a city where American presence has been felt for decades: 'historically, transnational actors such as US citizens, illicit businesses, and corporations have constructed Juárez as a frontier where "anything goes" and people are dehumanized and disposable' (Morales et al. 2013, p. 84). Beyond individual actors indulging in the offerings of this 'city of vice', transnational corporations occupy the landscape along the Mexican side of the border, as they have built large factories and maquiladora villages. Along the periphery of these factories are the 'colonias', which are slums occupied by workers and transient migrants passing through the border.

The current landscape of Juárez is one that tells the history of ongoing US domination over Mexico. For example, the presence of transnational corporations was a result of the maquiladora programme that began in 1965, followed by Mexico's signing onto the General Agreement on Tariffs and Trade in 1986 and culminating with the North American Free Trade Agreement (NAFTA). NAFTA was signed in December 1993 and came into effect the following January. The agreement eliminated barriers to trade and investment and has been described as the 'continued pursuit of neo-liberal policies at the domestic level ... in a context where the U.S. is dominant' (Abu-Laban 2008, p. 341). NAFTA sought to open borders in very particular kinds of ways that systematically excluded the entrance of Mexican bodies into the United States. For example, it eliminated tariffs on agricultural products while allowing for mass importation of cheap American goods into the Mexican market. Small farmers were unable to compete with the prices of the American imported goods and were no longer able to earn their living. Indeed 'over 1.3 million small farmers in Mexico were pushed into bankruptcy by cheap American grain imports between 1994 and 2004' (Chacon and Davis 2006, p. 121). Millions of people were displaced by the economic policies instituted by NAFTA. Goods, capital and transnational corporations have the ability to cross borders while the migrant is perpetually locked out of the imperial metropole.

In Mexico, NAFTA was accompanied by general economic liberalization, reduction in government spending and increased privatization of social services. Export processing zones (EPZs) flourished. These zones transformed local spaces and economies, which came to rely fully on the presence of transnational corporations. These factors created large waves of internal migration of workers who travelled to the border to work in the EPZs and in the maquiladoras. In the mid-1990s, Juárez was one of the larger cities to which people migrated, looking for work (Abu-Laban 2008). The geo-political landscape of Juárez exemplifies Mohanram's assertion that 'space is always simultaneously enmeshed with systems of power and domination' (1999, p. 54). The historical movement of capital and bodies is marked on the landscape of Juárez and other Mexican border towns. The presence of the factories of transnational corporations dictated the geography of habitation, for example, where the colonias resided on the periphery of the maquiladora villages. Many of the factories have since been abandoned by corporations moving to safer zones outside Mexico that offer even cheaper unregulated labour. Today, criminality rules the city and the promise of development held out by the promoters of NAFTA is an empty one.

The reality of waves of migrants cannot be seen as a choice but must be framed as forced migration. As Marx wrote, capitalism is a system of 'forced labour – no matter how much it may seem to result from free contractual agreement' (1967 [1887], vol. 3, p. 819), where the wageworker is 'a man who is compelled to sell himself of his own free will' (ibid., vol. 1, p. 766). When people are forced to migrate they are already excluded from Cartesian subjectivity. Migrants are forced to follow the jobs provided by transnational corporations for survival. That corporations can so easily move elsewhere with no regard or concern for the well-being of the local community, that they come to be understood as human actors, that they can easily cross borders with authority and have power and control over their movement, and that they have authority over the land that they occupy – these facts are demonstrative of their access to Cartesian subjectivity; they are the exemplars of both Cartesian subjectivity and global citizenship.

Today Juárez is considered one of the most dangerous cities in Mexico because of the control the drug cartels have on the territory. The Mexican side of the border is not patrolled by agents of the law but rather by cartels. Indeed many cite the perpetual neoliberalization of the economy, always in favour of the United States, as the reason there is such a violent drug war in Mexico currently. The displacement experienced by so many workers in the aftermath of NAFTA 'opened the door for the replacement of [the exportation of] fruits and vegetable crops with something that is more marketable – illicit drugs' (Morales et al. 2013, p. 85). Border towns still act as exporting zones but the product is far more dangerous. Migrants looking to cross the US–Mexican border become particularly vulnerable to violence, as they have no permanency in the city and can easily be disappeared by cartel members and police alike.

There is a growing crisis in Mexico. Cartels are gaining more power over territories. The US Congressional Research Service estimates that there have been 150,000 deaths due to 'organized criminal violence' since 2006, and that 'in 2018, the number of drug-related homicides in Mexico rose to 33,341, a 15 percent increase from the previous year—and a record high' (Council on Foreign Relations 2019).

While there is a state response to this violence, the state is entangled in the culpability of it as well (see Paley 2014). The disappearance of 43 Mexican students in September 2014 highlights the involvement and investment of all levels of government in organized crime. These students were arrested by state officials and handed over to a cartel. The investigation is 'ongoing' but it is said that the students were subsequently murdered and their bodies burned. Given the combination of a weak, corruptible government, the lack of a welfare state, rampant poverty, few employment opportunities and the overwhelming presence of organized crime, the 'choice' of migrating 'illegally' is an illusion. The 'choice' to move out of one's homeland is reserved for the Cartesian subject and global citizen.

The United States is not innocent in this violence: 'the United States has spent approximately $3 billion to fund the so-called war on drugs in Mexico' (*Democracy Now* 2014). Since that war began under President Felipe Calderón in 2006 it has had the consequences noted above. The imperial US state has invested in strengthening a corrupt government and yet takes no responsibility for the violence of Mexico. Instead it criminalizes those who seek to escape the violence, the very violence that their policies have had a role in creating.

The border, especially its non-porous areas, serves to keep the criminality and assumed degeneracy of the violence, poverty and ugliness of Mexico hidden from the Cartesian subject's view. The very need to escape the violence of Latin America constitutes it as a land of degeneracy. Latin America is taken up as a homogeneous unit of criminality, a criminality with no connection to American policies. Stories telling of gang violence and unbearable life are told without any attempt to understand how this violence came about. Beginning the story with the violence creates the degenerate. Representation of entire nations and geopolitical areas as entrenched in violence comes to re-legitimize the presence of a strong border. The border creates a barrier preventing this violence from spilling over. Even if this is not the case in reality, it certainly is representationally.

If the American investment in border control exemplifies the wealth of the empire, the fence on the Mexican side of the border is experienced in very different ways. It is adorned with 'ofrendas' (offerings) for those who died or disappeared during their travels 'to the other side'. It is a daily reminder to many of lost loved ones, but also of those who successfully crossed. Many undocumented migrants attempt crossing more than once (Jimenez 2009). The fence is the visible barrier between the migrant and the 'good life', between the migrant and the Cartesian subject/global citizen. It acts as a threat of death but one that is always worth it if you make it across alive. In its magnitude the fence contradicts the logic of deterrence theory, since it represents to the migrant the promise of the 'American Dream', one that grants access to wealth. The 'American Dream' exists on the other side of the fence, and the fence embodies a false confirmation of the migrant's journey to 'safety'.

Constructed death zones: constructing a Cartesian global citizen

Stasiulis and Bakan (2005, p. 2) note, 'while citizenship appears to be an inclusive, universalistic concept, in reality all state citizenships are not equivalent; nor are all state citizenships allocated in equivalent ways'. The Cartesian subject, for example, as a citizen of the imperial state can cross all borders easily and safely. Their universal and materially experienced global citizenship grants them legitimized access, occupation and use of all space. The undocumented migrant, conversely, risks disability and death, perpetrated by the imperial state with impunity, when crossing borders. The imperialist US state, for example, constructs death zones in an attempt to safeguard the pure white Cartesian subject, while catching, killing and disabling undocumented migrants along their journey to safety. The journey of undocumented Latinx migration claims many lives. Most bodies and/or body parts never get identified (Maril 2011). The journey of undocumented migration is one that disappears people at high rates with little to no public reaction and total impunity.

Falfurias traffic checkpoint, and other checkpoints of its kind, exemplify the murderability of undocumented people. Falfurias is located in the interior of Texas and is specifically designed to catch undocumented migrants who have managed to cross the border. There are 33 permanent traffic checkpoints inside the United States (Jimenez 2009), which operate as internal manifestations of the border. Instead of risking driving through these checkpoints, undocumented migrants will walk around them. Most deaths occurring during the journey of avoiding these checkpoints are attributed to dehydration and heat stroke, as the land is dry and desolate. Undocumented migrants must walk for days with the constant risk of running out of water and food as they are exposed to the harsh elements of the land. Migrants are at the mercy of the land they travel across rather than being in control of it. The rational occupation and control over land is a right reserved to the truest citizen, the Cartesian subject. The migrant in contrast travels through a designed death world constructed to legitimize and safeguard the power of the Cartesian subject.

The checkpoints are strategically positioned to 'deter' migrants from attempting to go around them. The intentional threat of death surrounds the checkpoint. According to the institutionalized logic of deterrence theory, the migrant will cross through the checkpoint and subsequently be caught by government officials in order not to risk dying. Deterrence theory concludes that if the undocumented migrant 'chooses' to walk around the checkpoint then they are also choosing to expose themselves to possible death. Mbembe articulates what a death world is:

> Michel Foucault has argued that biopower is, to a large extent, power's hold over the right to preserve life and administer death. He also showed how modern societies that function through biopower can justify the killing of populations only through appeals to race or racism, that very 'pre-condition

that makes killing acceptable'. By 'killing', Foucault meant not simply 'murder as such, but also every form of indirect murder: the fact of exposing someone to death, increasing the risk of death for some people, or, quite simply, political death, expulsion, rejection, and so on.'

(Mbembe and Foucault, quoted in Mbembe 2004, p. 392)

The establishment of the checkpoint pushes undocumented migrants to travel through these spaces that kill many of them or succumb to political death resulting from deportation. The deadly terrains are left untouched for the passing of migrants with the goal of limited survival rates. Furthermore, humanitarian interventions, which seek to make these passages less murderous, are criminalized. For example, one can be charged with littering for leaving water jugs out for migrants. Some 'volunteers have been charged with "aiding and abetting" for transporting seriously ill migrants' (Jimenez 2009, p. 43).[4] Another incident demonstrating the maintenance of these spaces as death worlds was reported by the American Civil Liberties Union. The non-governmental organization 'Water Station' campaigned for safety measures to be added to the All American Canal in order to prevent the drowning of transient undocumented migrants. The Imperial Irrigation District ignored this campaign and funded the design and production of a crane to scoop dead bodies out of the canal instead (ibid., p. 39). There is perpetual maintenance and protection of the deadly aspects of these spaces. These spaces are designed and maintained as a space for death, particularly the death of undocumented migrants.

Creating the conditions that allow for so many undocumented migrants to succumb to the dangers of the terrain they traverse keeps the migrant in a state of bare life. These death worlds are scattered with bodily remains, which decompose quickly in the heat. Mass graves, burial sites and abandoned belongings pepper the terrain (*The Real Death Valley* 2014) of these death worlds, all physically marking the terrain with the state-invested project of creating the undocumented migrant as disposable. The murderability of the undocumented migrant positions the migrant in a pre-modern state of bare life, which in turn legitimizes their disposability. The fact that few of these bodies are successfully identified, and thousands have been disappeared by this trek, exemplifies the construction of the undocumented migrant as little more than bestial in nature.

The rates at which Latinx migrants are killed locks them into a physical and political space of non-humanity, which in turn keeps them out of citizenship. The relationship between human subjectivity and citizenship is a reflexive one. Gombay (2015) refers to Hacking's (2007) 'looping effect' to understand this relationship, wherein personhood grants subjectivity, which in turn grants citizenship, which, in a looping manner, grants personhood. One cannot be granted citizenship until they are deemed acceptable and welcomed into the human fold. At the same time, one's citizenship informs one's human subjectivity. The content of this reflexive relationship changes with time as different bodies come to be accepted into the fold. Gombay (2015, p. 13) writes, people's subjectivities are both the product and the object of external institutions that seek to control people, not simply in overt external ways, but so that they come to be conscious of and know themselves as a consequence of these defining mechanisms. They thus become subject of and subjects to these institutions of power.

This looping effect moves forward with time, always changing and expanding outwards. It is not stagnant and individuals gain access to human-ness and citizenship in various ways despite being caught up in it. Some bodies cannot gain this access due to class, disability, status and race. Those that are excluded from the fold are subjects that the institutions of power have deemed as wholly expendable and exploitable. The Cartesian subject, by contrast, is always already human and citizen. It embodies the exploiting class and benefits most from the constructed presence and perpetuation of the non-human migrant.

Detention/deportation exemplifying the impossibility of global citizenship

If one manages to survive without capture and make it to their desired destination they are far from escaping danger. The undocumented migrant has to perpetually avoid deportation, which makes them particularly vulnerable to violence, as reporting violence acted upon them would most likely lead to their detention and/or deportation. Furthermore, undocumented bodies are taken up as cheap, exploitable and expendable labour in the US economy. The undocumented migrant exists as a surplus labour force 'or reserve army [which is useful for the maintaining of the U.S. imperial economy] as it pressure[s] workers to accept lower wages, limited benefits, intensified production processes, dangerous and stressful working conditions, limits to the hours of the work and so on' (Merrill 2011, p. 1548). The undocumented migrant must accept these working conditions, which can also include being exposed to abuse, disablement and death, out of the need to survive in an economy that does not recognize them as a legitimate workforce.

The undocumented Latinx embodies the fallibility of Cartesian borders, and therefore cannot be humanized without challenging the superiority of the Cartesian subject. Their presence must then be delegitimized through a re-establishing of the rightful owner of the US land, namely the white European American. As the binary opposite of the undocumented migrant whose 'passage' is described in the previous section, the white settler is incarnated as the truest American, as the builder of modern society. Fausto-Sterling notes (1995, p. 21), 'human racial difference, while in some sense obvious and therefore "real", is in another sense pure fabrication, a story written about the social relations of a particular historical time and then mapped onto available bodies'. The Cartesian subject configures the boundaries of a nation, not just spatially, temporally and demographically but 'real-ly'.

The result of being caught as an undocumented migrant is detention and subsequent deportation. 'When the state punishes, say, a murderer, it not only removes a threat from the body politic, it also authoritatively repudiates the criminal person as an offending individual not deserving recognition as a citizen' (Kumar and Silver 2008, p. 61). The undocumented migrant is always already understood as criminal. When they are detained they lose all rights to citizenship.

> As a technology of citizenship, detention is based on the creation of spaces and practices of *transition*, in which a person's subjectivity can be transformed from that of a citizen, or a political subject with rights, into that of a quasi-citizen or non-citizen with fewer rights or, by removing the right to have rights altogether, into an abject subject … [It] (un)makes this citizen subject position and turns other mobile subjects, such as migrants and asylum seekers, into abject subjects.
> (Rygiel 2010, pp. 156–7; see also Nyers 2006)

In Canada, undocumented migrants face indefinite detention while in the United States they are thrown into the detention industrial complex: 'this type of industry operates with a market that pursues private profit not only at the expense of the taxpayers but also those who are held in immigration detention' (Welch 2012, p. 30). Both the profiting from detainees living under conditions worse than citizens in correctional detention facilities, and that the Canadian government can indefinitely detain undocumented migrants, reify the undocumented migrant's status as non-human. Detainees cannot enter the fold of humanity and can therefore not enter any kind of citizenship. Even once released, this constructed criminality follows them, keeping them outside citizenship. The criminal cannot embody the global citizen as their movements are restricted and monitored. Furthermore, the altruistic humanist citizen imagined to embody global citizenship is not imagined as the criminal, demonstrating once again the limitations of this rhetoric. The sovereignty of the individual (Teune 2008) celebrated under global citizen rhetoric always already refers to a specific type of individual, one who can move freely and safely through the world, bridging gaps across borders. The undocumented, the criminal and the poor themselves cannot do so.

Most detainees face deportation upon release. The forcible removal of undocumented migrants again points to the fact that some bodies (those of Cartesian global citizens) have control over where and how their bodies move while others have none. Deportation then is the returning of the degenerate to the space of degeneracy ('where they came from'), which is always already affirmed as such due to the vast numbers of people trying to escape it. Deportation re-establishes the borders instituted by the Cartesian subject, and therefore re-affirms the legitimacy of Cartesian subject settler-rule and imperial dominance. Furthermore, once 'returned' to their 'homeland' many are still unable to embody citizenship. Indeed,

> deportees frequently experience removal as an exile *from* their home [vs a return *to* home]. This sense of exile is often reinforced by the reactions of fellow citizens in their countries of origin, who perceive and treat deportees

as outsiders, foreigners, and/or violent criminals threatening state security. Second, deportees and their family members experience a post-deportation victimization that confounds popular perception of the migrants as troublemakers who, at a minimum, have violated prohibitions on unauthorized entry.

(Dingeman-Cerda and Coutin 2012, p. 114; emphasis in original)

Their criminality is not specific to the site of detention but rather is treated as inhering within *them*. Hence, even after living as documented citizens they are still understood and often understand themselves as non-citizens, looping them out of humanity and subjectivity and ultimately out of any possible embodiment of global citizenship.

Conclusion

'The question for the future of citizenship is whether a "global" citizenship can transcend citizenships defined by "local" states on the basis of blood and birth or through an act of the state itself. That is beginning to happen' (Teune 2008, p. 249). The answer is unequivocally no, and I reject any claim that this is beginning to happen for anyone outside those embodying the Cartesian subject. To suggest that global citizenship is a current possibility is only to reify the dominance of the Cartesian subject at the expense of marginalized 'others', as it celebrates the movement and access to the occupation of territory of some bodies over and at the expense of others. The idea of global citizenship would have it that our loyalty be to humanity as a whole, to all humans around the world, with a particular emphasis on speaking and advocating for the global poor. Global citizenship is taken up as a call to action for people in the global North to act for and save people in the global South under a mirage of unity and allyship. And yet global citizens are always 'privileged individuals who have the opportunity to learn about the world, often through travel' (Roddick, quoted in DeCaro 2014, p. 8). No sources that I found that celebrate global citizenship offer a concrete critique of the neoliberal world order, nor do they recognize the legacies of and ongoing colonization projects that allow some to embody the global citizen over others. Furthermore, few call for individuals to hold their own states to account or to act against them. Rather they are encouraged to envisage themselves as stateless, classless, sovereign individuals that come from nowhere. We cannot just suddenly transmute into global citizens when the global economic system does not allow for the deterritorialisation of the world. To suggest otherwise is neoliberal propaganda that only serves to reaffirm the global supremacy of the Cartesian subject, as it, in its various forms, is the only figure to truly embody the global citizen.

Notes

1 Parts of this chapter are adapted with permission, and enlarged, from a section of Chapman, Ruiz-Chapman and Eglin (2018).

2 The analysis presented here may be considered a case study extrapolating and sharpening the systematic, book-length treatment of citizenship as biopolitics, border controls as technologies of citizenship and detention practices as (un)making citizens and abject subjects by Kim Rygiel (2010). See also Johnson (2014).
3 Much the same has been said about women's bodies, as in Durkheim's *Suicide* (1951: 215–16).
4 It is heartening to see that not all Americans agree with these policies:

> An Arizona jury on Wednesday found human rights activist Scott Warren not guilty of 'harboring' undocumented migrants, charges that were levied by federal prosecutors after the geography teacher [a member of the humanitarian aid group No More Deaths] provided food, water, and shelter to two men traveling through the desert in 2018.
>
> (Johnson and Corbett 2019)

References

Abu-Laban, Y 2008, 'Migration in North America', in Y Abu-Laban, R Jhappan and F Rocher (eds), *Politics in North America: redefining continental relations*, 339–52, Broadview Press, Peterborough, Ontario.

Chacon, JA and Davis, M 2006, *No one is illegal: fighting violence and state repression on the U.S.-Mexico Border*, Haymarket Books, Chicago, IL.

Chapman, DD, Ruiz-Chapman, T and Eglin, P 2018, 'Global citizenship as neoliberal propaganda: a political-economic and postcolonial critique', *Alternate Routes*, vol. 29, pp. 142–66.

Cisneros, JD 2014, *The border crossed us: rhetorics of borders, citizenship and Latina/o identity*, University of Alabama Press, Tuscaloosa.

Council on Foreign Relations 2019, *Global conflict tracker: criminal violence in Mexico*, viewed 3 December 2019, www.cfr.org/interactive/global-conflict-tracker/conflict/criminal-violence-mexico.

Da Silva, DF 2001, 'Towards a critique of the socio-logos of justice: the analytics of raciality and the production of universality', *Social Identities: Journal for the Study of Race, Nation and Culture*, vol. 7, no. 3, pp. 421–54.

DeCaro, L 2014, 'Who is a global citizen?' *Citizenship Education Research Journal*, vol. 4, no. 1, pp. 3–12.

Democracy Now 2014, 'Are Mexico's missing students the victims of U.S.-backed drug war?' *Democracy Now*, 13 November, viewed 17 November 2019, www.democracynow.org/2014/11/13/are_mexicos_missing_students_the_victims.

Dingeman-Cerda, MK and Coutin, SB 2012, 'The ruptures of return: deportation's confounding effects', in CE Kubrin, MS Zatz and R Martinez Jr. (eds), *Punishing immigrants: policy, politics and injustices*, 113–37, New York University Press, New York and London.

Durkheim, E 1951, *Suicide: a study in sociology*, trans. JA Spaulding and G Simpson, Free Press, New York, original work in French published 1897.

Fausto-Sterling, A 1995, 'Gender, race, and nation: the comparative anatomy of "Hottentot" women in Europe, 1815–1817', in J Terry and J Urla (eds), *Deviant bodies: critical perspectives on difference in social and popular culture*, 19–48, Indiana University Press, Bloomington and Indianapolis.

Global Citizen 2012–2019, 'Global Goal Live: the possible dream', viewed 23 November 2019, www.globalcitizen.org/en/2020/.

Gombay, N 2015, '"There are mentalities that need changing": constructing personhood, formulating citizenship, and performing subjectivities on a settler colonial frontier', *Political Geography*, vol. 48, September, pp. 11–23.

Hacking, I 2007, 'Kinds of people: moving target', *Proceedings of the British Academy*, vol. 151, pp. 285–318.

Harvey, D 2003, *The new imperialism*, Oxford University Press, New York.

Jimenez, M 2009, 'Humanitarian crisis: migrant deaths at the U.S. Mexican border', *American Civil Liberties Union*, 1 October, viewed 21 September 2019, www.aclu.org/legal-document/humanitarian-crisis-migrant-deaths-us-mexico-border.

Johnson, V 2014, *Borders, asylum and global non-citizenship: the other side of the fence*, Cambridge University Press, Cambridge, UK.

Johnson, J and Corbett, J 2019, 'Attempt to "criminalize basic human kindness" fails as activist Scott Warren found not guilty on all charges', *Common Dreams*, 21 November, viewed 3 December 2019, www.commondreams.org/news/2019/11/21/attempt-criminalize-basic-human-kindness-fails-activist-scott-warren-found-not?utm_campaign=shareaholic&utm_medium=referral&utm_source=facebook&fbclid=IwAR1Dp1TSYej1r73h0AKZJD0kkfehKMXFCKwZJwaWzQU-_atzvdmWfpblkGk.

Kirby, K 1998, 'Re: mapping subjectivity: cartographic vision and the limits of politics', in N Duncan (ed.), *Bodyspace: destabilizing geographies of gender and sexuality*, 45–55, Routledge, New York.

Kumar, R and Silver, D 2008, 'The ethics of exclusion', in JV Ciprut (ed.), *The future of citizenship*, 55–75, MIT Press, Cambridge, MA and London.

Lipsitz, G 2007, 'The racialization of space and the spatialization of race: theorizing the hidden architecture of landscape', *Landscape Journal*, vol. 26, no. 1, pp. 10–23.

Loomba, A 1998, *Colonialism/postcolonialism*, Routledge, London and New York.

Maril, RL 2011, *The fence: national security, public safety, and illegal immigration along the U.S.-Mexico Border*, Texas Tech University Press, Lubbock, TX.

Marx, Karl 1967, *Capital: a critique of political economy*, 3 vols, International Publishers, New York, original work in English published 1887.

Mbembe, A 2004, 'Aesthetics of superfluity', *Public Culture*, vol. 16, no. 3, pp. 373–406.

Merrill, H 2011, 'Migration and surplus populations: race and deindustrialization in northern Italy', *Antipode*, vol. 43, no. 5, pp. 1542–72.

Mignolo, WD and Walsh, CE 2018, *On decoloniality: concepts, analytics, praxis*, Duke University Press, Durham, NC and London.

Mohanram, R 1999, *Black body: women, colonialism, and space*, University of Minnesota Press, Minneapolis.

Morales, MC, Morales, O, Menchaca, AC and Sebastian, A 2013, 'The Mexican drug war and the consequent population exodus: transnational movement at the U.S.-Mexican border', *Societies*, vol. 3, no. 1, pp. 80–103.

Nyers, P 2006, 'The accidental citizen: acts of sovereignty and (un)making citizenship', *Economy & Society*, vol. 35, pp. 22–41.

Paley, D 2014, *Drug war capitalism*, AK Press, Chico, CA.

Quijano, A 2000, 'Coloniality of power: eurocentrism and Latin America', *Nepantla: Views From South*, vol. 1, no. 3, pp. 533–80.

Razack, S 2010, 'A hole in the wall', *Critical Race Inquiry*, vol. 1, no. 1, pp. 90–108.

Rygiel, K 2010, *Globalizing citizenship*, University of British Columbia Press, Vancouver.

Sierra Club 2019, 'Real ID Waiver Authority compromises our borderlands', *Sierra Club Borderlands*, viewed 23 November 2019, www.sierraclub.org/borderlands/real-id-waiver-authority-compromises-our-borderlands.

Silver-Greenberg, J and Kitroeff, N 2018, 'Miscarrying at work: the physical toll of pregnancy discrimination', *New York Times*, 21 October, viewed 25 November 2019, www.nytimes.com/interactive/2018/10/21/business/pregnancy-discrimination-miscarriages.html.

Stasiulis, DK and Bakan, AB 2005, *Negotiating citizenship: migrant women in Canada and the global system*, University of Toronto Press, Toronto.

The Real Death Valley: A Weather Channel and Telemundo Investigation 2014, documentary, The Weather Channel, produced by S Granatstein and S Efran, viewed 19 September 2019, http://stories.weather.com/realdeathvalley.

Teune, H 2008, 'Citizenship deterritorialized: global citizenship', in JV Ciprut (ed.), *The future of citizenship*, 229–52, MIT Press, Cambridge, MA and London.

Tuck, E and Wang, KW 2012, 'Decolonization is not a metaphor', *Decolonization: Indigeneity, Education and Society*, vol. 1, no. 1, pp. 1–40.

United Nations n.d., *Academic impact: global citizenship*, viewed 24 November 2019, https://academicimpact.un.org/content/global-citizenship.

Welch, M 2012, 'Panic, risk, control: conceptualizing threats in a post 9/11 society', in CE Kubrin, MS Zatz and R Martinez Jr. (eds), *Punishing immigrants: policy, politics and injustices*, 17–41, New York University Press, New York and London.

Chapter 4

Global capitalism, immanent borders, and corporeal citizenship

Charles T. Lee

Introduction

Since the modern inception of the concept, citizenship has always been implicated in both the sovereign and social mechanisms of inclusion and exclusion. While many embrace the ideal of citizenship for its promise of social inclusion, political belonging, and democratic rights, it has also always entailed insidious layers of exclusion. Sandro Mezzadra and Brett Neilson address this immanent exclusion as the 'borders of citizenship' (2013, p. 249), which are manifested when particular social groups marked as different from the dominant sociocultural norms due to their race, indigeneity, class, gender, sexuality, culture, homelessness, disability, and/or immigration status experience unequal access to rights, political participation, and social recognition (Young 1989; Isin and Wood 1999; Kapur 2007). As Engin Isin (2002) articulates it, this exclusionary dynamic of citizenship is not merely an external occurrence that happens to citizenship but is immanent to its constitution. Citizenship is only made possible by what it excludes: the alterity/other (i.e. strangers, outsiders, aliens). The very formation of citizenship and citizen-subjects 'requires the constitution of these others to become possible' (ibid., p. 4). The immanent boundaries and borders that replicate and reproduce exclusion and abjection are constitutive of the liberal citizenship system (Lee 2016).

Current governmental, corporate, educational and philanthropic discourse on 'global citizenship', despite its rhetoric of inclusivity of and loyalty to all humanity across sovereign boundaries, cannot resolve this immanent exclusion of citizenship. Emanating from the Westernized, neoliberal, ideological, and biopolitical force that configures the contemporary citizenship system (ibid.), global citizenship discourse constructs a mirage of all-embracing cosmopolitan inclusion that conforms to the capitalist instrumentalist motif (Chapman, Ruiz-Chapman, and Eglin 2018) while perpetually regenerating exclusion and abjection as its 'constitutive outside' (Butler 1993, p. 3). This impossibly smoothes over the colonial, racial, class, gender, and sexual differences and inequities that have always already existed in citizenship and are being continually reproduced by global capitalism, resulting in the immanent proliferation of 'global non-citizens', that is, subjects who continue to lack de jure and/or de facto access to rights, political participation, and social recognition in the midst of neoliberal globalization.

But while exclusion is always inherent in the mechanism of citizenship and it may be impossible to transcend this problematic, it is also misleading to understand citizenship as being in a fixed and static relationship (Isin and Nyers 2014, p. 2). As Isin argues, citizenship is not only defined by membership but also dynamically constituted through political subjectivity. As such, excluded subjects may 'enact citizenship ... that invent new ways of becoming political subjects as citizens' (Isin 2012, p. 568). Specifically, the problematic of exclusion that is immanent to citizenship also generates immanent struggles within the constitution of citizenship, and these immanent struggles register what Étienne Balibar calls the 'permanent reinvention' of citizenship (2004, p. 10). By way of these immanent struggles and permanent reinvention, excluded subjects can become 'key actor[s] in reshaping, contesting, and redefining the borders of citizenship' (Mezzadra and Neilson 2013, p. 257). In this dynamic sense, not only can the *scope* of citizenship be expanded beyond national sovereignty, but the *ways* of becoming citizens and claiming rights may also be expanded through channels beyond state recognition. Thus germinated in the threshold space between the *immanent exclusion* of citizenship and the *permanent reinvention* of citizenship, these extrastatal forms of citizenship culminate in mutating and varied forms of citizenship contestations in the global capitalist landscape.

Drawing on my fieldwork on the Asian restaurant industry in Southern California that is densely populated with immigrant populations, this chapter specifically examines the intricate dynamics under global capitalism as Asian and Latinx immigrants working in the industry jostle between the immanent borders of citizenship that insidiously exclude them *and* their everyday attempts to reinvent and revive their citizenship by informally improvising their own 'contributions' and 'rights' as citizens through ethnic culinary commerce. As I suggest, these immigrants' improvisation of inclusion, belonging, and rights through the commercial space of ethnic restaurants is at once illusive and real: *illusive* because it is complicit in reinscribing the global capitalist structure that places them in a precarious condition of 'differential inclusion' (Mezzadra and Neilson 2013); *real* because it underlines immigrants' aspirations for psychosomatic inclusion and belonging at the immanent borders that remain perpetually unfulfilled by global (neoliberal) citizenship.

My discussion will proceed as follows. First, I point to the disconnect between the euphoric aspirations for global citizenship and the immanent production of global non-citizens on the ground by examining the unfulfilled inclusion and belonging among Asian and Latinx subjects in Southern California. These immigrant subjects are seemingly well situated in the capitalist circuits of global citizenship but are in fact afflicted by an ongoing sociohistorical process of differential racialization that unsettles and fractures the chimera of global (neoliberal) citizenship.

Second, precisely because they lack formal or effective means to be meaningfully included in the U.S. polity, I suggest that Asian and Latinx immigrants resort to everyday spaces such as ethnic restaurants that are situated in the midst of global capitalist commerce to invent and improvise what I call 'corporeal citizenship' in their everyday life. While Teena Gabrielson and Katelyn Parady's (2010) prior work articulates an intrinsic, non-instrumental notion of corporeality in their advocacy for a democratic progressive vision of corporeal citizenship rooted in normative environmental justice concerns, I develop an alternative conception of corporeal citizenship embedded in the historical-material context of global capitalism, using it to describe the material, affective, and biological dimensions of inclusion, belonging, and 'rights' that immigrants actualize through their everyday participation in ethnic culinary commerce. Corporeal citizenship constitutes an informal and improvisational way by which many immigrants living and working in the global economy engender their own 'citizenly contributions' and 'nonexistent rights'.

Next, drawing on field interviews with two immigrant restaurant workers – a Chinese waitress and a Latino kitchen worker – I analyze the ways in which they enact corporeal citizenship at their workplace to actualize their contributions and rights as well as the inherent limitations of their informally acquired inclusion and belonging under global capitalism. What is also notable here is the differential inclusion between these two immigrant subjects given their respective racial-class-occupational positioning within the Asian restaurant industry in particular and the liberal capitalist citizenship system at large. Lastly, I conclude with a brief reflection on the political implications of corporeal citizenship.

Immanent borders between the local and the global: contextualizing Asians and Latinxs in Southern California

As an immigrant gateway with a high concentration of Asian restaurants and immigrant populations, Southern California is reputable among Asian Americans and immigrants for its diverse and abundant offering of 'authentic' Asian food in the United States. Indeed, traveling from the San Gabriel Valley in Los Angeles County (crossing cities such as Alhambra, Arcadia, Monterey Park, Pasadena, Rowland Heights, and Rosemead) to the various suburbs in Orange County (e.g. Anaheim, Costa Mesa, Fountain Valley, Fullerton, Garden Grove, Huntington Beach, Irvine, Tustin, Westminster, and Yorba Linda), one can find plenty of restaurants serving Chinese, Filipino, Indian, Japanese, Korean, Taiwanese, Thai, and Vietnamese cuisines.

Such a vibrant Asian restaurant scene, without doubt, is encapsulated in the global capitalist and neoliberal entrepreneurial development. Corresponding to what the geographer Wei Li (1998) observes as the shift of the ethnic landscape from the Chinatown communities situated in downtown Los Angeles to the emergence of 'ethnoburbs' (i.e. suburban residential and commercial areas with significant ethnic minority populations that tend to be more affluent and diverse in terms of race, ethnicity, and age) in the surrounding San Gabriel Valley since the 1980s, the Asian food scene in Southern California has undergone significant transformation. Not only has there been a blossoming of Asian gourmet restaurants, eateries, cafes, and pastry and bakery stores (some of which are international chains hailing from Asia) in these multiethnic suburbs, these establishments regularly import and bring in the latest (or the most trendy) food dishes and products that are offered in many Asian immigrants' homelands. Moreover, fierce competition drives many Asian restaurateurs to constantly update their food offerings in order to distinguish their establishments from competitors or newcomers in the industry that 'copy' their specialties. Surrounded by a high density of Asian-based commercial plazas, supermarkets, boutiques, and music records stores that cater to Asian middle-class and professionals, the young generation drawn to K-pop, and multiethnic consumers in general, the Asian restaurant industry in Southern California can be said to be enclosed in a material environment of 'global (neoliberal) citizenship' that is simultaneously inclusive and competitive, as ethnic minorities and immigrant subjects access their inclusion, belonging, and freedom through the commercial activities of entrepreneurship, work, and consumption as (transnational) entrepreneur- and consumer-citizens.

This seemingly all-encompassing (neoliberal) inclusion, however, jostles uneasily with the larger sociopolitical context of the differential racialization of ethnic minorities and immigrants in the region under the hegemonic construct of (white) liberal citizenship. As Wendy Cheng articulates the distinctive racial political history and landscape in California:

> [I]t was here that whiteness was solidified by both literal and figurative Asian exclusion and troubled by the 'doubly colonized' and ambiguous racial status of Mexican Americans. Racialized labor competition in California served as the impetus for the Chinese Exclusion Act of 1882, as well as the exclusion of Asians as 'persons ineligible for citizenship' from property ownership. The 'ideological baggage' that developed hand in hand with such laws prevented Asians from full participation in civil society and enabled and perpetuated their containment in segregated spaces. The ambiguous racial and social status of Mexican Americans was also formed to a great degree in California, where, after the vast majority of what is now the American Southwest was ceded by Mexico to the United States in 1848, Mexicans wishing to remain in the United States were granted access to naturalized, American citizenship and therefore legal whiteness. ... At the same time, however, Mexican Americans were regularly denied the full social and material benefits of whiteness, and the constant presence of a large Mexican immigrant and Mexican American working class, in tandem with shifting immigration policies, led, during the second half of the twentieth century, to the racialization of Mexicans as the archetypal 'illegal alien'.
>
> (2013, pp. 15–16)

In fact, despite their internal diversity in terms of ethnicity, class, gender, sexuality, generation, and immigration status, the positioning of Asians and Latinxs is significantly impacted by their differential racialization in relation to the liberal ideal of universal citizenship, which was and continues to be, aligned with whiteness. As Cheng further explicates,

> With regard to Asian Americans and Latinas/os, one must also pay attention to differential racialization vis-à-vis Asian American model minority discourse and the ambiguously white status of Mexican Americans (referring to both day-to-day experiences of 'passing' and historical and legal factors). These differentiated statuses of relative valorization coexist with a 'forever foreign' racialization of Asian Americans – stemming from a long history of exclusion from citizenship, civic participation, and even the nation itself – and a combined 'foreign' and devalorized class stigma for Mexican Americans, whose position in the racial hierarchy shifted over the course of the last century to reflect many Mexican immigrants' niche in the American economy as cheap labor. All these discourses paper over the tremendous ethnic, class, political, generational, and racial (in the case of Latinas/os) heterogeneity of U.S. Asians and Latinas/os – yet all 'Asians' and 'Latinas/os' must contend with the effects of the most salient racialized meanings.
>
> (ibid., p. 15)

This differential racialization in a regional and historical context reverberates in a generalized condition that characterizes the racialized predicament of Asian and Latinx subjects in the way they *experience* citizenship in their day-to-day life in contemporary United States. Thus, as Claire Jean Kim points out in her analysis on the 'racial triangulation' of Asian Americans, while hegemonic whiteness positions Asian Americans as a racially valorized 'model minority' given their economic success relative to blacks, it simultaneously marks them as 'immutably foreign and unassimilable with Whites on cultural and/or racial grounds in order to ostracize them from the body politic and civic membership' (1999, p. 107). Takeyuki Tsuda specifically observes that the indiscriminate racialization of Asian Americans as non-American foreigners or noncitizen outsiders results in their frequent encounter with the 'where are you really (or originally) from?' question in their everyday life which, though 'seemingly innocuous and inoffensive, ... indicates that peoples of Asian descent in the United States are considered to be non-American outsiders, and therefore lack ... citizenship and belonging' (2016, p. 139). Tsuda writes, 'The denial of their Americanness by virtue of their race ultimately brings their status as American citizens into doubt, making their daily lives a struggle for racial inclusion and belonging, or racial citizenship' (p. 135).

A similar yet different predicament of racialization exists for Latinxs as well. As Vilma Ortiz and Edward Telles (2012) observe,

> Persuasive anti-immigrant sentiment and treatment have also worked against all Mexicans whether immigrant or born in the United States. Viewed as alien and low status, Mexican immigrants were (and continue to be) scapegoated

and targeted for mistreatment. Even though immigrants were a minority of all Mexican Americans up to the 1980s, the perception of all Mexican Americans as low status immigrants has been pervasive. ... [I]n the eyes of many White Americans, all Mexicans are 'illegals' and all 'illegals' are Mexican.

(n.p.)

Raymond Rocco (2014) specifically uses the term 'exclusionary inclusion' to characterize the racialized position of Latinxs in the United States. As he indicates, while Latinxs have been included, they are included

> on a differentially exclusionary basis, ... [which is] based on a racialized ideological trope that has constructed Latinos *as perpetual foreigners*, ... result[ing] in a marginalized mode of Latino political membership that, despite significant progress since the 1970s, still characterizes the condition of a majority of Latinos to this day.
>
> (p. xxx; emphasis in the original)

Indeed, given that liberal citizenship in its material reification is 'inescapably racialized and thoroughly contaminated by the civilizing engineering of whiteness/ Westernness' (Lee 2016, p. 46), the racially different/othered Asians and Latinxs (even when granted the formal status of citizenship) are not the same kind or level of citizens as whites but are marked by and entrenched in their corporeal difference and exclusion. These differential experiences of inclusion and belonging underline their racialized relations to citizenship. As Iris Young (1989) has long noted, the presumption of 'equality as sameness' in the liberal construct of universal citizenship does not consider the structural exclusion of minority social groups in terms of their difference in norms, perspectives, and interests as well as their difference in power, representation, and access to influence legislation and policies. This immanent structural exclusion generates shifting, subordinating dynamics and internal borders of citizenship within liberal democracies that shape the political, social, and cultural lives of racial minorities and immigrants. Concomitantly, these immanent borders within liberal citizenship also unsettle the mirage of all-encompassing inclusion emanating from the neoliberal trajectory of global citizenship in Southern California that is undergirded by the processes of economic restructuring, ethnoburbanization, and immigrant entrepreneurial development.

In fact, the immanent exclusion in liberal citizenship cannot possibly be resolved by the corporate, governmental, and educational discourse on global citizenship. As Debra Chapman, Tania Ruiz-Chapman, and Peter Eglin point out, the notion of global citizenship belies an underlying neoliberal political-economic structure of '"global monopoly-finance capitalism" ... – what Harvey ... calls "accumulation by dispossession" via privatization and market liberalization ... [that] extols the primacy of private property rights and ... the commodification, privatization and deregulation of everything except state protection of these very rights' (2018, p. 145). They assert: 'the concept of citizen implies the liberal state. The concept of global citizenship implies the neoliberal state' (p. 145). Like its forebear of liberal citizenship, global citizenship conjoins liberalism with its inextricable components of 'capitalism, imperialism, ableism and the patriarchal state' (p. 147). This renders 'the white subject ... [as] the truest embodiment of the American nation-state and the Cartesian subject [of science and logics]' while dissociating nonwhite bodies 'from full, enlightened subjectivity', as illustrated by the Latinx undocumented 'migrants who are perpetually deported to the site of non-humanity and global non-citizenship' (pp. 154–5). As such, not only is global citizenship unable to smooth over the immanent borders within liberal citizenship, but it has also regenerated and proliferated them in insidious forms.

Yet in spite of global citizenship's internal boundaries and exclusions, the neoliberal ethnoburban development in Southern California that has proffered economic opportunities and sociocultural diversity to minorities and immigrants in the last few decades also suggests a more complex picture than a straight trajectory of unilateral exclusion. Arguing that borders do not merely reflect 'the image of the wall [that] can ... entrench the idea of a clear-cut division between the inside and the outside as well as the desire for a perfect integration of the inside' (Mezzadra and Neilson 2013, p. viii), Sandro Mezzadra and Brett Neilson have reconceptualized borders as boundaries of sociopolitical relations in global capitalism that are always already in our midst, permeating, proliferating, and constantly shifting. As they suggest, this proliferation of shifting boundaries and borders immanent to global capitalism simultaneously engenders and multiplies border struggles and resistance within, producing crisscrossing 'tensions and conflicts that blur the line between inclusion and exclusion ... as well as ... the profoundly changing code of social inclusion in the present' (ibid.).

Invoking the concept of 'differential inclusion', Mezzadra and Neilson argue that borders do not simply exclude and reject; rather, they include selectively, fluidly, and differentially to optimize extraction, subordination, and exploitation in the global capitalist assemblage. As they observe, 'filtering, selecting, and channeling migratory movements – rather than simply excluding migrants and asylum seekers – seems to be the aim of contemporary border and migration regimes' (ibid., p. 165). In fact, 'figures such as benched body shop workers, "illegal" migrants, deportable subjects, banlieusards, and international students ... make the idea of a clear-cut distinction between inclusion and exclusion increasingly problematic' (p. 165). For them, differential inclusion underlines how 'inclusion in a sphere or realm can be subject to varying degrees of subordination, rule, discrimination and segmentation' (p. 159). That is to say, the ineradicable and shifting immanent borders in liberal and global (neoliberal) citizenship do not produce a *fixed* constitutive outside; rather, there are heterogeneous internal differentiations within the outside that are contingently included and excluded. This unstable and precarious global capitalist assemblage operates intricately with the internal racial, gender, and sexual boundaries of the liberal state, producing multiple laboring subjects and political subjectivities that become constitutive of the immanent border struggles. These border struggles, while slippery and perilous, also

> open a new contingent of political possibilities, a space within which new kinds of political subjects, which abide neither the logics of citizenship nor established methods of radical political organization and action, can trace their movements and multiply their powers.
>
> (pp. 13–14)

Building on Mezzadra and Neilson, I argue that Asian and Latinx immigrants in Southern California can be understood as situated differentially in the immanent borders between the local and the global where they engage in interstitial border struggles vis-à-vis their entrenched exclusion. Looking into the everyday labor practices in Asian restaurants, I suggest, can uncover unseen political possibilities as immigrants negotiate their material and psychosomatic inclusion and belonging that remain perpetually unfulfilled by both liberal citizenship and global (neoliberal) citizenship. These immigrant labor practices culminate in what Balibar underlines as the permanent reinvention of citizenship. In the context of Asian restaurants, this permanent reinvention takes form as a daily improvisation of corporeal citizenship.

Conceiving corporeal citizenship in global capitalism

Gabrielson and Parady (2010) have previously articulated a conception of 'corporeal citizenship' embedded in environmental justice concerns. Proceeding through an ontological, posthumanist paradigm, they conceive corporal citizenship as involving ' "a dance of agency" that includes the human, nonhuman nature and artifice, … [and] emphasises the dynamic connectivity and co-constitutive interactions between human bodies and the nonhuman natural world' (p. 383). As they assert,

> in beginning from an ontological perspective that envisions human bodies as porous but resistant, plural, connected and inescapably embedded in both social and natural contexts, one of the advantages of corporeal citizenship is that it is *inherently*, rather than *instrumentally*, green.
>
> (p. 381; emphasis in the original)

This intrinsic, non-instrumental corporeality is at the root of their vision for 'an inclusive and democratic conception of green citizenship' (p. 386).

While Gabrielson and Parady's ontologically inflected posthumanist approach to corporeal citizenship is significant and deserves a more detailed examination beyond this chapter, what I wish to emphasize here is that, by grounding corporeal citizenship on a plainly normative vision of intrinsic ecological/environmental ends, they render a corporeality that is unfiltered by the instrumental effects of global capitalism. This exclusive focus on non-instrumental corporeality misses a keen consideration of the ways in which corporeal citizenship may take on distinctive instrumental forms when it is situated and manifested in everyday life under the historical-material context of global capitalism. Taking this as a point of departure, I adapt 'corporeal citizenship' to the worldly context of ethnic restaurants in contemporary multiethnic suburbs and use the term to delineate the material, affective, and biological dimensions of inclusion, belonging, and 'rights' that immigrants actualize through their everyday production and consumption of ethnic food.

Conceived in this way, I thus understand corporeality to refer not only to the physical or bodily components of humans; rather, following Elizabeth Grosz (1994, p. 22), I conceptualize it as encompassing both mind and body, affect and biology in a co-extensive constitution of 'psychical corporeality'. We can also call these (co-constitutive and co-extensive) affective and biological dimensions of corporeal citizenship 'psychosomatic'. As I suggest, corporeal citizenship is enacted when immigrant participants in the Asian restaurant industry improvise and generate their own 'citizenly contributions' and 'nonexistent rights' in ways that encompass both tangible (material) and intangible (psychosomatic) dimensions.

For instance, the 'nonexistent rights' (rights that are not yet existing or codified in law) that immigrants improvise encompass rights in the material dimension such as the rights to enterprise, work, consumption, and residency as well as rights in the psychosomatic dimension such as the rights to affective inclusion, biological wellbeing, and sociocultural belonging.[1] These rights are not constitutionally protected rights and do not have state recognition even for formal citizens, but improvising these nonexistent rights may achieve some de facto and meaningful (albeit differential) results for the immigrant subjects in the absence of the official recognition of these rights. In fact, corporeal citizenship can be understood as a particular form of what I articulate in another context as 'nonexistent citizenship – that is, inclusion, belonging, equality, or rights that are not formally guaranteed and codified' (Lee 2016, p. 27). From this perspective, corporeal citizenship thus 'enables a viewing horizon of the liminal change and movement that are effected in the hegemonic liberal terrain' (p. 27) even as it generates its own immanent exclusion within the structure of global capitalism.

Immigrant workers enacting corporeal citizenship in ethnic restaurants

Drawing on field interviews with two immigrant restaurant workers, Sherry (a Chinese waitress) and Caesar (a Latino kitchen worker), here I first provide their work narratives and then proceed to discuss how they can be understood as improvising corporeal citizenship to reinvent themselves as citizens through the 'citizenly contributions' they see themselves as making and the kinds of 'nonexistent rights' they are improvising and obtaining. As we shall see, by helping provide a dining atmosphere of affective comfort and cultural vibrancy through their physical, mental, and affective labor, immigrant workers can derive a sense of personal wellbeing, contentment, and achievement in their cultural-economic contributions as they actualize both the tangible (material) and intangible (psychosomatic) dimensions of inclusion, belonging, and 'rights'. At the same time, the intensity of the direct exertion of their labor (sometimes even exploitation) can limit their affective and bodily experiences at their workplace. In fact, configured by the immanent borders within global capitalism from which it emanates, such improvisational enactment of corporeal citizenship is also *differentially* realized in correspondence to the differential racial-class-occupational positionings of the immigrant subjects within the Asian restaurant industry.

Sherry

Sherry, a nineteen-year-old college student from China who works as a server at the Taiwan-originated transnational chain restaurant in Irvine, Chef Hung Taiwanese Beef Noodle, expressed how she derives great pleasure from being in a position to 'directly bring happiness to others' through her service, and thought it particularly interesting being able to interact with customers of different personalities and backgrounds as it expands her knowledge and horizon of human social relations. Although she has never been to Taiwan, she feels a sense of pride when her Taiwanese customers mention to her that this restaurant is famous in Taiwan and offers the most 'authentic' Taiwanese beef noodle (a popular and well-known dish on the island). In her words, she feels she is contributing 'something valuable' for helping continue the cultural heritage and disseminate the 'homeland taste' for her Taiwanese customers. And when she introduces and explains different menu items to American-born or other non-Taiwanese customers who are not familiar with the cuisine, she feels she is 'doing a good deed' by helping them understand what those dishes are. In fact, she noted,

> when the customers comment to me that I have a sweet smile when I serve or that this is the best meal they've ever eaten, that'd totally make my day, more so than I do well at my own school tests[!]

At the same time, one valuable lesson she has learned at work is to be 'calm and patient when facing customer complaints'.

What is notable in Sherry's narratives here is her provision of affective labor that is recognized and affirmed by her customers, which contributes to her affective sense of inclusion and belonging within the culinary economy at her workplace. Importantly, Sherry indicated that she does not think she will be as happy working in an American restaurant for several reasons: (1) the English menu items will be harder for her to memorize; (2) she would have a harder time socializing and getting along with her coworkers because she may not understand their conversations coming from a different cultural background; and (3) she would get less out of her interactions with the customers because if they make some jokes, she may not be able to understand them. In these little and myriad ways, Sherry reveals her sense of foreignness as an Asian-looking and Chinese-speaking subject in English-speaking white America, and the positive affect she is experiencing at Chef Hung is tied to the ethnic-based establishment where she can feel at ease 'using ... my Chinese-speaking ability on my job'. In fact, Sherry thinks ethnic restaurants help immigrant workers transition to life in America and chase the 'American Dream' by allowing them to have a job and accumulate savings while providing them with 'emotional sustenance' in a culturally and linguistically new land.

Yet Sherry's positive sense of material security, social inclusion, and cultural belonging derived from her cultural-economic contributions is often tempered by the reality of her physical and mental labor that is integral to the ethnic culinary economy. For example, Sherry commented that her job is not difficult because most of the tasks are usually manageable, but when the restaurant gets busy it can get very tiring for her. When I asked her in what aspects she got tired, she remarked:

> Physically. And sometimes, my brain also gets tired because you have to memorize many things: 'Here here ... There there ...' And you'd give yourself a lot of pressure. ... But if you actually take it easy – you know I realized when I started [on my job] at the beginning I got nervous easily because sometimes all of a sudden all the things were coming at you. There were things you had to handle here and handle there. But then I realized I seemed to be the only one who acted so busy while everyone else just chilled, doing one thing at a time. I felt strange why my coworkers were not busy like me ... I mean I even ran [in the restaurant]! Then I discovered if you got yourself too busy, it actually didn't make you more efficient. ... You had to calmly handle one thing at a time and put things in order: pouring water first or taking out the noodles? Taking care of the things here while making other customers wait or asking other servers to cover for you? ... I felt I gradually learned a lot about the ways to do things around here.

What has also been indispensable to the Asian restaurant business is thus the coordination of physical and mental labor on the part of the restaurant servers, which becomes the way for them to derive (or exchange for) cultural, social, economic, and emotional benefits from the ethnic culinary commerce.

The physical dimension of her service work is further underlined when Sherry noted that as a server she has to be constantly standing and walking and cannot sit down. She said, 'If you sit down, then you don't need to bother to come [to work], you can go home tomorrow [laugh]. Even if there is no customer, you need to keep walking back-and-forth'. Though mostly unnoticeable, such a physical dynamic of walking is intricately connected to the need to sustain and animate the vibrancy of ethnic restaurants even during a downtime.

In another instance, Sherry also mentioned the need to endure the heat of carrying the big hot noodle soup bowls as another aspect of her corporeal labor:

> When I started out at the beginning, I felt the noodles were so hot. Our noodles were really hot, and they [the management] expected us to carry the noodle soup bowls on both of our hands when we took them to the customers. On top of it, the soup bowls felt heavy and even oily and slippery, and sometimes the customers were sitting a bit far from you and you had to walk a long way to get the food to them. So I felt it was difficult and challenging for me to do. The food was just so hot and there was no way to get around it. One time I was carrying two noodle soup bowls to customers, and it took me four trips (laugh)! They were so hot and I had to come back and take a break before I took them out again but only stopped in the midway to take another break [laugh]. ... But eventually I got used to it. I met some coworkers who used materials like Band-Aid to wrap around their fingers and that made the soup bowls feel not as hot. So people came up with different methods to deal with the heat. I eventually learned to carry the soup bowls by holding onto their edges [where they were less hot] rather than onto their bottoms [where they were the hottest]. Initially it felt unstable when I did so, but over time it worked out for me.

Although Sherry recounts her experience with humor, the narrative here accentuates the direct exertion of intense bodily and physical labor, which again is integral to the ethnic culinary economy that sustains her informal acquisition of inclusion and belonging.

Of course, as mentioned earlier, Sherry's labor is not only physical but affective as well. Her volition to bring a smile when serving, and learning to keep calm and patient when facing customer complaints, are all part and parcel of the detailed work that helps infuse elements of cultural vibrancy and affective comfort into the ethnic restaurant, a culturally affective atmosphere that she herself also partakes in.

Notably, Sherry commented that while working at an Asian restaurant has opened up her horizon and enabled her to 'discipline and train herself', she intends to work at Chef Hung only temporarily and plans to quit her job in a year or two. As a college student, she said, she still wants to keep her focus on her studies and enter into a professional field in the future. Reflecting the gradations of material, affective, and bodily comfort and inclusion within the capitalist class system, the toil of manual labor and relatively lower pay compromise and circumscribe the extent of inclusion and belonging Sherry acquires at the Asian restaurant, but her class and educational positionings also open a door for her to seek out better economic and life opportunities in the long run.

Caesar

For immigrant workers from Latinx backgrounds, the exertions of their bodily labor can take on even greater intensity given their lower status in the echelon of the Asian restaurant economy. Caesar, a twenty-eight-year-old Mexican worker, was taken to the United States by his parents who crossed the border when he was eight months old. Coming from a family of restaurant workers and without U.S. citizenship and with only high school education, he has been working in the kitchens at many different Asian restaurants (including Korean, Vietnamese, Japanese, and Chinese) since he was sixteen, and in job positions that varied from food preparation worker to dishwasher to line cook. Caesar commented that ethnic food is important for immigrants because 'their tastes are different' and that it is also important in helping people cross cultural boundaries (e.g. for himself, having worked at a Chinese restaurant 'makes me learn about the Chinese New Year'). In fact, he added that at his family gatherings, everyone (including his relatives) 'cooks and brings different kinds of food because we work in so many different kitchens'. For Caesar, there is an affective excitement brought about by culinary diversity.

Having been a worker at Asian restaurants for a significant part of his life, Caesar recognizes these establishments for playing a role in helping him chase the 'American Dream': e.g. getting paid, raising a family (with four children), owning a car, and renting an apartment. In fact, Caesar informed me that he has the aspiration to open a Japanese restaurant someday because he likes the flavors of Japanese food and because 'it'd be a family business' drawing on the culinary skills and knowledge of his father, brother, and himself who all have had the experience working at the same Japanese restaurant in Tustin. He explained that his father used to be a cook at the Japanese restaurant and 'knows all the recipes of authentic Japanese food'; his brother used to be 'the sushi man and knows everything about the rolls'; and he himself also knows how to make teriyaki chicken/beef, tempura, and California rolls. For Caesar, the Japanese restaurant owner whom his family worked for played a critical role in teaching the recipes to the Mexican workers and enabling them to potentially start their own business as cross-cultural ethnic restaurateurs in the future.

However, these positive attributes of Asian restaurants in enabling Caesar's material, affective, and cross-cultural inclusion as an undocumented immigrant are complicated by his work experiences at the other establishments. For instance, while noting that some of his managers were compassionate and caring and would buy drinks for the workers 'even though it's not their responsibility', some of the restaurant owners he worked for 'made me do so many things from food prep, dishwashing, cooking, to cleaning the kitchen' even though his job position was just a dishwasher, leading him to conclude that he was not adequately paid for his labor. For instance, recounting his recent experiences of working at a Chinese restaurant in Westminster, Caesar complained that the owner made the workers work late into the night (from 10 p.m. to 2 a.m.) after the restaurant's regular business hours and did not pay them. In one incident, he accidentally cut off the skin of his ear while working in the kitchen and was bleeding badly, and after his coworkers helped put a Band-Aid on him, the restaurant owner simply told him to 'keep on working'. When he tried to talk to the owner about 'the work condition', he was 'told to leave if [he] didn't like it'. Caesar noted that because he had to pay the rent, he stayed on working there, but he did leave his job at that restaurant eventually. He contrasted this negative incident with a positive experience at the Japanese restaurant mentioned earlier where once when he was sick, he was 'sent home with pay' by the restaurant owner.

While Caesar faces similar challenges like Sherry in needing to adjust to the tempo and conditions of restaurant work (e.g. he mentioned at one point that he adapts to the kitchen heat by 'drinking a lot of cold water'), it is notable that his differential racialization and occupational status as a Mexican kitchen worker who labors in the back (rather than the front) of the restaurant complicates his improvisation of corporeal citizenship. On one hand, in spite of his 'devalorized class stigma' in the American economy (Cheng 2013, p. 13), Caesar has relied on the same operations of the Asian restaurant economy – to which he contributes through his *culinary* (e.g. making teriyaki chicken), *affective* (e.g. making customers happy by bringing them different tastes), *physical* (e.g. cleaning the kitchen), and *bodily* (e.g. keeping on performing his labor in spite of the ear injury he suffered at work) labor – to engender his own inclusion and belonging as an undocumented worker. On the other hand, as a Mexican kitchen worker whose low-wage labor fits the niche of the restaurant economy, Caesar exists as a racialized foreigner within the racially foreign Asian restaurants in mainstream America, rendering effects akin to what Cathy Cohen (1999) calls 'secondary marginalization' as he stands in an even more marginalized and precarious position under the power structure of hegemonic whiteness. Immigrants' improvisation of corporeal citizenship thus does not materialize in an universal and equal way but is itself internally differentiated by the racial-class hierarchy within the Asian restaurant industry – which itself exists in an ethnically unequal culinary commerce[2] – reproducing discrepant effects as they negotiate and reinvent citizenship in global capitalism.

Improvising 'citizenly contributions' and 'nonexistent rights': benefits and limits

As signaled in both Sherry's and Caesar's narratives above (as well as in my larger interview sample), immigrant workers at Asian restaurants see themselves as making several 'citizenly contributions' through the ethnic culinary realm. Materially speaking, they see themselves as working and consuming to help sustain and boost the U.S. economy while paying taxes to increase state revenues. On a deeper, intangible level, they see themselves as helping sustain and enhance the affective and bodily lives of immigrants by preparing, cooking, and delivering revitalizing homeland/comfort food that is integral to their psychosomatic embodiment. Furthermore, they also help disseminate and reinvent the cultural heritages of culinary traditions that in turn facilitates and revitalizes ethnic diversification in immigrant America. Rather than proceeding through conventional civic and political institutions and channels, they offer these citizenly contributions through their corporeal (i.e. affective, mental, and physical) labor at the commercial sites of ethnic restaurants. At the same time, Caesar's account of labor abuse shows how his 'citizenly contributions' can be compromised and taken advantage of by certain Asian restaurateurs, thus limiting his contributory experience.

Alongside these citizenly contributions, immigrant restaurant workers can also be understood as improvising a set of 'nonexistent rights'. For instance, both Sherry and Caesar expressed having derived a sense of economic security from the ability to work in their chase of the 'American Dream'. This can be understood as actualizing nonexistent rights in the material dimension such as the rights to work, consumption, and residency (which, in Caesar's case, is perhaps especially significant given his nonstatus that supposedly bars him from even having an opportunity to pursue such rights in the U.S. territory). Notably, such material acquisitions yield complex and asymmetrical results. For Sherry, while feeling like a foreigner in many respects of American life (including her reservation about working as a server at American restaurants), her work experience at Chef Hung functions as a springboard for her to achieve greater material inclusion and wellbeing as she continues on with her educational-professional endeavors within global capitalism, illustrating how the Asian restaurant materially buttresses her acquiring of corporeal citizenship in the process. At the same time, her intent to eventually exit the ethnic restaurant industry reveals the limits of this improvisation given the relatively low socioeconomic positioning of restaurant labor and the toil it involves.

As for Caesar, while his ability to raise a family, own a car, and rent an apartment underscores how his labor in Asian restaurants enables him to acquire better material wellbeing and the de facto rights to work, consumption, and residency in spite of his nonstatus, he is not only afflicted by the exploitation of his labor in some instances but also faces greater challenges in climbing up the socioeconomic ladder with only high school education and without a legal path to U.S. citizenship. In this context, his determination to further material success by enacting the nonexistent right to enterprise – through his aspiration to co-open a Japanese restaurant with his family someday given the culinary knowledge/skills they have acquired – is particularly noteworthy.

It is also clear from Sherry's narratives that her work as an Asian restaurant server allows her to realize nonexistent rights in the psychosomatic dimension such as the rights to affective inclusion and sociocultural belonging. The significance of such informal rights is accentuated if one were to place Sherry in the setting of a (predominantly white) American restaurant, where she would occupy a different positionality as someone whose Chinese communicative skills serve little use and where her Asian racial-linguistic *foreignness* would be marked (and her sense of contributions and self-esteem likely diminished). This, in fact, speaks to the ways in which such informal attainment of nonexistent rights both empowers the immigrant subjects in the particular context of Asian restaurants but also remains limited by hegemonic whiteness in the larger American society.

For Caesar, a differentiated outcome again occurs. While working in a space that is not of his own culture, Caesar expressed his excitement at being situated in a context that involves learning about and crossing over culinary traditions. His thought that ethnic food is important for immigrants because 'their tastes are different' signals his belief that a multicultural environment is dynamic and beneficial. His desire in co-opening a Japanese restaurant is also suggestive of how he acquires the informal rights to affective inclusion and sociocultural belonging from his working experiences at Asian restaurants – and he can further strengthen and enhance the actualization of such rights if he were to become the co-owner of an Asian restaurant operated by his own Mexican American family. Yet, unlike Sherry, for Caesar the informal acquisition of these nonexistent rights is doubly compromised by his continuing racialization as a 'lower-class undocumented Mexican kitchen worker' both in the larger societal context of hegemonic whiteness *and* within the particular setting of certain Asian restaurants that take advantage of his corporeal labor precisely because of his racialized vulnerability.

Conclusion

By improvising their own citizenly contributions and nonexistent rights in informal but de facto ways, it is notable that immigrant restaurant workers carve out a surprising opening in the midst of immanent borders and exclusions as they draw on the instrumental circuits of global capitalism to regenerate their material and psychosomatic inclusion, belonging, and 'rights' in an existential sense. In the current conjunctures of transnational migration and global capitalism, corporeal citizenship becomes an informal way for them to renew their citizenship life in U.S. capitalist democracy.

To be sure, such improvised citizenship can be illusive, for the kinds of informal inclusion, belonging, and rights that are acquired through the circuits of global capitalism, while meaningful for the workers in their immediate or particular contexts, remain contingent and precarious. In fact, as shown in the cases of Sherry and Caesar, the immanent (racial-class-occupational-educational) borders within global capitalism condition corporeal citizenship to be *differentially* realized, rendering its enacting subjects differentially included as their 'inclusion in a sphere or realm [in this context, Asian restaurants] can be subject to varying degrees of subordination, rule, discrimination and segmentation' (Mezzadra and Neilson 2013, p. 159). Corporeal citizenship thus at once illuminates the possibility of change and movement for the global non-citizens and its own complicity and limits in reinscribing the global capitalist structure that leads to differential inclusion and discrepant outcomes.

At the same time, immigrants' improvisation of corporeal citizenship through ethnic commercial spaces also suggests something deep and real, for it underlines their existential aspirations for psychosomatic inclusion and belonging that remain perpetually unfulfilled by both liberal citizenship and global (neoliberal) citizenship. In fact, if immanent borders will always be here with us in any existing circuits/systems of citizenship, it follows that any contestatory or dissonant citizenship formation must proceed through the given borders and exclusions to reinvent and extend a *nonlinear* possibility of life in global capitalism (Tsing 2015; Lee 2016). That is to say: if there is any value in the limits of corporeal citizenship, it is that it presents precisely such a nonlinear possibility of life for the global non-citizens in their perpetual border struggles, and it awaits an unconventional form of political intervention to further reorient such unorthodox rights-claiming toward even more progressive and transformative ends.

Acknowledgements

I would like to thank the Institute for Humanities Research at Arizona State University for providing me with a seed grant that supported the fieldwork for this project. I also thank the respondents for offering their time to share their experiences and perspectives in the study. Lastly, I am thankful to Peter Eglin, Debra Chapman, and Tania Ruiz-Chapman for inviting me to contribute to this volume and for their thoughtful comments and suggestions on this chapter.

Notes

1 I borrow the term 'nonexistent rights' from Jacques Rancière who uses the term 'the staging of a nonexistent right' (1999, pp. 24–5) to refer to the ways in which subjects without formal status/standing to participate politically have historically claimed rights in advance of sovereign recognition through democratic contestations. Expanding on Rancière, I suggest that immigrants in the Asian restaurant industry may also resort to the informal, commercial, and nondemocratic venture of ethnic restaurants to improvise and acquire 'rights' that do not (yet) have sovereign recognition.
2 One notable indicator of this is what Krishnendu Ray (2016) observes as the differential prices that Americans are willing to pay for different kinds of ethnic food, revealing an ethnic hierarchy of tastes and certain presumptions regarding race, class, and social status of different ethnic groups.

References

Balibar, É 2004, *We, the people of Europe? Reflections on transnational citizenship*, Princeton University Press, Princeton, NJ.

Butler, J 1993, *Bodies that matter: on the discursive limits of 'sex'*, Routledge, New York.

Chapman, DD, Ruiz-Chapman, T and Eglin, P 2018, 'Global citizenship as neoliberal propaganda: a political-economic and postcolonial critique', *Alternate Routes*, vol. 29, pp. 142–66.

Cheng, W 2013, *The Changs next door to the Díazes: remapping race in suburban California*, University of Minnesota Press, Minneapolis.

Cohen, CJ 1999, *The boundaries of blackness: AIDS and the breakdown of black politics*, University of Chicago Press, Chicago, IL.

Gabrielson, T and Parady, K 2010, 'Corporeal citizenship: rethinking green citizenship through the body', *Environmental Politics*, vol. 19, no. 3, pp. 374–91.

Grosz, E 1994, *Volatile bodies: toward a corporeal feminism*, Indiana University Press, Bloomington.

Isin, EF 2002, *Being political: genealogies of citizenship*, University of Minnesota Press, Minneapolis.

Isin, EF 2012, 'Citizenship after orientalism: an unfinished project', *Citizenship Studies*, vol. 6, no. 5–6, pp. 563–72.

Isin, EF and Nyers, P 2014, 'Introduction: globalizing citizenship studies', in EF Isin and P Nyers (eds), *Routledge handbook of global citizenship studies*, 1–11, Routledge, New York.

Isin, EF and Wood, P 1999, *Citizenship and identity*, Sage, Thousand Oaks, CA.

Kapur, R 2007, 'The citizen and the migrant: postcolonial anxieties, law, and the politics of exclusion/inclusion', *Theoretical Inquiries in Law*, vol. 8, no. 2, pp. 537–69.

Kim, CJ 1999, 'The racial triangulation of Asian Americans', *Politics and Society*, vol. 27, no. 1, pp. 105–38.

Lee, CT 2016, *Ingenious citizenship: recrafting democracy for social change*, Duke University Press, Durham, NC.

Li, W 1998, 'Ethnoburb versus Chinatown: two types of urban ethnic communities in Los Angeles', *CyberGeo: European Journal of Geography*, viewed 15 September 2019, https://journals.openedition.org/cybergeo/1018.

Mezzadra, S and Neilson, B 2013, *Border as method, or, the multiplication of labor*, Duke University Press, Durham, NC.

Ortiz, V and Telles, E 2012, 'Racial identity and racial treatment of Mexican Americans', *Race and Social Problems*, vol. 4, no. 1, viewed 15 September 2019, www.ncbi.nlm.nih.gov/pmc/articles/PMC3846170/.

Rancière, J 1999, *Dis-agreement: politics and philosophy*, University of Minnesota Press, Minneapolis.

Ray, K 2016, *The ethnic restaurateur*, Bloomsbury Academic, London.

Rocco, R 2014, *Transforming citizenship: democracy, membership, and belonging in Latino communities*, Michigan State University, East Lansing.

Tsing, A 2015, *The mushroom at the end of the world: on the possibility of life in capitalist ruins*, Princeton University Press, Princeton, NJ.

Tsuda, T 2016, *Japanese American ethnicity: in search of heritage and homeland across generations*, New York University Press, New York.

Young, IM 1989, 'Polity and group difference: a critique of the ideal of universal citizenship', *Ethics*, vol. 99, pp. 250–74.

Part III

Global citizenship and the universities

Chapter 5

Global citizenship in the neoliberal Canadian university[1]

Debra D. Chapman

Introduction

Global citizenship is a concept steeped in Northern privilege implicating and implicated in neo-colonial relationships with the global South. 'The rhetoric of global citizenship often serves to obscure the North's complicity in perpetuating systems of dominance that ultimately create an imbalance of power between the North and the South' (DeCaro 2014, p. 3). While having roots in earlier ideas of international citizenship and international education (see Zemach-Bersin, this volume), the idea of *global citizenship education* (GCE) emerges within the neoliberal political-economic model that emphasizes, as stated in the Introduction, 'one's life as the enterprise of oneself'. On the basis of an extensive empirical study Schattle (2008, p. 75) finds that it is in educational institutions (compared to governments, businesses and civil society organizations) that the discourse is most prominent. He holds that its aim is '[to] promot[e] moral visions for a more just, peaceful and sustainable world and [to] enhance[e] the academic achievement, professional competence and economic competitiveness of the next generation' (ibid.). It is, in short, a blend of benevolence and self-interest. What it does *not* do, I argue, is educate young people about their actual place in the neoliberal world order of accumulation by dispossession, carried out by transnational corporations and managed, supervised and protected by imperialist Northern states, above all the United States. It thus serves as propaganda for that very order.

This chapter examines global citizenship discourse as found in the neoliberal Canadian university (Newstadt 2008; Eglin 2013; Fanelli and Evans 2015) with particular reference to international service/experiential learning, and will argue that privilege and marketing drive the concept. Affluent Canadian students, many of whom accrue large debt to pay for their studies, tout the title 'global citizen' in recognition of their knowledge of global politics and/or societal norms abroad, a title they believe places them above their fellow students. Universities themselves claim to produce global citizens (see Clifford and Montgomery 2014). Students who participate in international service learning projects, where they travel to Southern countries and provide services, adopt the concept as a given. They consider their travels to the global South entitle them to be global citizens, whereas, of course, the very people they are serving will never meet the prerequisite. As Biccum (2010, p. 107) states,

> the figure of the global citizen – which for the moment only seems to inhabit metropolitan spaces that are increasingly closed to the rather more specific citizenships of people coming from [the global South] ... see developing countries having to wait for their arrival into 'development' before they can lay claim to [global citizenship].

What I hope the extensive data reported in this study demonstrate is that for the neoliberal university itself, bent as it is on operating like a corporation (Angus 2009, pp. 65–88) and focused on 'bums in seats', the title of global citizen serves as little more than a marketing tool. By offering courses, programmes and certificates in global citizenship, universities hope to recruit students drawn to grandiose claims that station them above the average Canadian citizen.

Description of the data

Canadian universities are so-called 'public' institutions with the exception of a few privately owned ones, most of which have a religious or international foundation, which is not to say that they do not also receive public money. The data collected for this chapter derive from information provided by solely the 'public' universities. 'Public' here refers to institutions of higher education that receive funds primarily from their respective provincial governments (ultimately from the Federal Government of Canada), are bicameral with a board of governors and a senate, and are registered and recognized through the Ministry of Colleges and Universities (or similar body) of the province concerned. Nearly all of them are established by their own Act of the provincial government. While thought of as 'public', Canadian universities are legally private, autonomous, self-governing institutions. They are 'publicly assisted' but not publicly owned or operated.

> In a recent interview in the York Gazette, York University Secretary and General Counsel Harriet Lewis was quoted as saying: 'The most correct way to describe [York] University is that it is a private, charitable corporation, which is "publicly assisted"'.
>
> (Shaker 2002, p. 12)

Without regard to legalities, the 'public' universities are, substantively, 'semi-private' insofar as the amount of public funding they receive has diminished so much since the 1970s that about half of their revenue now comes from tuition fees and private donations.

I found that the concept of global citizen(ship) is used repeatedly and pervasively on Canadian university websites. While most commonly occurring in the Social Sciences, programmes across the university claim to be providing the tools for students to become global citizens. The concept is used in the self-descriptions of programmes including economics, engineering, fine arts, global studies, history, international development studies, languages, nursing, philosophy, political science and religious studies. The concept is typically not defined on such websites so that it tends to have the character of a buzzword or mantric charm.

To determine the specific uses of the concept global citizen(ship) at Canadian universities, all 96 of the 'public' universities in Canada were examined, including their professional, natural science, humanities and social science programmes. Data were collected through the website search engines of each university and then categorized by type of use. That is to say, the expression 'global citizen' was entered into the search engine on the front page of each university's website and whatever results were obtained were collected as the data for the research project.[2] To organize what is a significant amount of material the data were sorted into the following categories, and are presented in this order: definitions of global citizen, vision/mission/strategy, programmes/courses/clubs, events, international student opportunities, awards/certifications/donations, GCE and research, student testimonials, and study abroad/international service learning (ISL). Since space does not permit a display of the whole corpus the following may be regarded as a representative sampling.

Definitions of global citizen

Although the great majority of uses of the concept global citizen are not accompanied with a definition, there are cases where university officials have attempted to give it a definition. According to these definitions, global citizenship is about helping and respecting others, and being aware of and understanding global interconnectedness.

Thus, when asked what the term global citizen meant, President Indira Samarasekera of the University of Alberta (UA) responded,

> a citizen has rights and responsibilities, so a global citizen is someone who has a very clear understanding of his or her rights as a global citizen and therefore what his or her responsibilities are — not only in preserving those rights but in enhancing those rights, which means helping others. You know, I really think it's about each one of us being able to live life to its fullest potential. That's what global citizens are able to do.

Western University's (WU) Dr Larsen is interested in examining the extent to which students who participate in the ISL programme become 'critically engaged global citizens'. It is in this context that she describes a global citizen as 'someone who "becomes aware of difference, global issues, as well as one's identity, positionality, privilege and responsibilities" and "can respond to injustices and inequities that exist in the world today"'. She continues,

This can be as simple as recycling and buying fair-trade goods, and expand to more direct involvement such as participating in one's local, provincial and national community. The most engaged global citizens strive to change belief systems, values and assumptions within institutions and other power structures.[3]

Vision/mission/strategy

This section captures ways university administrations frame their entire programmes to attract students. Through vision, mission and strategic planning statements global citizenship has, in some cases, come to be synonymous with the conferring of a university degree. The examples that follow demonstrate these uses of the concept.

The University of British Columbia's (UBC) Vision Statement asserts that the university 'creates an exceptional learning environment that fosters global citizenship, [and] advances a civil and sustainable society'. The University of Victoria (UVic) has the mantra engraved in its mission statement: 'We are committed to ... promote civic engagement and global citizenship ... The university will enhance its leadership with regard to ... the development of global citizenship'.

Mount Allison University's (MAU) student affairs strategic plan 'challenge[s] students to become leaders as local and global citizens'. In addition, the university's 2016 Internationalization Strategy states, 'International education has the potential to develop well-rounded global citizens'.

Trent University (TU) is one of the Canadian universities most attuned to global citizenship. In fact Champlain College at TU 'has established itself as the college of choice for those who are passionate about adventure, discovery and global citizenship'. MacEwan University's (MEU) vision 'is to become a university of global significance, relevance and value, and [its] goal is to foster a culture of internationalization that creates global citizens'. Furthermore, 'At MEU, we value global citizenship ... [we] hope that we can have more diversity and that our students will be global citizens'.

In response to the question 'Who are we?', Kwantlen Polytechnic University (KPU) states that it 'is committed to providing curriculum and services necessary to prepare our students to be global citizens'. In fact 'all KPU graduates are prepared for global citizenship and rewarding careers'. Furthermore, 'the Arts create responsible, engaged, global citizens'. The Fashion Design and Technology, Health and Wellness and Anthropology programmes at KPU seek to ensure that all their students graduate as global citizens.

The 2025 vision for the University of the Fraser Valley (UFV) includes providing a place for students 'to learn how they can be better global citizens' as well as being a 'centre for intellectual and social development'. Brandon University's (BranU) mission statement considers all Canadian citizens to be global citizens.

Memorial University of Newfoundland's (MUN) strategic plan includes 'Educating global Citizens' as one of its themes. The claim is that by enrolling at MUN you will be equipped 'with the attributes of global citizenship'. This is accomplished by 'providing students both a global perspective and a richer, better rounded set of competencies on the road to a successful career and a meaningful life'.

According to Acadia University's (AU) mission statement, they 'will continue to provide the best undergraduate learning experience in Canada and that [their] graduates will continue to be great leaders, innovators, entrepreneurs and philanthropists, and will understand the true meaning of civil society and being a global citizen'. One of five distinguishing features mentioned in its strategic plan is the 'emphasis on responsible, global citizenship'. According to the president of the Student Union, 'AU is an institution that prides itself not only in providing the best undergraduate education in the country, but transforming its students into responsible global citizens'.

According to Brock University's (BRU) Strategic Plan,

> we encourage students to acquire the life skills and knowledge that will allow them to be prepared for local, global and digital citizenship. This entails being prepared for life long learning and responsible global citizenship in an ever changing global workplace.

BRU is 'compelled by an ever strengthening imperative to graduate global citizens'.

According to Ontario College of Art and Design University's (OCAD) Academic Plan, 'the institution's core mission and vision as an art and design university with a local and global scope ... provides students with the capabilities to be successful global citizens and creative participants in a complex world'.

Ryerson University's (RU) 2017 Internationalization Strategy speaks of 'creating a Global Citizenship Program that would reflect a student's global engagement through a transcript notation ... [which in turn would serve] to incentivise student engagement'. RU also has a 'social venture' called 'Shoppinglee' which is a 'social e-commerce enterprise'. On its website its proponents describe themselves as 'proud global citizens that believe in the interconnectivity of all people'. The periodic review of the Journalism programme at RU declares, 'one of our goals is ... engag[ing] the world as a global citizen, recognizing one's place and interaction in the widest of spheres'.

'Looking ahead' in Wilfrid Laurier University's (WLU) 'Laurier Strategy: 2019–2024' one reads, 'The next decade will bring significant changes to the way we live, learn and work. Engaged and aware global citizens are needed to address challenges such as economic and social inequality, cultural divisions, environmental change, and rapidly changing technology'. Moreover, 'The Strategy' speaks of a 'Thriving Community' as follows: 'Laurier excels at creating a culture of engagement that develops the whole person and builds reciprocal community relationships' by, among other things, 'increasing internationalization of the university to cultivate global citizens with strong intercultural competence'.

The University of Ottawa's (UO) Service Excellence guidelines have five pillars. By subscribing to these five pillars the university is 'creating a better university experience for everyone and helping prepare the leaders, innovators and global citizens of tomorrow ... UO plays a key role in developing global citizens'. Furthermore, 'studying languages and culture is essential ... to become a global citizen'.

WU's mission statement reads: 'WU creates, disseminates and applies knowledge for the benefit of society through excellence in teaching, research and scholarship. Our graduates will be global citizens whose education and leadership will serve the public good'.

Following a visit to Hong Kong, the President of the University of Prince Edward Island (UPEI) stated, 'I was so excited to speak to these prospective students about UPEI's applied programs because we share a mission with their current school: to guide students in becoming global citizens, and our leaders of tomorrow'. At the 2019 convocation ceremony the President addressed the Class of 2019 'as a freshly minted group of global citizens'.

In a 2015 speech at the Canadian Club of Montreal, the President of Concordia University (CU) said:

> I would like to suggest some opportunities for improving the formation of the next generation of Canadians. Like it or not, they will be global citizens ... Rather than a march along the familiar pathway, global citizenship and global employment may be more of a free-form improvisation in the future ... In an epoch of global citizenship, we need all to be at least amateur anthropologists.

In a welcoming speech to the members of CU's Garnet Key Society, the Dean of Students stated 'you're part of something that is much larger than what's in this room ... Having seen you in action, I would say it's more like an inclusive gathering of energized and engaged global citizens'.

An announcement coming from the Office of the Deputy Provost stated 'McGill University [McGU] is uniquely placed to foster students' development as global citizens empowered to meet local challenges'. McGU provides students 'with a network of support to ensure that they thrive in McGill and in Montreal as they develop their full potential as students and global citizens'.

The University of Regina (UR) has found a unique way of marketing itself as a global citizen hub by labelling one of its student housing facilities 'Global Citizen'.[4]

Programmes/courses/clubs

Many universities offer programmes, courses and clubs to do with global citizenship. Programmes other than GCE programmes are highlighted in this section. Courses can be found throughout the different programmes and are often multidisciplinary. Some universities also have clubs where global citizens can gather and organize awareness activities.

Among the variety of programmes designed to enhance or create global citizenship at UBC are midwifery, English for Global Citizens, the Global Citizens stream within the Coordinated Arts Program and a 'Road to Global Citizenship' educators' toolbox that is a joint initiative with the United Nations Children's Fund (UNICEF) and the (former) Canadian International Development Agency (CIDA).

Dalhousie University's (DU) International Development Studies (IDS) programme actively recruits students looking for a GCE. The IDS programme at DU 'teaches [students] how to be ... responsible and informed global citizens'. The International Studies programme at St. Mary's University (SMU) 'combines critical thinking with practice in everyday life aimed at enhancing the ability of all global citizens to actively participate in society to confront the world's most pressing social, economic, political and environmental problems'.

St. Thomas University (STU) promotes many of its programmes as fostering global citizens. It states that the liberal arts 'are the best preparation for a life as a leader, a professional and a global citizen'. The Spanish and Latin American studies programme fosters 'global citizens through exposure to the diversity of Hispanic cultures through literature, cultural media, cinema and art'. Likewise the Romance Languages 'department seeks to foster global citizens by exposing students to the diversity of Francophone, Hispanic, and Italianate worlds'. The French language programme 'seeks to foster global citizens by exposing students to the diversity of Francophone worlds'. The history department promises to 'produce thoughtful and informed global citizens who appreciate the fascinating and diverse charter of the world'.

The Global Health programme at MUN raises 'awareness about global health issues amongst students and the general public ... developing projects which are sustainable and aim to ... create a university wide community of global citizens' (see also the Community Health Program at the University of Saskatchewan [US]). The Faculty of Humanities and Social Science at MUN launched a new degree programme in 2017 'designed to prepare students for a future as global citizens'. MUN also promises 'to ensure [that] engineering graduates are engaged global citizens'. The Religious Studies programme creates 'global citizens with the capacity to engage in both sympathetic understanding and vigorous critique of the place of religion in today's religiously diverse world'.

Université Sainte Anne (USA) offers a literature and environment course. It is described in the following way: 'the examination of environmental degradation and other ecological concerns is a vibrant facet of contemporary literary criticism, a crucial aspect of social justice studies, and an urgent, timely enquiry for global citizens, learners and educators'.

The University of Windsor (UWin) declares in its pitch to law students,

> University is not just a place to secure a career ... it's a place to become a good global citizen and break down the walls of injustice ... [we are] committed to nurturing global citizens and attracting students with a diversity of

thoughts, background and experience, who are ready to make a real difference in local communities and beyond ... Thanks to our rich diversity, we all learn how to think and act as responsible global citizens.

Asian Studies courses at the University of Toronto (UofT) 'are designed to delve deep into the social, cultural and economic trends that have defined East Asia ... [by taking these courses students] can become ... more effective and well-versed global citizen[s]'. Political Science 101 at Capilano University (CapU) will 'prepare students to become global citizens'.

Martin Luther University College at WLU offers a BA in Christian Studies and Global Citizenship. In this programme, students 'will learn to think critically about [their] faith, the world, and [their] place within it'. The WLU Global Studies programme also offers a fourth year course on Global Citizenship.

The economics department at Queen's University (QU) considers all its students to be global citizens. Its website states that the study of 'economics will help [students] make better decisions in [their] personal life, in [their] business life and as a global citizen'.

UPEI offers a unique opportunity through the Veterinarian/farming programme. The title of the project is Integrating Innovative Research and Training for Improved Sustainable Livelihoods in a Smallholder Dairy Farming Region. The programme 'aims to develop Canadian and Kenyan students into global citizens through enriching courses, community engagement, research and development projects in Canada and Kenya'. The course will 'enhance [students'] research, communication and leadership skills as global citizens'.

The Climate Change graduate programme at Bishop's University (BU) states that 'finding solutions to the problems brought on by climate change requires educating a new generation of global citizens well-versed in the concepts, issues and challenges associated with such a complex topic'.

The Nursing and Health programmes at McGU hold that 'as global citizens, all of us have an obligation to make a contribution towards addressing [international] challenges [namely SARS, Ebola, Avian Flu]'. On World Health Day 2018, the University's focus was 'Educating Nurses to be global citizens and agents for change'. Its health programme 'coordinates the University's global health work, and is making strategic investments and partnerships to make sure McGill's faculty and students are actively engaged as global citizens'.

UR has a Global Citizen Youth Leadership Program tied to its Bachelor of Education programme. The Chinese Language programme prepares students 'to be wiser and more informed global citizens'. The Tourism and Hospitality programme at Royal Roads University (RRU) allows students to 'build competencies in the areas of global citizenship ... [students] will leave this program ... as responsible global citizens'. The Communications and Culture interdisciplinary programme gives students the opportunity to 'possess a well-developed perspective as a global citizen'. They 'develop global citizens'.

The Global Citizenship course at McMaster University (McMU) offers an interdisciplinary introduction to globalization through a critical engagement with the idea of 'global citizenship' in the contemporary context ... [in this course] students will reflect upon what it means to be a 'global citizen' in light of how such dynamics shape questions of identity, agency, power and resistance.

Political Science students are

> able to pursue a specialization in Global Citizenship which includes a term abroad or work experience/internship on a global issue ... This specialization is designed to prepare students for their roles as citizens in a globalized world. It examines global citizenship in relationship to some of the main challenges faced by contemporary politics ... with the aim of showing how [students] can enact themselves as global citizens.

The Social Responsibility for Sports, Recreation and Health course at BRU examines 'the role of social responsibility for sport, recreation and health with focus on organizational and individual orientations of social responsibility and global citizenship'. BRU also offers a Hosting a Migrant Worker forum. This is a course designed for 'creating global citizens by starting in our own backyard'. BRU 'wants to make sure that all of [their] students, staff and faculty from across the University have an opportunity to be actively and positively engaged as global citizens'. This is done through Brock International and the courses connected to this programme.[5]

Events

Global Citizen Week is an annual event held at Vancouver Island University (VIU). The event includes visiting speakers and classroom discussions that explore 'issues of global development at home and abroad'. They also hold a Global Citizens' Soccer tournament. The Atlantic Council for International Cooperation holds an annual International Development Week challenge. It 'encourages schools to be ACTive Global Citizens by participating in the ACT4 Global Change Challenge. Dalhousie University has actively participated in this challenge'.

SKILL21, which is a series of interdisciplinary workshops at McGU 'aims to provide students with opportunities to become contributing global citizens in the 21st century'. The Spiritual Fair 2019 is another event held annually where students can 'learn about different faiths [which is] an important part of being a global citizen and a first step toward understanding each other's world view'. In 2018, UR held a conference titled 'Educating Global Citizens: Stories and Strategies'. The Global Village event at US 'is a student-led intercultural celebration [that] explores what it means to be a global citizen in Canada and on Treaty 6 Territory'.[6]

International student opportunities

While most global citizen designations, courses and programmes are designed for national students, some universities offer opportunities for international students to become global citizens. Based on the definitions offered by some universities, one would expect international students to be true global citizens as they are aware of the local and the global through opportunities their privilege permits. International students' tuition fees are substantially higher than those of national students.

UA offers a Global Learning Summer Program for students from Beijing and Harbin. 'The purpose of the programme is to provide a unique learning opportunity for students to explore our vibrant campus and province and to engage with concepts related to global citizenship'. The programme description states, 'an understanding of cross-cultural nuances is an essential part of becoming a global citizen'.

International students at TU can apply for Global Citizenship Scholarships and Awards. In partnership with the Aga Khan Foundation Canada, the university has organized a Going Global Together Exhibit that 'inspires students to be Global Citizens'. As mentioned in the Introduction to this volume, one of the interactive components is an online quiz that claims to 'determine what type of global citizen' one is (Aga Khan Foundation Canada n.d.).

RRU offers scholarships to international students and refugee students who enrol in the Global Leadership MA programme. The award recipients must 'demonstrate their global citizenship through outstanding contributions to their community'. Conversation circles are offered at MUN for new Canadians. They hold that 'combining locals and new Canadians provides a great opportunity to take an action role in global citizenship'.

The MPower Global Citizen Scholarship is available to international students enrolled full-time in a Canadian or US university. The Schulich School of Business at York University (YU) encourages its international students to apply for the scholarship that is worth up to $5,000.[7]

Awards, certifications and donations

Global Citizenship awards take the concept one step further as they often require financial resources to travel abroad, a privilege only available to the more affluent students. If not through financial privilege the other ways to qualify for an award are through knowledge acquisition, by becoming aware of difference and by offering voluntary services to the underprivileged sectors of society.

The University of Guelph (UG) offers a Certificate in Civic Engagement and Global Citizenship as well as Global Citizenship awards. In 2007, ten 'renowned Global Citizens' were given honorary degrees at convocation. One of the recipients, Paul Rusesabagina of *Hotel Rwanda* fame, was invited to participate in a panel discussion on Canada's role as a global citizen. This example instructs us as to how the reference of the concept of global citizen may be extended from a person to a collective entity such as a country or a state.

The Government of Alberta's 2013 International Strategy had four objectives. The second was to 'build Alberta's reputation as a global citizen' (Government of

Alberta 2013). As a provincially funded and mandated institution the University of Lethbridge (UL) reflects this objective through its 'Certificate of Global Citizenship', its reference to a 'global citizenship cohort' and its proposal 'to develop global citizenship from a gender perspective'.

The University of Calgary (UC) offers a $6,000 Research Fellowship in Global Citizenship. The two- to eight-month fellowship is for those who understand 'the true meaning of citizenship'. Mount Royal University (MRU) offers the Calgary Peace Prize to what is described elsewhere as 'an exceptional global citizen'. In 2013 the University announced, 'Scotia Bank's gift to International Education helps MRU students become global citizens'. The bank donated $500,000 'to make international experiences a real possibility for hundreds of students by offsetting the significant costs of studying and living abroad'.

If a student wants to become a member of the Global Citizens Network at VIU, they will receive a $500 stipend in exchange for 15 hours of volunteer work. The annual Shirley Case Leadership Award for Global Citizenship is open to Atlantic province students who have 'demonstrated a spirit of global citizenship in a local, national or international capacity and who [have] helped create a more just and sustainable world'.

UofT offers a Global Citizenship Certificate. It 'prepares [students] for working and succeeding in a culturally diverse and rapidly changing world'. Certification involves a five-stage process with five workshops. Once completed, students will receive a certificate of completion and a reference letter.

For over 25 years UR has been granting Global Citizen Awards. 'These ... awards recognize ... people who make ... contributions to international development, cooperation, peace and justice'. 'More than 100 people and organizations have received' these awards.

At US the Gail Appel Global Citizenship Award is 'offered annually to an undergraduate student who exemplifies the spirit of global citizenship'. The Global Studies programme also offers a certificate to

> students from various academic backgrounds [giving them] ... the opportunity to come together with a common focus – a commitment to developing an understanding of various facets of the global village, gaining international experience, and becoming more aware and active as global citizens.

Another way to tout your global citizen designation is with the Certificate of Proficiency in Jewish and Christian Origins. This certificate 'will give you a new insights and critical perspectives from a variety of disciplines ... that will help to make you an informed global citizen'.[8]

GCE and research

GCE is offered at universities across the country and has been studied extensively (see this volume, Part I; Biccum, this volume, Chapter 7). 'The concept of educating for global citizenship encourages students to adopt a critical understanding of globalization, to reflect on how they and their nations are implicated in local and global problems and to engage in intercultural perspectives' (Pashby 2012, p. 9). GCE courses are designed to give educators the tools to teach global citizenship, to give teachers a better understanding of global issues such as poverty and AIDS, and to enhance students' knowledge of their responsibility in the world (ibid.; see also Jefferess 2012). Here are a few examples of some of the GCE programmes offered.

MRU has a Centre for Global Citizenship Education and Research. According to their vision statement, the centre 'heightens consciousness and understanding of issues of GCE in order to contribute to the collective development of societies that provide basic social justice and human rights'.

WU's Faculty of Education has created a Global Citizen Kit. The 'kit … provide[s] Grade 6 teachers with a cutting-edge curriculum resource to empower educators and students to make a difference in the world'. The kit comprises 'more than 40 lessons and assessment strategies on the theme of global citizenship'.

Graduate Students in the Education programme at the Université de Sherbrooke (USher) have the opportunity to take a course titled Global Citizenship in Teaching and Learning (PED607). The course prepares students to

> understand the responsibility of fostering the development of the attributes of global citizens in college students [and allows] participants to broaden their understanding of what global citizenship means and will find ways to foster the greatest attributes of a global citizen in the students they teach.[9]

Student testimonials

Here are just a few comments made by students who studied abroad or saw themselves as global citizens. I have removed all references to programmes and context as what I am trying to demonstrate is how students have bought into the global citizenship discourse.

> [It allowed me to] keep an open mind when brought to situations outside of [my] previous comfort zone [and it] allowed [me] to grow as a person but also as a global citizen.
>
> (Thompson Rivers University [TRU])

> I believe that as a global citizen, it is my responsibility to understand the world outside of the bubble I've always known.
>
> (MUN)

> It's made her a better person … It's made me a good global citizen … It's made me aware of my own actions. But it's also made me aware that I have a responsibility, and I have the ability to make changes to make the world a better place.
>
> (AU)

[It allowed me to] expand on my previous community engagements to learn what it means to be a global citizen.

(DU)

I travelled [abroad], where I learned more about social justice and my role as a global citizen.

(St. Francis Xavier [StFX])

My graduate education has helped me build my critical thinking, teamwork skills, collaboration and global citizen mindset ... The most humbling aspect of the trip overall for me was the chance to know what it truly means to be a global citizen.

(BU)

[T]hat's where I first discovered what it means to be a global citizen. ... What I didn't anticipate, however, was how it would allow me to unite with people around the world and truly understand how we as global citizens can ignite change on an international level ... My role as a global citizen has just begun.

(CU)

[I] could explore contemporary Canadian ... issues ... through different viewpoints ... [I have] been able to think of Canada as an outsider, as an insider, and, more importantly, as a global citizen.

(CU)

I think LU can really prepare you for your future because it teaches you to be a global citizen and to be the best you can be in your career. For me, having different clubs and people from different cultures and nationalities all working together at the same school helped me become a more global citizen ... Educating students to be global citizens is part of LU's mission and strategic plan.

(Lakehead University [LU])

I think I have become a more well-rounded global citizen because I have completely adapted to a new way of living while still maintaining my Canadian roots ... [It] helps you learn so much, become a better global citizen and broaden your horizons.

(WU)

I don't really know if travelling is for everyone, however, I think getting involved helps you to become a global citizen because it allows you to feel empathy, understand diversity and incorporate those experiences into who you are.

(University of Waterloo [UofW])

ISL/experiential learning/study abroad

International service/experiential learning and volunteer abroad programmes, which have flourished throughout Canadian universities over the past 15 years in blind ignorance of Ivan Illich's (2012 [1968]) stunning denunciation of the practice, typify the neo-colonial relationship between North and South (see also Krabill 2012). It is expressed in the Northern values, culture and political-economic outlook students bring to their placements (see DeCaro 2014, p. 10). The concept of global citizen is appropriated by Canadian students and teachers providing 'services' to people in small communities in the global South, people who will never be seen by themselves or by others to be global citizens (see Andreotti 2006, p. 9; see also Larsen and Searle 2017, p. 202).

Whether designed to facilitate student recruitment and research opportunities, to give students an alternative learning experience or simply to create so-called global citizens, ISL raises several troubling ethical concerns (Tiessen and Huish 2014; Chapman 2016) that reveal not only the neo-colonial character of the *practice* of global citizenship but also its neoliberal colouring. Zemach-Bersin (2009, p. 303) warns that ISL programmes appeal to students' 'sense of entitlement, consumerism and individualism'. As evident in the examples of global citizenship at Canadian universities above, 'foreign destinations and their citizens are products or commodities' (ibid., p. 305) that can be bought through ISL course enrolment and used to enhance Canadian students' self-perception. In order for them to turn into global citizens, 'the locals serve as "backdrops [or] props"' (ibid.). Furthermore, '[b]oth study abroad advertisements and participating students discuss international education as an entitlement, a non-academic adventure, and an experience primarily for personal advancement' (ibid., p. 313). The following are examples of how experiential learning is framed.

The Exercise Science, Physical and Health Education (ESPHE) programme at UVic states that 'programs offered by ESPHE provide opportunities ... to study abroad on international exchange or combine work with study to help prepare you for life as a responsible global citizen'. UofW 'creates global citizens in a global economy'. It encourages students to become global citizens through its International Experience programme, and through the Global Citizen Internships offered by its Faculty of Environment. TU's volunteering abroad programme allows students to 'become ... global citizen[s]'. Through the Impact programme, students can take a workshop on 'becoming a global citizen'.

MEU offers a study-abroad, community service-learning course in the Ukraine titled Global Health Perspectives (HLST 400). It promises to connect students 'with policy makers, health care workers, students, faculty and health care agencies from the Ukraine, gaining a deeper understanding of current and future global health issues and opportunities and [their] role as a global citizen and a healthcare professional'. UL's experiential learning graduate programme promises to set students 'apart as ... knowledge maker[s] and informed global citizen[s]'. It offers courses and research beyond the classroom, but not internationally.

Students can 'learn and practice the skills of a global citizen and become a transformative agent of social change' by spending three weeks in Ghana as part of the Service Learning Field School at KPU.

The Global Learning Program at RU 'helps students find opportunities to learn about other cultures ... gain new perspectives ... and engage the world as a global citizen'. This can be accomplished by attending an international conference or volunteering abroad.

UO offers a Global Recognition Program (uOGlobal) that has been funded by Power Corporation to nurture global citizens. Power Corporation donated $1.5 million to the programme that 'will encourage more students to get involved in cross-cultural activities'.

> The uOGlobal [programme] will help [students] set [themselves] apart in the eyes of employers because [students] will be better prepared for working in a global labour market ... [after all] employers are looking for people with intercultural skills and global citizenship values.

The Global Studies Experience offered through the Global Studies programme at WLU 'helps students to reflect on their privilege, their preconceived notions of other cultures, and the ethical dilemmas they face as global citizens'. Students who went to Ghana as part of the Kenneth Woods Portfolio Management Program were described as having 'found a way to grow into global citizens'.

HEC Montreal's Campus Abroad Program

> is intended to widen participants' global awareness, by focusing on learning through experience so that they can: understand the economic context and the cultural and socio-political aspects of another country; compare business practices; ... [and] integrate the intercultural knowledge they acquire, to become more involved global citizens.[10]

Political-economic analytic commentary

Canadian universities have experienced a neoliberalization or corporatization of their practices and organizational structures over the past 40 years. How well an institution, programme or course curriculum 'contributes to the knowledge economy' has become the yardstick commonly used to measure the effectiveness of universities. More vocationally oriented curricula, more publicly sourced research grants requiring private partners, more reliance on debt to finance students' education, more use of short-term, part-time, contractual employment for faculty, larger class sizes, higher tuition fees, greater reliance on international student recruitment and the lowering of student admission requirements have all been instituted. This is not to mention the greater contracting out of university services like student accommodation and food to private providers. While the idea of the university being a corporation was noted by Randolph Bourne around the time of the First World War (Chomsky 1969, p. 46), there's little doubt about its acceleration and growth in this direction under neoliberalism: 'If "universities are not corporations" ever was a good argument, it isn't anymore because universities, always corporations in financial fact, become increasingly corporate in spirit every day' (Fish 2011).

Côté and Allahar (2011, p. 11) point out that

> because the majority of the public do not attend university and are not attuned to what goes on there, they are ... understandably more likely to be interested in practical outcomes ... and in curricula that promise tangible returns on governments' spending of their tax dollars.

Practical outcomes come from skills-based learning and certifications such as global citizenship certificates that promise to give students a ticket to better employment. In the social sciences this means a transformative shift from the classics to instruction manuals (ibid.). The idea that 'knowledge is capable of being its own end' (Newman, as cited in Côté and Allahar 2011, p. 13) has been lost. As curricula change to accommodate skills-based learning, some of the notable changes include courses in social entrepreneurship being offered in the social science stream (see Chapman 2017) rather than through the business faculty, flourishing community engagement and international service learning opportunities, and interdisciplinary programmes that are replacing the traditional subjects in order to provide the job training skills graduates will need. Historically, job training and skill development were provided through college education while critical thinking and knowledge-based historical, political, social, economic and cultural analyses were acquired through university education. Côté and Allahar (2011, p. 25) describe the university as 'a "space" where complex ideas are unpacked, dealt with in abstraction, and then recombined in the form of concepts, theories, hypotheses, and ultimately policies applied back to the outside world'. These lines between college and university education have become blurred as universities move towards more skills-based education due to the pressures on university programmes to be more marketable. At the root of the change is the reduction in state funding of higher education.

In the 1950s and 1960s public higher education grew in demand and with it there was an increase in government funding. In 1955 the Canadian federal government covered 55 per cent of all university operating costs and by 1970 that amount increased to 75 per cent, peaking at 84 per cent in 1978. There was an increase of 13 new universities across the country from 1960 to 1969 with an additional five campuses of the Université du Québec (UduQ) (see Tudiver 1999, pp. 24–5, 66). Higher education was booming. It was considered a 'profitable investment' by both the public and private sectors (ibid., p. 43). With this rapid expansion came an unanticipated interest and opening for the corporate world. Representatives on university boards came to include corporate leaders who sought to influence the curriculum, internal administrative decisions and enrolment levels. The transition that opened the board and the senate to outside influence could be construed as the start of the corporatization of the university. In 1977, funding from the federal government for higher education became a provincial responsibility. This gave the provinces greater control over spending. Thus it is that neoliberal globalization has been experienced in Canadian universities since the late 1970s in the form of declining government funding (in real dollars) (ibid., p. 203): 'per student funding from the government (primarily provincial) ... dropped from $17,900 in 1980–81 to $9,900 in 2006–2007' (Damaskinos 2008). Ontario universities were hit particularly hard with 17 per cent cuts to operating grants from the Government of Ontario in 1995 (ibid.). Fish (2008, pp. 154–5) documents the comparably drastic 40-year decline in the public funding of universities in the United States.

As mentioned above, massive cuts to public higher education have forced public universities to seek other sources of revenue. Henry Giroux's (2012, p. 129) description of the changes experienced in today's university is particularly telling. He states that the changes include:

> a growing shift in governance away from faculty to administrations that largely define themselves in corporate terms; a growing restriction on academic freedom; a diminution of faculty rights; a growing army of part-time and nontenured faculty; the privileging of academic subjects and credentials tied to market-based principles; the rise of accountability measures that devalue critical thought and engaged scholarship; the blurring of lines between the university and the corporate world; the shaping of faculty research in the direction of corporate interests and priorities; and the appropriation of a corporate discourse in which students are viewed as customers, faculty as entrepreneurs, and university presidents as CEOs ... Or, to put it more specifically, the consequence of such dramatic transformations has resulted in the near-death of the university as a democratic public sphere.

The framing of higher education as described above provides a segue into consideration of how the concept of global citizenship is used within the corporatized university. Taking into account how the university has adopted a corporate approach to delivering education as a response to reduced funding helps to explain how marketing an image has become the necessary tool required to succeed. The value of free, open-ended and critical enquiry as an end in itself has been replaced with an emphasis on the number of bums in seats and relationships with corporate donors. Inviting students to go abroad to gain global citizenship status or offering a roster of selected courses designed to grant students a global citizenship certificate – both make a mockery of higher education.

Dower (2008, p. 39) argues, however, that 'we are all global citizens' and that as such we don't actually need to educate students to become global citizens but rather teach them how to 'become aware of themselves as having this status'. As students become aware of their status as global citizens (see Pike 2008, p. 225) they will in turn take it upon themselves to act globally and work to improve the lives of others. Whether thought of as an inherent characteristic of citizenship in a globalized neoliberal world or something learned at school, Dower rejects the view that global citizenship is an elitist idea, neglecting to acknowledge 'citizens' of the global South who lack the means to act globally, not least because they would be the recipients of the services provided by the elite global citizens to whom Dower refers. Global citizenship *education*, according to Dower (2008, p. 40), is for the purpose of creating 'the future "movers and shakers" of the world' or simply to make students aware of their inner global citizen. In response to this surely false assumption that we are all global citizens, I would invite Dower to look at the political-economic inequalities in *Northern* countries where the marginalized lack the opportunities afforded to Northern 'elites' to act globally.

In *For Love of Country?* Martha Nussbaum presents four arguments justifying 'making world citizenship ... the focus for civic education' (1996, pp. 11–14). Her arguments range from the importance of Northerners learning about and understanding the widely varying norms and practices of peoples throughout the world, that they can then use to compare with and modify their own practices, to people in the privileged North having a moral obligation to take care of and respond to the needs of people in the global South suffering from poverty, inequality and social injustice. Global citizenship in this context is something we learn through education and which we then apply benevolently at home and abroad.

But then '[t]he ambiguity of "global" and "citizenship" together reveal that the term is too vague to be useful' (Osiadacz 2018, p. 46). To suggest global citizenship is actually a meaningful concept logically requires 'a world of universal values, generally shared moral concerns, a real international human rights culture, widespread institutions ... and so on' (Dower 2008, p. 44; see also Pike 2008, p. 225; Falk 1994). A world passport or certificate would presumably follow. This vision derives, of course, from a literal interpretation of the concept, but this interpretation is very far from the world we live in today. If universities tend not to conceive of global citizenship literally, nevertheless, as revealed in the data displayed above, the concept is used in empirical ways that suggest students can actually become global citizens with the right education and lived experiences, such that it could become a legitimate form of self-description or description by another. For Dower (2008, p. 45), 'what makes someone a global citizen is a certain form of consciousnesses ... someone who cares about world poverty, or joins Amnesty International'.

The use of the concept global citizen becomes most problematic when it is used in this way as a personal claim or descriptor that is attainable through the right training and knowledge acquisition. To be blunt it is simply a fallacy to suppose that global citizenship can be attained through education. Osiadacz (2018, p. 45) points out that 'global citizen education means anything from attending a "Me to We" day to a sleepover in the gym without dinner to recognize global poverty and hunger'. In fact, the idea is preposterous, as I hope this chapter demonstrates in detail. Whether through travel abroad for the purpose of international service learning or simply from passive labelling, students who are themselves already privileged are receiving the wrong message. There is a latent understanding that holds that through education, global citizenship provides an edge over other students and certainly an edge over the impoverished, vulnerable populations of the Global South. This view and the more egalitarian notion of a 'universal moral status' plus the standard benevolence obligation – all are laced with Northern elitism and profoundly misleading to the students themselves.

Conclusion

It is important to state that learning about political, economic, cultural and social aspects of the globalized world of the twenty-first century does *not* give students a modified or enhanced citizenship status. History, geography and social studies have been subjects in Canadian secondary schools and institutions of higher education for a very long time. Degrees in these disciplines did not come with labels. Neither schools nor colleges and universities granted students a certificate that made them more employable or superior to their peers or citizens in the global South just because they could now speak knowledgeably about international relations. It has been the thesis of this chapter that the idea of global citizenship touted by Canadian universities, being empty of substance, is little more than a marketing tool, one that has unfortunately become all too common-place, and one that conveys the ideological affordance of 'one's life as the enterprise of oneself'. Brustein (2007, p. 384) puts it like this, 'The surge in global citizenship education programmes can be seen as a marketing tool to attract students looking for attributes to make them competitive in the global workforce'.

David Harvey (2005) sums up the global problem of inequality in his analysis of 'accumulation by dispossession'. He argues that corporations in the global North take advantage of the economic and material wealth of nations in the global South to generate profits and grow their financial wealth while dispossessing local citizens of their resources and financial opportunities. It is hard to imagine how the concept of global citizen could fit into Harvey's political-economic analysis, other than as ideology. His political-economic framing highlights power relations, economic inequality, the North–South divide and the inherent aspects of capitalism that leave people behind. One might ask, if we could remove the inequalities generated by the capitalist mode of production, would we need 'global citizens'? Or would the people of the earth then simply be global citizens?

Notes

1 Parts of this chapter are adapted with permission, and enlarged, from a section of Chapman, Ruiz-Chapman and Eglin (2018).
2 To avoid encumbering the chapter with an inordinately long list of university website urls suffice it to say that the data were assembled between mid-2016 and mid-2019 in the way stated in the text. Anyone wishing to corroborate them need only replicate the specified steps required, that is, Google the desired university, enter 'global citizen'

in the website search engine and see what turns up. While it is true that programme, course and other descriptions change, enough of them will be the same or close enough to verify the general point being made here about the pervasive use of the concept throughout the university sector in Canada.
3 See also University of Manitoba (UM), UO, UofT Mississauga and BU.
4 See also US, BU, McMU, UC, YU, WLU, Nipissing University (NU), LU, Carleton University (CarlU), UL and CapU.
5 See also University of Northern British Columbia (UNBC) Global Studies, UFV, VIU, TRU, WU and UG.
6 See also MUN and MEU.
7 See also New College at UofT and UNBC.
8 See also UFV, UBC, UA Faculty of Education, MUN, UM, WU Global Opportunities Award for Medical Students and YU.
9 See also UR Faculty of Education, BU, LU and VIU.
10 See also UFV, TRU, McGU, YU, University of Ontario Institute of Technology, BRU, NU, RRU, BU and CarlU.

References

Aga Khan Foundation Canada n.d., 'Together: take the global citizen quiz', viewed 30 October 2019, http://together.akfc.ca/exhibit/en/.

Andreotti, V 2006, 'Soft versus critical global citizenship education', *Policy & Practice: A Development Education Review*, vol. 3, pp. 40–51.

Angus, I 2009, *Love the questions: university education and enlightenment*, Arbeiter Ring, Winnipeg, MB.

Biccum, A 2010, *Global citizenship and the legacy of empire: marketing development*, Routledge, London and New York.

Brustein, W 2007, 'The global campus: challenges and opportunities for higher education in North America', *Journal of Studies in International Education*, vol. 11, no. 3–4, pp. 382–91.

Chapman, DD 2016, 'The ethics of international service learning as a pedagogical development practice: a Canadian study', *Third World Quarterly*, doi:10.1080/01436597.2016.1175935.

Chapman, DD 2017, 'Emprendimiento social y las ciencias sociales: evaluación de una practica de desarrollo pedagógico neoliberal', *Revista Observatorio del Desarrollo. Investigación, Reflexión y Análisis*, vol. 6, no. 16, pp. 31–8.

Chapman, DD, Ruiz-Chapman, T and Eglin, P 2018, 'Global citizenship as neoliberal propaganda: a political-economic and postcolonial critique', *Alternate Routes*, vol. 29, pp. 142–66.

Chomsky, N 1969, 'The function of the university in a time of crisis', in R Hutchins and M Adler (eds), *The great ideas today*, 41–61, Encyclopaedia Britannica, Chicago, IL. (Reprinted, 1973, as chap. 6 in Chomsky, *For reasons of state*, Vintage, New York.)

Clifford, V and Montgomery, C 2014, 'Challenging conceptions of western higher education and promoting graduates as global citizens', *Higher Education Quarterly*, vol. 68, no. 1, pp. 28–45.

Côté, JE and Allahar, AL 2011, *Lowering higher education: the rise of corporate universities and the fall of liberal education*, University of Toronto Press, Toronto.

Damaskinos, J 2008, 'Are Canadian universities underfunded?' *IMPRINT* (University of Waterloo's Official Student Newspaper), 11 July, front page.

DeCaro, L 2014, 'Who is a global citizen?' *Citizenship Education Research Journal*, vol. 4, no. 1, pp. 3–12.

Dower, N 2008, 'Are we all global citizens or are only some of us global citizens?' in AA Abdi and L Shultz (eds), *Educating for human rights and global citizenship*, 39–53, State University of New York Press, New York.

Eglin, PA 2013, *Intellectual citizenship and the problem of incarnation*, University Press of America, Lanham, MD.

Falk, R 1994, 'The making of global citizenship', in BV Steenbergen (ed.), *The condition of citizenship*, 127–40, Sage Publications, London.

Fanelli, C and Evans, B 2015, 'Neoliberalism and the degradation of education', *Alternate Routes: A Journal of Critical Social Research*, vol. 26, viewed 18 July 2018, http://alternateroutes.ca/index.php/ar/article/view/2233.

Fish, S 2008, *Save the world on your own time*, Oxford University Press, New York.

Fish, S 2011, 'We're all badgers now', *New York Times opinionator*, 21 March, viewed 3 November 2019, http://opinionator.blogs.nytimes.com/2011/03/21/were-all-badgers-now/.

Giroux, H 2012, *Twilight of the social: resurgent publics in the age of disposability*, Paradigm, London.

Government of Alberta 2013, 'Alberta's international strategy, 2013: fact sheet' viewed 18 April 2017, https://open.alberta.ca/dataset/1cf4294e-c385-48ad-b4a8-1ab2526ae0e3/resource/c39ebff2-8046-4971-813aa179a25b47a4/download/zz-6597763-2013-05-AB-International-Strategy-2013-FactSheet.pdf.

Harvey, D 2005, *A brief history of neoliberalism*, Oxford University Press, Oxford.

Illich, I 2012, 'To hell with good intentions', in A Gilvin, GM Roberts and C Martin (eds), *Collaborative futures: critical reflections on publicly active graduate education*, 314–20, Graduate School Press, Syracuse University, Syracuse, NY, originally given as a speech to the Conference on Inter-American Student Projects in Cuernavaca, Mexico in 1968.

Jefferess, D 2012, 'Unsettling cosmopolitanism: global citizenship and the cultural politics of benevolence', in V de O Andreotti and LMTM de Souza (eds), *Postcolonial perspectives on global citizenship education*, 27–46, Routledge, New York and London.

Krabill, R 2012, 'American sentimentalism and the production of global citizens', *Contexts*, vol. 11, no. 4, pp. 52–4.

Larsen, MA and Searle, MJ 2017, 'International service learning and critical global citizenship: a cross-case study of a Canadian teacher education alternative practicum', *Teaching and Teacher Education*, vol. 63, April, pp. 196–205.

Newstadt, E 2008, 'The neoliberal university: looking at the York strike', *Bullet*, 5 December, viewed 8 December 2017, www.socialistproject.ca/bullet/bullet165.html.

Nussbaum, M 1996, *For love of country?* Beacon Press, Boston, MA.

Osiadacz, E 2018, 'Global citizenship', *Brock Education Journal*, vol. 27, no. 2, pp. 44–7.

Pashby, K 2012, 'Questions for global citizenship education in the context of the "new imperialism": for whom, by whom?' in V de O Andreotti and LMTM de Souza (eds), *Postcolonial perspectives on global citizenship education*, 9–26, Routledge, New York and London.

Pike, G 2008, 'Reconstructing the legend: educating for global citizenship', in AA Abdi and L Shultz (eds), *Educating for human rights and global citizenship*, 223–38, State University of New York Press, New York.

Schattle, H 2008, 'Education for global citizenship: illustrations of ideological pluralism and adaptation', *Journal of Political Ideologies*, vol. 13, no. 1, pp. 73–94.

Shaker, E 2002, 'Following the money: the growing corporate presence in education', *Ontario Confederation of University Faculty Associations Forum*, fall.

Tiessen, R and Huish, R 2014, *Globetrotting or global citizenship: perils and potential of international experiential learning*, University of Toronto Press, Toronto.

Tudiver, N 1999, *Universities for sale: resisting corporate control over Canadian higher education*, Lorimer, Toronto.

Zemach-Bersin, T 2009, 'Selling the world: study abroad marketing and the privatization of global citizenship', in R Lewin (ed.), *The handbook of practice and research in study abroad*, 303–20, Routledge, New York.

Chapter 6

Global citizenship education and its discontents, from the global North to the global South

Polina Golovátina-Mora, Susan Harper, Jessica Smartt Gullion, Athina Karatzogianni and Tracy Simmons

Introduction: the premise and critiques of global citizenship education

At the top of the main web page on global studies at a large US research university, we see a young white man surrounded by Black children. He is teaching them the hand signal students use at university sporting events. They sit outside what appears to be a run-down building. As the children wear matching uniforms, one presumes this is a school. Below, the text reads that the university's academic mission is

> to educate leaders, create knowledge, and transform health and health care. [Our programme] takes that mission worldwide through innovative, interconnected and cross-border programs and partnerships that enrich students, scholars and alumni across disciplines and countries. Our global efforts strive to address and solve diverse challenges that make a positive impact around the world.

Global citizenship is a mainstay of Western university mission statements (Krabill 2012; Clifford and Montgomery 2014; Darian-Smith 2015) and is touted as a necessity in today's turbulent job market. Universities promote global engagement of their students, formation of 'the responsible citizens of the world' well equipped 'for today's globally engaged and culturally diverse society', as, for example, missions of some European universities claim. We see universities with missions to build economic development and sustainable healthcare systems in 'lesser developed' nations, students working on wildlife conservation in countries other than their own, medical and nursing students taking brief trips to assist in medical clinics in areas with health disparities and Alternative Spring Breaks in which students spend a week volunteering in a different country.

The global stage continues to shrink via technology. Humans can circumnavigate the globe within hours on aeroplanes, in seconds on computers. Ideas and products find their way en route as well. It is therefore not surprising that higher education would focus on the need to educate students on how to thrive and successfully function under globalization (Johnson, Boyer and Brown 2011; World Bank 2011; Sant and González Valencia 2018). At the same time, as the Global Citizenship Education Working Group (GCED-WG), together with a collegium of 90 organizations and experts in global education, emphasizes, 'global challenges such as climate change, migration, and conflict will require people to do more than just think about solutions' (Center for Universal Education at Brookings, 2017b, p. ix). As a result, as Dill (2012, p. 541) writes, 'schools around the world are focusing their curricular and extra-curricular attention on expanding the consciousness of their students to prepare them for the opportunities and challenges of a global society'. Universities are socializing this new generation of global citizens.

This chapter aims at deconstructing the idea of Education in/for Global Citizenship (GCE) starting with the idea of citizenship itself. Employing critical discourse analysis of the university missions, campus spaces and quotidian practices from the global North (specifically the United States and the United Kingdom), and the global South (Colombia), this chapter uncovers the insidious ways in which universities, with a hierarchical mindset, encourage the economic exploitation of resources (Southern nations, nature, human potential), in order to problematize the idea of citizenship itself in support of existing critical GCE literature.

The examination of these debates will draw on elements of critical discourse analysis approaches to textual analysis. The aim is to provide a selective qualitative study of these debates in order to develop a deeper understanding of the rhetorical strategies and themes that emerge out of the debates. In addition, appealing to the non-representational proposal of the nomad and new materialist framework we search to deepen and complexify the critique. The proposed analysis of the idea of global citizenship cannot only help to reveal certain narratives, but also deconstruct the social realities of these narratives, and how they may affect their respective societies. In the first section, we lay out the logic of the GCE initiatives based on the dialogue between the critical literature from both global North and South. In the following sections we examine specific examples from the United States, the United Kingdom and Colombia. We conclude with thoughts on confronting inequality structures and exclusionary logics in the GCE initiative, the contexts of its practical implementation as well as in the methodology of analysis itself.

GCE initiatives: further homogenization or opening the debates?

'Education for global citizenship' is not inherently a negative idea, and many of the people involved have altruistic motives and genuinely want to be helpful. The ability to work with diverse cultures in different settings *is* an important need for the workforce. Global citizenship discourse largely promotes the idea of a common and networked world and the values of social justice. For instance, the guiding principles, according to the Education 2030 Agenda of UNESCO (2017) are non-discrimination, transparency, horizontality ('all network members have an equal voice'), collaboration, solidarity, non-instrumentalization, respect and diversity (p. 20). Institutionalized by UNESCO (2015, 2016) the idea of education for global citizenship is seen as a response to planetary challenges and is intended as a 'means to help young people develop the knowledge, skills, behaviours, attitudes, and values to engage in effective individual and collective action at their local levels, with an eye toward a long-term, better future at the global level' (Center for Universal Education at Brookings 2017b, p. ix), and as one that 'prepares people to live with these immortal tensions and to devise the institutions that can guarantee human rights and ensure opportunities for democratic participation' (Papandreou and Shapiro 2017, p. 12).

Educational institutions as agents of global citizenship values and education would become the transformative factor for the world (Aguilar Forero and Velásquez 2018; UNESCO 2017). The initiative aspires to make education more inclusive, democratic, sustainable and fair (Cho 2016; Aguilar Forero and Velásquez 2018), and 'to reach a more effective, holistic, and equitable education for every child in the world' (Center for Universal Education at Brookings 2017a, p. 5). The initiative expands beyond the global North and has been generally accepted in the global South and other regions (Aguilar Forero and Velásquez 2018; Cho 2016; Davies et al. 2018; Peraza Sanguinés 2016; de Wit, Gacel-Ávila and Knight 2005).

The number of studies criticizing, rejecting, critically revising or cautioning against some aspects of the initiative, however, is increasing (Aktas et al. 2017; Andreotti 2006, 2011a, b; Chapman, Ruiz-Chapman and Eglin 2018; Davies et al. 2018; Krabill 2012; Pais and Costa 2017). The central concern could be summarized as follows: hidden behind the term 'global citizenship', are spectres of imperialism and colonization (Andreotti 2006, 2011b; Chapman, Ruiz-Chapman and Eglin 2018; Darian-Smith 2015; Davids 2018; Krabill 2012; Pashby 2011, 2012; Shultz 2018). Likewise, the marriage of global citizenship with the job market belies neoliberal underpinnings (for example, Aktas et al. 2017; Engel, Fundalinski and Cannon 2016). As Aguilar Forero and Velásquez (2018, p. 940) sum it up, 'the discourses of global citizenship and global competitiveness appear as synonyms'.

The discourse of education for/in global citizenship originates from the global North and Western Enlightenment thought (Aguilar Forero and Velásquez 2018; Davies et al. 2018; Cho 2016). Aguilar Forero and Velásquez (2018, p. 944) mention the study by Parmenter (2011) who mapped the discourse of GCE in its development between 1977 and 2009. According to Parmenter (2011), the number of papers has increased significantly since 2000, with 85 per cent of them coming from the United States, United Kingdom, Australia or Canada and discussing the situation in these regions. The balance has been slightly improving in the last five years with the increase of academic and institutional attention to the situation in other regions.

The idea of global citizenship inspired and informed by Western liberal democratic ideals is seen as obvious, natural and a universal good (Aguilar Forero and Velásquez 2018; Balarin 2011; Engel, Fundalinski and Cannon 2016; Pais and Costa 2017; Sant and González Valencia 2018). Therefore, the discussion generally does not invite debate or explore the alternatives, but rather explores the ways of its more efficient implementation throughout the globe. As Aguilar Forero and Velásquez (2018, p. 940) summarize the situation, 'GCE is imposed as a moral obligation … in the world, that is the fact, globalized and impossible to change'.[1] Citizenship is discussed as a set of pre-established values, beliefs, actions or criteria to comply with, which does not imply there is room for critical reflection (Cho 2016; Cyupers 2004; Duhan Kaplan 1991; Larsen 2014; Melo-Escrihuela 2008; Sant and González Valencia 2018). It corresponds to the 'mechanistic, static, naturalistic, spatialized view of consciousness', as Freire (2000, p. 77) elaborates it. The terms from the university mission statements tend 'to have the character of a … mantric charm' (Chapman, Ruiz-Chapman and Eglin 2018, p. 149) or of an empty signifier (Pais and Costa 2017).

While more radically critical voices, such as Andreotti (2006, 2011a, b), Balarin (2011) or Davies et al. (2018), call for a more scrutinizing review of the initiative's 'underlying assumptions' (Pais and Costa 2017, p. 3), many even critically inclined authors question the mechanisms for application rather than the idea itself. For example, Pais and Costa (2017), referring to Camicia and Franklin (2011), outline the tension between the following two discourses: 'one focused on individual achievements and self-investment (neoliberalism), and another one focused on active, responsible citizenship (critical democracy)' (p. 3). Pais and Costa (2017) propose that the discourse of GCE cleared of empty signifiers (Laclau 1994) could potentially harmonize the 'antagonisms that pertain to current education' (p. 3) and, therefore, could be the space for dreaming and hope, considered central to any social change initiative.

The same concepts that in academia are critical of the existing social and discourse orders, become instruments of branding effectively used by neoliberal political and economic actors, who popularize the academic concepts without their critical potential (for example, Camicia and Franklin 2011; Cyupers 2004; Duhan Kaplan 1991; Gremaud 2014; Laclau 1994, 2005) or they confuse their meaning (Pais and Costa 2017, p. 3). Pais and Costa (2017, p. 3) caution that 'global citizenship education, although it might rest on the principles of critical democracy, is still going to be implemented in highly commoditized schools and universities, by people who are immersed in the dynamics of capitalist economics'.

Developing Braidotti's (2006, p. 2) characteristics of the contemporary world's paradox – 'the potentially innovative, de-territorializing impact of the new technologies is hampered and tuned down by the reassertion of the gravitational pull of old and established values' – we can speak of the 'prevailing sense of anxiety' fuelled by the vast disparities in life chances 'that today seem to be widening still further' (Cope and Kalantzis 2000, p. 10). Such disparities are strengthened by the increasing conflict between the discursive push for homogenization of the sense of citizenship and further diversification 'in the nature of public, community and economic life' that leads to emergence of 'ever more diverse and subculturally defined groupings', new lifestyles that expand the opportunities for some and exclude others 'in ways that are increasingly related to the outcomes of education and training' (ibid., p. 10). The idea of education for/in global citizenship together with its application will be contradictory until the concepts of 'global' and 'citizenship' are revised from the perspective of social justice and beyond the dominating, Western Enlightenment, liberal-democratic thought framework. The role of education and academia here, we agree with other scholars (Gacel-Ávila et al. 2005; Sant and González Valencia 2018), is to generate and secure space for such a revision.

United States: postcolonial sentimentalism of the global North GCE initiatives

The primary theme of global citizenship in the North American universities is one of a saviour mentality, a holdover from America's colonialist roots. This is not surprising given both the paternalistic, racist trope that people of colour need to be rescued by liberal whites, and modern-day US imperialistic global policies. We do not dismiss the fact that useful work can be accomplished by students on trips abroad engaged in international service learning (such as building someone a home or helping out at a medical clinic); these are short-term interventions in which Western students swoop in with their 'superior' knowledge and then leave, with little long-term impact and even less collaboration (see Chapman, this volume, Chapter 5). Such projects are feel-good in nature for the students, and seldom have any transformative impact (for example, Larsen 2014). Developing a model of Critical GCE, Larsen (2014, p. 5) emphasized that central is the 'dialectical relationship' between awareness and engagement, each of which consists of several components; without taking this into account we will continue speaking about the white burden to help the rest of the world. A critical and responsible approach implies, according to Larsen (2014), the recognition of one's own privilege and power 'over other cultures as a result of colonization processes' (p. 6) and their mobilization 'to make a difference in the lives of those who are not as privileged as oneself' (p. 7). The global citizen, she continues, 'removes him/herself from the "centre" of the Us-Them binary of social relations ... and constructs a new relationship based on mutuality, openness, and dialogue rather than domination and oppression' (p. 7).

As Darian-Smith (2015, p. 166) worries, 'future historians may call the field of global studies the "handmaiden of neo-liberalism"'. Increasingly in the United States, higher education is seen not as a public good, but as a means for securing a well-trained labour force. Some states require educators at public universities to include lists of 'marketable skills' for each of their courses, directly linking curricula with employment (see Chapman, this volume, Chapter 5, for comparable Canadian data). Beyond this, a visible sub-culture of Americans (notably supported by the current US administration) argues that universities are liberal enclaves without social value.

The question then for American universities is how to decolonize global initiatives. As Darian-Smith (2015) notes, voices from the countries to which American students go for service learning – particularly those in the global South and global East – are largely absent from the field. Likewise, Western scholars tend to be the power bearers in this exchange: they come to a country, work on a project for a (usually brief) time period and leave feeling good about themselves. Too often these global citizens bring along their own values and expect the othered to conform, rather than embarking on relationships of collaboration and mutual respect. Dill (2012, p. 541) writes that

> a subtle contradiction lies at the heart of global citizenship education: it demands moral commitment and empathy beyond the individual and his/her own interests, but at the same time it sacralizes the individual autonomous chooser above all other forms. The implicit effort attempts to make students into secular, liberal, consumer-oriented cosmopolitan subjects.

Krabill (2012, p. 53) writes that the global citizenship of American universities is grounded in 'emotion-based claims to moral superiority and as justification for one's actions'. He writes about three dangers of the sentimentalism of the ways in which US universities promote global citizenship. The first is that a certain kind of productivity is associated with that goal. The second is the ways in which oppositional categories of global citizen and global other are created and maintained. The third is 'the illusion that awareness and enthusiasm are sufficient for social change' (ibid., p. 54). Krabill (2012) notes that the saviour identity provides both an emotional boost and validates one's privilege. It is not about collaboration and mutual understanding, but about domination. He writes, 'U.S.-based students become global citizens, while residents of the Global South become subjects of a global world order, in which they are seen as lacking agency' (ibid., p. 54).

Rather than a global village, most cultural exchanges remain steeped in ethnocentrism. If there is any doubt that this is a project of modernity and neoliberalism to bring forth a homogenizing imperialism, one should only imagine how American students would respond to a group of university students from the global South or global East coming to their campus for a week to teach them how to do something the 'right' way.

On the surface, global citizenship is presented as a noble effort, one filled with peace, sustainability and equity. Indeed, participation in such a context is desirable, for one feels good about oneself when one believes one is contributing to these goals. Yet Clifford and Montgomery (2014) write about the hidden facets of global citizenship: power, exclusion, oppression and marginalization. The false consciousness of the initiative actions inspired by the sentimentalism render their colonizing and imperialistic outcomes invisible.

Social and environmental problems exist; however, awareness of them is not enough to bring about social change. Yet awareness seems to be at the heart of most global citizenship endeavours – to learn about, to see, the problems of the world – to put the 'other' on display. If solving these problems is integrated into the mission, this largely comes about through the imposition of Western solutions rather than collaborative exchanges. Krabill (2012, p. 54) writes,

> U.S. students (and professors) inherently have the power – often conferred by some combination of access to disposable income and social media – to solve global problems, unlike those whom they are helping, who then come to be understood merely as victims or as actors playing minor roles in the drama of the student's global education.

Global citizenship and the differences of the 'others within'

Citizenship, generally, is understood in the Enlightenment tradition, 'in terms of individual conduct or participation' rather than 'as referring to the question of the "infrastructure"', which affects 'our sense of self, our ways of becoming, our modes of expression, our practices of relating to others', elements 'central to the development of the political desires that drive us' (Rieder 2018, p. 102). GCE and global citizenship are discussed as an abstract term, outside power relations; separately from the everyday life experiences of a person, whether travelling abroad or not; separately from the variety of actants (Latour 2004) that may not be conventionally considered a political subject yet who produce political effects (Karatzogianni and Schandorf 2016; Rieder 2018); separately from the trans-corporeality of the world (Alaimo 2018) and its network of relations and thoughts.

Seen rather as a unidimensional outgoing process, the GCE initiative ignores the benefits for the global North that the incoming other from the global South brings, with their differences, skills, challenges and contribution to diversity. International students 'generate invaluable economic, societal and cultural benefits' (Universities UK 2017, p. 1) and support jobs in the local communities both in the United Kingdom and the United States according to the existing reports (Association of International Educators [NAFSA] 2017; Universities UK 2017). The number of Chinese international students' enrolment in UK higher education, for example, reached 91,215 during the academic year 2015–2016, far exceeding any other non-European Union (EU) countries (Higher Education Statistics Agency 2017). The portrayal of the image of international students in terms of their approaches to learning, however, can often be unfavourable and unfair within UK higher education discourses (Sovic and Blythman 2013). The dichotomy between 'Western' and 'Confucian' approaches to learning fails to take account of the complexities among individual learners and it overlooks difference within two educational cultures (Ryan and Louie 2007) and attributes undesirable activities such as plagiarism and non-critical thinking to 'Confucian education'.

Feminist posthumanist authors (e.g. Alaimo 2018; Braidotti 2006) call for an ethical view of the diversity and the unknown of the other, especially when the other is within. In the following section, using examples from the United States and the United Kingdom, we will focus on such contexts of GCE as sexual difference and exclusionary migration policies in order to further problematise the GCE initiative itself and the possibility for its application by revealing 'the lack of coherence of the narratives that compose the social text' (Braidotti 2006, p. 28) of GCE discourse.

While institutions do not position their GCE initiatives as gender-specific, these programmes engage (or not) with gender diversity both in terms of the students they send abroad and in the communities they (purport to) serve. If global citizenship is invariably positioned as white, it is also largely positioned as cisgender and heterosexual. Observation of different college and university websites and revision of the critiques of mission trips and other service projects that are part of service learning reveal the gendered pattern. White women feature prominently in images of white people engaging in 'service' in the global South, and especially in projects that involve engaging with children or performing other traditionally 'feminine' tasks such as working with educational initiatives, food provision and other classically domestic tasks. Men, on the other hand, are more likely to be pictured doing construction or other such labour. Images of both men and women tend to feature relatively gender-conforming individuals, and there is virtually no representation of gender non-conforming or LGBTQ students. While it can of course be difficult to discern a person's gender identity or sexual orientation in a visual medium such as a university's webpage, it is worth noting that the students featured in these media at least outwardly present cisgender heterosexuality. Even institutions that have robust LGBTQ communities on their campuses and offer protections to LGBTQ students may choose to reify the image of the global citizen as cisgender, gender conforming and heterosexual-presenting. This leads to important questions about who counts as a citizen in this world.

While public universities may unintentionally erase LGBTQ students in the GCE initiatives and advertising, this may be much more intentional on the part of private, religiously affiliated institutions. Religiously affiliated institutions, particularly those with a Christian mission, commonly have policies that either forbid LGBTQ students from attending or, more often, allow them to attend as long as they do not engage in any same-sex/same-gender relationships or pursue gender confirmation (in the case of trans students) (Villareal 2019). Thus, these institutions make explicit that their ideal of citizenship is exclusively cisgender and heterosexual.

In the field, particularly in the global South sites that much GCE prefers, the positioning of global citizenship as exclusively heterosexual and cisgender has real impacts on students. As of 2019, 72 countries outlaw same-sex/same-gender sexual activity, and many of these also have laws explicitly outlawing forms of gender expression (Human Rights Watch n.d.). Most of these are in the global South. While many countries are making moves towards abolishing these laws, others still impose strict penalties up to and including the death penalty for those convicted of such offences. This poses potential danger to LGBTQ students who participate in GCE initiatives in these locales – students who may be unaware that such laws exist in their service location, since universities do not commonly include such information in describing their service projects. At a minimum, LGBTQ students may simply decline to participate in such GCE projects if they know of the destination country's laws and policies. At worst, LGBTQ students who do participate find themselves in situations where they may be at risk of legal repercussions or feel as though they need to hide who they are during the length of the project. While adherence to social norms about sexuality and behaviour generally are important lessons when engaging with a culture different from one's own, there is a vast difference between cultural courtesy and actively being afraid or overtly lying about one's identity. Universities that conduct GCE projects in countries and locales hostile to LGBTQ people send a message that they are not bothered by such policies or by the maltreatment of LGBTQ people in those countries – a message which impacts LGBTQ students. This can be an especially jarring situation when the institution itself has robust protections for LGBTQ students, and even more so when the institution is located in a US state that has state-level protections for LGBTQ people.

This echoes and therefore reproduces the biased citizenship policies altogether. For example, as some scholars argued (Andanaes and Wintemute 2001; Kofman 2011; Phizaclea et al. 2000; Stychin 2003), EU directives related to family reunion for non-EU migrants continue to be underpinned by gendered, racist and classed assumptions of who is a desirable migrant. The United Kingdom's approach to family reunion has historically been formulated on colonialist and sexist lines and depicts a privileging and hierarchy of rights around marriage and specific subjectivities of first world white men (Cohen 2001; Simmons 2008). As Richardson (2018) in her recent work on sexuality and citizenship argues, 'neoliberal processes can also lead to resistance to sexual and gender equality' (p. 142). Family reunion policies seek to selectively incorporate 'desirable' queer migrants, those that can be the motors of the economy, whilst making families (but only certain types, children entering as a unit of cost) engage in social reproduction of domestic life and being placed outside welfare resources and support.

The complex interconnectivity of the world requires looking at discourse as at infrastructure that affects and shapes our thinking of citizenship within it and simultaneously is being shaped by the concept of citizenship. The 'solutionism' tendency, that as we discussed above marks the GCE discourse – 'the belief that every social problem can and should be solved' (Rieder 2018, p. 104) by the mere implementation of the paradigm – is an oppressive, 'necrophilic' (Freire 2000) and mechanistic approach to an abstract citizen-machine that ignores the relational character of the world. Such themes as gender, migration or digital technologies shake up the field, question the representative model of the citizenship and emphasize the complex performativity of citizenship.

The GCE initiative in Colombia: the desirable values

The GCE initiative does not find much resistance in Latin America because the educational system adopts European academic paradigms and overall shares the intellectual background of Western European Enlightenment thought (Gacel-Ávila et al. 2005; Sant and González Valencia 2018). This thought has never been seriously contested as the independence movement led by criollos – European descendants, ideologically highly influenced by the Enlightenment and supported by some European countries (Sant and González Valencia 2018, p. 68) – was not the result of decolonization but rather part of further colonization.

Later on, the European influence was replaced with the greater economic and political influence of the United States. And, as Sant and González Valencia (2018, p. 69) point out, with the general stigmatization of any left-wing ideas 'economic openness did not open the political sphere' by the end of the twentieth century. Some authors emphasize that Latin American educational institutions 'still appear to be reacting to initiatives coming from national and, in particular, international organizations' (Gacel-Ávila et al. 2005, p. 354) instead of more proactive proposals based on indigenous knowledge, cosmovision and practices, and with consideration of the local conditions of extreme poverty and deep social inequality, of forced migration and social and political conflict, local hierarchies and access to resources coupled with global hierarchies (Aguilar Forero and Velásquez 2018; Andreotti 2006; Balarin 2011; Castles 2003; Martín-Cabello 2017; Sant and González Valencia 2018; Skrbis and Woodward 2013; Soong 2018), rural agricultural practices and natural biodiversity and resources, especially keeping in mind their potential role in the context of climate change.

At the moment, perception of the GCE initiative varies from country to country throughout Latin America, with an overall acceptance of it as strategy for development and participation in global competition. Yet the anti-imperialist movements of the second half of the twentieth century and the beginning of the twenty-first century, such as liberation theology, critical pedagogy, indigenous rights, human rights and LGBTQ rights, have their impact on the debates and define the directions for critical discussion (see, for example, Sant and Valencia González 2018). For example, in the context of the adopted 'pragmatic approach' towards the GCE initiative in Colombia, 'where it tries to incorporate the benefits of a more global knowledge society into the traditional, more national, and autonomous culture of higher education' (Gacel-Ávila et al. 2005, p. 356), the missions of many Colombian universities do not directly include references to GCE, but rather appeal, as we discuss later, to the universal human values and universal principles of personal development for local and global well-being.

Sant and González Valencia (2018) mention that as a result of these movements the alternative proposals of globalization and global citizenship education emerge with the demand for globalization 'from "below" – framed by social justice and democratic principles' (p. 71; Torres 2015). Intergovernmental research and educational organizations such as the Latin American Social Sciences Institute (FLACSO) and the Latin American Council of Social Sciences (2015) promote the idea of ecologies of knowledges for critical thought and emancipatory practices based on a more active South–South dialogue and cooperation in resistance to the geopolitics of knowledge and neoliberal hegemony. The logic of most proposals as well as the adopted practices of organization, however, rarely go beyond the established hierarchy of power within academia, which makes any proposal come off as appearing to opt for redistribution of power without the radical change of the system of power hierarchy itself (Wallerstein 1991, 2004). In fact, saviour identity extends to the souls of the global other. Recent programmes of teaching Spanish initiated by the Ministry of Foreign Affairs of Colombia, as a cultural diplomacy strategy, focus on the less developed countries within the framework of the South–South dialogue. The classes are mostly directed to 'the higher officers of the country' to ensure more successful economic cooperation (Ministerio de Relaciones Exteriores 2013). One Colombian private university reports on its participation in the programme in the following quite messianic form even if only jokingly: 'Ghana and Vietnam speak Spanish with the accent of the [University name]'.

In their contextualization of GCE in Latin America, Sant and González Valencia (2018) stress that the concept of citizenship and citizenship education 'is mainly constructed in relation to the nation' in Latin America in general and Colombia in particular (p. 78). The concept of citizenship, whether national or global, Sant and González Valencia argue, is seen as membership marked with rights and obligations. Citizenship is mostly associated with the peaceful coexistence and advancing of the peace movement in Colombia and in Latin America more broadly (ibid., pp. 73–8) in the context of the continuous, decades-long, violent conflict. Peace is understood predominantly in opposition to the conflict and therefore is seen as source of consolidation of the nation. The nation-state is presented as a guarantor of the rights and the peace process. In support of this logic,

> the desirable nation is ... understood as peaceful and ideologically homogeneous. Discussions on ideological differences within the nation are often avoided and, when recognized, they are identified as the source of violent historical and contemporary conflicts (e.g., coup d'états, guerrilla movements).
>
> (ibid., p. 75)

Sant and González Valencia emphasize that, consequently, 'the nation is constructed simultaneously as diverse and without differences' (p. 73), and 'discussions on socioeconomic and ideological differences and conflict are avoided or considered to be a problem to be solved' (p. 75), 'in the name of freedom, order, and social peace (that is, the peace of the elites)', as Freire (2000, p. 78) would put it. While expressing the belief that GCE could be the space for reflection on the 'complex nature of most identities' (p. 79), Sant and González Valencia (2018) note that global citizenship is mostly understood as being both 'culturally and ethnically diverse' (p. 77) and difference free.

Colombia GCE discourses and practice of the 'commoditized schools'

The mission statements of the Colombian universities that we reviewed for this study support the conclusions of the above-mentioned authors and the paradox they described: the principle of inclusion pronounced as a universal value coexists with the principle of exclusion in exercising social justice. Starting with the announcement of the benefits for humanity, university missions generally end as if ensuring the primary interests of the city and nation. While it may be the application of the idea of 'thinking globally – acting locally', it can also express the limitations of the idea of the citizenship as discussed above. For instance, the mission of one Colombian public university aims at

> democratization of access to knowledge to ensure, on behalf of the society and with the State's surveillance, the social right for citizens to achieve a higher education corresponding to the standards of excellence, fairness, and competitiveness. Generation and dissemination of knowledge are based on the principle of autonomy and focus on the sociocultural development and progress of [the city], the Nation and in extension to all their areas of influence.

The second public university as a 'centre of culture and science' with 'special social responsibility' confirms in their mission statement their commitment to the search for new knowledge and solutions for social problems from a humanistic and universal perspective, and states that their actions are for 'the benefit of human and scientific growth in reaffirmation of the nation's values, its ethnic and cultural diversity' based on the principles of 'respect for different ideologies; expansion of creativity and appreciation of culture; protection and taking advantage at the national level of the natural resources within an ecoethical approach'. The third public university stresses its 'contribution to the national project and enrichment of the cultural, natural and environmental heritage of the country'.

The missions of the private universities are quite similar to those of public universities with possibly slightly smaller emphasis on the national project. One Colombian private university mentions the crucial importance of lifelong education in the demanding and globalizing world. In their general mission they speak about tolerance and pluralism in 'critical and ethical education for consolidation of social and civil responsibility'; the goal of research, according to their mission, is 'to contribute to the development of the country and its international projection'.

A second private university positions itself as a university with 'a global vision and regional and local impact'. In their mission, they speak about their contribution to the sustainable development of humanity. Their principles and goals are to 'promote lifelong learning, discovery and creativity, encourage interaction with the environment based on the spirit of integrity, excellence, pluralism and inclusion'. A third private university lists patriotism together with the injunction to 'obey out of conviction, respect the hierarchy and comply with authority' as the core characteristics of their identity and the identity of everyone who shares the institutional spirit. The mission emphasizes that such spirit is 'not the result of vigilance, imposition or calculus but the spontaneous fruit of one's individual and institutional consciousness'; while proclaiming respect for integrity, creativity and diversity as any other university does, it does not recognize the actual difference of a subject or the subjects themselves altogether. Not following these principles is openly recognized as 'bad'. These very principles appear in the psychological test as part of the interview for the potential employee.

As Mill (1869) wrote, 'society, from its highest place to its lowest, is one long chain, or rather ladder, where every individual is either above or below his nearest neighbour, and wherever he does not command he must obey' (chap. 2). The university, as part of such a social structure that 'regards men as adaptable, manageable beings' (Freire 2000, p. 73), as a 'spectator, not re-creator' (ibid., p. 75), is, transposing Mill's words, 'the school of despotism, in which the virtues of despotism, but also its vices, are largely nourished' (1869, chap. 2). As a replica of the society, the university reproduces the same citizenship relations within its space. Quite often the values and principles stated in the mission statements are left without further elaboration. However, the micro-actions and everyday practices in the university routine, in the built environment of the campus and in the inner organization of inter-personal relations complement, clarify and complexify the mission's statements, revealing the incorporated hidden relations of power.

> Shortly before the accreditation, boards exhibiting the values of the University mission were placed in every classroom and office space in a private Colombian university. At the entrance to one office, one of these boards was glued to the wall not above the switch but partly covering it and limiting the access to it. By the following day, the board fell and was put behind a desk by the employees occupying the office.

While it could be a single unfortunate case, it yet manifests the absence of care, of belonging or sharing the values the board displayed as a result of the systemic denial of subjectivity and absence of any transparent infrastructure for feedback. The summarizing slogan on the bottom of the board – 'We evaluate ourselves for excellence. Integral education for social and human transformation' – augments the systemic contradictions. The university's mission speaks about the pursuit of truth, but also 'reaffirmation of values from the perspective of Christian humanism for the sake of the society's good', with the aspiration for ethical, scientific, managerial and social leadership at the service of the country, thus emphasizing the criteria for truth selection. While being a private university, they may set their own rules of the game. Yet, the logic of private property then directly confronts here the etymology of the word 'university' itself.

The examples are many. The inspiration for the campus reconstruction was the idea of the university's openness to the neighbouring community. The first thing that was built was the new fence. The sculpture complex by the main entrance consists of the three figures of the university's founding fathers. The figures are hardly recognized by the majority of the university employees, students or local visitors, to say nothing about a foreign visitor. Right at the entrance, they manifest the exclusivity rather than inclusivity that generally is stressed in most speeches and manifestos of the university. An abstract sculpture symbolizing key values of the university, designed by the students or faculty members, on the other hand, would develop a better sense of relation and belonging.

Despite the emphasis on a family-oriented discourse, no small playground was built or extra trees planted by the entrance square intended for the broader public. The university does not provide day care for younger children of the faculty members or secure housing for the new faculty members with a family. Solidarity-oriented discourse is not supported by transparent bottom-up communication and does not have an infrastructure for civil participation in the decision-making process concerning curriculum change, institutional reorganization or campus design and planning. The evaluation process hits harder the faculty members, who receive at least double evaluation by the students and their immediate coordinators, while students and university administration of any level have only evaluation from above. Faculty members are the disposable material. Finally, the old fence with the spiky wire has never been removed even with the certification of the university campus as environmentally conscious. Pigeons with mutilated legs skipping all over campus are a metaphor for the essentially exclusive institutional logic.

Black plastic bags with the slowly drying up saplings surround a billboard that announces the environment conscious campus certification for more than a week, revealing so the *necrophilic* and the narcissistic (Feyerabend, 1993; Pais, 2017) institutional policy rather than sincere and profound understanding of responsibility that comes with such an award for environmental consciousness.

Conclusions: confronting the inequality structures and the exclusionary logic in GCE

'The only school of genuine moral sentiment', Mill (1869) wrote, 'is society between equals', where to be an equal is not to be an enemy (chap. 2). In other words, we are not speaking of a member of a closed system, such as the politico-legal construction of citizenship (Leydet 2017), but the open system of community-based mutual responsibility, recognition of difference of the Other and Self and constant deconstruction of one's own personal and collective identity in the relations of care. Unpacking the meaning of global, Larsen (2014, p. 6) points out that 'we need to see that we are all a part of the problem, as well as a part of the solution(s)' in a world of dynamic, networked relationships, and not as isolated individuals but as parts of one shared whole.

Unfortunately, even when proposing a critical global citizenship model, Larsen (2014) speaks about a one-way road. But hierarchies do not just affect but form the meaning and the use of the concept 'global citizenship': age, language, origin, passport, social and economic status to name a few. The term is mostly applied to younger people from the global North and more specifically from its English-speaking part. While learning the destination language is encouraged, the language of the incoming 'global citizen' would most likely be prioritized over the local languages as the citizen is the one who brings the skill.

A language exchange programme called 'Keep talking' with the slogan 'Be fluent – be global. Be a global citizen' illustrates this well: the web page uses Chekhov's phrase about the practical importance of any knowledge. The next message that appears says to practise your second language, English, every day with people from the United States, Australia, United Kingdom and Sweden. Actively engaged in free language exchange organized in the expats bars and cafés in Medellín (Colombia), 'Keep talking' focuses on English/Spanish exchange, ignoring, for instance, the fact that 65 indigenous and two creole languages are officially spoken in Colombia. Promotional pictures on the organization's webpage and Facebook event pages show young, smart, casually and European style dressed, fit people in their 20 or 30s with broad and snow-white smiles, often with a slim laptop, and drinks. Whether it is intended to project the future or reflect the present, the old, poor, sick, fat, indigenous, 'ethnic', hungry, homeless, disabled or those willing to study a less popular language are excluded from the category of the global citizen.

The reality, however, is that global citizenship is a multidirectional process and includes more dimensions than usually discussed in the literature. People move from the global North to the global South or East, from the global South to the global South, and from the global South or East to the global North; it is not a straight, predefined road, but an individual case by case experience. The dangers and difficulties of such an experience result from the tension between the striated or structure-oriented spaces and the smooth or mobile, nomadic ones: obstacles are posed by bureaucracy, racism, nationalism, militarism and threats to one's life, to name just a few. Finally, the global citizenship experience does not happen automatically when someone travels abroad but when the known space gets deterritorialized by the unknown other, using the vocabulary of Deleuze and Guattari (2005). The examples can include learning the new language, reading, meeting an exchange student at your home university or even a visitor from another city or even sometimes from another neighbourhood of the same city. The global citizenship experience is in the bodily work of deterritorialization, of the deconstruction of the known space, meaning and identities that would ideally result in creating a more just world and community.

The contradiction discussed in the critical literature on GCE results in the contradictory meaning of both 'citizenship' and 'global'. The most often heard conclusions are to carefully revise the meaning of the concept of global citizenship. Considering the limitations of the concepts themselves and the potential harm they may cause to the initial intention and cause, we propose altogether not to use an expression that is so politically charged but to leave the space for multiple interpretations and focus on the organic, open-ended, self-transformative, collaborative, social organization that would promote social justice; on the social organization of no name and therefore not the final goal. Non-teleological education for social justice would be the space for understanding its meaning; and community-based, collaborative, participatory, action research the space of cognition and communication, using Freire's words (2000). Continuing Freire's logic, the truth is, however, that the oppressed are not 'marginals', are not people living 'outside' society. They have always been 'inside' – inside the structure which made them 'beings for others'. The solution is not to 'integrate' them into the structure of oppression, but to transform that structure so that they can become 'beings for themselves'. Such transformation, of course, would undermine the oppressors' purposes.

(2000, p. 74)

As a form of membership (Leydet 2017), citizenship, whether seen as a sentiment or as legal formality (Giraldo Jiménez 2000, p. 142), is based on exclusion, as the critical studies keep on emphasizing. As Papandreou and Shapiro (2017, p. 9) point out, in Antiquity the right of citizenship was extended 'to those who were free – not only from slavery, but also free from burdens such as high debt, lack of time, or incapacity to contribute to the economy'. Riley (1999, p. 38) defines membershipping as 'a range of discursive practices involved in the social construction of identity' of a mainly regulatory nature. Membershipping strategies, he argues, appeal to 'social categorisations which may legitimate their right to perform certain acts, or which might impose or prohibit the obligation to do so on their interlocutors' (ibid., p. 38).

Critical citizenship studies propose going beyond any individualistic, representative or necrophilic paradigm that 'begins with a false understanding of men and women as objects' (Freire 2000, p. 77) towards one that is more participatory, community-based (Leydet 2017; Melo-Escrihuela 2008; Vogel 1991) and biophilic (Freire 2000), that recognizes the subjectivity and agency of human as well as non-human subjects (Braidotti 2006, 2018).

The dangers of the reductionist, representational tendency, as elaborated, where 'everything is explained by the situation of the child in relation to its father, or of the man in relation to castration, or of the citizen in relation to the law', relying on the 'pseudoconstant' of content and of expression, could be avoided, according to Deleuze and Guattari (2005, p. 94), with 'placing-in-variation', 'because it builds a continuum or medium without beginning or end'. Instead of the causal coupling 'matter-form' they propose 'the coupling material-forces' (ibid., p. 95). In her interview, Braidotti (2018) summarizes the reality in place (Baugh 2016) of the nomad, post-identitarian and non-unitary subjects that do not belong to one location but are conceptualized as in a process of becoming and transformation through the 'multiple ways of belonging, each depending on where our particular location is and how we grow' (Braidotti 2018, n.p.). In accordance with the nomad and new materialist perspective, Alldred and Fox (2019, p. 689) declare that 'citizenship is not a state or status to be acquired, lost or refused by an individual (Sabsay, 2012, p. 610). Rather, it is an emergent capacity of a material and relational network', a posthumanist 'assemblage of bodies, things, places, thoughts, memories etc. that produces all kinds of capacities in bodies, groups and communities', which 'is not about being or belonging, but about becoming' (Fox and Alldred 2016, slide 21; see also Karatzogianni and Robinson 2010, 2017; Patton 2011).

Such a perspective, Alldred and Fox (2019) suggest, deconstructs the hierarchical, top-down approach from within or onto-epistemologically as it breaks the human centred vision of citizenship: according to it, citizenship is not a human product, but the result of 'the everyday material interactions in which humans are involved' (p. 670). As such, it transforms the structure (Freire 2000) built on the binary of 'inclusion and exclusion, security and insecurity, legitimation and transgression' (Alldred and Fox 2019, p. 670) and makes it organically participatory, collective and inclusive. It is based on the multiple, ever transforming group-allegiances instead of one 'master-allegiance' (ibid., p. 670) or 'herd mentality … basis of all narrow "nationalisms" (of ethnicity, race, religion and creed)' (Baugh 2016, p. 352), and 'substitutes a citizenship macro-politics of social groups, laws and government with a micropolitics of localised interactions' (Alldred and Fox 2019, p. 670).

To understand citizenship as becoming, a relational and ever transforming process, is, as Braidotti (2018) argues, to make an eco-philosophical and ethical shift. It is a transversal and collective process based on empathy and, as Mill (1869, chap. 2) wrote, on the idea of justice,

> grounded as before on equal, but now also on sympathetic association; having its root no longer in the instinct of equals for self-protection, but in a cultivated sympathy between them; and no one being now left out, but an equal measure being extended to all.

Lastly, as Braidotti (2018, n.p.) suggests 'planetary, almost global' citizenship is based on the recognition of 'collective responsibility in a non-reciprocal manner, covering humans and nonhumans'. In other words, we propose to speak not about global citizenship, but rather about the responsible, empathic 'citizens' in the global.

Note

1 All the non-English citations are personal translation by one of the authors of this chapter.

References

Aguilar Forero, N and Velásquez, AM 2018, 'Educación para la ciudadanía mundial en Colombia: oportunidades y desafíos', *Revista Mexicana de Investigación Educativa*, vol. 23, no. 78, pp. 937–61.

Aktas, F, Pitts, K, Richards, JC and Silova, I 2017, 'Institutionalizing global citizenship: a critical analysis of higher education programs and curricula', *Journal of Studies in International Education*, vol. 21, pp. 65–80.

Alaimo, S 2018, 'Trans-corporeality', in R Braidotti and M Hlavajova (eds), *Posthuman glossary*, 435–8, Bloomsbury, London.

Alldred, P and Fox, NJ 2019, 'Assembling citizenship: sexualities education, micropolitics and the becoming-citizen', *Sociology*, vol. 53, pp. 689–706.

Andanaes, M and Wintemute, R (eds) 2001, *Legal recognition of same-sex partnerships: a study of national European and international law*, Hart, Oxford.
Andreotti, V de O 2006, 'Soft versus critical global citizenship education', *Policy & Practice: A Development Education Review*, vol. 3, pp. 40–51.
Andreotti, V de O 2011a, 'The political economy of global citizenship education', *Globalisation, Societies and Education*, vol. 9, pp. 307–10.
Andreotti, V de O 2011b, '(Towards) decoloniality and diversality in global citizenship education', *Globalisation, Societies and Education*, vol. 9, pp. 381–97.
Balarin, M 2011, 'Global citizenship and marginalisation: contributions towards a political economy of global citizenship', *Globalisation, Societies and Education*, vol. 9, pp. 355–66.
Baugh, B 2016, 'The open society and the democracy to come: Bergson, Deleuze and Guattari', *Deleuze and Guattari Studies*, vol. 10, pp. 352–66.
Braidotti, R 2006, *Transpositions: on nomadic ethics*, Polity, Cambridge.
Braidotti, R 2018, 'On nomadism: a conversation with Rosi Braidotti', *Krytyka Polityczna & European Alternatives*, 24 July, viewed 15 September 2019, http://politicalcritique.org/world/2018/nomadism-braidotti/.
Camicia, SP and Franklin, BM 2011, 'What type of global community and citizenship? Tangled discourses of neoliberalism and critical democracy in curriculum and its reform', *Globalisation, Societies and Education*, vol. 9, pp. 311–22.
Castles, S 2003, 'Jerarquías de ciudadanía en el nuevo orden global', *Anales de la Cátedra Francisco Suárez*, vol. 37, pp. 9–33, viewed 15 September 2019, http://revistaseug.ugr.es/index.php/acfs/article/view/1084.
Center for Universal Education at Brookings 2017a, *Meaningful education in times of uncertainty: skills for a changing world*, viewed 30 September 2019, www.brookings.edu/research/meaningful-education-in-times-of-uncertainty/.
Center for Universal Education at Brookings 2017b, *Measuring global citizenship education*, 11 April, viewed 30 September 2019, www.brookings.edu/research/measuring-global-citizenship-education/.
Chapman, DD, Ruiz-Chapman, T and Eglin, P 2018, 'Global citizenship as neoliberal propaganda: a political-economic and postcolonial critique', *Alternate Routes: A Journal of Critical Social Research*, vol. 29, pp. 142–66, viewed 15 September 2019, www.alternateroutes.ca/index.php/ar/article/view/22450.
Cho, HS 2016, 'The gaps between values and practices of global citizenship education: a critical analysis of global citizenship education in South Korea', PhD thesis, University of Massachusetts Amherst, viewed 15 October 2019, https://scholarworks.umass.edu/dissertations_2/736.
Clifford, V and Montgomery C 2014, 'Challenging conceptions of Western higher education as promoting graduates as global citizens', *Higher Education Quarterly*, vol. 68, pp. 28–45.
Cohen, S 2001, *Immigration controls, the family and the welfare state: a handbook of law, theory, politics and practice for local authority, voluntary sector and welfare state workers and legal advisors*, Jessica Kingsley, London.
Cope, B and Kalantzis, M 2000, *Multiliteracies: literacy learning and the design of social futures*, Routledge, New York.
Cyupers, SE 2004, 'Critical thinking, autonomy and practical reason', *Journal of Philosophy of Education*, vol. 38, pp. 75–90.
Darian-Smith, E 2015, 'Global Studies: the handmaiden of neoliberalism?' *Globalizations*, vol. 12, no. 2, pp. 164–8.

Davids, N 2018, 'Global citizenship education, postcolonial identities, and a moral imagination', in I Davies, L-C Ho, D Kiwan, CL Peck, A Peterson, E Sant and Y Waghid (eds), *The Palgrave handbook of global citizenship and education*, 193–207, Palgrave Macmillan, London.

Davies, I, Ho, L-C, Kiwan, D, Peck, CL, Peterson, A, Sant, E and Waghid, Y (eds) 2018, *The Palgrave handbook of global citizenship and education*, Palgrave Macmillan, London.

Deleuze, G and Guattari, F 2005, *A thousand plateaus: capitalism and schizophrenia*, trans. B Massumi, University of Minnesota Press, Minneapolis.

Dill, JS 2012, 'The moral education of global citizens', *Society*, vol. 49, pp. 541–64.

Duhan Kaplan, L 1991, 'Teaching intellectual autonomy: the failure of the critical thinking movement', *Educational Theory*, vol. 41, pp. 361–70.

Engel, LC, Fundalinski, J and Cannon, T 2016, 'Global citizenship education at a local level: a comparative analysis of four U.S. urban districts', *Revista Española de Educación Comparada*, vol. 28, pp. 23–51.

Feyerabend, P 1993, *Against method*, Verso, New York.

Fox, NJ and Alldred, P 2016, 'The micropolitics of embodiment: citizenship, activism, posthumanism', PowerPoint presentation slides, viewed 20 September 2019, www.researchgate.net/publication/291332788_The_micropolitics_of_embodiment_citizenship_activism_posthumanism.

Freire, P 2000, *Pedagogy of the oppressed*, Continuum, New York.

Gacel-Ávila, J, Jaramillo, IC, Knight, J and de Wit, H 2005, 'The Latin American way: trends, issues, and directions', in H de Wit, IC Jaramillo, J Gacel-Ávila and J Knight (eds), *Higher education in Latin America: the international dimension*, 341–68, World Bank, New York.

Giraldo Jiménez, FH 2000, 'Ciudadanía y globalización', *Estudios Políticos*, vol. 16, pp. 141–50.

Gremaud, A-SN 2014, 'Power and purity: nature as resource in a troubled society', *Environmental Humanities*, vol. 5, pp. 77–100.

Higher Education Statistics Agency 2017, *Higher education student enrolments and qualifications obtained at higher education providers in the United Kingdom 2015/16*, viewed 25 September 2019, www.hesa.ac.uk/news/12-01-2017/sfr242-studentenrolments-and-qualifications.

Human Rights Watch n.d., '#OUTLAWED "The love that dare not speak its name"', viewed 10 October 2019, http://internap.hrw.org/features/features/lgbt_laws/.

Johnson, P, Boyer, M and Brown, S 2011, 'Vital interests: cultivating global competence in the international studies classroom', *Globalisation, Societies and Education*, vol. 9, pp. 503–19.

Karatzogianni, A and Robinson, A 2010, *Power, resistance and conflict in the contemporary world: social movements, networks and hierarchies*, Routledge, London and New York.

Karatzogianni, A and Robinson, A 2017, 'Schizorevolutions versus microfascisms: the fear of anarchy in state securitisation', *Journal of International Political Theory*, vol. 13, pp. 282–95, viewed 12 September 2019, http://journals.sagepub.com/doi/abs/10.1177/1755088217718570.

Karatzogianni, A and Schandorf, M 2016, 'Surfing the revolutionary wave 2010–2012: a technosocial theory of agency, resistance, and orders of dissent in contemporary social movements', in A Ornella (ed.), *Making humans: religious, technological and aesthetic perspectives*, 43–73, Interdisplinary Press, Oxford.

Kofman, E 2011, *Family reunion legislation in Europe: is it discriminatory for migrant women?* European Network of Migrant Women and European Women's Lobby,

Brussels, viewed 15 September 2019, www.migrantwomennetwork.org/IMG/pdf/Family_reunification_ENoMW_201 1.pdf.

Krabill, R 2012, 'American sentimentalism and the production of global citizens', *Contexts*, vol. 11, no. 4, pp. 52–4.

Laclau, E 1994, 'Why do empty signifiers matter to politics?' in D Howarth (ed.) 2015, *Ernesto Laclau: post-Marxism, populism and critique*, 66–74, Routledge, London.

Laclau, E 2005, *On populist reason*, Verso, New York.

Larsen, MA 2014, 'Critical global citizenship and international service learning: a case study of the intensification effect', *Journal of Global Citizenship & Equity Education*, vol. 4, no. 1, pp. 1–43.

Latin American Council of Social Sciences 2015, *Grupos de trabajo seleccionados para el período 2016–2019*, viewed 12 October 2019, www.clacso.org.ar/grupos_trabajo/detalle_gt.php?ficha=604&s=5&idioma=.

Latour, B 2004, *Politics of nature: how to bring the sciences into democracy*, trans. C Porter, Harvard University Press, Boston, MA.

Leydet, D 2017, 'Citizenship', in EN Zalta (ed.), *The Stanford encyclopedia of philosophy*, viewed 18 September 2019, https://plato.stanford.edu/archives/fall2017/entries/citizenship/.

Martín-Cabello, A 2017, 'Ciudadanía global: un estudio sobre las identidades sociopolíticas en un mundo interconectado', *Arbor*, vol. 193, no. 786, viewed 30 October 2019, http://arbor.revistas.csic.es/index.php/arbor/article/view/2233/3103.

Melo-Escrihuela, C 2008, 'Promoting ecological citizenship: rights, duties and political agency', *ACME: An International E-Journal for Critical Geographies*, vol. 7, no. 2, pp. 113–34.

Mill, JS 1869, *The subjection of women*, viewed 15 September 2019, www.earlymoderntexts.com/assets/pdfs/mill1869.pdf.

Ministerio de Relaciones Exteriores 2013, 'Cancillería le apuesta a la enseñanza del español en países de habla no hispana', *Colombian Ministry of Foreign Relations news page*, Bogotá, 11 January, viewed 17 October 2019, www.cancilleria.gov.co/en/newsroom/news/cancilleria-le-apuesta-la-ensenanza-del-espanol-paises-habla-no-hispana.

NAFSA 2017, *International student economic value tool*, viewed 31 October, www.nafsa.org/policy-and-advocacy/policy-resources/nafsa-international-student-economic-value-tool-v2.

Pais, A and Costa, M 2017, 'An ideology critique of global citizenship education', *Critical Studies in Education*, 22 April, pp. 1–16, viewed 15 September 2019, https://doi.org/10.1080/17508487.2017.1318772.

Pais, A 2017, 'The narcissism of mathematics education', in H Straehler-Pohl, N Bohlmann and A Pais (eds), *The disorder of mathematics education: challenging the sociopolitical dimensions of research*, 53–63, Springer, New York.

Papandreou, G and Shapiro, J 2017, 'An ancient education for modern democracy and global citizenship', in Center for Universal Education at Brookings, *Meaningful education in times of uncertainty: skills for a changing world*, 6–15, Center for Universal Education at Brookings, Washington, DC.

Parmenter, L 2011, 'Power and place in the discourse of global citizenship education', *Globalisation, Societies and Education*, vol. 9, pp. 367–80.

Pashby, K 2011, 'Cultivating global citizens: planting new seeds or pruning the perennials? Looking for the citizen-subject in global citizenship education theory', *Globalisation, Societies and Education*, vol. 9, pp. 427–42.

Pashby, K 2012, 'Questions for global citizenship education in the context of the "new imperialism": for whom, by whom?' in V de O Andreotti and LMTM de Souza (eds),

Postcolonial perspectives on global citizenship education, 9–26, Routledge, New York and London.

Patton, P 2011, 'What is Deleuzean political philosophy? *Crítica Contemporánea: Revista de Teoría Política*, vol. 1, pp. 115–26, viewed 25 September 2019, http://cienciassociales.edu.uy/wp-content/uploads/2013/archivos/patton.pdf.

Peraza Sanguinés, C 2016, 'Interpretaciones de la educación para la ciudadanía global en la reforma de la educación media superior en México', *Revista Española de Educación Comparada*, vol. 28, pp. 135–59.

Phizaclea, A, Kofman, E, Raghuram, P and Sales, R 2000, *Gender and international migration in Europe*, Routledge, London.

Ryan, J and Louie, K 2007, 'False dichotomy? "Western" and "Confucian" concepts of scholarship and learning', *Educational Philosophy and Theory*, vol. 39, pp. 404–17.

Richardson, D 2018, *Sexuality and citizenship*, Polity, Cambridge.

Rieder, B 2018, 'Digital citizenship', in R Braidotti and M Hlavajova (eds), *Posthuman glossary*, 101–4, Bloomsbury, London.

Riley, P 1999, 'On the social construction of the learner', in S Cotterall and D Crabbe (eds), *Learner autonomy in language learning: defining the field and effecting change*, 29–39, Peter Lang, Frankfurt am Main.

Sabsay, L 2012, 'The emergence of the other sexual citizen: orientalism and the modernisation of sexuality', *Citizenship Studies*, vol. 16, pp. 605–23.

Sant, E and González Valencia, G 2018, 'Global citizenship education in Latin America', in I Davies, L-C Ho, D Kiwan, CL Peck, A Peterson, E Sant and Y Waghid (eds), *The Palgrave handbook of global citizenship and education*, 67–82, Palgrave Macmillan, London.

Shultz, L 2018, 'Global citizenship and equity: cracking the code and finding decolonial possibility', in I Davies, L-C Ho, D Kiwan, CL Peck, A Peterson, E Sant and Y Waghid (eds), *The Palgrave handbook of global citizenship and education*, 245–56, Palgrave Macmillan, London.

Simmons, T 2008, 'Sexuality and immigration: UK family reunion policy and the regulation of sexual citizens in the European Union', *Political Geography*, vol. 27, pp. 213–30.

Skrbis, Z and Woodward, I 2013, *Cosmopolitanism: uses of the idea*, Sage, London.

Soong, H 2018, 'Transnationalism in education: theoretical discussions and the implications for teaching global citizenship education', in I Davies, L-C Ho, D Kiwan, CL Peck, A Peterson, E Sant and Y Waghid (eds), *The Palgrave handbook of global citizenship and education*, 165–77, Palgrave Macmillan, London.

Sovic, S and Blythman, M 2013, *International students negotiating higher education: critical perspectives*, Routledge, London.

Stychin, C 2003, *Governing sexuality*, Hart, Oxford.

Torres, CA 2015, 'Global citizenship and global universities: the age of global interdependence and cosmopolitanism', *European Journal of Education*, vol. 50, pp. 262–79.

UNESCO 2015, *Global citizenship education: topics and learning objectives*, UNESCO, Paris.

UNESCO 2016, *Educación 2030: Declaración de Incheon y Marco de acción para la realización del objetivo de desarrollo sostenible 4*, viewed 30 September 2019, www.unesco.org/new/fileadmin/MULTIMEDIA/FIELD/Santiago/pdf/ESP-Marco-de-Accion-E2030-aprobado.pdf.

UNESCO 2017, *Global citizenship education in Latina America and the Caribbean: towards a world without walls: global citizenship education in the SDG 4 – E2030*

Agenda, conclusions from the Latin America and the Caribbean Regional Network Meeting on Global Citizenship Education, 23–24 October, Santiago, Chile.

Universities UK 2017, *Briefing: the economic impact of international students*, viewed 31 October 2019, www.universitiesuk.ac.uk/policy-and-analysis/reports/Documents/2017/briefing-economic-impact-international-students.pdf.

Villarreal, D 2019, 'College kicks out trans student for having top surgery', *LGBTQ Nation*, 11 August, viewed 15 August 2019, www.lgbtqnation.com/2019/08/baptist-college-kicks-trans-student-top-surgery/.

Vogel, U 1991, 'Is citizenship gender-specific?' in U Vogel and M Moran (eds), *The frontiers of citizenship*, 55–85, Palgrave Macmillan, London.

Wallerstein, I 1991, *Geopolitics and geoculture: essays on the changing world-system*, Duke University Press, Durham, NC.

Wallerstein, I 2004, *World-system analysis: an introduction*, Duke University Press, Durham, NC.

Wit, H de, Jaramillo, IC, Gacel-Ávila, J and Knight, J (eds) 2005, *Higher education in Latin America: the international dimension*, World Bank, New York.

World Bank 2011, *Learning for all: investing in people's knowledge and skills to promote development – World Bank Group education strategy 2020: executive summary*, no. 64487, viewed 15 September 2019, http://documents.worldbank.org/curated/en/685531468337836407/Learning-for-all-investing-in-peoples-knowledge-and-skills-to-promote-development-World-Bank-Group-education-strategy-2020-executive-summary.

Part IV

Global citizenship and the international institutions

Chapter 7

Global citizenship and neo-republicanism?
Problematising the 'neoliberal subjectivities' critique

April Biccum

Introduction

This chapter problematises the 'neoliberal subjectivities' critique of Global Citizenship Education (GCE), by arguing that as it has recently been incorporated into the Sustainable Development Goals (SDGs) and coupled with the Preventing Violent Extremism through Education (PVE-E) and Youth Engagement Initiatives, it is better understood as part of a Polanyian style 'double movement' and as an attempt at constructing a 'republican citizen' in the absence of a 'global republic'. In its pamphlet the 'ABCs of Global Citizenship Education' (see Appendix), the United Nations Education, Scientific and Cultural Organization (UNESCO) defines GCE as follows:

> The goal of global citizenship education is to empower learners to engage and assume active roles both locally and globally to face and resolve global challenges and ultimately to become proactive contributors to a more just, peaceful, tolerant, inclusive, secure and sustainable world. Global citizenship education has three conceptual dimensions. The cognitive dimension concerns the learners' acquisition of knowledge, understanding and critical thinking. The socio-emotional dimension relates to the learners' sense of belonging to a common humanity, sharing values and responsibilities, empathy, solidarity and respect for differences and diversity. The behavioural dimension expects the learners to act responsibly at local, national and global levels for a more peaceful and sustainable world.

Labelled by advocates as the fastest growing educational reform movement (Dill 2012), GCE has been championed by a variety of actors in a networked assemblage of Global Education Governance (GEG) (comprising educators, non-governmental organisations (NGOs), academics, policy makers, international organisations (IOs) and some private actors) as a solution to global problems through the production of 'change makers'. GCE is part of a two-pronged shift in approaches to education since the 1970s, one that links education exclusively with the market and productivity (human capital), and one that links education to social justice outcomes. Both approaches have coalesced within a thickening networked space of GEG since the 1990s and have become progressively intertwined, minimally via the Millennium Development Goals (MDGs), and explicitly within the SDGs.

Most critiques of GCE argue that it is either an exercise in 'neoliberal subject production', or a reconfiguration of imperial relationships through epistemic framing. It has been criticised using postcolonial, decolonial, Zizekian ideology critique, and Ferguson's 'anti-politics machine', as producing depoliticized 'neoliberal subjects' with sanitized aggregate and panoptic knowledge that masks the reality of globalising capital and thwarts the capacity for genuine critique (Andreotti 2011; Pais and Costa 2017; Gough and Scott 2006). The common refrain of these critics is that it offers the production of highly individuated cosmopolitan subjectivities that are endowed with knowledge that can be simultaneously capitalised upon for better market outcomes. Following the Foucauldian approach to theorising neoliberalism as more than just economic policy, Wendy Brown understands neoliberalism as a modality of governance which devolves itself to the level of the individual and 'responsibilizes' and constrains the subject into acting in capital enhancing ways (2016).

While these critiques are not without their merit, this chapter argues that the inclusion of GCE into the SDGs, its coupling with the PVE-E agenda and the securitisation of 'youth' are an integral part of the Post-Washington Consensus (PWC); together, they are *a response to* the contradictions unleashed by neoliberalism. While there is some debate about how much the PWC constitutes a departure from the neoliberalism of the 1980s, it is nevertheless understood as widespread acknowledgement of and/or disillusionment with the strict market policies of 1979–2000 (Stiglitz 2002; Piketty 2014; World Bank Group 2015) and a more comprehensive agenda of governance and regulatory reforms. Some scholars refer to the PWC as 'social regulatory neoliberalism', while others may understand it as an expanded architecture of governmentality to facilitate the further entrenchment of the market (Güven 2018). In development scholarship there is widespread acknowledgement that the MDGs and SDGs represent a significant shift in development policy accompanied by an expanded architecture of global governance and development cooperation (Caballero 2019).

There is ample scope for understanding these changes as a Polanyian style 'double movement' as Polanyi described a pattern of political-economic changes whereby various socialist, collectivist and fascist elements within society react to protect society from the market (Stewart 2018; Polanyi 1944). In addition to a renewed interest in the sociological approach to the market found in Karl Polanyi,[1] and a literature in International Relations (IR) harkening the coming of a world state (Ruggie 2002), these developments have been accompanied by a revival of Republican political thought in American Political Science that has generated an ambitious programme for institutional and political reform (Costa 2009, 2013; Dagger 2006; Klein 2017; Lovett and Pettit 2009; Petit 1996, 1997).

This chapter will argue that the 'neoliberal subjectivities' argument is no longer quite the right fit for understanding what is happening with the mainstreaming of GCE within GEG and its coupling with the youth and counterterrorism agenda. The chapter is organised as follows. Section 1 provides a theoretical discussion across four literatures – neoliberal governmentality, youth discourse, development and security, and the neo-republican revival literature – to elaborate a theoretical framework informing analysis. Section 2 will use ongoing documentary process tracing, network ethnography and secondary literature to provide a thick description of the three processes under consideration and the ways they intersect (Ball 2016). My argument is that while neoliberal governmentality is certainly evident in the way that GCE has been integrated into GEG, GCE is not itself neoliberal and is possibly better understood as neo-republican. Moreover, its combination with these other initiatives demonstrates that GCE is a *response* to the global dislocation produced by the market logic of the 1980s in a way that tries to domesticate critique. In section 3 I concretise this interpretation through documentary analysis through which these projects and policies are being articulated. I conclude by elaborating the shortcomings of the 'neoliberal subjectivities' account.

Development, security and neoliberal subjectivity?

A substantial volume of scholarship since the 1990s has been devoted to an application of a Foucauldian framework to international governance, specifically in the fields of global governance, security and development (Bratich, Packer and McCarthy 2004; Leask 2012; Stoler 1995; Escobar 1995). The application of Foucault to the architecture of global governance has had to undergo some theoretical legwork, because Foucault only turned his attention to neoliberalism towards the end of his life. Jason Read traces out how Foucault understands the shift from liberal to neoliberal governmentality as a discursive shift from a focus on *exchange* which naturalises the market as a rational system of distribution to a focus on *competition* and an extension of the market logic to all areas of social and economic life (Read 2009). While both have the ideal subject of 'homo economicus' as their referent object, the shift to neoliberalism is not simply an ideological shift, but a transformation in ideology. That is because it is not articulated by specific elites and their capture of state institutions, but instead is an ideology that permeates all institutions to become an image of society itself. It refers to the entirety of human existence. Predicating itself on knowledge of human nature it is intimately tied up to the government of the individual, attempting to reproduce a particular manner of living (Read 2009). This shift in focus to the individual also entails a redefinition of labour whereby the rebranding of the worker as 'human capital' is a collapse of two subjectivities – the capitalist and the worker – into one. 'Homo-economicus is an entrepreneur, an entrepreneur of himself', a subjectivity that should through 'lifelong learning' be continually investing in herself to increase returns on her 'human capital' (Read 2009, p. 28). While there is a substantial literature on neoliberal governmentality (Brady 2008; Ellison 2009; Walters 2012), Wendy Brown's work has done the most to theorise neoliberalism through the Foucauldian prism of power/knowledge (Brown 2015, 2016). The consensus is that neoliberalism as a governing technique involves the reproduction of power through its devolution to the individual through self-surveillance, bodily discipline, self-responsibilisation, techniques of the self, 'self-animation', 'self-government' and individuation (Gill 2008; Olssen and Peters 2005; Pathak 2014; Brockman and Eyal 2002). Brown describes how devolution combined with market entrenchment fractures a variety of social solidarities leaving the 'neoliberal subject' reliant on her own capabilities to withstand and adapt to the vagaries of the market.

> While the classical liberal ideal of individual autonomy and freedom is exploited through neoliberal devolutions of decision-making, agency and responsibility to the Individual, this ideal is hollowed out as de-regulation eliminates a range of public goods and social security provisions, unleashes the powers of corporate and finance capital, and dismantles classical twentieth century solidarities among workers, consumers, and electorates. The combined effect is to generate intensely isolated and unprotected individuals, persistently in peril of deracination and deprivation of basic life support, wholly vulnerable to capital's vicissitudes.
>
> (Brown 2016, p. 3)

This neoliberal subject is fundamentally different from *homo juridicus* – the legal subject of the state – and neoliberal governmentality is not about rights and laws but interest, investment and competition.

Mark Duffield also uses a Foucauldian framework to elaborate the knowledge/power nexus of 'human security' as another iteration in the devolution of governance to 'uninsured' populations which it seeks to render *adaptive, self-reliant* and *resilient*. Foucauldian framings of development policy and global governance (Escobar 1995; Duffield 2001) point out that development discourse over the twentieth and twenty-first centuries has undergone both profound change and yet has in many ways remained consistent. Beginning in the post-war period under the anti-communist modernisation paradigm of the cold war, development intervention sought to shift 'traditional' behaviour towards 'rational' instrumentalist and market-oriented behaviour. The shift to the neoliberal paradigm in the 1980s was accompanied by the assumption that these behaviours are naturally occurring and development interventions should simply shrink the size of the state to unleash the market. When poverty, inequality and an increase in conflict resulted from these policies by the 1990s, the shift to the PWC has been underpinned by the assumptions of behavioural economics which, incorporating the various social constructivist challenges of the twentieth century social sciences, presumes that market-like behaviour needs to be socially engineered and that people can be guided or 'nudged' into making 'rational choices'. An important part of this shift is a change in the role of NGOs, which have been increasingly integrated into the global governance architecture, or in the language of Mary Kaldor, domesticated (2003).

The work of Mark Duffield has been central to the literature in critical development studies that has identified a 'development–security nexus', characterised as a 'constellation of institutions, practices and beliefs' that has deepened in *response* to the political, economic and social fractures caused by the neoliberal development paradigm (Duffield 2010). There is now a voluminous academic literature and policy discourse articulating this paradigm (Hettne 2010; Jensen 2010; Kingebiel 2006; Stern and Ojendal 2010), but in brief, the development–security nexus can be summarised as: (1) the conditional use of aid for conflict resolution; (2) the policy framing that poverty is the cause of conflict and therefore increased economic well-being is the redress; and (3) a discursive subterfuge which masks the real causes of poverty, conflict and insecurity in the previous decade of neoliberal policy. Human security follows the devolutionary pattern identified by Brown in that donor interventions have changed their relationships with recipient states to focus on local populations. Calling this the 'liberal way of development', Duffield has argued that it is not at all new, that the development–security nexus is intrinsic to modernity and liberalism itself. If liberalism presumes a 'correct mode of life' that constructs those who live differently through an itinerary of 'lack', development is a governmental response to this lack that constructs itself as socially engineering an alignment through interventions designed to 'help'. This modality of development has no intention of actually spreading the 'correct mode of life' but instead is a means of managing and containing counter-insurgency, civil wars, and spontaneous or undocumented migration.

Another significant discursive and institutional shift in the 1990s is the designation of 'youth' as a global social category at the heart of the development and security agenda (Bersaglio, Enns and Kepe 2015; Sukarieh and Tannock 2018, 2011, 2008). The context for this reconstruction of 'youth' by IOs and the development establishment is the demographic observation of a 'youth bulge' in developing countries that has occurred as a consequence of these very same neoliberal policies. Although IOs do not cite these circumstances as the cause of the 'youth bulge', they nevertheless designate the 'surplus' populations of young people as the cause of conflict and increased insecurity as young people are idle, disaffected and easily radicalised. The World Bank's 2007 World Development Report cites unemployment, economic marginalisation and political exclusion as having the potential to foster resentment, oppositional identifications, defiance, indifference, political extremism, terrorism and revolutionary ideas among the developing world's burgeoning youth population (World Bank Report 2006, cited in Sukarieh and Tannock 2008, p. 307). According to the World Bank, 'countries with 40% or more youth (aged) 15–29 were twice as likely to break out in civil conflict in the 1990s' and that the 'costs of not investing in youth are staggering both politically and economically' (cited in Sukarieh and Tannock 2008, p. 305).

IO fears are not without warrant. In the same period under consideration (roughly 1995–2019) youth globally have been active in a variety of anti-systemic movements across the political spectrum: in the anti-globalisation movement, the Arab

Spring, Occupy Wall Street, various climate justice and anti-energy initiatives, and among many of the recruits of Al-Qaeda, ISIS, the agents of lone wolf and organised terrorist attacks and the swelling ranks of the far right globally. The literature observing and tracking this reconstruction of 'youth' notes that there is a longer genealogy which goes back to the economic dislocations of the nineteenth and twentieth centuries where a whole interventionist apparatus emerged within states to discipline unruly youth under the auspices of a scientific and pathologised category of 'juvenile delinquency'. Effectively, the socio-political capture of youth is vital to the reproduction of the economic system. What's changed according to the youth-as-discourse literature is that the framing has shifted from negative to positive in a 'scientific' academic discourse coming out of the United States known as the 'Positive Youth Development' (PYD) movement, which operates according to a duality of 'risk' (human security) and as an asset (human capital). Following the neoliberal 'responsibilisation' model, grooming tactics of IOs ultimately regard 'youth' as *responsible* for solving the problems related to youth and want to incentivise states to adopt the governance and regulatory model of 'youth engagement'. Therefore the youth discourse literature concludes that this is another attempt at the (re)production of the neoliberal subjectivities. Yet, there is here a very Polanyian-style contradiction in that the 'neoliberal responsibilisation' of the youth is done through a growing apparatus of *non-market* interventions and an implicit mandate that all states adopt the same education systems and same regulatory frameworks around young people. While the literature details how youth engagement is ultimately about employment, what is left underexplored is the possibility that the expanded architecture of global governance will require bureaucratic functionaries. The combination of GCE, PVE-E and youth-led governance initiatives creates a pool for this labour.

Following Karl Polanyi, we could consider the SDGs as a global institutional apparatus of public policy that moves to protect global society from the devastation caused by the market. But, unlike Polanyi's account of British economic history, this expanded architecture is trans- and intra-national and must be also understood following IR framings of the international system in terms of regime, polity, society or a world state in the making (Ruggie 2002; Buzan 2004; Wendt 2003). No small irony then that the 'coming of the world state' framing of IR is accompanied by the theoretical revival of republicanism in American political science. In reading GCE/PVE-E through this republican revival I am not arguing for a causal connection between the two – neo-republicans are largely ignorant of GCE and scholars and practitioners of GCE are largely ignorant of American political science. I am arguing that in the context of American political science and the PWC, a republican revival is significant. It is a departure from the formerly dominant rational choice theory (RCT) that underpinned American foreign and economic policy in important ways (Almond 1991; Eriksson 2011; Hindmoor 2006; Kiser and Hechter 1998). Following a Foucauldian understanding of knowledge/power, we would expect a change in orientation in American political science to correspond to changes in global institutions in which the United States has a dominant interest.

The revival of republicanism in the American academic sphere is traced to historiographic work in the twentieth century revising the classical scholarly reading of republican political thought in relation to negative and positive freedom. The work of Pocock and Quentin Skinner is most commonly attributed but the revival revolves around the work of Phillip Petit (1996, 1997), Cass R. Sunstein (1997) and Richard Dagger (2006, 1997).[2] Given the widespread acknowledgement of the failure of both market and socialist society a republican revival allows American political theorists to chart a middle path between Hayek and Marx which could be characterised as a way of preserving the market against the double movement. Neo-republicans offer their work as a 'post-socialist' critique of market society that doesn't abandon private property. Instead they insist that it is a requirement for personal independence and freedom, but they reject the free-market fundamentalism of the Chicago School and the economised political assumptions of RCT. They want to subsume market relations to the political as a way of protecting democracy, while rescuing the market from 'collectivisms' by preserving the assumed connection between market freedom and political freedom.

Richard Dagger defines republicanism as a belief that government is a public affair and should be directed by the makers of the public themselves. The public sphere is not a mere aggregation of private citizens, but a political space open to scrutiny and preserved from the corruption of the market (where politics is simply deal making by citizens and interest groups pursing their private preferences). The citizen of the republic is *not* the autonomous, self-aggrandising instrumentalist of the market society, but a self-governing individual who derives her identity from the polity. She takes her responsibility for the creation of a common good seriously and complies with laws that she has had a voice in the making. The construction of the republic by the self-governing individual should reflect and promote 'civic virtue' – that is the disposition to put the public good ahead of one's private interests. Freedom, from the neo-republican perspective, is not freedom from interference in the neoliberal mould, but freedom from domination, that is ensured by living under a rule of law. Republican institutions must ensure opportunities for equal citizens to govern themselves in a deliberative manner and politics should be conducted through discussion and debate. Importantly, neo-republicans reject the givenness of preferences articulated by RCT. Instead they embrace the critiques of a vast array of twentieth century social theory that describe the constructedness of preferences through institutions and social norms, and blame the market society for the decline in civic virtue. In alignment with socialism they deny that the market has inherent moral legitimacy, although it should remain the basis for the autonomy required for self-government. Following classical republicanism they argue *that the same skills the self-governing individual exhibits in the marketplace are the same set of rational and discerning skills that the republican citizen brings to the public sphere.*

> To be sure, there is an important sense in which the ability to engage in free exchanges in the marketplace enables people to be self-governing – the sense in which they are able to make decisions about how they live their lives.
>
> (Dagger 2006, p. 158)

I am not by any means offering a sympathetic reading of neo-republicanism. While Philip Petit claims to be against colonialism because it is clearly arbitrary domination and goes against his principle of freedom-as-nondomination, there is nevertheless a clear elision in his thought about the relationship between republican political thought and the history of empire. There is a substantial scholarship that situates republican *and* liberal political thought as indivisibly undergirding imperial projects (Mehta 1999; Muthu 2012; Pagden 1995; Irving 2008). Moreover, all of the republican experiments historically which neo-republicans cite as their tradition (the ancient Greek and Roman, the Renaissance, Enlightenment – especially French, and American) have also been imperial. This glaring omission on the part of the neo-republicans is also accompanied by frequent use of the phrase 'empire of laws' to characterise neo-republican governance. Philip Petit in particular advocates a very conventional American foreign policy predicated on democratic peace theory. My argument in observing the common inflections of GCE as articulated by IOs through neo-republican theory is not that the subjectivity of GCE is not *imperial*, simply that is it not *neoliberal*.[3]

Incorporation and coupling: GCE, PVE-E and youth engagement

What is observable in the twentieth century are two competing discourses on education, one that is socio-political, the other economic. I will describe first GCE's roots in the first and then the way it becomes a redress for the contradictions of the second. The genealogy of GCE is rooted in the socio-political approach and located in three different institutional/actor sites from the 1960s to the 1990s – states demonstrating increasing concern about public knowledge of and support for foreign aid; educators politicised by civil rights movements and global inequality; and NGOs using knowledge gained on the ground for lobbying and public awareness in the global North. It will be pointed out that even in its most deracinated market forms, education is always political. Educational policy is implicated in state formation, social compromise for the purposes of economic development and hegemonic extension of state architectures into colonial peripheries (Borg, Buttigieg and Mayo 2002; Boyd 1921; Dale 2000; Hall 2008; Tait 2015; Leask 2012; Meyer et al. 1977). Institutionalised educational apparatuses were an integral part of the elite and bureaucratic functionary making enterprises of various European and non-European empires (you can think of the public school system in England, or the examination system of Imperial China). During the nineteenth century education became an integral part of the state making and modernisation enterprises of European states through the expansion of public provision and its extension to colonial governance (you can think of Macauley's educational mandate of 1883). It is only late in the nineteenth and early twentieth centuries that education becomes associated with liberal tenets of democracy through personal betterment and also hitched to the mobilising tactics of social movements. Examples include the various articulations of anti-colonial nationalisms from the Spanish American war through to Indian mobilisation for independence and the awareness raising tactics of civil society movements in the 1960s across a number of sites (from the United States to South Africa and Australia).

In the twentieth century, educational practice becomes an ambivalent site, both the subject-making enterprise of hegemonic structures and the mobilising tactics of social movements. This is reflected in a variety of sites, such as educational scholarship and theory (Freire 1970), the emergence of a wide variety of 'adjectival' educations to reflect the various social movement uses of education (such as environmental education, intercultural education, anti-racist education, peace and conflict education), and the use of education as a mobilising tactic among a wide variety of civil society actors (Rugendyke 2007). Development Education (DE) has its genealogy here. In the 1970s and 1980s it was the recourse of politically motivated educators who wanted education to contribute to global social justice and lobbying efforts of NGOs. NGOs also began to develop their own internal public outreach and educational structures. Beginning as a loose partnership between these two constituencies it was first elaborated in the creation of Development Education Centres (DECs) which housed the educational resources produced by educators and NGOs and supplied support for educators wanting to introduce DE into their educational practice.

States began funding DE in the 1990s through their foreign aid arms (notably the British Labour government from 1999–2009). State funding has allowed the creation of large archives of educational materials, many of which are now being housed in online archives hosted by Oxfam and the UNESCO.[4] These educational resources cover a wide variety of civil society perspectives on global problems and can be used in a wide variety of ways by educators in classrooms. The intention of many educators is to remedy the contradictions of the globalising market economy. Through the production of 'critical consciousness' these educators are hoping to encourage anti-systemic response to globalising capital. It is through state funding initially and then through its take up in IOs (the European Union first then other IOs) that development education became Global Education, Global Learning and/or GCE. GCE is expressly intended to be an umbrella for all the variety of 'adjectival' social justice educations. Effectively what has happened is that the advocacy and social movement knowledge of 'development' has made its way into the educational policy being articulated at the global level. There is a variety of ways in which GCE can be co-opted, hijacked and marginalised but it is not *in itself* education for neoliberalism.

This genealogy of the twentieth century *politicisation of education* includes and is coterminous with shifts in educational scholarship and policy towards the marketisation of education. The market-based approach, as articulated best by a brief consensus among some economists, is that the state-centric bureaucratic system is inadequate for a world of free flows through information communication technologies (Boix 2016; Boix and Jackson 2011) and that educational provision is best determined by market forces where responsibilised individuals have direct access. This view of education was supported by the inclusion of education in the services industry via the General Agreement on Trade in Services (GATS) (Robertson 2005). While briefly the site of debate, the World Bank approach did not gain universal traction and IOs demonstrated a similar concern to NGOs about public support for foreign aid spending going back to the 1960s (Kilby 2015). So while educational policy at state and IO level during the 1980s was expressed in the 'human capital' paradigm (Bloom 2004; Robertson 2005), at the same juncture, there was also simultaneously a growing concern regarding how global changes (in markets and migration) could affect the legitimacy of state institutions and practices. In other words, there has emerged a countervailing pressure to preserve the political function of education for hegemonic purposes. It is not that education has not been marketised through the regime of intellectual property, the knowledge economy, the expansion of the services sector and the growth of edu-business (Ball 2012; Burbules and Torres 2000; Verger, Lubienski and Steiner-Khamsi 2016); it's just that education is a key site for the double movement because the expansion of educational provision is one of the mechanisms via which society protects itself from the market. Education also contains another 'fictitious commodity' not initially theorised by Polanyi – knowledge. These three approaches to education (free market, state hegemonic and social movement) mingle and merge through the construction of a regime of GEG.

As part of the double movement, education is prioritised in the PWC because neoliberal policies shrank state capacity for educational provision in the global South. While the MDGs were regarded with suspicion by many NGOs they are nevertheless a profound reframing of development (Burke and Rurup 2019). The double movement is expressed in an NGO- and IO-led global educational reform movement expressed at the Jomtien Education for All (EFA) conference (1990). While several multilateral organisations have been instrumental in shaping the EFA agenda from the start (most notably the World Bank, UNESCO, United Nations Development Programme and the Organisation for Economic Co-operation and Development (OECD)) (Tikly 2014), the EFA represents a clear departure from the narrower market-oriented approach to education of the neoliberal period. With the EFA, education becomes a key node in an expanded and reformed development discourse where education as public good linked to global justice is combined with human capital. The EFA is one of the mechanisms via which GCE (formerly Development Education) comes to be included in the SDGs.

GCE was informally a part of the MDGs. As MDG Goal 8 Building a Global Partnership for Development it prompted limited state funding for 'global education' in countries like Australia, the UK and Canada.[5] In the SDGs it has come to be explicitly articulated. SDG 4.7 reads:

By 2030, ensure that all learners acquire the knowledge and skills needed to promote sustainable development, including among others, through education for sustainable development and sustainable lifestyles, human rights, gender equality, promotion of a culture of peace and non-violence, *global citizenship* and appreciation of cultural diversity and of culture's contribution to sustainable development.

(United Nations 2015c, my emphasis (for details of UNESCO documents, see the Appendix table at the end of the chapter))

The SDGs are regarded as a further attempt to revolutionise development policy by incorporating environmental and social movement concerns (Caballero 2019). In education, a focus on access has expanded to include a focus on quality and therefore content. And the content of education needs to support the goals of access, by breaking down discriminatory barriers, particularly for women, girls and minority groups. The content of education therefore has become GCE, which enters the expanded architecture of GEG in two ways: one top down (the Global Education First Initiative (GEFI) of the then UN Secretary General Ban Ki-moon from 2012–2015),[6] and the other bottom up (the Muscat Agreement, following an extensive consultation process to establish the post-2015 educational agenda, including extensive involvement from NGOs and the Global Education Community).

With IOs and states driving their own educational agenda there has been a clear shift in the institutional balance of power. While UNESCO is nominally in a co-ordinating role, the OECD in particular has set itself up as a leader in the collation of knowledge for GEG, in some respects outpacing UNESCO in its leadership role (Allina-Pisano 2009; Grek 2009; Sjoberg 2014; see Costa and Ponte e Sousa, this volume, Chapter 8). It is the expanded global development and educational governance architecture itself which produces the apparatus of knowledge/power and devolution that is associated with neoliberal governmentality, not the aims, content or pedagogy of GCE itself. I will provide three brief examples. The UK was the forerunner of state funders of DE under the Labour administration from 1999–2009. The British state continued to fund DE after the election of the coalition government, but following the Conservative party's platform of devolution, DE was centralised under a consortium of actors in London called 'Think Global', one of which was a controversial edu-business outfit called Pearson Education. Its model of dissemination sidestepped the DECs and instead identified 'School Leaders' who would model Global Learning for other schools, incentivised to adopt the Global Learning Programme as a means to comply with school governance regulations already set by the state. The UN Secretary General's GEFI programme follows the same model of 'responsibilisation'. This was a short programme with three educational aims: (1) put every child in school; (2) improve the quality of learning; (3) foster global citizenship. Its structure followed the same centralising devolutionary pattern where the programme sought states to voluntarily take leadership roles on implementation. This model is followed again by the Global Citizenship Foundation based in India. Its executive board comprises mostly young people with marketing degrees, and it operates by identifying individual and institutional 'leaders' who will take forward the GCE programme and will be supplied with pre-prepared educational resources to do so. The awards and ambassadors scheme identifies 'social entrepreneurs'; the institutional partners scheme identifies schools, all of them elite. The Global Citizenship Foundation is exactly the kind of youth-led organisation of social entrepreneurs that is championed by the Youth Engagement Initiative.

The Youth Engagement Initiative, PVE-E and GCE all come to intersect with one another at key points. The Youth Engagement initiative began in 1985 with a series of statements and activities (such as the designation of a UN International Youth Year), with the Barcelona Statement acknowledging the usefulness of involving youth in planning, and with a World Congress on Youth in Spain. Youth consultations expanded in the early 2000s, with the Y8 meeting yearly from 2001 to 2018. And the 2011 General Assembly Resolution on Policies and Programmes involving youth urged member states to promote the full and effective participation of youth. The UNESCO Operational Strategy on Youth 2014–2021 builds on its Youth Forums 2015 and 2017 and overall Youth Programme. The PVE-E emerges from a shift away from militaristic and hard security strategies that informed counter-terrorism at the global level from 2001. The limitations of the former approach were increasingly recognised and the fifth review of the UN's Global Counter-Terrorism Strategy provided the opportunity to re-emphasise the importance of prevention and it welcomed the UN Secretary General's Plan of Action to Prevent Violent Extremism in 2016, which established the priority of education as a long-term strategy of prevention. The Plan recommends educational programmes which promote Global Citizenship. At the same time, UNESCO's executive Board Decision 197 in October 2015 was addressed to UNESCO's role in promoting education as a tool to prevent violent extremism and it linked PVE work with its wider commitment to promote Global Citizenship through education. The Youth Engagement Initiative comes also to be connected to education policy as reflected in the document 'Planning Education with and for Youth', but it is via UN Security Council Resolution 2250 on Youth, Peace and Security (S/RES/2250 9 December 2015) that the Youth Engagement Initiative intersects with counter-terrorism and education. Since then, the UN has stated its policy for youth engagement in PVE via the Forefronts document and youth delegations have been involved in the publication of several documents analysed below.

Document analysis

The documentation which is constitutive of this three-part agenda – GCE, PVE-E and youth engagement – is continually expanding and tends to be organised according to documents which articulate the agenda (UNESCO 2015a), or set out policy advice and guidance (UNESCO 2016a), or disseminate the latest research and/or address specific issues (UNESCO 2018a). The documents articulate broad policy objectives and aims for education, provide advice and guidance on how to implement and achieve those aims (which often include models of devolutionary governance) and they often detail and highlight projects which are considered model examples of implementation. This section has selected a small corpus of texts (see Appendix), analysed them thematically, conceptually, discursively and for process, that cut across and intersect. Each is implicated in the other in the following ways: GCE prepares young people for youth engagement by teaching the skills required; GCE is the appropriate education for PVE because of its emphasis on compassion, solidarity and respect for diversity; discussing VE in the classroom fosters the skills required by GC; and young people are conceived of as boundary agents in the process. They are posited as the most appropriate actors to act on PVE, to act as a bulwark against VE, and to formulate policy for PVE. This is an active site of policy formulation and implementation so new documents are being produced all the time. I will try to demonstrate my claims as much as possible through textual reference but the units of analysis cut across all documents and they have been analysed as a corpus for both within-text and intertextual inference on meaning and process.

The Education 2030 Agenda is significant in that it moves global educational policy away from the instrumental-economistic approach and understands education as transformative in two ways: first, education and the education system need to be transformed according to the tenets of the social justice approach to education; and, second, the new education should transform individuals into potential change makers and problem solvers. This account of education as humanistic, a human right and public good, transformative and contributing to 'global social cohesion' is present across three constitutive documents: The Incheon Declaration (UNESCO 2016c); Education Transforms Lives (UNESCO 2017a) and Rethinking Education: Towards a Global Common Good (UNESCO 2015a).

Critical, NGO and social movement approaches to education are in evidence in all framings of GCE. GCE is described as different pedagogically, in content and in learning outcomes, intending to shape recipient attitudes and values (including value and respect for diversity and a political commitment to inclusion and social justice) and inform recipient behaviour (including creating the capacity for specifically defined political activism and problem solving). Moreover, UNESCO's Rethinking Education report cites the writing of anti-colonial writer Rabinranath Tagore and other anti-colonial nationalists of the early twentieth century and includes postcolonial critiques of hegemonic knowledge systems as central to the need to build into education systems a respect for diversity.

> It is essential to recall – as have thinkers Frantz Fanon, Aime Cesaire, Rabindranath Tagore and others – that when we privilege one form of knowledge, we in fact privilege a system of power. The future of education and development in today's world requires fostering a dialogue among different worldviews with the aim of integrating knowledge systems originating in diverse realities, and to establish our common heritage.
>
> (UNESCO 2015a, p. 3)

In addition, the 'universal vision' for 'transformative education' set out by the Incheon Declaration will necessitate a reorientation of the governance and content of national education systems with a new type of education. What we see is that, while there are certainly hegemonic elements, GCE and global educational reform is not neoliberal, in Wendy Brown's sense, because it is a departure from the individualising, self-capitalising approach. It includes (at least at face value) the social justice approach to education and the pedagogical approaches informed by social movements, and its implementation actually requires a reversal of neoliberal policies on education that required a shrinking of state provision. Instead, it requires the globalisation of a specific type of education system including governance, teacher training, pedagogy and curricular content.

State-based education systems that formerly were an instrumental part of national identity construction are now being asked to reorient identity and political allegiances globally with a type of education that emphasises solidarity, respect for diversity and *political activism*. But what we see across the documents is a securitising objective where this activism is directed and circumscribed. So for example,

> Learners can be encouraged to think critically about, and to question, current situations and the status quo; to come up with new and creative approaches to common/global problems; and to find ways to take non-violent and constructive action to demonstrate their solidarity with others. These actions could include volunteerism, or obtaining more information from reputable institutions, NGOs and civil society organisations that work to help people in difficult circumstances and in need of support.
>
> (UNESCO 2016a, p. 35)

And, 'Schools can teach skills related to advocacy, campaigning, budgeting, organisation building and leadership, in order to facilitate engagement' (UNESCO 2016a, p. 40).

Education for activism will supply the skills required for 'youth engagement'. While this is clearly a discourse of responsibilisation and resilience, resilience is understood politically. Resilience is more than passive resistance to violent extremism. It necessarily includes a sense of personal responsibility and an engagement. In this respect, citizenship education, considered as an integral part of an education system, provides a means to overcome youth disengagement. If designed for this purpose, citizenship education can encourage and motivate learners to contribute constructively to society and support social change through non-violent ways in their local environment (UNESCO 2017c, p. 36).

A key part of this policy formulation is that one of the pull factors of extremist groups, namely that they supply a sense of meaning and purpose, will be replaced by the sense of solidarity, purpose and collective identity supplied by GCE. The Youth 2.0 project is described as aiming to help young people build new forms of 'global solidarity' and to support youth civic engagement and participation in peace building and including empowering and organising youth organisations, with a view to using these youth organisations as a 'multiplier effect' on the ground.

It is this sense of belonging combined with the capacity to contribute which makes GCE/PVE-E legible through the lens of neo-republicanism. The intended subject of both educations combined is endowed with active civic virtue, has a sense of belonging to the polity (in this case the global community), and is autonomous and sovereign, accepting the legitimacy of laws and institutions because they had a part in constructing them. So, for example, youth engagement adds value to the decision-making process because policies are more effective if young people have had a hand in formulating them. Youth involvement may also secure their buy-in to policies and increase their motivation to join efforts to change and improve the system (UNESCO 2015d, p. 30).

The report cites evidence that youth engagement produces lower drop-out rates, higher academic achievement, a greater sense of career direction and reductions in crime; and the self-confidence gained through participation produces character traits that contribute to peace building. The Teacher's Guide to VE defines GC as 'a sense of belonging to the global community and common humanity, with its members experiencing solidarity and collective identity among themselves and collective responsibility at the global level' (UNESCO 2016a, p. 15) and 'Education is one area where young people remain passive, but could become drivers of reform in a system of which they are a part' (UNESCO 2015d, p. 21).

GCE is further securitised through its tethering to the aim of strengthening the capacities of education systems to promote the rule of law (UNESCO 2018c), which enfolds it in the risk/asset duality of the positive youth development discourse. What we see here is that contra Wendy Brown above, the 'global citizen' *is also homo juridicus*. Combined with the youth engagement paradigm, GCE is the appropriate education for reproducing a culture of lawfulness, insofar as it creates youth capable of political and policy engagement, including involvement in educational planning (UNESCO 2015b), thereby exhibiting the republican subjectivity (after Petit) of one who complies with laws that she has had a voice in making.[7]

The aims of GCE are clearly about the promotion of 'civic virtue' in the neo-republican sense. For example, in its 2013 Consultation document in the lead up to the SDGs, UNESCO states that the aims of GCE are

> to equip learners with the following core competencies: a) A deep knowledge of global issues and universal values such as justice, equality, dignity and respect; b) cognitive skills to think critically, systemically and creatively, including adopting a multi-perspective approach that recognizes different dimension, perspectives and angles of issues; c) non-cognitive skills including social skills such as empathy and conflict resolution, and communicative skills and aptitudes for networking and interacting with people of different backgrounds, origins, cultures and perspectives; and d) behavioural capacities to act collaboratively and responsibly, and to strive for collective good.
>
> (UNESCO 2013)

These same civic virtues nevertheless are grounded in the same rationality required for market success in the classical republican formulation.

> Offering young people a seat at the table, and welcoming and encouraging their ideas, can help them to cultivate an entrepreneurial spirit, and to take an active interest in the world and in those with whom we share it.
> (UNESCO 2015d, p. 5)

and,

> Although causality is not always clear, voluntary social activism, of which participation in policy planning is one example, appears to build civic skills and social consciousness in young people, as well as social psychological and academic skills and, not least, transferable skills for the world of work.
> (UNESCO 2015d, p. 10)

Thus, more than simply the construction of market-wise individuals instrumentally capitalising on their knowledge and capabilities, the institutionalisation and grooming of 'youth' through GCE and PVE-E becomes another platform in the development-security nexus that mitigates the double movement through the production of 'neo-republican' subjectivities redirected away from anti-systemic political mobilisation and fit for employment in the expanded global governance architecture.

Conclusion

My aim in this chapter has been to problematise the neoliberal subjectivities account in respect of GCE. I have done so through an analysis of the way that GCE has been coupled with PVE-E and the Youth Engagement Initiative in its incorporation into GEG. I have demonstrated that the inclusion of GCE represents in effect the inclusion of the knowledges of critique of neoliberalism gathered by social movements and NGOs and therefore its inclusion into GEG provides a mechanism via which it can make its way into national education systems through the pressure of IOs and transnational advocacy networks (TANS). This does not mean that the market emphasis has been excised, it has not, but careful empirical work needs to be done which traces out exactly how the incorporation of GCE marries up or not with the market logic. The networked structure of GEG and the slipperiness of the concept 'global citizenship' enables this assemblage of actors to mobilise in a way that makes such a co-opting possible (Mannion et al. 2011) through a hegemonic struggle that is ongoing. Thus, the mainstreaming of GCE is not simply another reiteration of neoliberal subject production, but about the domestication of the critique of social movements through incorporation. The inclusion of the knowledge produced by global civil society and global social movements into an expanded architecture of GEG is more likely the result of a political compromise. Moreover, it is not a foregone conclusion that GCE will form the major component of the realisation of the SDGs (if any part of it is indeed realised); it is just as likely to be sacrificed in favour of the more market-oriented components of SDG4.

The fact that GCE is at the forefront of a common educational policy platform of thickening networks of GEG means that education policy is being decided a priori at the international level. This will require the globalisation of a specific kind of education with corresponding educational systems and governance which many states either do not have (because of the state shrinkage effects of structural adjustment policies) or will not comply with, because of the role that education plays in constructing national identities and legitimating state authority.[8] Given the rise of ethno-nationalisms[9] (the other side of the double movement), the acceptance of GCE in the form articulated at national level is by no means a fait accompli (witness the recent US withdrawal from UNESCO). Third, the coupling of GCE/PVE-E means that the subjectivity intended by these educational reforms is as much about socially engineering appropriate activisms as it is about preserving market relations in the face of contradictions. It is therefore just as much about political behaviour as it is about economic behaviour. Finally, insofar as the intended subjectivity of GCE/PVE-E is a national citizen who identifies globally, and is the recipient of skills that will simultaneously equip them for both the market and democracy, it is a 'republican citizen'. If successful the project to spread global citizenship through global education governance would be one necessary step along the way towards the creation of a global republic.

Appendix

Appendix table

Document title	Year	Institution	Document type	Policy the document is linked to	Document author	Title of meeting/conference
Global Citizenship Education: preparing learners for the challenges of the 21st century	2014	UNESCO	Policy document	EFA post 2015 Agenda	UNESCO	–
Rethinking Education: Towards a Global Common Good?	2015a	UNESCO	Policy document	UNESCO	–	–
Empowering youth to build peace	2015b	UNESCO	Policy document	Operational Strategy on Youth	UNESCO	Youth and the Internet: Fighting Radicalisation and Extremism, 16–17 June 2015
Transforming our World: The 2030 Agenda for Sustainable Development	2015c	United Nations	Resolution document	Sustainable Development 2030	UN	–
Planning Education with and For Youth	2015d	UNESCO/IIEP	Report	WPAY	Anja Hopma and Lynne Sergeant	Engaging Youth in Planning Education for Social Transformation, 2012
Global Citizenship Education: Topics and Learning Objectives	2015e	UNESCO	Pedagogical guidance	GEFI 2012	UNESCO	–

A Teacher's Guide to the Prevention of Violent Extremism	2016a	UNESCO	Policy guidance	UNESCO's 197 Decision/GCED/ UN Plan of Action to Prevent Violent Extremism	UNESCO	—
Measuring Sustainable Development Goal 4	2016b	UNESCO	Booklet	Education 2030 and PIRLS	UNESCO	—
Education 2030: Incheon Declaration and Framework for Action of Sustainable Development Goal 4	2016c	UNESCO	Policy document	SDG Education 2030	UNESCO	World Education Forum, 19–22 May 2015
Education Transforms lives	2017a	UNESCO	Policy document	—	UNESCO	—
Measuring Global Citizenship Education	2017b	Brookings Institute	Policy guidance	—	Brookings, UNESCO, GEFI-YAG	—
Preventing Violent Extremism through Education: A Guide for Policy Makers	2017c	UNESCO	Pedagogical guidance	SDG Education 2030	Lynn Davies and Gabriele Gottelmann	—
Unesco in Action: Preventing Violent Extremism Worldwide	2017d	UNESCO	Policy guidance	—	UNESCO	—
Youth Waging Peace: Youth Led Guide on Preventing Violent Extremism Through Education	2017e	UNESCO/ MGIEP	Policy document	—	Carolyn Nash and Yulia Nesterova	—

continued

Appendix table continued

Document title	Year	Institution	Document type	Policy the document is linked to	Document author	Title of meeting/ conference
Preparing Teachers for Global Citizenship Education	2018a	UNESCO	Pedagogical guide	Education 2030	UNESCO	–
Global Citizenship Education: Taking it Local	2018b	UNESCO	Policy document	Education 2030	UNESCO	–
Global Citizenship Education for a Culture of Lawfulness	2018c	UNESCO/ UNODC	Meeting report	Promoting a Culture of Lawfulness	UNESCO	Expert Consultation Meeting, 15 March 2018
Global Citizenship Education and the Rise of Nationalist Perspectives	2018d	UNESCO	Policy document	Education 2030	UNESCO	Nationalistic Perspectives and their Implications for GCED, 28–29 June 2017, Seoul, Korea
Policy Brief: Youth Led Guide to Preventing Violent Extremism through Education	2018e	UNESCO/ MGIEP	Policy guidance	YouthWaging Peace	UNESCO	–
Frontlines: Young People at the forefront of Preventing and Responding to Violent Extremism	2019	UNDP	Research report	UNDP Global Youth Programme for Sustainable Development and Peace	–	–
The ABCs of Global Citizenship Education	–	UNESCO	Pamphlet/FAQ Document	–	–	–

Notes

1 An International Karl Polanyi Society was established at Wirtschafts University, Vienna in 2018.
2 The oeuvres here are far larger than I have the space to represent.
3 Note that the British Empire also shifted away from laissez faire policies in its period of hegemonic decline. For comparison see Go (2011).
4 Oxfam's database of educational resources can be found here: www.oxfam.org.uk/education/resources; UNESCO's database is hosted by the Asia Pacific Centre for Education and Intercultural Understanding (APCEIU) and can be found here: https://en.unesco.org/themes/gced/resources.
5 Australia funded a Global Education Project through its foreign aid arm only briefly (2002–2014) before Ausaid was incorporated into DFAT. Canadian support ceased with the same institutional change. The UK began funding development education under its Labour government and global education through the coalition and Conservative governments that followed.
6 Ban Ki-moon has moved on from his role at the UN to establish a 'Centre for Global Citizens' in partnership with former Austrian President Heinze Fisher.
7 Although UNESCO is clear that GCE does not entail promoting a supranational legal status (UNESCO [Brookings Institute] 2017b, see Appendix).
8 See Golovátina-Mora et al. (this volume, Chapter 6) for discussion of this point in relation to the countries of Latin America.
9 I use 'ethno-nationalism' over populism because I feel that populism doesn't capture the racialised, gendered and class contesting nature of the global lurch to the right, and the marshalling of the term populism in political science harbours a normative bias in favour of electoral systems presumed to be more 'rational', anything falling outside the parameters of conventional party politics on the left or right being 'populism' by default. This misapprehends the way that the globalisation of neoliberal capitalism has fractured and problematised partisan institutions that have their origins in the nineteenth century industrial order.

References

Allina-Pisano, J 2009, 'How to tell an axe murderer: an essay on ethnography, truth and lies', in E Schatz (ed.), *Political ethnography: what immersion contributes to the study of power*, 53–73, University of Chicago Press, Chicago, IL.
Almond, GA 1991, 'Rational choice theory and the social sciences', in K Monroe (ed.), *The economic approach to politics*, 32–52, Harper Collins, New York.
Andreotti, V 2011, '(Towards) decoloniality and diversality in global citizenship education', *Globalisation, Societies and Education*, vol. 9, pp. 381–97.
Ball, SJ 2012, *Global education inc.: new policy networks and the neo-liberal imaginary*, Routledge, New York.
Ball, SJ 2016, 'Following policy: networks, network ethnography and education policy mobilities', *Journal of Education Policy*, vol. 31, pp. 549–66.
Bersaglio, B, Enns, C and Kepe, T 2015, 'Youth under construction: the United Nations' representations of youth in the global conversation on the post-2015 development agenda', *Canadian Journal of Development Studies*, vol. 36, pp. 57–71.
Bloom, DE 2004, 'Globalization and education: an economic perspective', in MM Suarez-Orozco and DB Qin-Hilliard (eds), *Globalization: culture and education in the new millennium*, 56–77, University of California Press, Berkeley.
Boix, M 2016, 'How to be a global thinker: using global thinking routines to create classroom cultures that nourish global competence', *Education Leadership*, vol. 74, pp. 10–16.

Boix, M and Jackson, A 2011, *Educating for global competence: preparing our youth to engage the world*, Council of Chief State School Officers' EdSteps Initiative and Asia Society Partnership for Global Learning, Washington and New York.

Borg, C, Buttigieg, J and Mayo, P (eds) 2002, *Gramsci and education*, Rowman & Littlefield, Boulder, CO, New York and Toronto.

Boyd, W 1921, *The history of Western education*, Adam and Charles Black, London.

Brady, MJ 2008, 'Governmentality and the National Museum of the American Museum: understanding the indigenous museum in a settler society', *Social Identities: Journal for the Study of Race, Nation and Culture*, vol. 14, pp. 763–73.

Bratich, J, Packer, J and McCarthy, C (eds) 2004, *Foucault, cultural studies and governmentality*, State University of New York Press, Albany.

Brockman, J and Eyal, G 2002, 'Eastern Europe as a laboratory for economic knowledge: the transnational roots of neoliberalism', *American Journal of Sociology*, vol. 108, pp. 310–52.

Brown, W 2015, *Undoing the demos: neoliberalism's stealth revolution*, Zone Books, New York.

Brown, W 2016, 'Sacrificial citizenship: neoliberalism, human capital and austerity politics', *Constellations*, vol. 23, pp. 3–14.

Burbules, N and Torres, C (eds) 2000, *Globalisation and education: critical perspectives*, Routledge, London.

Burke, S and Rurup, BL 2019, 'Political thriller exposes the underbelly of global goals', *Global Policy*, vol. 10, p. 137.

Buzan, B 2004, *From international to world society? English school theory and the social structure of globalisation*, Cambridge University Press, Cambridge.

Caballero, P 2019, 'The SDGs: changing how development is understood', *Global Policy*, vol. 10, pp. 138–40.

Castel, C, Leicht, A and Ruprecht, L 2016, 'UNESCO's pedagogical guidance on global citizenship education: topics and learning objectives', *Curriculum Perspectives*, vol. 36, pp. 83–90.

Costa, V 2009, 'Neo-republicanism, freedom as non-domination and citizen virtue', *Politics, Philosophy and Economics*, vol. 8, pp. 401–19.

Costa, V 2013, 'Is neo-republicanism bad for women?' *Hypatia*, vol. 28, pp. 921–36.

Cox, RW 1987, *Production, power and world order: social forces in the making of history*, Colombia University Press, New York.

Dagger, R 1997, *Civic virtues: rights, citizenship and republican liberalism*, Oxford University Press, New York.

Dagger, R 2006, 'Neo-republicanism and the civic economy', *Politics, Philosophy & Economics*, vol. 5, pp. 151–73.

Dale, R 2000, 'Globalisation and education: demonstrating a "common world educational culture" or locating a "globally structured educational agenda"?' *Educational Theory*, vol. 50, pp. 427–48.

Dill, JS 2012, 'The moral education of global citizens', *Society*, vol. 49, pp. 541–64.

Duffield, M 2000, *Development, security and unending war*, Polity Press, Cambridge.

Duffield, M 2001, *Global governance and the new wars: the merging of development and security*, Zed, London.

Duffield, M 2010, 'The liberal way of development and the development-security impasse: exploring the global life-chance divide', *Security Dialogue*, vol. 41, pp. 53–76.

Ellison, J 2009, 'Governmentality and the family: neoliberal choices and emergent kin relations in Southern Ethiopia', *American Anthropologist*, vol. 111, pp. 81–92.

Eriksson, L 2011, *Rational choice theory*, Palgrave Macmillan, New York.

Escobar, A 1995, *Encountering development: the making and unmaking of the Third World*, Princeton University Press, Princeton, NJ.

Freire, P 1970, *Pedagogy of the oppressed*, Herder & Herder, New York.

Gill, R 2008, 'Culture and subjectivity in neoliberal and postfeminist times', *Subjectivity*, vol. 25, pp. 432–45.

Go, J 2011, *Patterns of empire: the British and American empires, 1688 to the present*, Cambridge University Press, Cambridge.

Gough, S and Scott, W 2006, 'Education and sustainable development: a political analysis', *Educational Review*, vol. 58, pp. 283–90.

Grek, S 2009, 'Governing by numbers: the PISA "effect" in Europe', *Journal of Education Policy*, vol. 24, no. 1, pp. 23–37.

Güven, AB 2018, 'Whither the post-Washington consensus? International financial institutions and development policy before and after the crisis', *Review of International Political Economy*, vol. 25, no. 3, pp. 392–417.

Hall, C 2008, 'Making colonial subjects: education in the age of empire', *History of Education*, vol. 37, pp. 773–87.

Hettne, B 2010, 'Development and security: origins and future', *Security Dialogue*, vol. 41, pp. 31–52.

Hindmoor, A 2006, *Rational choice*, Palgrave Macmillan, New York.

Irving, S 2008, *Natural science and the origins of the British empire*, Pickering & Chatto, London.

Jensen, S 2010, 'The security and development nexus in Cape Town: war on gangs, counterinsurgency and citizenship', *Security Dialogue*, vol. 41, pp. 77–98.

Kaldor, M 2003, *Global civil society: an answer to war*, Polity Press, Cambridge.

Kilby, P 2015, *NGOs and political change: a history of the Australian Council for International Development*, Australian National University Press, Canberra.

Kingebiel, S (ed.) 2006, *New interfaces between security and development*, German Development Institute, Bonn.

Kiser, E and Hechter, M 1998, 'The debate on historical sociology: rational choice theory and its critics', *American Journal of Sociology*, vol. 104, pp. 785–816.

Klein, S 2017, 'Fictitious freedom: a Polanyian critique of the republican revival', *American Journal of Political Science*, vol. 61, pp. 852–63.

Leask, I 2012, 'Beyond subjection: notes on the later Foucault and education', *Educational Philosophy and Theory*, vol. 44, pp. 57–73.

Lovett, F and Pettit, P 2009, 'Neorepublicanism: a normative and institutional research program', *Annual Review of Political Science*, vol. 12, pp. 11–29.

Mannion, G, Biesta, G, Priestley, M and Ross, H 2011, 'The global dimension in education and education for global citizenship: genealogy and critique', *Globalisation, Societies and Education*, vol. 9, no. 3–4, pp. 443–56.

Mehta, US 1999, *Liberalism and empire: a study in nineteenth century British liberal thought*, University of Chicago Press, Chicago, IL, and London.

Meyer, JW, Ramirez Francisco O, Rubinson, R and Boli-Bennett, J 1977, 'The world educational revolution, 1950–1970', *Sociology of Education*, vol. 50, pp. 242–58.

Muthu, S (ed.) 2012, *Empire and modern political thought*, Cambridge University Press, Cambridge.

Olssen, M and Peters, MA 2005, 'Neoliberalism, higher education and the knowledge economy: from the free market to knowledge capitalism', *Journal of Education Policy*, vol. 20, pp. 313–45.

Pagden, A 1995, *Lords of all the world: ideologies of empire in Spain, Britain and France, c.1500–c.1800*, Yale University Press, New Haven, CT.

Pais, A and Costa, M 2017, 'An ideology critique of global citizenship education', *Critical Studies in Education*, 1–16, DOI: 10.1080/17508487.2017.1318772.

Pathak, G 2014, 'Presentable: the body and neoliberal subjecthood in contemporary India', *Social Identities: Journal for the Study of Race, Nation and Culture*, vol. 20, pp. 314–29.

Petit, P 1996, 'Freedom as anti-power', *Ethics*, vol. 106, pp. 576–604.

Petit, P 1997, *Republicanism: a theory of freedom and government*, Oxford University Press, Oxford.

Piketty, T 2014, *Capital in the twenty-first century*, Harvard University Press, Cambridge, MA.

Polanyi, K 1944, *The great transformation: the political and economic origins of our time*, Beacon Press, Boston, MA.

Read, J 2009, 'A genealogy of homo-economicus: neoliberalism and the production of subjectivity', *Foucault Studies*, vol. 6, pp. 25–36.

Robertson, SL 2005, 'Re-imagining and rescripting the future of education: global knowledge economy discourses and the challenge to education systems', *Comparative Education*, vol. 42, pp. 151–70.

Rugendyke, B (ed.) 2007, *NGOs as advocates for development in a globalising world*, Routledge, London and New York.

Ruggie, J 2002, *Constructing the world polity: essays on international institutionalisation*, Routledge, London.

Sjoberg, S 2014, 'PISA and global education governance', *Eurasia Journal of Mathematics, Science and Technology Education*, vol. 1, no. 1, pp. 111–27.

Stern, M and Ojendal, J 2010 'Mapping the security-development nexus: conflict, complexity, cacophony, convergence?' *Security Dialogue*, vol. 41, pp. 5–30.

Stewart, F 2018, 'Changing approaches to development since 1950: drawing on Polanyi', *History of Political Economy*, vol. 50, pp. 17–38.

Stiglitz, J 2002, *Globalization and its discontents*, Penguin Books, New York.

Stoler, AL 1995, *Race and the education of desire: Foucault's history of sexuality and the colonial order of things*, Duke University Press, Durham, NC, and London.

Sukarieh, M and Tannock, S 2008, 'In the best interests of youth or neoliberalism? The World Bank and the New Global Youth Empowerment Project', *Journal of Youth Studies*, vol. 11, pp. 301–12.

Sukarieh, M and Tannock, S 2011, 'The positivity imperative: a critical look at the "new" youth development movement', *Journal of Youth Studies*, vol. 14, pp. 675–91.

Sukarieh, M and Tannock, S 2018, 'The global securitisation of youth', *Third World Quarterly*, vol. 39, pp. 854–70.

Sunstein, CR 1997, *Free markets and social justice*, Oxford University Press, New York.

Tait, G 2015, *Making sense of mass education*, Cambridge University Press, Cambridge.

Tikly, L 2014, 'Review: the World Bank and education', *Comparative Education Review*, vol. 58, no. 2, pp. 344–355.

UNESCO 2013, 'Outcome document of the Technical Consultation on Global Citizenship Education: Global citizenship education – an emerging perspective', viewed 15 September 2019, https://unesdoc.unesco.org/ark:/48223/pf0000224115.

Verger, A, Lubienski, C and Steiner-Khamsi, G (eds) 2016, *The global education industry*, Routledge, New York.

Walters, W 2012, *Governmentality: critical encounters*, Routledge, London and New York.

Wendt, A 2003, 'Why a world state is inevitable', *European Journal of International Relations*, vol. 9, pp. 491–542.

World Bank Group 2015, *World Development Report 2015: mind, society and behaviour*, International Bank for Reconstruction and Development, Washington, DC.

Chapter 8

International policy influencers and their agendas on global citizenship

A critical analysis of OECD and UNESCO discourses

Francisca Costa and Pedro Ponte e Sousa

Introduction

Global citizenship is a trending concept, due both to globalisation and the rise of multi-level governance, and it is so among nation-states, non-governmental organisations (NGOs), global and regional international institutions, and many other national and international actors. It has even changed the traditional main pillars of national citizenship, promoted by education and national cultural initiatives, as national traditions and law have been challenged by the new global order. In this context, global citizenship has been taken up and advanced by a whole range of international institutions, from the World Bank to the many agencies of the United Nations (UN). In this chapter we aim to describe and critically analyse the discourse and practice of global citizenship of the Organisation for Economic Co-operation and Development (OECD) and the United Nations Educational, Scientific and Cultural Organization (UNESCO).

These organisations were chosen due to their global influence and social impact, particularly in relation to educational theory and practice. We will analyse, in their own narrative, how and why they seek to advance global citizenship, not least in relation to the values they seek to promote to young people. Adopting a technocratic and so-called 'apolitical' stance such policy influencers promote young people's 'skills for the twenty-first century' including not only how they should act in the international scene but also those aptitudes and attitudes relevant to the labour market.

While the bulk of the chapter critically analyses the discourse and practice on global citizenship of the OECD and UNESCO, we begin with a background discussion on global citizenship, globalisation, international organisations and critical theories, which attempts to establish a link to and, more importantly, the need for a critical study of the concept of global citizenship. The research for this chapter is based on the critical analysis of documentary sources within a theoretical framework combining elements from globalisation studies, (global) citizenship studies and international relations. While this is not an extensive analysis on the entirety of strategies, goals and policies advanced by these actors, we will attempt, in the final section of the chapter, to draw some general conclusions about the actions of these organisations. We will locate their professed desire to promote cosmopolitanism, conscious and critical reflection upon global inequalities and disparities, and labour market 'skills for the twenty-first century' in the context of the actual opportunities for global citizenship experienced by the mass of the world's population.

Conceptualising global citizenship in a globalised framework

Conceptual investigations of the idea of global citizenship have ancient roots and have arisen both in different socio-political contexts (Haraway 1988) and different disciplines. Our interest lies in its contemporary manifestation in a time of global capitalism.

The idea that citizenship refers to more than the geographical nation-state is, contrary to what may be thought, rather longstanding. In Greek and Roman ancestral societies some thinkers such as Socrates or Diogenes thought of themselves as 'citizens of the world', in a conception based on human freedom, full enjoyment of their rights and political participation (Follesdal 2002). Nonetheless, citizenship in close association with the nation-state has prevailed over time, despite it assuming so much, and, at the same time, leaving so much out (Isin and Nyers 2014). Moreover, although citizenship is not a uniquely Western institution, its dominant version can be seen as 'ignoring or neglecting the specific ways that citizenship is enacted globally and working with an all-encompassing idea of "liberal democracy"' (ibid., p. 7).

Given Isin and Nyers's view of citizenship as 'an "*institution*" mediating rights between the subjects of politics and the polity to which these subjects belong' (2014, p. 1), we must take into account 'legal and extra-legal belongings' (ibid.) due to the hybridity of profiles of residents across countries and the variety of ways they can (or cannot) exert their rights and duties as citizens under fluid relations with the state and the world. The authors do so by addressing 'the term "polity" to move away from the idea that the state is the sole source of authority for recognizing and legislating rights' (ibid.). According to these authors, there are 'international polities such as the European Union or the UN as well as many other covenants, agreements and charters that constitute polities other than the state' (ibid.). In other words, although the contemporary dominant polity institution is the state, even its dominance is now in intimate relation with several international agendas, demands and orientations, deriving from 'apolitical' guidelines from international organisations and their agreements, conventions or covenants (ibid.). Moreover, it is important to note that so-called politics 'for' citizenship depend on how the inter-relationship between state and supra-state organisation is regulated, in terms of who is implicated in the mediation of rights, when and how it occurs and also what rights are the focus of such mediation (ibid.). Furthermore, to perform citizenship, some profiles (especially from non-dominant groups such as migrants) might find some tensions related with their rights beyond their legal status. This also might happen regarding such 'expanded social rights' as cultural or environmental ones, which increase the tensions attending their novelty. All these new phenomena came with globalisation, often at the hand of intergovernmental agencies, being therefore responsible for the explicit debate on cosmopolitanism, the international community and global citizenship in the first place.

Globalisation has gone from scientific discourse to political discourse and from this to the common language (Santos 2002). According to Boaventura de Sousa Santos (2002), globalisation is a concept that aims to describe network interdependencies at the global level (Robertson 1992; Held et al. 1999; Castells 1996, 1997, 1998; cf. Waters 2001), and which is based on ideas such as determinism (that globalisation and its effects are inevitable in the way they present themselves) or the disappearance of knowledge of the 'South'. More specifically, Giddens (1990) describes the phenomenon of globalisation as the intensification of social relations around the world, linking to distant localities in such a way that local events can be influenced by events that occur thousands of miles away. These ideas are not infrequently contested in public debate by proponents of global citizenship who argue that the global South has been particularly neglected due to the dominance of the Western framework of action on the globalisation scene. We will look further into this later in this chapter.

Globalisation is based on a historical process of change, where some argue that it is technological progress that has created a global world (Castells 1996; see Held and McGrew 2013), with intense communications and mass circulation among countries, markets and people, while others maintain that it is the dissemination of capitalism with a truly global scope that is, in its essence, globalisation (see Robinson 2007): 'thus far globalization has left capitalism as entrenched as ever, if not more so, to the point that one could even speak of an onset of "hyper capitalism"' (Scholte 2005, p. 24). In line with such global interconnection across time, Almeida (2003) summarises two major dimensions of globalisation: hegemonic globalisation, focused on global trade and its objectifiable dividends in capitalist accounting; and counter-hegemonic globalisation, centred on civil society, social movements and individual and collective rights and duties. Both inevitably came to be considered in global citizenship analysis (see Biccum, this volume, Chapter 7, on Polanyi's 'double movement' thesis).

It should be noted that the discourse on globalisation (and globalisation itself) does not entail neutrality (Magalhães and Stoer 2003): it represents itself as an 'inevitability' that, due to the times and spaces in which it occurs, just happens to serve a specific set of interests (Risse 2007), thereby supporting Foucault's argument that globalisation translates processes of domination and subordination. Andreotti (2014a) explains the postcolonial nature of such phenomena happening under the auspices of globalisation as, in her view, the continuous reproduction of relations of power and violence of the hegemonic and dominant groups over the non-dominant ones (p. 58).

Under such hegemonic tendencies, which contribute to the construction of high 'walls' resulting from historical, political and social differences and miscomprehension, some societal forces have been arguing for what they call a patriotic, nationalistic approach to citizenship. Despite the positive condition of national roots, one of the effects of the instigation of national citizenship (among others, both positive and negative) is the potentiation of a 'competition game' between 'us/we' and 'them', advocating division and segregation, rather than an appeal to global union as implied by the idea of global citizenship. Larsen (2014), following Said (1978), refers to the proliferation of 'binary ideas' (such as developed/ undeveloped, skilled/unskilled) that create an opposition of 'us' and them in a process known as 'othering'. Under this concept, there is an implicit (and sometimes explicit) differentiation and segregation between 'us', Westerners, and the so-considered underprivileged ones, 'the others', who do not possess certain competences seen as relevant in the so-called 'developed world' (see Brubaker and Laitin 1998; Sen 2007; Soguk 2014; Lederach 1995). By this means, an immediate relation of moral supremacy and paternalism is put in place (Andreotti 2014a).

Social Psychology has been explaining that prejudice can be defined as a favourable or unfavourable attitude towards members of a group, not necessarily because of its individual characteristics, but mainly because we are either part of it or not, and we either recognize it as a positive value or we do not, according to the beliefs we have about that group unit (Neto 1998). Discrimination is thus the behavioural manifestation of prejudice, and may take different forms, such as avoidance, antilocution (hostile dialogue) or physical attack.

Such social (and psychological) mechanisms and further common understandings are deeply rooted in the main central beliefs of people, since they might also be socially inherited. As a way to counter and critically reflect upon such understandings (as well as the complex processes behind it), global citizenship emerges as a strategy and a pedagogy to challenge such beliefs and broaden the scope of citizenship, attending both to the history of structural inequalities as well as the current global phenomena that maintain polarities and segregation.

According to Andreotti (2015), 'humanity has been divided between those who are perceived to be leading progress, development and human evolution; and those who are perceived to be lagging behind' (p. 7). According to her view, this problem is the product of the violent dissemination of a dominant modern/ colonial global imaginary based on a single story of progress.[1] This single story puts economic development and technology, generally possessed by the so-called 'developed world', at the centre of decision-making and world leadership. This modern(/colonial) mythology positions, in Andreotti's words (2015), 'knowledge holders' and 'aid dependents' on opposite sides which, we conclude, generates either tensions, pity or a sense of powerlessness. These polarities apply to the inequalities reproduced between the so-called global North and global South, a geographical metaphor that helps to understand the mechanisms of symbolic violence (Bourdieu and Passeron 1990) projected from dominant groups towards non-dominant ones. According to Spivak (2004), in Andreotti's words (2014a, p. 62), the professional global elite (constituted by privileged people coming from both the so-called 'first world' and 'third world') tends to project its common ethnocentric myths and beliefs on its subordinates. These polarities are reproduced across centuries, through the intentional maintenance of inequalities and power supremacy in relations between dominant groups and those they dominate. The central reason for such continuous polarity lies in the myth that the universal knowledge (in the hands of the global North) should prevail (and be accepted) over the diverse set of traditions and values of non-dominant communities across the globe (the global South). This establishes a 'cause–effect' chain through which people respond to the explicit and public inequalities as immediate obligations instead of seeing that those considered 'dominants' are, in our view, and under the postcolonial paradigm (Andreotti 2010, 2014a, 2014b; Pais and Costa 2017), part of both the problem and the solution (Larsen 2014).

In order to promote comprehension of the processes through which these beliefs are sustained and naturalised, reflexive thinking must come into force to dissect the reasons for such polarities. *Critical* global citizenship *scholarship* is such an endeavour.

Thus, global citizenship, though it does not have a legal status, is seen as giving a sense of belonging and collective accountability to a shared world, aiming to bridge the failures of globalisation, particularly through education (Andreotti 2014a). Global citizenship, in Linder's words (2012), reflects a belonging to a 'single family', humanity, grounded in human rights, equality and dignity, based on a perspective of cooperation. It highlights the need to foster a 'moral community', through which people are connected due to the shared condition and responsibility of being 'human'. In our view, global citizenship aims to foster a shared sense of belonging under a critical view where people, regardless of their location and position in the world, are able to contribute to global welfare and a sustainable world, with more equality, fairness and social justice action under an effective awareness and understanding of the complexity of global issues, as well as the interconnectedness of events and people.

In Andreotti's (2014a) view, a critical global citizenship:

- focuses on structural inequalities and lack of fairness, instead of poverty by itself;
- targets power relations as a main issue at the centre of world problems and disparities between the global North and global South;
- aims to promote individual and collective responsibilities towards the other;
- its reasons to act are not just humanitarian, but mainly political and ethical;
- aims to promote change in systems, institutional actions and personal and one-sided common beliefs;
- sees people's role as active contributors to the problem, and therefore with capacity to act on the solution for the global issues;

- requires people to question themselves on their own actions;
- promotes the establishment of a committed relationship towards a shared world and a common humanity;
- fosters critical thinking, supported by information and ethics;
- in short, requires people to act as concerned citizens with a participatory role to change policies and practices that instigate the continuous reproduction of inequalities across the globe.

Larsen states that in order to achieve such a critical global citizenship, it is essential to reach two important dimensions as an individual/member of the world community: the first is '*Awareness/Analysis*' and the second '*Engagement/Action*' (2014, p. 5). The first dimension includes '*Difference Awareness*' (respecting diverse ideas and other knowledges), '*Self Awareness*' (comprehending one's own identity and taking the personal view as naturally limited), '*Global Awareness*' (as the recognition of the social and political differences that frame the world, as well as the main global issues) and '*Responsibility Awareness*' (the idea of striving for collective responsibility and that 'we are all part of both the problem and the solution') (pp. 5–6). The second dimension includes '*Self Action*' (change through day-to-day actions, such as recycling), '*Civic Action*' (participation in the community and getting involved in civic and social issues) and '*Social Justice Action*' (actions that foster change in systems and social structures that reproduce injustices). All the different components of these two dimensions constitute a framework to reach the status of a critical global citizen. Thus, and for global citizenship education (GCE) to work towards the awareness, reflexivity, analytical skills and capacity to act, critical literacy (Andreotti 2010, 2014a, 2014b) is perceived as a key ability. However, this is seen as a complex task, given the modern social structure of society, which makes it difficult to experience global citizenship and the idea of common identity and belonging in pursuit of a profound self- and social-critical analysis (Larsen 2014).

For instance, the current global situation of intensifying movements of migrants and refugees coming from different countries and socialised in very different contexts forces us to reflect on ways in which greater understanding and respect for the 'different other' should be created (Cortesão 2000), through a clear comprehension of the conflicts that produce such flows of desperate people. With socially challenging phenomena such as the circulation of more diverse people and cultures, increasing information (and hence fake news) and the power of social networks in consolidating perspectives, more space is created for hateful attitudes and behaviours, as well as discrimination.

Therefore, a context of difficult multicultural interaction is produced, in which pacifying and informing responses are sought, as in the proposal to promote global citizenship. This, in turn, gives rise to the ambition to be transformative, namely at the psychological level of the subject, through the understanding and interaction between diverse sociocultural egos, without falling into the webs of uniformisation or division (Linder 2012).

'Global competence' from the perspective of the OECD

For the purpose of this chapter, we reviewed the OECD's and UNESCO's official documentation such as reports, studies and other primary sources as found on their institutional websites. In this analysis, the importance of the development of competences for the promotion of global citizenship particularly in the context of education is highlighted.

The OECD has taken a proactive stance in the search to improve processes and interventions in education in the various educational systems around the world, in particular through *PISA – Program for International Students Assessment* (OECD 2018a). When we search for 'global citizenship' and 'OECD' what is most noticeable is that global citizenship is presented within the framework of the idea of 'global competence'. While 'global citizenship' is actually quoted several times in institutional documents and related information, the central topic is 'global competence'. Despite the crosscutting concerns on 'competencies for the twenty-first century', which have always dominated the discourse of this organisation, the idea of *global* competence has only recently become an explicit focus (aligned with the 'historical' OECD educational focus) and subject to monitoring.

In recent years, the OECD, as a policy-making adviser institution at the macro level, has sought to operationalise strategies for the promotion of youth skills through schooling, in order to contribute to the *United Nations Decade for Education for Sustainable Development* (UNESCO 2014a). Under the title of 'Development Education', the OECD assumes that it can contribute to the development of key competencies that should be promoted in the most diverse educational systems: through the use of tools and resources in a dynamic and interactive way; through socialisation with heterogeneous and diverse groups; through the promotion of individuals' autonomy. Strategies to develop such competencies and contents are adapted to the different educational stages (primary, secondary, tertiary) (Stevens n.d.). The ultimate goal is to seek for the establishment of connections between different contents by developing skills of comprehension and analysis based on individuals' age group. Some of the possible contents would relate, for example, to global economic and social issues, to governance and politics, both in the individual dimensions of the subject's own life and in their social surroundings.

This framework of competencies arises in an effort to promote a path to the 2030 Agenda for Sustainable Development, once again in harmony with the work promoted by the UN. In the context of the OECD, and given the type of information and action they foster, this work is based on the establishment of innovative resources, access to more information and empowerment of different ways of working, which requires new ways of thinking about global development and what this means for different nations and people.

Following this approach focused on competencies and contents, the OECD discourse emphasises 'reinforcing global competencies'. In its report *Preparing our*

Youth for an Inclusive and Sustainable World: The OECD PISA Global Competence Framework, the OECD states:

> Against a context in which we all have much to gain from growing openness and connectivity, and much to lose from rising inequalities and radicalism, citizens need not only the skills to be competitive and ready for a new world of work, but more importantly they also need to develop the capacity to analyze and understand global and intercultural issues.
>
> (2018b, p. 1)

Therefore, according to the organisation, it is fundamental that citizens, especially those in training and education, (a) develop 'competitive' competencies (from a labour market point of view), and (b) be equally prepared to analyse and understand global and intercultural themes. The above report also refers to the need to develop emotional and social competences, as well as values such as respect, solidarity, self-confidence and sense of belonging, as fundamental elements to promote opportunities for all, along with human dignity.

Concern for 'global skills' has become more explicit recently, despite the fact that the OECD's work on Education and Citizenship is understood to be operating at the global level. It is therefore important that at the OECD, in the words of Andreas Schleicher, Special Adviser for Educational Policy to the Secretary General of the OECD, initiatives such as the Sustainable Development Goals (SDGs, OECD 2019) are closely linked to raising awareness, particularly in the classroom context (OECD 2018b, p. 1). Within the framework of the OECD, 'global competence' means the following:

> Global competence is a multidimensional capacity. Globally competent individuals can examine local, global and intercultural issues, understand and appreciate different perspectives and world views, interact successfully and respectfully with others, and take responsible action toward sustainability and collective well-being.
>
> (ibid., p. 4)

Global competence encompasses the labour market and work dimension; it also includes the training of 'communicative' professionals who are able to adapt and transfer their knowledge in varying situational contexts. Indeed, according to the above-mentioned report, work in multicultural contexts should be celebrated; individuals must be respectful and know how to interact with diverse subjects, and how to understand the specificities and effects of globalisation in their own context.

The OECD's work in the field of global competence is effected through monitorisation – carried out through PISA – of four essential factors for the development of said 'global competence'. The 'Building blocks of global competence' (ibid., p. 12) include 'Knowledge', 'Skills', 'Attitudes' and 'Values'. In the OECD's words, any of the goals established by the organisation 'require knowledge of a particular issue, the skills to transform this awareness into a deeper understanding, and the attitudes and values to reflect on the issue from multiple cultural perspectives, keeping in mind the interest of all parties involved' in order for global competencies to be attained and successfully mobilised (ibid.). Below we provide a brief explanation of each of those elements.

'Knowledge' includes the core of information and content of a given topic with global influence. It is considered essential for the existence of greater awareness about a particular topic, that the individual has significant knowledge about it, so as to better discern and reflect on it. Regarding 'Skills', the cognitive, socio-emotional and communicational levels stand out, as they constitute an essential 'reading grid' for the individual to problematise 'global issues'. In addition to the importance of information rationalisation, the document also highlights the effectiveness of communication, based on respect for, and interiorisation of, the possible expectations and characteristics of the subjects and/or groups with whom communication takes place (in this regard, speaking more than one language is considered an intercultural advantage). At this level, the competence to take into consideration the position of the 'other' is also highlighted; one is to be the kind of person able to understand the existence of multiple perspectives, and to be influenced by different sociocultural vectors; the ability to adapt is also seen as essential in diverse cultural environments, where subjects are able to deal with so-called 'cultural shock'. Regarding 'Attitudes', it is important to acquire 'openness' to people from different cultural realities, based on sensitivity, curiosity and willingness to interact regardless of individuals' backgrounds. 'Respect' is an essential vector at this level, seeking to develop and stimulate an intrinsic 'value' of positive appreciation and understanding of the other, in parallel to the avoidance of unfounded judgements. Furthermore, this dimension also includes so-called 'global mindedness', a way of looking at the world in the holistic perspective of an interconnected global community, in which mutual responsibility for the other is enhanced (even if located in another part of the world). With regard to 'values', importance is attached to the value of human dignity and cultural diversity; values are thus like filters through which individuals process information about other cultures, and how to engage with others in the world. These values, when promoted, trigger greater understanding and motivation to combat exclusion and discrimination, as well as other inequalities and injustices in the world.

According to the OECD (2018c), the global competence concept includes building specific cognitive and socio-emotional skills. The purpose of 'global competence' is to prepare people (students) for the complexity of global society (ibid.). According to the organisation:

> Globally competent students can draw on and combine the disciplinary knowledge and modes of thinking acquired in schools to ask questions, analyse data and arguments, explain phenomena, and develop a position concerning a local, global or cultural issue …

and

> they can retain their cultural identity but are simultaneously aware of the cultural values and beliefs of people around them, they examine the origins and implications of others' and their own assumptions. And they can create opportunities to take informed, reflective action and have their voices heard.
>
> (ibid., p. 9)

In order to assess the levels of global competence of young people from different countries of the world, *PISA 2018* seeks to integrate, from a single instrument, a variety of dimensions. It is thus constituted by an exam which draws on cognitive capacities focused on the construction of 'global understanding', where intercultural challenges and issues are the goal of the analysis and are required to be solved; it also includes a set of items on a questionnaire that aims to assess the competences and attitudes of young people on certain global and cultural problems.

In this assessment, the cognitive test affords the attaining of scores, which will rank students on a scale, to the extent that their answers are correct, partially correct or wrong; in the case of items focused on how to understand socio-emotional attitudes and competences, the methodology might consider an analysis under response patterns, since it is more difficult to measure these items, influenced as they are by a greater degree of subjectivity.

In sum, as far as the OECD is concerned, there is a more recent concern in terms of understanding the global competence of young people around the world, despite the OECD's mission to work on skills-building in order to 'respond to the twenty-first century'. The OECD's proposal is aligned with the identification of standards and the obtaining of results through standardised tests that, in the organisational view, is a cautious methodology and framework of analysis designed to neutralise cultural bias.

The connection to global citizenship can be found in the introduction to *Preparing Our Youth for an Inclusive and Sustainable World* (OECD 2018b). The introduction is titled 'The Importance of an International Global Competence Assessment'. In answer to the question 'Why do we need global competence?' the document offers four reasons: 'to live harmoniously in multicultural communities', 'to thrive in a changing labour market', 'to use media platforms effectively and responsibly' and 'to support the sustainable development goals'. The last reads as follows:

> To support the Sustainable Development Goals
> Finally, educating for global competence can help form new generations who care about global issues and engage in tackling social, political, economic and environmental challenges. The 2030 Agenda for Sustainable Development recognises the critical role of education in reaching sustainability goals, calling on all countries 'to ensure, by 2030, that all learners acquire the knowledge and skills needed to promote sustainable development, including,

among others, through education for sustainable development and sustainable lifestyles, human rights, gender equality, promotion of a culture of peace and non-violence, *global citizenship* and appreciation of cultural diversity and of culture's contribution to sustainable development.'

(Target 4.7, Education 2030, *Incheon Declaration and Framework for Action*, p. 20) (ibid., p. 5, emphasis added)

Thus, the work developed by the OECD also follows other international guidelines and agendas. Indeed, Auld and Morris (2019) argue that the organisation's interest in the concept of 'global competence' was driven by the will to become a player in monitoring the fulfilment of the SDGs and, matching our own conclusion, that the discourse on 'global competencies' also relates to its economic mission. Therefore, it is evident that the OECD recognises the relevance of global citizenship but only within the framework of global competence.

Global citizenship as a way to promote peace, according to UNESCO

Within the framework of the UN, UNESCO 'seeks to build peace through international cooperation in Education, the Sciences and Culture. UNESCO's programmes contribute to the achievement of the SDGs defined in Agenda 2030, adopted by the UN General Assembly in 2015' (UNESCO 2019a). Among its principles and 'mission values' are tolerance, pluralism, respect for human rights, freedom and dialogue. In line with this view, democracy is promoted at various levels, and education for peace and human rights are highlighted as essential for global citizenship (UNESCO 2019b). To this extent, UNESCO seeks the promotion of global citizenship through education, alongside other partners of the UN, at the forefront of initiatives such as the *World Program for Human Rights Education* as well as the promotion of *Education for Global Citizenship*.

UNESCO perceives GCE as an empowering response to interconnected challenges:

> While the world may be increasingly interconnected, human rights violations, inequality and poverty still threaten peace and sustainability. Global Citizenship Education (GCED) is UNESCO's response to these challenges. It works by empowering learners of all ages to understand that these are global, not local issues and to become active promoters of more peaceful, tolerant, inclusive, secure and sustainable societies.
>
> (UNESCO 2019c)

Therefore, educating for global citizenship entails the need to foster the learning of 'living together' (UNESCO n.d.; Delors 1996).

Among several initiatives and official documents pertaining to global citizenship are the Universal Declaration of Human Rights (UDHR), the Education

Agenda 2030 and Framework for Action, the Agenda for Sustainable Development and the Education Recommendation for International Understanding, Cooperation and Peace. In the UDHR (UN 1949) the dimension of 'brotherhood' among all men, born equal in rights and dignity, who must seek to act for one another, is essential. This declaration, among others, shows principles of solidarity and cooperation, seen as key dimensions of the concept of global citizenship.

In this context, UNESCO's work focuses in particular on education and training for global citizenship, through specific topics or main issues aligned with social and political circumstances such as the Prevention of Violent Extremism (UNESCO 2019d) through GCE, Holocaust Education and Genocide, or even the promotion of the rule of law through Education for Global Citizenship.

UNESCO collaborates with various entities that support the promotion of global citizenship, such as other UN agencies and intergovernmental organisations. One of the initiatives launched by the UN (n.d.a) was the Global Education First Initiative, which incorporates GCE as one of its priorities along with access to, and quality of, education (see also Costa 2015). This initiative begins a 'new era' from the educational point of view, where concerns about humanity and awareness of the issues that affect us all are explicitly framed as a direct goal of the educational process. Moreover, since 2015, GCE has been included in the SDGs (Goal 4.7):

> By 2030, ensure that all learners acquire the knowledge and skills needed to promote sustainable development, including, among others, through education for sustainable development and sustainable lifestyles, human rights, gender equality, promotion of a culture of peace and non-violence, global citizenship and appreciation of cultural diversity and of culture's contribution to sustainable development.
>
> (UN n.d.b, p. 19)

Global citizenship for UNESCO is viewed from an educational perspective as a way, a strategy and a vision through which young people and adults can take an active role in solving global problems on a path towards a more peaceful, tolerant, inclusive and secure world (UNESCO 2014b). UNESCO undertakes actions to raise awareness and to train several publics for these topics, covering three main domains of personal development: 'Cognitive', 'Socio-emotional' and 'Behavioural'. The first refers to people acquiring knowledge, understanding and critical thinking about global issues, as well as a solid comprehension of the interdependence between different problems and nations; the second emphasises the need to develop a sense of belonging to a common humanity, through the promotion of empathy, solidarity towards others and respect for difference; finally, the third domain (based on the promotion of previous ones) implies responsible action at both local and global levels (UNESCO Associated Schools Network n.d.).

The UNESCO Associated Schools Network promotes global citizenship through initiatives such as the 2014–2021 Global Network of Schools addressing

Global Challenges. It aims to cultivate a respect for democracy and the rights of 'the other' not only by targeting students in all school levels and through different educational approaches and structures, but also by reaching teachers and other educators as central figures in the effort to shift the paradigm for action (see also Costa 2015).

UNESCO's work, then, is very much focused on establishing recommendations and promoting education initiatives aligned with the promotion of human rights, fundamental values and a shared sense of humanity among people; consequently, the actions promoted have to do with awareness-raising and, through this, engagement with social and political causes for the welfare of all. For example, a recent report from UNESCO states that there are still insufficient teacher training programmes on the Guiding Principles of the *Recommendation concerning Education for International Understanding, Co-operation and Peace and Education relating to Human Rights and Fundamental Freedoms* (which was adopted in 1974).

This is an ongoing effort. For example, in 2019, UNESCO held a major conference called 'UNESCO 2019 Forum on Education for Sustainable Development and Global Citizenship' (UNESCO 2019e) focused on learning and teaching for peaceful and sustainable societies, from early childhood to primary to secondary education. It is possible to conclude that, despite having people from all ages and professions participate, the particular focus was children and young people, as the future working generation, who will (and must) participate in society and take part in the leadership of, or contribute to, its organisations and companies. This event, among others, targeted policy-makers and professionals from several backgrounds and contexts, as both 'influential' and 'multiplication' actors to work towards global citizenship and support learners across the world to act socially and politically on the main world problems. Maybe some of them will be able to *think educationally* (as Andreotti [2015] says) about forms of GCE. Nevertheless, considering that UNESCO's work is based on a model similar to that of 'mentoring' – that is, one that focuses on the support of education practitioners, NGOs, community organisations, experts, policy-makers, the private sector, etc. – it remains unclear how and in what directions UNESCO guidelines and tools have been appropriated by the mentioned groups.

A critical analysis of the discourse of the OECD and UNESCO[2]

It is evident from the foregoing description of global citizenship discourse in documents emanating from the OECD and UNESCO that while its themes are closely related there is an important difference in emphasis. Whereas UNESCO is focused on awareness-raising and educating for global issues through different initiatives (some of them falling into more 'theoretical' and policy-oriented stances), the OECD is focused on assessment of 'global competence' as a primary set of skills to foster economic and social development. Moreover, the OECD is an instrument of world order focused on 'economic development' that presents itself as technocratic and apolitical, including with respect to education. Thus, its educational rhetoric is not limited to the promotion of access and quality, but embraces the importance of training for the 'competencies of the twenty-first century'. These competencies integrate cognitive and socio-emotional valences, but also competencies for employment and the labour market and, equally importantly, skills that inform 'living with' ('living with' being explicit in the view of UNESCO on global citizenship).

The OECD

As we have said, the OECD does refer to global citizenship but only in the context of what is a rather different concept, namely global competence, and specifically as part of 'educating for global competence'. From what we analysed, global competence is a recent trend within the framework of action of OECD, nonetheless being aligned with both its paradigm on skills to prepare people for the future labour market and its methodology for studies and measurement. No doubt these ideas will influence national and international actors across the globe. The OECD is also aligned with the SDGs, to which it responds by advocating 'global' skills. It is very much focused on the knowledge and skills required for cognitive and socio-emotional development according to age. Cultural background, however, is missing from its definition of skills to be promoted and its methodology of measurement. Its emphasis on formal schooling is perhaps at the expense of informal schooling. For the OECD, education is closely related to global competencies, and so proposed measures are related to education and training, particularly in formal settings such as schools, as the necessary means for the acquisition of knowledge, development of skills and promotion of attitudes and values. For this reason, and under the framework of PISA, OECD is interested to assess the 'global' level of competence of young people under a 'technical', 'apolitical' and, in their vision, an 'acultural' way. Its main targets are children and youth, while nothing is being said for adults, which would also be – in our view – extremely important.

The references to global competence include skills such as reasoning with information, knowing how to communicate in diverse intercultural contexts, perspective-taking, conflict resolution, adaptability, openness towards people from different cultural backgrounds and respect for them, as well as global-mindedness. Nevertheless, although the skills comprising global competence might be useful for global citizenship, we do believe that the discourse stops short of addressing the essence of global citizenship. The OECD's focus is encapsulated within the framework of competence for the global economy as an important tool to achieve success in a neoliberal environment. Following Andreotti's work on critical global citizenship, it is evident that the OECD's concept of global competence is distant from such self- and social-critical stances; after Larsen's work we may also say that the (self) awareness, engagement and action he sees as defining critical global citizenship are, at least currently, not part of the idea of global competence.

We would also like to emphasise that the validity of the kind of results obtainable from the OECD global competence questionnaire is questionable given the methodology of measurement proposed by and for PISA (Engel, Rutkowski and Thompson 2019), in light of the varying social, cultural and political backgrounds of respondents. Moreover, whether these data might actually help in the practical daily life of global citizens across the globe is something that requires both additional argumentation and further research by the OECD.

The OECD model may be further criticised for not adequately addressing the current threats the world faces from global polarities and inequalities to ignorance and hatred of the 'other' (see Introduction, this volume, for further elaboration). Under the framework promoted by OECD, the divide between the global North and South is not considered. Instead, the organisation promotes a 'western, cognitive and rational, late modern discourse' over a more plural one (Grotlüschen 2018, p. 12; see also Engel, Rutkowski and Thompson 2019).

UNESCO

UNESCO clearly focuses on global citizenship across several topics, from sustainability to peace, identifying large themes and global issues to which people around the world should pay attention; occasionally, it also identifies specific polarities and inequalities, including global power imbalances. As with the OECD, the proposal from UNESCO considers cognitive and socio-emotional development, the privileged targets being children and youth.

UNESCO prioritises civilisational development and the promotion of fundamental values such as solidarity and respect. To this extent, UNESCO has a content-centric approach based on principles and moral values, clearly emphasised in its mission and mandate. The OECD welcomes many of these principles, but its focus is on 'competence' as a capability that can be measured and understood in a context of 'standards of analysis'. In UNESCO's line of work there are proposed methodologies and initiatives to raise awareness on global themes and to foster competencies, including producing supporting documentation for these purposes.[3]

While, unlike the OECD, UNESCO includes other actors, national and international, in its activities the question remains of the extent to which its recommendations and proposals are actually taken up and applied by such actors across the globe, whether, that is, and to what extent, its attempts to build capacity bear fruit. While UNESCO does move in the direction of a critical global citizenship, its actions are limited to raising awareness and knowledge production. This leaves it open to critics such as Bourn (2015) who argue that UNESCO's promotion of global citizenship in the context of global education is actually in the service of global economic integration, being not so focused as it should be on acting on global issues that affect non-hegemonic populations.

Final remarks

This chapter has discussed global citizenship at the international level, seeking to reinforce the study of this practice beyond the domestic realm of the state.

There are two reasons for this: the state is almost exclusively the preferred level of analysis to study and understand citizenship (and policies that affect it); and also international institutions have a significant role in promoting (their take on) global citizenship across countries, and among other national and international actors. Thus, this chapter overcomes the domestic–international divide regarding (global) citizenship, emphasising the role of international key actors in domestic policy while noting differences in conceptual usage in the analysed international organisations.

The importance of discussing this topic lies in the current global challenges requiring civic action and a true sense of care, in order to bring more peace, sustainability, equality and mutual understanding to our lives. Here we have advocated for the role of critical global citizenship in addressing such issues. Moreover, we recognise the crucial role key international players such as the OECD and UNESCO have in moving education and social policies towards a meaningful citizenship that it is not confined to the borders of a nation-state. We do believe that through processes of transformative pedagogy and critical literacy the idea of global citizenship can foster a better life for all people by creating a shared consciousness of our interdependence across the world, one where 'all are part of both the problem and the solution'. For this, it is important to acknowledge that cosmopolitanism is not the full answer by itself, but adopting a critical global citizenship approach may help to cultivate the qualities and attitudes of citizens (Ide 2018) necessary to reach a fairer international community. Our critical purpose herein has been, then, to demonstrate that it is relevant for these organisations to take a more critical approach to global citizenship, and that it is pertinent for scholars to resort to a more critical approach to assess the means and goals of such institutions in the promotion of global citizenship.

The international organisations that we have analysed in this chapter – the OECD and UNESCO – have been developing activity on global citizenship and global competence through various strategies and tools. Via these means they have, first, introduced global citizenship and global competence to the international debate (which is highly important) and, second, made a contribution to the improvement of our planet on key issues by raising consciousness and awareness, to instigate important skills for the future and, in more specific cases, making a contribution to global civic action. This 'internationalism' overcomes the limits of nations (Isaacs 2018) and has the potential to engage people to be part of a wider and concerned community.

That said, it is clear that while referring to global citizenship the OECD's focus is on global competence whereas UNESCO's is mostly related to global education, what may be thought of as a prior step to (critical) global citizenship itself. From this perspective it may be said that the discourse of both bodies is still lacking a critical approach to global citizenship (Andreotti, 2010, 2014a, 2014b), with particular reference to critical literacy (ibid.). In a Freirean reading global citizenship should be based on processes of awareness, in the logic of cooperation, in order to promote the acquisition of knowledge and understanding on topics such as global injustice, in pursuit of action directed towards social change and liberation from structural oppression (Freire 1998).

Despite the important step of producing guidelines and tools to enhance understanding of the current state of global society through debate and awareness-raising, the task of addressing in material terms the fundamental roots of inequalities and disparities across the world to bring about effective structural change in its social and political systems is not nearly as close as it should be to being taken up. An effective identity change and a true cosmopolitan sense of belonging to a shared world, under a conscious and critical reflection upon the structural dynamics of the polarities still existing between the global North and global South, is not to be fully found in the actions of these international intergovernmental institutions.

Notes

1 For a brilliant demolition of the 'single story' see Adichie (2009).
2 For discussion of the European Union's (limited) uptake of the concept of global citizenship see Ross and Davies (2018) and Tonkiss (2014).
3 For a comparison of the OECD and UNESCO global education policy documents regarding the 2030 Agenda for Sustainable Development, and how these organisations' notions of global citizenship and agendas are distinct and divergent, see Vaccari and Gardinier (2019).

References

Adichie, CN 2009, The danger of a single story, viewed 1 October 2019, www.youtube.com/watch?v=D9Ihs241zeg&t=154s%29.

Almeida, J 2003, *Cidadania sem governo/Estado: Noções Para uma Cidadania Global No Quadro do Sistema Internacional Contemporâneo* [Citizenship without a government/state: concepts for a global citizenship in the context of the international contemporary system], Master's dissertation in Sociology 'As Sociedades Nacionais Perante os Processos de Globalização' [National societies on the globalization processes], Faculty of Economy, University of Coimbra, Portugal.

Andreotti, V 2010, 'Postcolonial and post-critical "global citizenship education"', in G Elliot, C Fourali and S Issler (eds), *Education and social change: connecting local and global perspectives*, 233–45, Continuum, London.

Andreotti, V 2014a, 'Educação para a Cidadania Global' ['Soft versus critical'] trans. Tânia Neves and Teresa Corte-Real, *Sinergias: diálogos educativos para a transformação social* [Synergies: educational dialogues for social change], 1, 57–66 (Original Andreotti, V 2006, 'Soft versus critical global citizenship', *Policy and Practice: A Development Education Review*, vol. 3, autumn, pp. 40–51).

Andreotti, V 2014b, 'Critical and transnational literacies in international development and global citizenship education', *Sisyphus: Journal of Education*, vol. 2, no. 3, pp. 32–50.

Andreotti, V 2015, 'Global citizenship education otherwise: pedagogical and theoretical insights', in A Abdi, L Shultz and T Pillay (eds), *Decolonizing global citizenship education*, 221–30, Sense Publishers, Rotterdam.

Auld, E and Morris, P 2019, 'Science by streetlight and the OECD's measure of global competence: a new yardstick for internationalisation?' *Policy Futures in Education*, vol. 17, no. 6, pp. 677–98.

Bourdieu, P and Passeron, J 1990, *Reproduction in education, society and culture*, Sage, London.

Bourn, D 2015, *The theory and practice of development education: a pedagogy for global social justice*, Routledge, Abingdon.

Brubaker, R and Laitin, D 1998, 'Ethnic and nationalist violence', *Annual Review of Sociology*, vol. 24, pp. 423–52.

Castells, M 1996, *The rise of the network society. Vol. I of The information age: economy, society, culture*, Blackwell, Oxford.

Castells, M 1997, *The power of identity. Vol. II of The information age: economy, society, culture*, Blackwell, Oxford.

Castells, M 1998, *End of millennium. Vol. III of The information age: economy, society, culture*, Blackwell, Oxford.

Cortesão, L 2000, *Ser professor: um ofício em risco de extinção? Reflexões sobre práticas educativas face à diversidade, no limiar do século XXI* [Being a teacher: a job at risk of extinction? Reflections on educational practices in the face of diversity, at the threshold of the 21st century], Edições Afrontamento, Porto.

Costa, F 2015, *From policy to practices: global education in Portugal and England. A comparative case-study à propos of an internship at the Development Education Research Centre of the Institute of Education, University College London*, Faculdade de Letras da Universidade do Porto, Porto.

Delors, J 1996, *Learning: the treasure within*, Report to UNESCO of the International Commission on Education for the twenty-first-century, UNESCO, Paris.

Engel, L, Rutkowski, D and Thompson, G 2019, 'Toward an international measure of global competence? A critical look at the PISA 2018 framework', *Globalisation, Societies and Education*, vol. 17, no. 2, pp. 1–15.

Follesdal, A 2002, 'Citizenship: European and global', in N Dower and J Williams (eds), *Global citizenship: a critical reader*, 71–83, Edinburgh University Press, Edinburgh.

Freire, P 1998, *Pedagogy of freedom: ethics, democracy and civic courage*, Rowman & Littlefield, Oxford.

Giddens, A 1990, *The consequences of modernity*, Stanford University Press, Stanford, CA.

Grotlüschen, A 2018, 'Global competence: does the new OECD competence domain ignore the global South?' *Studies in the Education of Adults*, vol. 50, no. 2, pp. 185–202.

Haraway, D 1988, 'Situated knowledge: the science question in feminism as a site of discourse on the privilege of partial perspective', *Feminist Studies*, vol. 14, no. 3, pp. 575–99.

Held, D and McGrew, A 2013, 'Introduction: current controversies about the demise of globalisation', in D Held and A McGrew, 2nd edn, *Globalization/anti-globalization: beyond the great divide*, 1–12, Polity, Cambridge.

Held, D, McGrew, A, Goldblatt, D and Perraton, J 1999, *Global transformations: politics, economics and culture*, Polity, Cambridge.

Ide, K 2018, 'Living together with national border lines and nationalisms', in I Davies, L-C Ho, D Kiwan, CL Peck, A Peterson, E Sant and Y Waghid (eds), *The Palgrave handbook of global citizenship and education*, 133–47, Palgrave Macmillan, London.

Isaacs, T 2018, 'Internationalism in global citizenship and education', in I Davies, L-C Ho, D Kiwan, CL Peck, A Peterson, E Sant and Y Waghid (eds), *The Palgrave handbook of global citizenship and education*, 149–63, Palgrave Macmillan, London.

Isin, EF and Nyers, P 2014, 'Introduction: globalizing citizenship studies', in EF Isin and P Nyers (eds), *Routledge handbook of global citizenship studies*, 1–11, Routledge, New York.

Larsen, M 2014, 'Critical global citizenship and international service learning: a case study of the intensification effect', *Journal of Global Citizenship and Equity Education*, vol. 4, no. 1, pp. 1–43.

Lederach, J 1995, *Preparing for peace: conflict transformation across cultures*, Syracuse University Press, Syracuse, NY.

Linder, E 2012, 'Fostering global citizenship', in M Deutsch and P Coleman (eds), *The psychological components of a sustainable peace*, 283–98, Springer-Verlag, New York.

Magalhães, A and Stoer, S 2003, 'Educação, conhecimento e sociedade em rede' [Education, knowledge, and network society], *Educação & Sociedade* [Education & Society], vol. 24, no. 85, pp. 1179–202.

Neto, F 1998, *Psicologia social* [Social psychology], Vol. I, Universidade Aberta, Lisboa [Lisbon].

OECD 2018a, *PISA: programme for international student assessment*, viewed 1 August 2019, www.oecd.org/pisa/pisa-2018-global-competence.htm.

OECD 2018b, *Preparing our youth for an inclusive and sustainable world: the OECD PISA Global Competence Framework*, viewed 1 August 2019, www.oecd.org/education/Global-competency-for-an-inclusive-world.pdf.

OECD 2018c, *OECD education and skills today: how to prepare students for the complexity of a global society*, viewed 1 August 2019, https://oecdedutoday.com/how-to-prepare-students-for-the-complexity-of-a-global-society/.

OECD 2019, *OECD and the sustainable development goals: delivering on universal goals and targets*, viewed 1 August 2019, www.oecd.org/dac/sustainable-development-goals.htm.

Pais, A and Costa, M 2017, 'An ideology critique of global citizenship education', *Critical Studies in Education*, 22 April, pp. 1–16, viewed 1 August 2019, DOI: 10.1080/17508487.2017.1318772.

Risse, T 2007, 'Social constructivism meets globalization', in D Held and A McGrew (eds), *Globalization theory: approaches and controversies*, 126–47, Polity Press, Cambridge.

Robertson, R 1992, *Globalization: social theory and global culture*, Sage, London.

Robinson, W 2007, 'Theories of globalization', in G Ritzer (ed.), *The Blackwell companion to globalization*, 125–43, Blackwell, Oxford.

Ross, A and Davies, I 2018, 'Europe and global citizenship', in I Davies, L-C Ho, D Kiwan, CL Peck, A Peterson, E Sant and Y Waghid (eds), *The Palgrave handbook of global citizenship and education*, 21–36, Palgrave Macmillan, London.

Said, EW 1978, *Orientalism*, Pantheon, New York.

Santos, B 2002, 'Os processos de globalização' [Globalization processes], *Eurozine*, viewed 1 August 2019, www.eurozine.com/os-processos-da-globalizacao/.

Scholte, JA 2005, *Globalization: a critical introduction*, 2nd edn, revised and updated, Palgrave Macmillan, London.

Sen, A 2007, *Identity and violence: the illusion of destiny*, Penguin Books, London.

Soguk, N 2014, 'Global citizenship in an insurrectional era', in EF Isin and P Nyers (eds), *Routledge handbook of global citizenship studies*, 49–61, Routledge, New York.

Spivak, GC 2004, 'Righting wrongs', *Southern Atlantic Quarterly*, vol. 103, no. 2–3, pp. 523–81.

Stevens, C n.d., 'OECD work on competencies on education for sustainable development (ESD)', viewed 1 August 2019, www.unece.org/fileadmin/DAM/env/esd/inf.meeting.docs/EGonInd/8mtg/ESDCompetenciesOECD.pdf.

Tonkiss, K 2014, 'Experiences of EU citizenship at the sub-national level', EF Isin and P Nyers (eds), *Routledge handbook of global citizenship studies*, 446–54, Routledge, London.

UN 1949, *Universal declaration of human rights*, viewed 1 August 2019, www.supremecourt.ge/files/upload-file/pdf/act3.pdf.

UN n.d.a, *Sustainable development goals: global education first initiative (GEFI)*, viewed 1 August 2019, https://sustainabledevelopment.un.org/partnership/?p=9696.

UN n.d.b, *Transforming our world: the 2030 agenda for sustainable development*, viewed 1 August 2019, https://sustainabledevelopment.un.org/content/documents/21252030%20Agenda%20for%20Sustainable%20Development%20web.pdf.

UNESCO 2014a, *Shaping the future we want: UN decade of education for sustainable development 2005–2014 (final report)*, viewed 1 August 2019, https://sustainabledevelopment.un.org/content/documents/1682Shaping%20the%20future%20we%20want.pdf.

UNESCO 2014b, *Global citizenship education: preparing learners for the challenges of the 21st century*, viewed 1 August 2019, http://unesdoc.unesco.org/images/0022/002277/227729E.pdf.

UNESCO 2019a, *UNESCO in brief: mission and mandate*, viewed 19 September 2019, https://en.unesco.org/about-us/introducing-unesco.

UNESCO 2019b, *Democracy and global citizenship*, viewed 1 August 2019, https://en.unesco.org/themes/democracy-and-global-citizenship.

UNESCO 2019c, *Global citizenship education*, viewed 1 October 2019, https://en.unesco.org/themes/gced.

UNESCO 2019d, *Preventing violent extremism*, viewed 1 August 2019, https://en.unesco.org/preventing-violent-extremism.

UNESCO 2019e, *UNESCO 2019 forum on education for sustainable development and global citizenship*, viewed 1 October 2019, https://en.unesco.org/themes/gced/esd-gced-forum2019.

UNESCO n.d., *The ABCs of global citizenship education*, viewed 1 August 2019, https://aspnet.unesco.org/en-us/Documents/The%20ABCs.pdf.

UNESCO Associated Schools Network n.d., *Global citizenship education*, viewed 1 August 2019, https://aspnet.unesco.org/en-us/Pages/Global-Citizenship-Education.aspx.

Vaccari, V and Gardinier, M 2019, 'Toward one world or many? A comparative analysis of OECD and UNESCO global education policy documents', *International Journal of Development Education and Global Learning*, vol. 11, no. 1, pp. 68–86.

Waters, M 2001, *Globalization*, 2nd edn, Routledge, London.

Part V

Global citizenship and the benevolent actors

Chapter 9

Benevolence, global citizenship, and post-racial politics[1]

David Jefferess

Introduction

Mahmood Mamdani characterized global politics at the beginning of the twenty-first century as demarcated by two contrasting narratives of 'Culture Talk': the first constructs a premodern Other as *not yet* modern while the second constructs this Other as *anti*-modern. Writes Mamdani (2005, p. 18), 'Whereas the former conception encourages relations based on philanthropy, the latter notion is productive of fear and preemptive police or military action'. While these two narratives – one of security, the other of humanitarian benevolence – are continuous with and reinforce one another, Mamdani focuses on the second narrative of Culture Talk: the way North Atlantic 'security' forces are arrayed against this threatening Other. Discourses of security, as Thobani (2007), Razack (2008), and Goldberg (2009) argue, construct difference in the terms of racial discourse; in the context of the 'war on terror', for instance, Islam is produced as a racial sign. In contrast, discourses of global citizenship, particularly in Canada, posit an end to race. In this chapter, I argue that global citizenship discourse, as centred in the states of the North Atlantic, and as performed through a politics of humanitarian action, articulates a post-racial ideal. I describe this as an ideal because global citizenship does not seek to contend with the historical and ongoing social implications of race thinking or dismantle the structures of racialized violence, but simply to transcend race.

Overt analyses of race and racism have largely been ignored within development studies (Khotari 2006; White 2002). Similarly, contemporary theories of global citizenship typically elide race and the history of colonialism. For instance, in *An Introduction to Global Citizenship*, Nigel Dower (2003, p. 41, emphasis added) seems dismissive of the dynamics of race and racism, characterizing 'identity politics' as the reaction of 'members of certain groups [who] may be disadvantaged in various ways (economic status, public recognition) and *feel* that it is because they belong to a certain group that they are disadvantaged or discriminated against'. The eradication of systems of marginalization would seem not to be a goal of the global citizen. While Kwame Anthony Appiah has most certainly engaged with the problem of race and racism, in his influential *Cosmopolitanism:*

Ethics in a World of Strangers (2006), ongoing and historical structures of racial thinking are not addressed as a dynamic in contemporary international conflicts; yet cosmopolitanism seems to figure as a post-racial ideal. *Cosmopolitanism* argues for 'our' obligations to the welfare of others and to value particular human lives and hence cultural diversity. This 'obligation' is framed specifically in terms of philanthropy, as the means to alleviate poverty, as if both the historical structures that have produced suffering and the very ideal of humanitarian philanthropy are not imbricated in colonial racism.

In this chapter, I critically examine two distinct pedagogical examples of the construction of the ideal of global citizenship in Canada to show how benevolence provides a 'structure of attitude and reference' (Said 1993, p. 253) for understandings of global social and economic inequality. As the performance of humanitarian benevolence, global citizenship reveals a complicated racial politics that seems to shun the patronizing and self-serving imperial subject produced through the 'white man's burden' to 'uplift' and 'civilize' others, but nonetheless presumes a moral hierarchy; what I call the signature of modernity. I begin by examining the construction of the figure of the global citizen as humanitarian in documentary films that focalize the trauma and compassion of Stephen Lewis and James Orbinski. Both men have held senior positions in humanitarian organizations: Lewis, as UN Special Envoy for HIV/AIDS in Africa; and Orbinski as President of the International Council of Médicins Sans Frontières (MSF). Their books and the documentaries that chronicle their work are often featured in global citizenship education resources, and both are regularly invited to speak to the issue of global citizenship.[2] I argue that the status of these men as humanitarian figures and models of the global citizen requires that they be constructed as non-racial, or as exhibiting attitudes that repudiate racial difference. Paradoxically, it is their coding in the films as white men that allows them to be the models of post-racial global citizenship.

I also offer an analysis of the Aga Khan Foundation Canada's (AKFC) travelling development-education exhibition, *Bridges that Unite*, which overtly addresses its audience as global citizens, constructing humanitarian work as the practice of global citizenship (Classroom Connections 2009). Specifically, I analyse its representation of 'Agents of Change' and engage with how the exhibit is informed by a discourse of benevolence that relies upon the ideal of cultural pluralism. Unlike earlier forms of European imperial benevolence – the 'white man's burden' – I argue that global citizenship presupposes, or seems to enact, an end to race. Taking up Cecil Foster's contention that multicultural Canada is poised to foster a new spirit of modernity, an era in which 'race does not matter' (2005, p. 25), I argue in the final section of the chapter that benevolence provides the signature of this new modernity. To be modern – to be fully human – is to have the responsibility to aid and uplift an Other, who is not (yet) modern. The performance of benevolence is not bound by race, but is indebted to, and rearticulates, race thinking in a way that belies the ongoing dynamics of colonial racism.

Global citizenship, benevolence, and imagined relations

Vanessa Andreotti (2006) argues that global citizenship, in its 'soft form', as articulated by development agencies, university initiatives, and cosmopolitan philosophers, posits an abstract global community bound by a shared humanity. In Canada, to be a global citizen requires helping Others in need, through humanitarian projects, for instance. According to Andreotti, global citizenship asserts a recognition of a shared humanity as the basis for conceiving of interconnection, relies upon a universalist vision of what the good life or ideal world constitutes, assumes the autonomy and agency of the global citizen to act or help, and enacts responsibility *for*, rather than *to*, the Other (2006, p. 6). In Patrick Reed's 2008 documentary, *Triage: Dr. James Orbinski's Humanitarian Dilemma*, Orbinski describes this responsibility while reflecting on his work with MSF in war zones in Africa:

> I still have – and I always will I think – the nearly uncontainable rage about what happened in Rwanda ... and Somalia ... and about what is happening now in many parts of the world. To see mothers and fathers and children dying of indifference, dying of neglect, of abuse, of somebody's political calculation ... It fills me first of all with just profound sorrow that they have to live that and die it. And then it fills me with rage frankly, and the question then is what do you do? What do you do with that? We are responsible for our lives and for our world and if we don't engage that responsibility no one else will, and we will live or die with the legacy of our failures.

Here, Orbinski articulates a moral obligation to act in the world in terms of his own sorrow, anger, and, significantly, shame; he articulates shame not in terms of being complicit in violence but in being part of a social community (Canada, the West) that has failed to 'help' those Others who suffer. The narrative he constructs to explain his humanitarian work positions him as outside the conflict and suffering he witnesses, and hence innocent, but still responsible for caring for those who suffer as a result of this conflict.

In Catherine Mullins's 2005 documentary *Their Brothers' Keepers*, Stephen Lewis affirms a moral obligation to ease suffering. Decrying the discrepancy between the financial cost of fighting wars in Afghanistan and Iraq with what has been spent during the same period on development aid, Lewis says:

> I don't understand the nature of the moral default. I love the words 'we are our brothers and sisters' keepers' – I'm not a biblically inclined person – but it is absolutely true that the reason you respond to people is out of an innate compassion and decency and solidarity when human beings are under siege.

Lewis defines humanitarian action in terms of a relation based on philanthropy; one has a moral obligation to an Other in need because that Other is also human.

For Lewis, the billions spent on war does not provide a key factor for *why* human beings elsewhere 'are under siege', but simply reveals a gross discrepancy in priorities. As Orbinski presents it, people die of *indifference* and *neglect*, not war, exploitation, and impoverishment. Conflict and poverty are dehistorized; 'our' relation to the suffering of Others is defined in terms of benevolence – our compassion and decency – rather than in terms of material inter-connection.

In *Cosmopolitanism: Ethics in a World of Strangers* (2006), Appiah examines the nature of the obligation of the affluent to those in the so-called 'developing world'. He argues for instance that 'most of us are in no danger of meeting ... [our] basic obligation', of help or aid to Africa (p. 170). Yet, he also contends that 'a genuinely cosmopolitan response begins with caring to understand *why* the child is dying' (p. 168). He identifies a host of causes for suffering, from poor infrastructure and governance in African states, to international trade and subsidy programmes that favour US and European industries, to the burden of debt for 'poor countries'. Focusing specifically on humanitarian crisis relief, such as rehydration for children suffering from diarrhoea or providing food aid, Appiah warns that our desire to help may actually be 'doing more harm than good' (p. 170). Yet, despite this framing of the structural causes and contexts of suffering, Appiah posits cosmopolitanism in the terms of personal morality and ethics: 'Whatever my basic obligations are to the poor far away, they cannot be enough, I believe, to trump my concerns for my family, my friends, my country' (p. 165). His normalization of 'country' as a privileged relationship (like family) both potentially undermines these structural arguments (as dumping grain into the African market benefits *my* Canadian agricultural industries even if it hurts African farmers) and naturalizes the stratification of moral obligation against the cosmopolitan interest in recognizing our shared humanity, across difference.

Appiah argues that specific forms of aid may actually cause suffering, but I want to suggest that the emphasis on the moral obligation to help or aid – to be benevolent – in fact serves to do more harm than good in that it elides the material conditions of both suffering and the global citizen's capacity to help. As Damien Riggs (2004a, p. 8) contends,

> the ability to be benevolent is always already predicated on the power to do so – it does not require the giving up of power, but rather is reliant upon an imbalance of power to instantiate the categories of giver and receiver.

Benevolence normalizes the position of the global citizen as helper and constructs the relationship between caregiver and beneficiary as beginning with the act of aid. Historically, Euro-American cultures have constructed benevolence of this kind specifically in terms of whiteness; indeed, it has been a way of asserting whiteness against difference. When the global citizen is constructed in this way, how is it indebted to this history of the 'white man's burden' and to what extent does it continue to perform it?

Humanitarian intervention depends upon the conception of a global community bound by a shared human dignity; as Didier Fassin argues through the notion of a 'politics of life', however, the contemporary (Western) moral economy of humanitarianism reflects a 'complex ontology of inequality' (2007, p. 519). Fassin explains that there are lives that can be risked and lives that can be sacrificed, and 'lives that can be narrated in the first person (those who intervene) and lives that are recounted only in the third person (the voiceless in the name of whom intervention is done)' (p. 519). Benevolence provides a structure of attitude and reference for global citizenship, and serves to redefine a material relationship of inequality as an ethical relationship aimed at helping the Other in need. In this chapter, I seek to contribute to the work of complicating 'benevolence as a presumed-to-be moral category, and instead understand it as a network of power that attempts to mask histories of colonisation' (Riggs 2004b). Ruth Frankenberg has noted the *historical* constitution of benevolence as a set of cultural practices whose whiteness goes unmarked and unnamed (1993, p. 1); however, this contemporary 'politics of life' continues to be informed by colonial racism, articulated in post-racial terms.

Global citizenship as the spectacle and erasure of whiteness

Lewis and Orbinski have come to prominence as spokespeople for the ideal of global citizenship and the causes of development aid and humanitarianism. They are in demand as speakers and each has been the subject of documentary films with mass distribution, primarily through television. In their writing, both identify causes of suffering and poverty, and Lewis, in particular, provides compelling critiques of the disastrous impacts of Western-mandated structural adjustment programmes in Africa (Lewis 2005; Orbinski 2008).[3] However, the documentaries produce them as figures of global citizenship in ways that elide an analysis of the causes of the suffering they witness, never mind an analysis of why these particular men are in the position to help. *Triage* chronicles Orbinski's return to many of the communities in which he worked with MSF. The film presents Orbinski's reflections on the violence he witnessed in Somalia, Rwanda, and the Democratic Republic of Congo, and provides a commentary on his suffering as well as the project of humanitarianism. While Stephen Lewis is not the subject of *Their Brothers' Keepers*, his face and voice narrate the stories of two child-headed households in Zambia. Lewis fulfils the expert role, providing context and analysis. The film begins with Lewis's claim that '*we* have failed to subdue the pandemic' and concludes with his invocation that '*we* are our brothers' keepers' (quoted in Mullins 2005, emphasis added). In contrast, in the CBC documentary, *The Value of Life: AIDS in Africa Revisited* (Jackson 2004), Lewis is the subject of an episode of *The Nature of Things*.[4] I characterize Lewis and Orbinski as 'figures' of global citizenship because they are publicly well known and are represented as physical embodiments of the ideal. They also reveal the ways in which global citizenship remains a primarily symbolic or metaphorical construct to be figured.

In these films, both men are constructed as noble actors who undertake the responsibility to alleviate the suffering of Others. In part, the men are figured in the tradition of the white male (colonial) saviour. Adapting S.P. Mohanty's argument (1991) that whiteness in colonial India was either invisible or eminently spectacular, I argue that while the representation of Lewis and Orbinski as global citizens relies on a spectacle of whiteness, whiteness is nonetheless erased rather than simply unmarked or unnamed; they are figured as performing a post-racial benevolence. In scene after scene in these documentaries, Lewis and Orbinski are shown in gatherings of African people in need, or with African friends and colleagues, arrangements that figure their presence in Africa as evidence of humanitarianism's post-racial ethic. However, the spectacle of their presence as white men in Africa and on screen is crucial to the films' messages. The men are positioned in such a way as to represent (i.e. describe) the suffering of Others elsewhere. Yet they also represent this Other in a political sense, in that they speak for them, often quite literally. For instance, in one scene in *Triage*, Orbinski asks a Somali man about the murder of an expatriate doctor, but Orbinski's retelling of the man's response is superimposed over the man's own voice. Further, the trauma these men experience as witnesses to the suffering of Others elsewhere is foregrounded in the films. The story of the individuated subject focuses on Lewis's and Orbinski's suffering, figuring the benevolence of the global citizen. As a reviewer of *Triage* puts it, 'the documentary affords a glimpse into Orbinski's heart, and by extension, the heart of humanitarianism: our capacity for decency' (Sibbald 2008, p. 1192). The films do not posit a relationship between the viewer and the person suffering somewhere else, but rather one between the viewer and the figure of global citizenship.

While the films document Lewis's and Orbinski's good deeds, the men are presented as benevolent, or as those who *are* good. *The Value of Life* begins with images of Stephen Lewis welcomed to a village by singing children. David Suzuki's introductory narration tells how the film will trace Lewis's journey 'from hope to despair to hope again' (Jackson 2004). In a voice-over, while he sits on the floor of a home with a child in his arms, Lewis states:

> I'd moved from frustration to anger; I've moved from anger to rage because I don't understand how people can't absorb the truth that in ten to fifteen years from now those countries will be falling apart. 'Till my dying day I will never forgive the western countries for all the lives that were needlessly lost.
> (Jackson 2004)

As the film traces his visits to a variety of African countries, Lewis's emotional distress is foregrounded in a way that dehistoricizes the suffering that affects him. As Sherene Razack (2004, p. 19) argues, we talk of the pain of the 'peacekeeper' in a way that forecloses recognition of the colonial violence of which the peacekeeper is a part. The emphasis on the stories and trauma of the figure of global citizenship reflects Fassin's (2007, p. 507) contention that within the 'politics of life' there is a distinction between 'the *zoe* of "populations" who can only passively await the bombs and the aid workers, and the *bios* of the "citizens of the world", the humanitarians who come to render them assistance'. The humanitarian worker is the speaking subject and the subject who willingly risks his safety. As global citizens, Lewis and Orbinski are admirable for achieving a post-racial ethic through which they regard the human dignity of the Other; but, paradoxically, it is precisely their positioning as white and male that provides for their spectacular benevolence. The pained expressions on the men's faces and the film's close takes of their eyes or hands make visible an emotional suffering that the figures also articulate through their stories. In contrast, those suffering from poverty and war are represented only as physical through photographs of their wounds or their bodies. The psychic aspects of their experiences are represented by Lewis and Orbinski. The global citizen's performance of compassion marks the repudiation of race, or its relegation to the past, but the spectacle of the feeling white man who bears witness to the suffering Other depends on Euro-American cultural norms of racial and gender identity. The compassion and decency of global citizenship is marked by the undoing of the expectations of white masculinity, an undoing that only a white male can perform.

As figures of global citizenship, Orbinski and Lewis are presented as men who have left their country to travel to an elsewhere, surrounded by human beings in need, all of whom are very specifically coded as black. Orbinski and Lewis are often depicted either interacting with African children or recounting stories of their interactions with these children. In *The Value of Life*, for instance, Lewis describes his desire to reconnect with a young girl he had met in Rwanda in 2001, who, he recounts over footage of the original visit, 'attached herself physically to me' (Jackson 2004). He describes how there was a look of abandonment in her eyes when he left, and how her 'sweet little face [was] etched in [his] mind'. His 'reunion' with her in 2003 depicts the two embracing as Lewis narrates, 'we are attached to each other'. He explains that 'the mother' is dying of AIDS and that she and her daughter are depressed and anxious. Lewis re-presents them in the sense that he makes meaning of their bodies, and he represents them in the political sense because the child and her mother do not speak. The image of Lewis physically embracing the child figures their relationship – which consists of two brief meetings two years apart – as a mutual and meaningful emotional bond, which belies the power relations inherent in the historically repeated image of the white male humanitarian and the redeemable black child (Dogra 2012).

Scenes like this, which recur so often within development marketing more generally, reflect the paradoxical positioning of whiteness within discourses of benevolence, where the object/Other is always racialized as not white, and is usually a child. Richard Dyer (1997, p. 45) describes how 'whites must be seen to be white, yet whiteness as race resides in invisible properties and whiteness as power is maintained by being unseen'. In the examples of these figures of global citizenship, benevolence needs to be both seen as white at the same time that whiteness, or race, appears to be repudiated. As feeling, benevolent people, Lewis's and Orbinski's authority to speak of and for the suffering of Others is reinforced by being (un)seen, and marked against the images of African children, and African friends and colleagues who are figured as peers, rather than bodies in need. In *The Value of Life*, Graça Machel, the African humanitarian, politician, and third-wife of Nelson Mandela, is presented as Lewis's colleague, standing beside him in a couple of scenes. The narrator explains how Lewis 'enlisted' this high profile African woman into the fight against HIV/AIDS (Jackson 2004). Similarly, in *Triage*, Orbinski is reunited with a Somali colleague named Lesto, who, the viewer is told, saved Orbinski's life on numerous occasions. However, it is Orbinski's story of paying to save Lesto from certain death that is narrated by Orbinski in the film. Unlike the colonist saviour of the white man's burden, the figure of the global citizen is authenticated by the assertion of emotional bonds to Africans.

Lewis and Orbinski's ability to speak of and for those suffering seems to reflect the way they undo race or subvert their whiteness. In one scene in *Triage*, Orbinski visits the King Faisal Hospital in Kigali, where MSF was stationed during the Rwandan genocide. The film presents Orbinski entering a room to meet a group of his Rwandan colleagues from 1994. Rather than showing this reunion, the film cuts from the meeting to present an extended scene of Orbinski providing a tour to the current director general of the hospital, John Stevens, who is also white. Over images of Orbinski showing Stevens what he witnessed in the hospital during the genocide, a voice-over by Orbinski explains that the director was unaware of what had happened and that his ignorance of the genocide as 'the defining moment of that country' is a 'huge tragedy' (Reed 2008). Orbinski reflects on the importance of cultural memory and speaks with the authority of the native. As the tour guide, Orbinski is the object of the gaze for both the viewer and Stevens and it is *his* experience of witnessing the genocide that is narrated in place of the experiences of his Rwandan colleagues. In this scene, Stevens's apparent ignorance of the place seems marked by *his* whiteness and foreignness. As a figure of the global citizen, Orbinski is situated against Stevens's ignorance and insensitivity, his whiteness. Orbinski's implicit castigating of Stevens is a spectacular performance of how he has transcended race, or whiteness, to perform a post-racial identity.

There is one moment in the film, however, where race, or 'culture', is overtly referenced, and it troubles the ideal of a common humanity that Orbinski otherwise seems to be presented as figuring. Reflecting on the personal trauma that he experienced as a witness to the horrors of the Rwandan genocide, Orbinski states:

> My experience of coming back from Rwanda ... it was an experience of despair. How do you get out of this? This is what we are. I am this. I am capable of this. My culture is capable. We did it. You know? As this was happening, as genocide was happening here in Rwanda, war crimes, ethnic cleansing, rape, genocide was happening simultaneously in the former

Yugoslavia. At the very same time. That's our culture. That's where we come from. You know? We are capable of that.

(Reed 2008)

When Orbinski first utters the pronoun 'we' in this passage, he seems to be acknowledging that he was a part of the genocide, and not outside it as a foreign bystander or witness. But after introducing the simultaneity and similarity of the Yugoslavian war, he remarks that 'that's our culture' and that 'we are capable of that', statements that seem to represent a white/European 'we' rather than a postracial human 'we'. This monologue is accompanied by two photographs depicting the war in the former Yugoslavia: one of elderly women sitting by a fence and the other of the bare backs of emaciated men illuminated by the sun. These images contrast starkly with the film's graphic imagery of mutilated and suffering Rwandan bodies, from that country's genocide. This contrast reflects an example of 'the politics of life' Fassin identifies: the black body can be rendered, here for a Canadian audience, bare or abject in a way that the white body cannot.

Orbinski's reflections on 'our'/white capability to *also* commit genocide or the idea that Lewis is 'haunted by a world that looks the other way' (Jackson 2004), suggest the possibility of critical self-reflection, but, in both cases, these films construct Orbinski and Lewis, as innocent, outside, and intervening through a compulsion to help; as global citizens, they are separate from the Western governments who fail to act or contrasted with the 'bad' white person who is ignorant and insensitive. Yet, in the tradition of the white man's burden, these films reaffirm their responsibility to care for the suffering Other. As I have argued, while the rhetoric of global citizenship that informs these films presents these men as figures of benevolence in a way that seems to articulate a post- or nonracial cultural politics, such post-racialism serves to elide historical, structural, and racially experienced forms of domination and inequality. At the same time that global citizenship relies on the authority of the white male voice, this voice is paradoxically de-raced through the spectacle of the benevolent figure's positioning in Africa. In the next section I extend this analysis of the post-racial politics of benevolence to interrogate how global citizenship affirms the status of full humanity as benevolence. In other words, humanity, or the modern, is marked by the responsibility to help Others.

Bridges that Unite, pluralism, and benevolence

The travelling development-education exhibit, *Bridges that Unite*, was presented by the AKFC in seven cities between 2008 and 2010, including Halifax, where I viewed it in the autumn of 2009. The AKFC is part of the Aga Khan Development Network (AKDN), 'a family of private, non-denominational development agencies' that work in the areas of education, health care, microfinance, private sector enterprise, and the restoration of cultural sites, in order to 'improv[e] living conditions and opportunities for the poor, without regard to faith, origin or gender' (*Bridges that Unite* 2009). *Bridges that Unite* educates viewers on the work the AKDN has done in collaboration with the government of Canada over the past twenty-five years. More importantly, it seeks to challenge 'simplistic ideas of what development looks like' by depicting the successes of community-based and cooperative development projects (Shariff 2008). The exhibit and its supplementary materials (website, teaching resources, etc.) repeatedly invoke the idea of Canada's leadership role in development in the terms of global citizenship, with the figure of the global citizen articulated in a section of the exhibition highlighting 'Agents of Change'. The *Bridges that Unite* exhibit relies upon what Lilie Chouliaraki (2010, p. 112) describes as 'positive image appeals'. This strategy is unlike the ways in which development agencies have traditionally relied upon a 'moral emphasis of pity' or, more recently, brand-based relations of consumer affiliation with development agencies. The exhibition focuses on the work of local individuals and groups in their communities. These people are named and presented shaping their own futures, an exhibition strategy through which the foreign Other is presented to the Canadian viewer of the exhibit as having capabilities, and not simply need.

However, the exhibition by no means provides a radical reinterpretation of the problem of global poverty. Rather, by asserting that the AKDN provides 'a hand up instead of a handout' (Classroom Connections 2009, p. 1), the exhibit reflects the slow shift from charity towards the idea(l)s of exchange and partnership in North Atlantic-based development agency rhetoric. The development project nonetheless focuses on the problem of 'poverty' rather than structural inequality. Development is presented as remedying the Other's lack, which is defined against a normative notion of Canadian democracy, education, consumerism, and multiculturalism. There is no engagement with *why* Canadians are in a position to provide 'a hand up' or *why* people in Africa and Asia are in need of our aid or 'partnership'. Exhibit signs and descriptions reaffirm the idea that Canada empowers others, and that local development projects are *dependent upon* Canadian support. In the section on Afghanistan, for instance, elections, women's ability to access education, and the restoration of cultural landmarks is attributed to 'Canadian leadership'. While the exhibit states that Afghanistan has been 'ravaged by decades of war', there is no acknowledgement that Canada has been a military partner to the US and NATO political entities that Malalai Joya, a suspended Afghanistan parliament member, describes as having 'occupied my country' (Joya 2010). Suffering and poverty are localized, as if they exist outside global historical or social contexts, including the context of the racially coded security discourse of the 'war on terror'. The question, 'What is Canada's role in a world where poverty and hopelessness thrive?' on a large banner, welcomes viewers into the exhibition hall and shapes the exhibit's pedagogical strategies from the beginning. Although all of the projects depicted in the exhibit are sponsored by the AKDN, the history and structure of the network are marginalized within a narrative of Canadian goodwill. The sentence 'in a world that remains troubled,

Canada is needed more than ever' is repeated on panels and banners throughout the exhibition.

In her analysis of the Canadian peacekeeper mythology, Sherene Razack suggests that Canada is much more in need of the world than the world is in need of Canada to keep peace. She concludes that we use suffering Others 'to reconstitute ourselves as white knights and as victims, taking ourselves out of their histories' (2004, p. 166). Narratives of Canada's place in the world are historically constructed through race, at least implicitly. When the dynamic of race within development discourse has been taken up, critics have focused on critiquing development as the continuation of the colonial 'white man's burden'. In *Desire for Development* Barbara Heron (2007, p. 9) contends that 'whiteness is constituted through doing what is "right"'. The development enterprise validates northern bourgeois superiority within the enduring idea of progress, wherein the white subject gains a 'sense of *entitlement and obligation* to intervene globally' in order to better the lives of others (p. 36; original emphasis). In Heron's and Maria Eriksson Baaz's (2005) studies, research interviews with white European and Canadian development workers are used to argue that development work constitutes the performance of whiteness. As I argue above, race is crucial to understanding how Orbinski and Lewis are produced as figures of the global citizen. However, if we limit the examples of benevolence to the representation of white development workers, to what extent do we foreclose recognition of a more complex racial politics of contemporary formulations of benevolence?

Canada is marked as white when development agencies such as World Vision or Plan Canada appeal to Canadians to sponsor a child and 'give a gift of hope' (Plan Canada 2010). In these agencies' television appeals the spokespeople and Canadian sponsors are almost always coded as white, in contrast to the faces of the children in need of aid, who are always brown or black. The *Bridges that Unite* exhibit represents AKDN workers as 'Agents of Change', which suggests an overtly paternalistic relationship that contradicts the presentation of local individuals determining their own futures in the other components of the exhibit. The individuals profiled as 'Agents of Change' in scrapbooks and via computer terminals in the exhibition reflect Canada's racial, ethnic, and religious diversity, perhaps disproportionately so.[5] The collection of narratives and photographs provided by the AKFC workers reflects the Aga Khan's characterization of Canada as a model of pluralism, with a responsibility to share its 'national genius' with the rest of the world (Aga Khan 2008, p. 49). In *Where Hope Takes Root* (2008), the Aga Khan writes that Canada is 'able to harness the best from different groups, because [its] civil society is not bound by a specific language or race or religion' (p. 49).[6] As a result, the normative racial coding of the development enterprise is disrupted; the benevolent actor is not necessarily white.

This presumption of Canada as a pluralist state and meritocracy, and hence a model for cosmopolitanism, is in marked contrast to Thobani's contention that whiteness retains its exalted status within the politics of Canadian multiculturalism. Thobani (2007, p. 148) argues that within Canada's multicultural ethos, 'white people [are] constituted as tolerant and respectful of difference and diversity, while non-white people [are] instead constructed as perpetually and irredeemably monocultural, in need of being taught the virtues of tolerance and cosmopolitanism'. In the example of the Agents of Change narratives, however, it is predominantly non-white, non-Christian Canadians who expound upon Canada's moral leadership. In my analysis, I focus on the profiles of Agents of Change who appear racialized as not white. For instance, one Agent of Change asserts that Canada's 'approach to difference and diversity is important' and that 'Canada values a pluralist, multicultural society', unlike the United States. Another Agent who self-identifies as an immigrant who has chosen to live in Canada, contends that 'One of the unique things about Canada is its ethnic diversity. So when people are exposed to difference they realize that at the end of the day we are human'. More standard development rhetoric describing the 'chaos' of India or how helping others is personally satisfying is also evident in these narratives, though more often by Agents who I would read as coded as white. As well, photographs with captions that identify 'typical villages' and unnamed 'African girls', are features of many of the profiles. Despite the colonial echoes of the term 'Agent of Change' and the rhetoric of many of the narratives presented in the exhibition, the benevolence of the Agents is constituted not by whiteness, per se, but by the ideal of pluralism, both rhetorically and in the composition of the profiles of a diverse group of Agents.

If civility, tolerance, and cosmopolitanism have been produced as specifically white characteristics in the Canadian context, how do we account for this emphasis upon pluralism as necessary for the development project? In her work on transnational solidarity activists, Gada Mahrouse (2008, p. 90) defines whiteness as a discursive location that is not synonymous with skin colour and so 'the boundaries of whiteness shift over time and place'. Although her work focuses primarily on activists who self-identify as white, she contends that 'as Westerners who carry the Canadian passport, in those geographical contexts, the activists of colour also came to represent whiteness, albeit to a lesser degree' (Mahrouse 2009, p. 671). The way in which these boundaries shift makes this sense of whiteness particularly unstable and its privileges for the visibly not-white person tenuous. For instance, reflecting on her own position as a woman of colour working on development projects in Bangladesh, Uma Khotari (2006) identifies how expertise is often associated with white skin in the development context. Her position as an ex-patriot consultant *and* racialized (as not white) woman breaches 'the previously stable boundary between "us" and "them"' (p. 16).

Many of the Agent of Change profiles assert a celebratory Canadian pluralism as the basis for an Agent's desire to aid others; however, there are a couple of examples that trouble the hegemonic rhetoric of white-Canadian benevolence. One profiled worker, for instance, describes how he was able to utilize his skills in wireless technology to volunteer for His Highness the Aga Khan in Afghanistan. This narrative is one of the few that overtly identifies with the Aga Khan and the AKDN, rather than with Canada. While the exhibition repeats the notion that 'the world needs more Canada', the Aga Khan's assertion that 'the average Afghan wants the same things as every normal person' appropriates 'normal' from its Canadian associations with whiteness, while nonetheless constructing it within familiarly modern terms: 'normal' people want democratic elections, schools, and decent transportation systems. Another profiled Agent of Change describes how the childhood experience of being a Boy Scout taught him the value of volunteerism, which he describes as a critical dimension of Canadian identity and the humanistic principles of Islamic ethics. These two examples allude to the way in which we can see the AKDN's development philosophy as distinct from Western humanitarianism. While the AKDN provides examples of benevolence, they also reflect the way in which the structure of 'attitudes' that underwrite benevolence are neither singular nor reducible to the performance of white identity.

In *Where Hope Takes Root*, the Aga Khan expresses his frustration with Western media representations of the AKDN as philanthropic or entrepreneurial. He writes: 'What is not understood is that this work is, for us, a part of our institutional responsibility. It flows from the office of Imam to improve the quality of worldly life for the concerned communities' (2008, p. 126). While he emphasizes that the Islamic values of unity within diversity, patience, tolerance, and open communication, are consistent with Christian teachings, he argues that tolerance has come to be associated with the secular in the West, while religion is associated with intolerance. While many Canadian development non-governmental organizations (NGOs) continue to imply a Christian framework for the project of aid, the construction of Orbinski and Lewis as cosmopolitan figures, and the rhetoric of global citizenship more generally, reflect the way in which the obligation to aid others is produced as secular. For example, large orange signs throughout the *Bridges that Unite* exhibit identify various ways that development is 'the way forward for Canada'. In Canada, an attitude and frame of reference for benevolence is the presumption of Canadian exceptionality: Canada is fortunate, tolerant, and pluralist, apparently unlike other places in the world, particularly those places in need of aid. To some degree, the Aga Khan reaffirms this perception, arguing that Canadians have the obligation of 'sharing the many forms of human knowledge and experience that create and sustain a civil society of quality' (2008, p. 54). In order to do so, we 'must see real enrichment in life's purpose in [our] willingness to help' (p. 54). The Aga Khan's discomfort with Western understandings of humanitarianism and his proviso of how we understand our ethical role as helpers, reflects the limits of reducing the contemporary discourse of benevolence to whiteness.

In a presentation on the AKDN, Noha Nasser describes how Ismailis challenge traditional notions of nation and identity. As a de-territorialized community that has no desire to create a homeland, Ismaili identity is not imagined within the framework of the nation or country (Nasser n.d.). Ismailis conceive themselves as having a transnational identity, or both Canadian and transnational identities, which might suggest a somewhat different structure of reference for humanitarianism from that of the dominant framework for development and global citizenship in Canada. Lewis and Orbinski's status as global citizens is performed by leaving their home nation to help or represent Others elsewhere, in other countries. The *Bridges that Unite* exhibition, however, reinforces the notion of Canadian exceptionality in such a way as to almost completely usurp the Ismaili ethical framework. The Ismaili values the Aga Khan describes are absent from the exhibit, in any overt way, apart from the narratives of a few Agents of Change. Nonetheless, if the transnational is not simply an aspiration or ideal but a structure of reference that shapes one's understanding of place and identity, does the AKDN escape the colonial implications of benevolence? To what extent is the structure of reference for AKDN workers who conceive their identities as both Canadian *and* transnational different from the structure of reference for Lewis, Orbinski, or Heron's research subjects, who conceive their moral responsibility more in line with Appiah's cosmopolitan ethics, as exerting a will to care beyond family, community, or country?

Narda Razack (2009) suggests that a complex form of positioning and identity is common to all people in Canada who are racialized as not white. She argues that many racialized Canadians are marginalized and their ancestral homelands are regarded as degenerate. Many share mixed feelings about being Canadian, feelings which reinforce affiliations to the homeland and beyond that are distinct from white Canadian identity (Razack, N 2009, pp. 16, 17).[7] Reflecting on her own positioning during a work trip to her birth country Trinidad, Razack recognizes that she 'perceived how our scripts in the North are continuously tinged with the stains of neo and post colonialism and imperialistic traditions', and she recognizes that her 'context and struggles differed significantly from [her] "local" colleagues' (Razack, N 2000, p. 76). Similarly, Rasna Warah reflects on how her interview with Mberita Katela, a woman living in Nairobi's Kibera slum, served to translate the woman into little more than the example of a statistic:

> I was objectifying her, seeing her as part of a problem that needed to be solved ... This allowed me to perceive her as being 'different' from me and bestowed on her an 'otherness' that clearly placed her as my inferior, worthy of my sympathy.
>
> (Warah 2008, p. 4)

Although Warah is differently situated in the development context from the white volunteers that Heron and Baaz study, she has nonetheless internalized benevolence in a way she characterizes as distinctly 'self-serving'.

For those Agents of Change featured in the *Bridges that Unite* exhibition who are racialized as not white, development work overseas may also be seen as a way to assert their belonging to the nation in terms of the imaginary of tolerance and pluralism. Further, the words, actions, and photographic presence of development workers who are racialized as not white in the exhibition, reinforces the idea that Canada *is* the pluralist, tolerant state it purports to be; the diverse, educated group of Agents of Change provide proof of Canada's multicultural civility. However, the narratives that frame development work in terms of the ethics of Islam, rather than nation, trouble the idea that benevolence is distinctly white-Canadian. To return to Mamdani's formulation of Culture Talk, the representation of the Agents of Change emphasizes culture and difference over relations of power and privilege, and reflects ideals that can be associated with the good, modern, or respectable Muslim. Although I recognize that the AKFC may have a number of reasons for framing their work in terms of Canadian identity, the fact that the AKDN's history and philosophy is so muted in comparison to the rhetoric of Canadian exceptionalism and leadership, is particularly significant. In this respect it is important to remember that the contemporary discourse that underwrites global citizenship coexists with discourses of security through which the foreign/Muslim/Other is produced as a threat.[8]

While the figure of the global citizen who is racialized as not white or as Muslim is not the 'same' as the white male figure, it is nonetheless a figure of benevolence. These alternate narratives within the *Bridges that Unite* exhibit provide distinct structures of attitude (Islamic ethics) and reference (transnational identity) but ultimately reinforce the prevailing norm that 'we' Canadians are enablers and capacity builders in a world divided in structural terms between the fortunate and unfortunate. The exhibit reinforces hegemonic narratives of Canadian identity as innocent, peaceable, and exceptional. As such, it reaffirms the material politics of benevolence and our 'sense of *entitlement and obligation* to intervene globally' (Heron 2007, p. 36). I have sought to acknowledge a complex racial politics of the shifting, unstable positioning of the racialized or marginalized Canadian in reference to white normativity in the *Bridges that Unite* exhibit; however, the exhibit does not disturb the colonial politics of benevolence so much as reveal the way in which benevolence cannot be limited to whiteness. Rather, benevolence may be characterized as the signature of modernity.

Benevolence as the signature of modernity

I identify benevolence as the signature of modernity because the structure of attitude and reference that benevolence provides in the contemporary Canadian and North Atlantic context is not figured as the performance of whiteness. Rather, benevolence is articulated as the recognition of the dignity of the unfortunate Other as human, not regardless of race, but as if there is no history of race and racism. Benevolence has become associated with tolerance and pluralism, which ironically affirm Canadian distinction in the examples I have analysed. As Thobani (2007) argues, tolerance is associated with whiteness, maintaining the exalted status of the white citizen against the racialized Other who needs to be taught tolerance. Yet, I think tolerance and pluralism can also be seen as associated with a sense of the modern that is not always confined to white/Western identity. The Aga Khan invokes the idea of modernization in a way that seems consistent with theories of global citizenship, cosmopolitanism, and Canadian civility, although it is derived from a tradition and worldview that is not Western. Each of the examples I have discussed affirms the ideal of progress towards a modernity that Canada (and the North Atlantic) are presented as having already 'achieved': democracy, equality, human rights, multiculturalism. To argue that benevolence is the signature of modernity is not to suggest that benevolence no longer reflects racial discourses because colour-blindness is articulated through its rhetoric. As figures of global citizenship, Lewis and Orbinski articulate their humanitarian ethics and are represented in a way that shows the continued significance of the cultural capital of whiteness, and particularly white masculinity. They embody whiteness, but they perform modernity. They are the subject of reverence, or models of global citizenship, because (as white men) they espouse modern ideals of compassion, respect for others and colour-blindness.

While Paul Gilroy argues that forms of 'identity and solidarity that derive from class, gender, sexuality and region, have made a strong sense of racial difference unthinkable to the point of absurdity', he also contends that despite the lack of 'any strong belief in integral races', racism continues to be enacted (2005, pp. 120, 122). What I characterize as the signature of modernity reflects this deep ambivalence: what Gilroy describes as racism without race. Benevolence affirms our common humanity at the same time that discourses of security reconstitute a racially ordered world, constructing ever greater anxiety about who belongs and who does not belong to the nation. As Sherene Razack (2009, pp. 818–19) contends, however, the humanitarian impulse reflects a 'nasty racial subtext': 'Can a Canadian imagine himself without these bodies of colour?'

I have argued that benevolence is no longer confined to the white subject but it is still informed by race thinking. The racial subtext of benevolence is the fact that the body in need is always depicted as brown or black in the documentaries or the development education exhibit. The racial subtext is the way in which the humanitarian's spectacular assertions of the Other's dignity reinforce the humanitarian's distinction as more fully human. Following Fassin's 'politics of life', humanitarians are actors capable of self-awareness and self-representation, and their risk is marked and mourned against the expendability of the life of the Other. The 'poor' are homogenized and essentialized. Without history or character, they are to be represented, explained, pitied, and saved. Pheng Cheah (2006, p. 11) argues that 'the efficacy of these new cosmopolitanisms is generated by, and structurally dependent on, the active exploitation and impoverishment of the peripheral majorities'. Benevolence, as a structure of attitude and reference, produces violence and structural inequality as poverty and misfortune; our relationship with the Other in need begins when we ask ourselves how we can help. In this way, global citizenship is marked by both the performance of white civility and pluralism and tolerance; however, the performance of global citizenship as an act of will to care for distant Others denies histories of race and racism at the same time that it reinforces the complex ontology of inequality that is the ongoing legacy of colonial racism.

Notes

1 This chapter provides, with permission from University of Toronto Press, a revised version of an article published in *Topia: Canadian Journal of Cultural Studies*, vol. 25 (2011).
2 For instance, in November 2019, Stephen Lewis was the featured speaker at an event addressing the question of what a 'good global citizen' should do 'in an era of rising populism, cynicism and challenges to the post-war institutions of the West' (https://harthouse.ca/events/opportunity-lost-a-call-to-global-action-in-the-age-of-trump), educational materials for the Stephen Lewis Foundation address students as global citizens (www.stephenlewisfoundation.org/assets/files/SLF_Schools_Flyer_Dec2015.pdf), and his book *Race against Time* (2005) is listed as a resource for global citizenship in an issue of *Global Citizen Digest* (www.centennialcollege.ca/pdf/global_citizen_digest/Winter-2011.pdf). Similarly, a media release highlighting the participation of James Orbinski in a 2018 Water for Peace event is titled, 'Being Canadian Means Being a Global Citizen' (www.newswire.ca/news-releases/being-canadian-means-being-a-global-citizen-687321001.html), and both his memoir and the documentary *Triage* (2008) are featured as resources in Elementary Teachers Federation of Ontario resource, *Educating for Global Citizenship* (http://etfo.net/globaled/Educating4GlobalCitizenship.pdf).
3 While both critique global economic structures to some degree, their criticism of North Atlantic states focuses much more on their failure to do enough to 'help' rather than their role in producing underdevelopment. The action that they identify as the work of humanitarians emphasizes aid rather than structural change.
4 The CBC series, *The Nature of Things* has produced a second episode focusing on Lewis, *Stephen Lewis: The Man Who Couldn't Sleep* (2009).
5 Heron notes that Canadian development workers tend to be white women (2007, pp. 158–9). Because of their focus on white participants, the research of Heron and Baaz implies that development workers are homogeneously white.
6 The network was founded and is guided by His Highness the Aga Khan, the 49th hereditary Imam of the Shia Ismaili Muslims (AKDN 2007).
7 Currently there is limited research on the experience and motivations of development and solidarity workers who are racialized as not white. See: Eguren and Mahoney (1997), Khotari (2006), Ojelay-Surtees (2004), Weber (2006).
8 See Biccum (this volume, Chapter 7) for analysis of the connections between 'development' and 'security' discourses at the international level.

References

Aga Khan 2008, *Where hope takes root: democracy and pluralism in an interdependent world*, Douglas & Mcintyre, Vancouver.
Aga Khan Development Network (AKDN) 2007, *About us*, viewed 30 July 2010, www.akdn.org/about.asp.
Andreotti, V 2006, 'Soft versus critical global citizenship education', *Policy & Practice: A Development Education Review*, vol. 3, pp. 40–51.
Appiah, KA 2006, *Cosmopolitanism: ethics in a world of strangers*, WW Norton, New York.
Baaz, ME 2005, *The paternalism of partnership: a postcolonial reading of development and aid*, Zed, London.
Bridges that Unite 2009, Exhibition, Pier 21 Canadian Immigration Museum, Halifax, Nova Scotia.

Cheah, P 2006, *Inhuman conditions: on cosmopolitanism and human rights*, Harvard University Press, Cambridge, MA.

Chouliaraki, L 2010, 'Post-humanitarianism: humanitarian communication beyond the politics of pity', *International Journal of Cultural Studies*, vol. 13, no. 2, pp. 107–26.

Classroom Connections 2009, *Bridges that unite: an exploration of international development. A teaching resource for use in grades 5–8 social science, social studies and geography*, viewed 3 October 2019, www.classroomconnections.ca/en/btu.php.

Dogra, N 2012, *Representations of global poverty: aid, development, and international NGOs*, I.B. Tauris, London.

Dower, N 2003, *An introduction to global citizenship*, Edinburgh University Press, Edinburgh.

Dyer, R 1997, *White*, Routledge, London.

Eguren, L and Mahoney L 1997, *Unarmed bodyguards: international accompaniment for the protection of human rights*, Kumarian, West Hartford, CT.

Fassin, D 2007, 'Humanitarianism as a politics of life', *Public Culture*, vol. 19, no. 3, pp. 499–520.

Foster, C 2005, *Where race does not matter: the new spirit of modernity*, Penguin, Toronto.

Frankenberg, R 1993, *White women, race matters: the social construction of whiteness*, University of Minnesota Press, Minneapolis.

Gilroy, P 2005, *Postcolonial melancholia*, Columbia University Press, New York.

Goldberg, DT 2009, *The threat of race: reflections on racial neoliberalism*, Blackwell, Malden, MA.

Heron, B 2007, *Desire for development: whiteness, gender and the helping imperative*, Wilfrid Laurier University Press, Waterloo, ON.

Jackson, J Dir. 2004, 'The value of life: AIDS in Africa revisited', *The nature of things*, DVD, CBC Television, Toronto.

Joya, M 2010, 'Time Magazine's sneaky way of muffling the message of an Afghan peace activist', interview with Sonali Kolhatkar, *ZNet*, viewed 13 February 2020, https://zcomm.org/znetarticle/time-magazines-sneaky-way-of-muffling-the-message-of-an-afghan-peace-activist-by-malalai-joya/.

Khotari, U 2006, 'An agenda for thinking about "race" in development', *Progress in Development Studies*, vol. 6, pp. 9–23.

Lewis, S 2005, *Race against time*, House of Anansi, Toronto.

Mahrouse, G 2008, 'Race-conscious transnational activists with cameras: mediators of compassion', *International Journal of Cultural Studies*, vol. 11, pp. 87–105.

Mahrouse, G 2009, 'The compelling story of the white/Western activist in the war zone: examining race, neutrality, and exceptionalism in citizen journalism', *Canadian Journal of Communication*, vol. 34, pp. 659–74.

Mamdani, M 2005, *Good Muslim, bad Muslim: America, the Cold War, and the roots of terror*, Three Leaves/Doubleday, New York.

Mohanty, SP 1991, 'Drawing the color line: Kipling and the culture of colonial rule', in D LaCapra (ed.), *The bounds of race: perspectives on hegemony and resistance*, 311–43, Cornell University Press, Ithaca, NY.

Mullins, C Dir. 2005, *Their brothers' keepers: orphaned by AIDS*, DVD, Bullfrog Films, Oley, PA.

Nasser, N n.d., 'The Aga Khan Development Network: an Ismaili perspective on culture, transnationalism, and development in Pakistan', viewed 30 July 2010, bcgit.berkeley.edu/nasser_ppt.ppt.

Ojelay-Surtees, B 2004, 'Diversity in Oxfam GB: engaging the head and turning the heart', *Gender and Development*, vol. 2, pp. 56–67.

Orbinski, J 2008, *An imperfect offering: humanitarian action in the twenty-first century*, Doubleday, Toronto.

Plan Canada 2010, 'Gifts of hope', viewed 30 July 2010, http://plancanada.ca/Page.aspx?pid=1334.

Razack, N 2000, 'North/South collaborations: affecting transnational perspectives for social work', *Journal of Progressive Human Services*, vol. 11, pp. 71–91.

Razack, N 2009, 'Decolonizing the pedagogy and practice of international social work', *International Social Work*, vol. 52, no. 1, pp. 9–21.

Razack, S 2004, *Dark threats and white knights: the Somalia affair, peacekeeping, and the new imperialism*, University of Toronto Press, Toronto.

Razack, S 2008, *Casting out: the eviction of Muslims from Western law and politics*, University of Toronto Press, Toronto.

Razack, S 2009, 'Afterword', *University of Toronto Quarterly*, vol. 78, no. 2, pp. 815–20.

Reed, P Dir. 2008, *Triage: Dr. James Orbinski's humanitarian dilemma*. DVD, New Video Group, New York.

Riggs, D 2004a, 'Constructing the national good: Howard and the rhetoric of benevolence', Paper presented to the Australasian Political Studies Association Conference, University of Adelaide, Adelaide, Australia, viewed 30 July 2010, www.adelaide.edu.au/apsa/docs_papers/Others/Riggs.pdf.

Riggs, D 2004b, 'Benevolence and the management of stake: on being "good white people"', *Philament*, vol. 4, viewed 30 July 2010, http://sydney.edu.au/arts/publications/philament/issue4_Critique_Riggs.htm.

Said, E 1993, *Culture and imperialism*, Vintage, New York.

Shariff, K 2008, 'Why the world needs more Canada', *Vancouver Sun*, 12 June, viewed 30 July 2010, www2.canada.com/vancouversun/news/editorial/story.html?id=76d606cd-04fb-4df3-bb94-2a9cec821656.

Sibbald, B 2008, 'Human being', *Canadian Medical Association Journal*, vol. 178, pp. 1191–2.

Thobani, S 2007, *Exalted subjects: studies in the making of race and nation in Canada*, University of Toronto Press, Toronto.

Warah, R 2008, 'The development myth', in R Warah (ed.), *Missionaries, mercenaries, and misfits: an anthology*, 3–22, AuthorHouse, Milton Keynes.

Weber, C 2006, *Visions of solidarity: U.S. peace activists in Nicaragua from war to women's activism and globalization*, Lexington Books, Lanham, MD.

White, S 2002, 'Thinking race, thinking development', *Third World Quarterly*, vol. 23, pp. 407–19.

Chapter 10

The social entrepreneur as global citizen

A critical appraisal of a theory of social change

John Abraham

Introduction

In the first decade of the new millennium, Social Entrepreneurship (SE) appeared to offer a wellspring in what had become an otherwise parched political and economic policy landscape. This hybrid approach, and its allied concepts such as social innovation, seemed to address a deep-seated urgency to strike out in new directions where the old tried and tested approaches had failed. However, despite the much-heralded examples of its success, it remains unclear whether SE offers either a genuine break from the past or whether it can even claim unadulterated success. In this chapter, I will argue that in the current era of globalization, SE emerged as the individual personification of an attempt to resolve the failures of the left–right political antinomy in the Anglo-American sphere (Blond 2010). As such, it provided a means of preserving the myths of citizen vitality and empowerment, particularly at the global level, in the midst of political banality and economic uncertainty.

This chapter problematizes the emergence and consolidation of SE against the backdrop of Anglo-American politics of the late twentieth century. In the USA, the accentuation of urban poverty in the 1980s was met by a range of proposals that included everything from a more robust citizen volunteerism in 'a thousand points of light' to the ultimately misguided strategy of expanding home ownership through credit deregulation (Rajan 2010). Meanwhile the stillborn politics of the 'Big Society' in the UK, intended to supplant the eventual disenchantment with New Labour, failed to generate a rejuvenated citizen-led Conservatism (Jordan 2012). Ironically, rather than nurturing a revived global citizenry, both trajectories created the conditions for a resurgent nationalism, evident in Brexit and the election of Trump. In the problematic circumstances that generated these torrid outcomes, SE was proffered as a universal strategy utilized by dynamic and virtuous global citizens to initiate radical social transformations. These transformations had the seemingly additional advantage of requiring neither tax revenue nor charity.

The limits of this strategy, however, quickly become apparent when SE is understood both in its origins as well as in the manner in which it functions. I will begin by defining the social entrepreneur as a concept allied with the global citizen. I will then use the Marxist school of regulation theory to describe SE as an institutional form alongside current regimes of accumulation. Explained this way, the emergence of SE can be described as an ironic strategy to maintain the mode of regulation by depicting this very tool of the status quo as a transformative catalyst. I then show how the typical profile of the social entrepreneur demonstrates their embeddedness within existing institutional forms, implicating them as possible agents of the status quo rather than exclusively agents of change. I conclude with a short case study demonstrating how this positionality can fatally compromise the very goals of the social entrepreneur.

Global citizenship and the social entrepreneur

I begin by making the claim that the social entrepreneur and global citizen are allied and mutually supporting notions within a larger matrix of a neoliberal, political-economic order. As Chapman, Ruiz-Chapman and Eglin (2018) demonstrate, the notion of global citizenship assumes a particular type of subjectivity whose origins and positionality are obscured both to these subjects as well as those who subscribe to this notion. Classic definitions of SE (Dees 1998; Martin and Osberg 2007) describe it as the practice of particular actors who combine entrepreneurial initiative and empathetic awareness to create initiatives that maximize desirable social impacts while also being financially sustainable. To be sure, there are many possible modalities of SE (Lenssen et al. 2005; Zahra et al. 2009). However, implied across these descriptions is a social entrepreneur who acts as an external agent, articulating an otherwise obscure social challenge and using a set of specialized skills to simultaneously generate financially self-sustaining solutions.

Leaving aside the questionable entropic feasibility (Georgescu-Roegen 1971) of a self-replicating social activity that can at once generate greater order (more desirable social outcomes) while also producing the financial resources to sustain (and even grow) itself, such definitions are problematic for several reasons. For example, implicit in such a definition is that communities experiencing problems are not themselves able to generate their own solutions. They assume a priori that it is the skillset of entrepreneurship that comprises the essential tools required to enact positive and lasting change, rather than advocacy, design, traditional knowledge, activism and community-based organization. This is clearly not the case, as a growing body of research handily demonstrates (Ostrom 1990; Armitage, Charles and Berkes 2017).

It might still be argued, however, that many of the practices engaged by such communities could be described under the rubric of SE or its allied concepts. In many cases, SE is merely the label (or more accurately the brand) given to agents who enact such changes, whether or not they engage in practices that could narrowly be described as entrepreneurial. In such cases, change agents are unwitting social entrepreneurs and even include historical figures including Gandhi and

Florence Nightingale (Bornstein 2007). This seemingly innocent and descriptive application of the term SE is, however, deeply problematic. While this is at least an awkward anachronism, the application of such terminology potentially risks misunderstanding the core philosophy and methods of such figures (such as *satyagraha*) which may well run against the grain of SE. I will return to the significance of the flexible use of this term later in the chapter.

Furthermore, these definitions obfuscate the positionality of the social entrepreneur. The social entrepreneur typically constitutes an agent able to access higher education, and leverage substantial social and financial resources that would not otherwise be available to members of the communities they serve. In typical portrayals of social entrepreneurs, these attributes are often included incidentally, or even obscured, in favour of those that portray them as dynamic and innovative agents of change. In this there is much overlap with the individual attributes associated with the global citizen. These concepts, however, remain distinct due to the individual trajectories through which they have emerged. The significance of this is that the social entrepreneur therefore remains embedded within the culture, values and networks of the very restrictive systems they seek to disrupt. A rhetorical strategy used to resolve this seeming contradiction is to portray the social entrepreneur as a maverick and outsider, at once able to use these resources from within the system while effectively deploying them against the system. At the very least, this makes the social entrepreneur's activity fraught with the likelihood of unintentional but inevitable compromise. Once again, I will return to this later in the chapter.

I will conclude this section with an acknowledgement that within the broader stream of literature on the allied field of social innovation, there are questions around the prominent role ascribed to 'heroic' social entrepreneurs at the expense of multiple actors and stakeholders engaged in a process of social change (Dey and Steyaert 2010). Ultimately, the valorization of the social entrepreneur, and the celebration of the social transformation ascribed to their efforts, may well conceal the role that these actors play in maintaining rather than transforming the very circumstances they seek to change. In order to understand why, this chapter outlines the historical and political background to the emergence of SE using the analytical tools of regulation theory.

The historical trajectory of SE

In order to properly understand the operation of the concept of SE, it is necessary to understand its political and economic origins. In this section, I argue that SE emerged as a response to the particular economic context of the 1980s and, in particular, the emergence of the neoliberal economic order. I argue that SE seeks to 'normalize' the social and economic disparities that emerged during this decade, by offering ostensible solutions to these problems within the prevailing political and economic ideology of the era.

Drawing from the work of the Regulation School (Boyer and Saillard 2002, p. 36; Jessop and Sum 2006), I argue that SE is one response to the tendency that capitalism has towards crisis. According to this school, economic crises occur when a regime of accumulation cannot be supported by an existing mode of regulation. A mode of regulation 'normalizes' the inherent contradictions that exist and accumulate within a capitalist system. Modes of regulation are in turn underpinned by corresponding institutional forms. Institutional forms are defined as legal, economic and moral frameworks and norms, which allow for the contracting and constraining of economic activities. Within these institutional forms are embedded regimes of accumulation that constitute forms of wage relation and the accompanying modes of production particular to distinctive types of capitalist economies. A mode of regulation comes into existence when institutional forms and regimes of accumulation are articulated into a coherent form (Dunford 1990, p. 301). A mode of regulation reproduces the fundamental social relations that enable institutional forms and regimes of accumulation to operate and coordinate the many decentralized decisions required for this operation.

Modes of regulation are dynamic and have been shaped by successive economic crises over the twentieth century. These crises necessitated the development of new institutional forms and regimes of accumulation. Among the key institutional forms of the current mode of regulation is the idealization of SE. This idealization emerged at a time when social welfare was increasingly viewed as a matter of private rather than public priority. To understand the significance of this shift, it is necessary to recount the evolution of this current mode of regulation through the twentieth century from a time when the institutional forms that provided for social welfare moved from the public towards the private domain.

For this I begin with the global economic system that emerged at the beginning of the last century that was characterized by the eclipse of mercantile colonial empires by new industrial nation states. In creating the industrial consumer economy, these states applied the efficiencies of wartime industry to the domestic economy to create a mode of regulation characterized by increasing productivity gains, competition and investment in equipment. However, such a system was susceptible to instability and the economic crisis of the 1930s necessitated the shift in the mode of regulation to one characterized by high productivity, institutional forms of collective bargaining and regimes of accumulation emphasizing rising standards of living and mass consumption. The relations of production instituted by Henry Ford's eponymous company became the locus of a new regime of accumulation in which profits were maximized through waged, semi-skilled labourers who in turn could buy manufactured products (Jessop 1992).

Together, these arrangements constituted the post-war settlement in the Anglo-American sphere. While there is some debate on the actual form of this settlement (Toye 2013) the era was particularly marked by its orientation around the new ideals of the 'American Way' and the proposals for state welfare beginning with the Beveridge report and universal healthcare in the UK and the Great Society programmes in the US (Wall 2009). Highly regulated national economies employed a Fordist regime of accumulation and were reinforced by the global institutional form of the Keynesian consensus (Ikenberry 1992). Rejecting the laissez faire of the inter-war period, government fiscal policy was the preferred economic tool of democratically elected welfare states in Europe and the US, which would ensure sufficient economic demand through the course of the business cycle. Welfare states in turn guaranteed protections from personal tragedies. The post-war mode of regulation was therefore supported through institutional forms and regimes of accumulation guaranteeing social welfare and personal prosperity.

The significance of the post-war settlement and mode of regulation was the separate framing of personal human welfare within the ambit of the state and prosperity within that of the market. Until this time, individual human welfare largely remained vulnerable under existing legal frameworks (such as the Poor Laws) and relied on the interventions of religious groups and civil society organization for relief (Gladstone 1999). Such groups played an important role in allaying some of the most severe consequences of the growth of global capitalism over the previous two centuries. However, the inherent instability of this monopolist mode of regulation became apparent through the increasing costs of the state welfare systems (the Great Society programmes in the USA) as well as strategic conflicts in South East Asia (Vietnam, Cambodia) and the Middle East (Israel) that spelled the end of the Keynesian consensus. The introduction of price and wage controls by the Nixon administration did not effectively improve either inflation or unemployment until the formal abolishment of the post-war order by removing the American dollar from the gold peg. The political watershed of the late 1970s brought the global Keynesian economic system to its conclusion (Gilpin and Gilpin 2001).

Following this disruption in the global economic system, a new regime of accumulation and corresponding institutional forms emerged through a new ideological consensus that had been developed among a small group of émigré academics in the UK and the US. Several members within this group had experienced both the sclerotic bureaucracy of the declining Hapsburg Empire and the subsequent chaotic socialist revolutions in Europe. The members of the Mont Perelin Society argued against state intervention in the functioning of the economy and in favour of a greater emphasis on free markets (Hayek 1944; Friedman 1962). Following the formation of the Society in 1947, this ideological proposal percolated through a network of universities (namely the University of Chicago), industry funded think tanks (American Enterprise Institute, Cato Institute), media (Hoover Media Fellowships) and among prominent political champions (Goldwater 1960). The significance of this was the emphasis on autonomous individuals for human welfare and a corresponding negation of collective responsibility, implying the need for new institutional forms and regimes of accumulation that would shift the responsibility for human welfare from the collective to the individual sphere.

Within a decade of the Nixon shocks the Reagan and Thatcher governments implemented these ideas through a policy programme of economic 'neoliberalism'. In addition to the ideological orientation, allied institutional forms were created through reductions in public spending, the deregulation of prices and cuts to corporate and personal income taxes (Harvey 2007). For the first time since the post-war settlement, the role of the state in providing economic security was intentionally and drastically reduced in favour of an expanded role for economic markets. The institutional forms of this new ideological and policy consensus were accompanied by a newly emerging post-Fordist mode of accumulation characterized by specialization and flexible wages (Jessop 1996).

The effect of these policies was an extended period of economic growth, most intensively across global financial markets. This led to consequent expansions in credit, and a new cultural emphasis on individual consumption (Schor 1999). The collapse of the communist bloc countries ushered in a global, free market, liberal, political consensus (Fukuyama 1989), further entrenching these regimes. The gains of growth largely accumulated among limited sectors of the population, increasing socio-economic disparities and creating a climate for policy corrections (Irvin 2011). By the late 1980s, successive waves of fiscal austerity in the United States established a renewed urgency for the role of the non-profit sector in providing services for communities that the former welfare provisions of the public sector were no longer able to deliver. It is within this climate that the notion of SE was articulated as a solution to the unequal social and economic circumstances deriving from the new ideological and political consensus. Diverse meanings of the combination of the words 'social' and 'entrepreneur' are evident in various literatures prior to this time (Falk 1978; Johnson 1988). However, it is within this era that this concept begins to emphasize those attributes related to individual resourcefulness, as opposed to public spending, and targeting deep systemic change. Throughout the ensuing two decades, the notion of SE was further refined to this end (Waddock and Post 1991; Leadbeater 1997).

The new neoliberal consensus was further ratified when newly elected Democratic and Labour parties retrenched and even expanded these priorities under a 'Third Way', which advocated high economic growth in order to supposedly replenish welfare services that were starved over the previous decade (Giddens 1998, p. 129). After losing credibility in the post-cold war environment, remnants of the Left regrouped around the new policy orientation of the 'extreme middle' and its civil society counterpart, a newly emerging theory of social innovation (Mulgan 2006; Westley and Antadze 2010). Combining theoretical insights from ecology and community development, the social innovation framework has been used to understand how positive and lasting changes have been effected on seemingly intractable problems that emerge from the failure of government and markets.

As Third Way governments began to implement neoliberal economic agendas, SE became a beachhead into the mainstream for some elements on the political left that were twice marginalized through the delegitimization of socialism and the Third Way emphasis on positive social outcomes. After this contrived alliance between economic growth and public welfare collapsed in the global financial crisis, exacerbating social inequalities to levels not seen since the 1980s, the concept of SE gained currency as a method of radically transforming the circumstances of individuals supposedly without the ideological baggage of either side of the political argument. In what seemed to be a final attempt to mobilize the state to engender transformation, the British Conservative Party's promising Big Society programme was ultimately stillborn and failed to deliver its promise of a reinvigorated civil sector. Instead, the lasting legacy of the party's tenure in power appears to be the deeply divisive achievement of Brexit, making the need to break out into new directions even more urgent. But is the social entrepreneur a worthy and legitimate agent of change for the present circumstances? In order to properly weigh this question, I turn to a critical examination of the social entrepreneur as an agent of change.

Who is a social entrepreneur?

In much the same way as the global citizen implies the neoliberal state (Chapman, Ruiz-Chapman and Eglin 2018, p. 4), I argue that the social entrepreneur implies a particular arrangement of social and economic relationships supported by the institutional forms and regimes of accumulation associated with economic neoliberalism. Much as global citizens exemplify the socially and economically unhindered liberal subjects of this new order, social entrepreneurs appear as a manifestation of the institutional forms of this order. They are the unencumbered and virtuous citizens of the post-welfare era in which the highest aspiration is of 'everyone a changemaker' (Drayton 2006). Individuals are no longer simply citizens carrying out their civic responsibilities but agents who transform the undesirable circumstances experienced by others. All that is required for an individual to catalyse such a transformation is the appropriate combination of empathy, ingenuity and unyielding determination. Such transformational activity is no longer the role of elected government or of robust civil society but of individual social entrepreneurs. To be sure, social entrepreneurs must engage with both government and community in order to enact such transformation. However, these estates are no longer the catalysts of transformation; indeed they are, more often than not, the very source of the problem to which the social entrepreneur is responding.

Who is the social entrepreneur who initiates such transformations? While the literature dubiously refers to transformational figures of the past in such terms, I will limit the analysis in this section to the post-war era in the Anglo-American realm. This is partly because I view the application of this terminology to past figures as an anachronistic application of a concept rooted in the post-war era. To be sure, the idea of profit-making, socially impactful forms of organization had certainly existed before the 1980s, but the use of this language to describe lone, resource mobilizing individuals catalysing massive change in a financially sustainable manner is largely unique to this latter period.

The search for such figures quickly yields suitable candidates, most prominently the British politician, social researcher and activist Michael Young. Young was among the first to earn the epithet of social entrepreneur after founding a series of organizations in reaction to failures of post-war institutional forms and regimes of accumulation, in addressing the economic needs and concerns of working-class communities. These include the Institute for Community Studies, the Mutual Aid Centre, Language Line and the precursor to the Open University;

they are still in operation today. Contemporary portrayals of Young describe him as a tirelessly inventive and somewhat maverick figure developing ingenious, socially based solutions to problems that remained on the margins of the political process (Briggs 2001).

However, Young is probably best known for his argument against the very kind of meritocratic elitism (Young 1958) that seems to permeate the profiles of many social entrepreneurs. In this volume, Young criticized the unjust tendency for society to retain influence and opportunity amongst a class of meritocrats while systemically and increasingly denying these for others. The wide misapplication of his thesis and term 'meritocracy' is itself illustrative of the tone-deaf reception to genuine criticisms of the prevailing social and economic order. The significance of this cannot be overstated in that it acts as a corrective to viewing Young's work as an exceptional form of enterprise, only in as far as he was able to mobilize the education, networks and other social resources that he gathered through his lifetime.

More contemporary case studies of social entrepreneurs (Bornstein 2007) present social entrepreneurs in a standard narrative encompassing middle-aged (often middle class), educated individuals identifying a systemic problem and applying entrepreneurial initiative and determination to create a sustainable solution with only meagre material resources and little regard to financial reward. One of the better-known creation myths in Bornstein's seminal volume describes the foundation of 'Ashoka: Innovators for the Public', possibly the most prominent organization engaged in the promotion of SE in North America. The founder, Bill Drayton, is the product of an elite education (Philips Academy, Harvard, Oxford, Yale), followed by a corporate career at a global management consulting organization (McKinsey and Company) and a stint in government as Assistant Administrator of the Environmental Protection Agency (EPA) in the Carter administration. In a typical profile, Drayton's own professional milestones are described as his entrepreneurial activities in school and college, a trip to India to study Gandhian activism and initiating emissions trading as a policy innovation at the EPA. All of these typify the well-educated, socially privileged, social entrepreneur with the capacity to therefore defy problematic circumstances.

Drastic reductions in public spending under the new Reagan administration (including at the EPA where Drayton worked) allowed Drayton to devote himself entirely to his initiative. The evolving operating model sought to identify particular attributes among individuals who would then receive salary support for three years while they mobilized, developed and leveraged the necessary resource networks to achieve their intended social goals. In accounts of the early recruits to Ashoka, much stress is laid on the exceptional qualities of these individuals. Once again, the narrative masks, or at least de-emphasizes, other attributes that would have contributed equally to their success. In Drayton's own case, professional contributions of former Ivy League classmates and corporate colleagues, a grant from the MacArthur Foundation and generous donations from personal associates enabled the organization to establish itself into what is now the most well-known organization focusing on SE in North America.

The argument being made here is twofold. First, the depiction of social entrepreneurs often obscures access to resources that form a significant basis of their success. If this is the case, then what is called SE requires access to a unique set of resources that may be beyond the reach of many individuals. This leads to the second argument: that SE cannot therefore be a universal strategy for social change. The archetypal social entrepreneurs described above were able to utilize their educational and accumulated social capital to enact change. While popular profiles of these social entrepreneurs reveal these advantages, the stress of these profiles is on their demonstrated ingenuity, ethical motivation and empathy, and not on the considerable economic and social advantages they were able to access to engender their intended social impacts. While each of these former traits may be desirable, what is problematic about such profiles is their selective emphasis on these while obscuring their level of access and ability to leverage resources to attain their goals. In both Young's and Drayton's cases this included a network of well educated, wealthy and influential professional associates.

The legitimacy of SE as a universal method for change is therefore called into question. It might be argued that the point of proposing SE as a universal strategy simply intends for a more active citizenry, engaged with social and economic challenges as they emerge. However, much as the notion of a global citizen assumes a fictitious universal access and mobility, the universalization of SE also assumes a universal level of agency. This ignores widespread inequalities in opportunity, individual capabilities (Gasper 1997) and uncritically universalizes the attributes of an increasingly narrow socio-economic group (Florida 2002). Significantly, what is emphasized in this universalization are not the attributes of citizenship but of motivation and enterprise.

This raises further questions about the adequacy of the language of SE to properly describe the character and mechanisms of social change that are in fact taking place. If not purely based on the unique skills or attributes of an individual, then SE is an insufficient explanation of the mechanism of social change. However, rather than being further interrogated or discarded, SE, now unmoored from particular mechanisms, has ironically evolved into an all-encompassing way of describing social change with important implications. This results in a cooptation of other forms of social transformation under an all-encompassing rubric. Any form of change in any domain can now be described as SE or social innovation, further delegitimizing other forms of social transformation, especially in the way agents are able to describe their transformative values and practices in their own language. In addition, entrepreneurial initiatives are now also being increasingly portrayed as social innovations.

The significance of this is difficult to overstate. Major corporations now depict what might have formerly been termed 'corporate social responsibility' as social innovations (Herrera 2015). The measurement of 'social impact' initially developed as a policy tool, is now increasingly gaining currency in the corporate sector (Mirvis et al. 2016). In these ways, activities that have traditionally been allied with public policy or activism are being coopted into the goal of profit maximization.

This is significant since it indicates a further translation of the notion of SE and its allied concepts from their original formulation. An initial movement comprised the selective depiction of a rich variety of legitimate social changes under the rubric of SE. The second movement is the depiction of activities that are primarily intended for purposes other than social change under this rubric. The dilution of SE to mean any activity that might purportedly have a positive social impact has significant implications that go much further than the accurate use of terminology. It is the final step in the cooptation of this supposedly disruptive concept into the existing institutional forms of the global social and economic system. By using an illustrative case study below, I will trace the evolution of this conceptual translation and its implications.

SE in crisis

If SE is an attribute of the institutional forms that support rather than transform the existing global social and economic order we should expect that attempts to harness this concept and apply it to transform social outcomes will inevitably manifest irreconcilable contradictions that may lead to their failure. A narrow indication of failure would mean the inability to achieve the intended social impact while being financially self-sustaining. More broadly, failure would be illustrated by an organization's mission drift towards the social and economic status quo. The argument I make in this section is not that every initiative that claims to follow an SE model is doomed to failure. My goal rather is to show how this happens and that in at least one prominent case, failure looked like the organization's inability to not only reconcile financial sustainability with social impact but its eventual integration and cooptation into the prevailing economic system.

One of the better-known models of SE is the microfinance institution (MFI) which gained increased attention after both the Grameen Bank and its founder, Muhammad Yunus, were given the endorsement of the Nobel Peace Prize committee in 2006. Microfinance has its roots in traditional forms of informal community-based lending in the global South (Tsai 2004) and emerged as a formalized method of community development in the Comilla community development projects in Bangladesh which involved multiple stakeholders including international aid, government organizations, universities and communities (Khan 1979). Yunus based the group lending model of the Grameen Bank on lessons learned from the Comilla experience.

Yunus's own biography aligns closely with the archetypical social entrepreneur. After training as a Fulbright scholar at Vanderbilt University, he initiated his own microfinance activities while observing the hardships of villagers living adjacent to the university where he was working as a professor. By making the case that microfinance was capitalism for the poor, the Bank received crucial support from the Ford Foundation throughout the 1980s (Morduch 1999). This situates the origins of the Grameen model of microfinance as an institutional form within the broader context of a global capitalist economy. The shortcomings of the Grameen model have been well documented elsewhere (Bateman 2010) so I will now turn to the case that illustrates my argument more clearly.

For this I turn to an account of the first major microfinance organization in India that reads as something of a morality tale of good intentions corrupted through neoliberal intervention. The Swayam Krishi Sangham (SKS) was founded in 1997 as a non-profit organization, lending microloans to rural communities in the Indian state of Andhra Pradesh. After an education at Yale, the University of Chicago and the Fulbright programme, founder Vikram Akula created the organization while working at the global management consulting firm McKinsey and Company (Akula 2010). The story of the organization's early years reads like a standard account of a small but impactful social enterprise. In its first six years, SKS had made loans to approximately 85,000 clients and claimed a 99 per cent recovery rate (Perez and Ben-David 2012).

What was not as conventional was a momentous change of course in the operating model of the organization. Within six years of its founding, claiming that the non-profit model had reached its 'limits' and was insufficient to meet the scale and demand of its recipients, SKS transformed into a private for-profit organization (Knowledge@Wharton 2010). The new private company raised funds through several successful rounds of investment from a number of private actors and expanded to neighbouring states within India. Investments into SKS included a first-round investment in 2007 from the prominent Silicon Valley Private Equity fund, Sequoia Capital ($11.5 million), followed by more substantial investments from other global investment funds and an eventual initial public offering (Brennan 2007; Chen et al. 2010). At this point, the engagement of SKS with global capital markets was overt, and the stake of major global investment funds in the organization removed any pretence that the organization was aiming to disruptively transform the financial services sector.

Still, it could be argued that in seeking to serve those 'bottom billions' (Collier 2007) who would otherwise be unable to access financial services, SKS served as a conduit for global finance to be extended to otherwise financially disenfranchised individuals. In this way, it might still effect transformative change for the individuals it was seeking to service. However, such a sentiment does not stand up to scrutiny, and confirmed some of the persistent criticisms of the microfinance sector (Bateman and Chang 2012). Soon after the change in its operating model, the organization started to show cracks. Turnover among senior executives of staff indicated disagreement amongst its major stakeholders, especially with the global financial funds newly on the company's Board. The company's current Chief Financial Officer indicated in a later interview that despite the changing operational model of the organization, its brand was still associated with values that it could no longer subscribe to exclusively – namely the empowerment of the poor (Bandyopadhyay and Unnikrishnan 2013). This organization's social mission drift was initially not properly acknowledged, even amongst its leadership. A rash of farmer suicides provoked the state government of Andhra Pradesh, where SKS had its most significant presence, to investigate. The investigation implicated the microfinance industry as a cause of these suicides, specifically steep interest rates and harsh loan recovery practices, including public shaming and the use of loan shark networks (Kinetz 2012).

In response to this finding, the state government of Andhra Pradesh instituted a new law around the lending practices of MFIs, targeting harsh payment collection and aggressive over-lending practices (Ghate 2007). These measures had the inevitable effect of collapsing the company's stock price. In the ensuing weeks, the shuttering of numerous MFIs was described in some mainstream media as the 'other' financial crisis of the decade (Wichterich 2012). Akula was removed as chairman of the Board and SKS was recently bought out by a large financial institution, IndusInd Bank, making it a full part of the mainstream financial system (Bandyopadhyay 2017).

This case is significant in the way in which the arc of the narrative extends further than the embeddedness of the social entrepreneur within the institutional form of the current era. Akula typifies a version of the socially and economically endowed social entrepreneur. However, the point of this case extends further. Here, the very model of the social enterprise was eventually overwhelmed by the institutional forms that ultimately support (rather than disrupt) the global neoliberal economy. On such a reading, it is not surprising that an organization founded by a social entrepreneur deeply embedded in the prevailing institutional forms should ultimately also be coopted into this system.

Conclusion

I must begin this conclusion with the clarification that my point in this chapter is not to vilify the social entrepreneur. In most of the cases I have read or observed, these individuals are engaged in their work out of good intentions and possess many of the positive ethical, professional and personal attributes for which they are heralded (a recognition gained, in many cases, against their wishes). In addition, I am not arguing that this work is illegitimate – only that its selective depiction is ultimately self-defeating.

In a global, social, environmental and economic system characterized by conflict, disequilibrium and steep inequalities in access, SE was proposed as a novel pathway that ordinary people with extraordinary determination could engage for lasting change after decades of ideological rancour, policy debacles and market failures among elites. On the above analysis, however, such a prescription reveals itself to be the result of a very selective retelling of the sources of social change. This selective retelling is oriented in such a way as to obscure the participation of these purported agents of change in the very systems they wish to change. Rather than simply being myopic, such an approach may ultimately support rather than disrupt the existing status quo, with sometimes disastrous consequences for the very people that were the intended beneficiaries.

What does this mean? Should social entrepreneurs return to their armchairs, abandon their initiatives and leave their intended beneficiaries to their own devices? This is not the argument being made in this chapter. However, what would be more instructive in both the depiction and implementation of social change would be to account for how lasting social change is being engendered using a variety of understandings, methods and resources. Such a narrative would constitute a rich retelling of the complexities and contingencies that are involved in a process of social change. It could then engender a richer, transparent, more democratic, inclusive response to existing social challenges, beyond the solitary social entrepreneur as global citizen.

References

Akula, V 2010, *A fistful of rice: my unexpected quest to end poverty through profitability*, Harvard Business Press, Cambridge, MA.

Armitage, D, Charles, AD and Berkes, F 2017, *Governing the coastal commons*, Routledge, London.

Bandyopadhyay, T 2017, 'The untold story behind IndusInd Bank-Bharat Financial merger', *Livemint*, viewed 7 November 2019, www.livemint.com/Opinion/9ZWgRWMtD11ts6xe7ygAmJ/The-untold-story-behind-IndusInd-BankBharat-Financial-merge.html.

Bandyopadhyay, T and Unnikrishnan, D 2013, 'SKS Microfinance: the inside story', *Livemint*, viewed 7 November 2019, www.livemint.com/Industry/hvWN2IbllrX5hXKj3keERL/SKS-Microfinance-The-inside-story.html.

Bateman, M 2010, *Why doesn't microfinance work? The destructive rise of local neoliberalism*, Zed Books, London.

Bateman, M and Chang, HJ 2012, 'Microfinance and the illusion of development: from hubris to nemesis in thirty years', *World Economic Review*, vol. 1, pp. 13–36.

Blond, P 2010, *Red tory: how left and right have broken Britain and how we can fix it*, Faber & Faber, London.

Bornstein, D 2007, *How to change the world: social entrepreneurs and the power of new ideas*, updated edn, Oxford University Press, New York.

Boyer, R and Saillard, Y 2002, *Regulation theory: the state of the art*, Routledge, London.

Brennan, M 2007, 'Sequoia invests $11.5 million in microfinance fund', *CNBC.com*, 27 March, viewed 7 November 2019, www.cnbc.com/id/17844093.

Briggs, A 2001, *Michael Young: social entrepreneur*, Palgrave Macmillan, London.

Chapman, DD, Ruiz-Chapman, T and Eglin, P 2018, 'Global citizenship as neoliberal propaganda: a political-economic and postcolonial critique', *Alternate Routes: A Journal of Critical Social Research*, vol. 29, pp. 142–66.

Chen, G, Rasmussen, S, Reille, X and Rozas, D 2010, 'Indian microfinance goes public: the SKS initial public offering', *Focus Note*, 65, CGAP, Washington, DC.

Collier, P 2007, *The bottom billion: why the poorest countries are failing and what can be done about it*, Oxford University Press, New York.

Dees, JG 1998, 'The meaning of social entrepreneurship', viewed 10 November 2019, www.redalmarza.cl/ing/pdf/TheMeaningofsocialEntrepreneurship.pdf.

Dey, P and Steyaert, C 2010, 'The politics of narrating social entrepreneurship', *Journal of Enterprising Communities: People and Places in the Global Economy*, vol. 4, pp. 85–108.

Drayton, W 2006, 'Everyone a changemaker: social entrepreneurship's ultimate goal', *Innovations: Technology, Governance, Globalization*, vol. 1, pp. 80–96.

Dunford, M 1990, 'Theories of regulation', *Environment and Planning D: Society and Space*, vol. 8, pp. 297–321.
Falk, N 1978, 'Growing new firms: the role of the social entrepreneur', *Built Environment*, vol. 4, pp. 204–12.
Florida, R 2002, *The rise of the creative class*, Basic Books, New York.
Friedman, M 1962, *Capitalism and freedom*, University of Chicago Press, Chicago, IL.
Fukuyama, F 1989, The end of history? *National Interest*, vol. 16, Summer, pp. 3–18.
Gasper, D 1997, 'Sen's capability approach and Nussbaum's capabilities ethic', *Journal of International Development*, vol. 9, pp. 281–302.
Georgescu-Roegen, N 1971, *The entropy law and the economic process*, Harvard University Press, Cambridge, MA.
Ghate, P 2007, 'Consumer protection in Indian microfinance: lessons from Andhra Pradesh and the microfinance bill', *Economic and Political Weekly*, vol. 42, pp. 1176–84.
Giddens, A 1998, *The third way*, Polity, Cambridge.
Gilpin, R and Gilpin, JM 2001, *Global political economy: understanding the international economic order*, Princeton University Press, Princeton, NJ.
Gladstone, D (ed.) 1999, *Before Beveridge: welfare before the welfare state*, Civitas, Choice in Welfare No. 47, Institute of Economic Affairs, London.
Goldwater, B 1960, *The conscience of a conservative*, Victor Publishing Company, Shepherdsville, KY.
Harvey, D 2007, *A brief history of neoliberalism*, Oxford University Press, New York.
Hayek, FA von 1944, *The road to serfdom*, Routledge, London.
Herrera, MEB 2015, 'Creating competitive advantage by institutionalizing corporate social innovation', *Journal of Business Research*, vol. 68, pp. 1468–74.
Ikenberry, GJ 1992, 'A world economy restored: expert consensus and the Anglo-American postwar settlement', *International Organization*, vol. 46, pp. 289–321.
Irvin, G 2011, 'Inequality and recession in Britain and the USA', *Development and Change*, vol. 42, pp. 154–82.
Jessop, B 1992, 'Regulation and politics: the integral economy and the integral state', mimeograph, Department of Sociology, University of Lancaster, UK, pp. 1–30.
Jessop, B 1996, 'Post-Fordism and the state', in B Greve (ed.), *Comparative welfare systems: the Scandinavian model in a period of change*, 165–83, Palgrave Macmillan, London.
Jessop, B and Sum, NL 2006, *Beyond the regulation approach: putting capitalist economies in their place*, Edward Elgar Publishing, Cheltenham, UK.
Johnson, C 1988, 'Enterprise education and training', *British Journal of Education and Work*, vol. 2, pp. 61–5.
Jordan, B 2012, 'Making sense of the "Big Society": social work and the moral order', *Journal of Social Work*, vol. 12, pp. 630–46.
Khan, AR 1979, 'The Comilla model and the integrated rural development programme of Bangladesh: an experiment in "cooperative capitalism"', *World Development*, vol. 7, pp. 397–422.
Kinetz, E 2012, 'Small loans add up to lethal debts', *Hindu*, 25 February, viewed 7 November 2019, www.thehindu.com/news/national/Small-loans-add-up-to-lethal-debts/article13325024.ece.
Knowledge@Wharton 2010, 'Capitalism vs. altruism: SKS rekindles the microfinance debate', 7 October, viewed 7 November 2019, https://knowledge.wharton.upenn.edu/article/capitalism-vs-altruism-sks-rekindles-the-microfinance-debate/.

Leadbeater, C 1997, *The rise of the social entrepreneur*, no. 25, Demos, London.
Lenssen, G, van den Berghe, L, Louche, C, Roper, J and Cheney, G 2005, 'The meanings of social entrepreneurship today: corporate governance', *International Journal of Business in Society*, vol. 5, no. 3, pp. 95–104.
Martin, RJ and Osberg, S 2007, 'Social entrepreneurship: the case for a definition', *Stanford Social Innovation Review*, vol. 11, Spring, pp. 29–39.
Mirvis, P, Herrera, MEB, Googins, B and Albareda, L 2016, 'Corporate social innovation: how firms learn to innovate for the greater good', *Journal of Business Research*, vol. 69, no. 11, pp. 5014–21.
Morduch, J 1999, 'The role of subsidies in microfinance: evidence from the Grameen Bank', *Journal of Development Economics*, vol. 60, pp. 229–48.
Mulgan, G 2006, 'The process of social innovation', *Innovations: Technology, Governance, Globalization*, vol. 1, no. 2, pp. 145–62.
Ostrom, E 1990, *Governing the commons: the evolution of institutions for collective action*, Cambridge University Press, Cambridge.
Perez, YV and Ben-David, Y 2012, 'Internet as freedom: does the internet enhance the freedoms people enjoy?' *Information Technology for Development*, vol. 18, pp. 293–310.
Rajan, RG 2010, 'How inequality fueled the crisis', *Project Syndicate*, 9 July, viewed 7 November 2019, www.project-syndicate.org/commentary/how-inequality-fueled-the-crisis?barrier=accesspaylog.
Schor, JB 1999, *The overspent American: why we want what we don't need*, Harper Perennial, New York.
Toye, R 2013, 'From "consensus" to "common ground": the rhetoric of the postwar settlement and its collapse', *Journal of Contemporary History*, vol. 48, pp. 3–23.
Tsai, KS 2004, 'Imperfect substitutes: the local political economy of informal finance and microfinance in rural China and India', *World Development*, vol. 32, pp. 1487–507.
Waddock, SA and Post, JE 1991, 'Social entrepreneurs and catalytic change', *Public Administration Review*, vol. 51, pp. 393–401.
Wall, WL 2009, *Inventing the 'American Way': the politics of consensus from the New Deal to the civil rights movement*, Oxford University Press, New York.
Westley, F and Antadze, N 2010, 'Making a difference: strategies for scaling social innovation for greater impact', *Innovation Journal: The Public Sector Innovation Journal*, vol. 15, no. 2, article 2.
Wichterich, C 2012, 'The other financial crisis: growth and crash of the microfinance sector in India', *Development*, vol. 55, pp. 406–12.
Young, M 1958, *The rise of the meritocracy*, Thames & Hudson, London.
Zahra, SA, Gedajlovic, E, Neubaum, DO and Shulman, JM 2009, 'A typology of social entrepreneurs: motives, search processes and ethical challenges', *Journal of Business Venturing*, vol. 24, pp. 519–32.

Part VI

Global citizenship and the multi/trans-national corporations

Chapter 11

Constructing 'progressive neoliberal' citizens

The political economy of corporate global imaginaries[1]

Kevin Funk

Introduction

From nearly ubiquitous television advertisements to posters competing for passengers' attention in jet bridges all over the globe, consumers are continuously subjected to messages affirming the inception of a 'flat', borderless world (Friedman 2005). Such discourses suggest that time–space compression is inexorably bringing humanity together into a globally connected, cosmopolitan world order based on a shared, global citizenship. As the below Emirates Airlines advertisements put it: 'Tomorrow brings us all closer'; 'The world is your playground' (which boasts of 'A multilingual cabin crew from over 100 nations'); 'Beijing. Once Forbidden. Now daily.'; and, '7 billion people. One bridge that connects us all'.

Figure 11.1 Emirates tagline 1.
Source: https://khatijaliaqat.wordpress.com/2016/05/21/taglines-of-emirates-airline/ (viewed 15 January 2017).

Figure 11.2 Emirates tagline 2.
Source: https://khatijaliaqat.wordpress.com/2016/05/21/taglines-of-emirates-airline/ (viewed 15 January 2017).

'Progressive neoliberal' citizens 213

Figure 11.3 Emirates tagline 3.
Source: https://khatijaliaqat.wordpress.com/2016/05/21/taglines-of-emirates-airline/ (viewed 15 January 2017).

Figure 11.4 Emirates tagline 4.
Source: https://khatijaliaqat.wordpress.com/2016/05/21/taglines-of-emirates-airline/ (viewed 15 January 2017).

Such assertions of borderless creed and global belonging motivate the following questions: What understanding of globality do corporations attempt to 'sell' through advertisements, how do they sell it, and what effect does this have on audiences? What is the corporate interest in promoting an ethos of 'banal cosmopolitanism'[2] among consumers 'in which everyday nationalism is circumvented and undermined and we experience ourselves integrated into global processes and phenomena' – though in some cases, as observed below, with a regional or local twist (Beck 2002, p. 28)? These corporate messages focus on globalization's 'humanistic' side, as they highlight cross-cultural exchange, limitless travel, and our belonging to a universal community. After all, for capitalism to 'persuade', it requires an accompanying – and appropriately pleasant – narrative (García Canclini 2014, p. 42). In these and other cases, hyper-globalist and 'futurist' imaginaries have indeed proven to be quite successful at seducing audiences (Tsing 2000, p. 334).

This assertion of a multiculturally inclusive and globally integrated, borderless world order, premised on a spirit of global citizenship, possesses a potentially 'subversive' edge, for it challenges existing material and epistemological hierarchies by claiming to open an uneven global playing field to those often excluded from participation (Chandra 2013). That is, those who hail from what Vijay Prashad (2007) labels the 'darker nations': global Southerners, immigrants, asylum-seekers, hijab-wearers, and others whose stubborn existence (and, perhaps, lack of the 'right' citizenship papers) 'interrupts the flat earth, borderless world, and smooth space conceits of globalists, highlighting asymmetry and inequality amidst intensifying global interdependency' (Sparke 2007, p. 117; see also Meena 2016 and Smith 2005). Yet beneath this humanistic, cosmopolitan, inclusive, and visually alluring imaginary – complete with pithy, memorable slogans regarding global citizenship and related themes, written over lush, seductive backgrounds – lurks a self-interested, ideological mission. That is, of course, the corporate *raison d'être*: to seek profit. Specifically, transnational corporations convey to consuming classes around the world (and those who aspire to join them) the desirability and inevitability of a borderless economy that cannot be regulated and in which they may roam unfettered.

These advertisements thus aim to perform two simultaneous tasks: that is, to evoke a globe-spanning 'imagined community' (Anderson 2006) that appears politically liberal if not subversive, while also 'selling' teleological global capitalism and corporate globalization as the 'end of history' (Fukuyama 1992) to various publics, who are meant to accept this fait accompli, if not embrace it outright and participate in it. Accordingly, this chapter delineates *how* these polyvalent advertisements operate at multiple levels to convey related but distinct messages about 'the global', and more specifically 'global citizenship', to audiences. In short, an inclusive, cosmopolitan, and people-first globalization, based on the universal principle of global citizenship, is the superficial idea meant to attract audiences upon first glance. However, the deeper meaning that is transmitted more subtly is that capitalism's global march is unstoppable. To borrow from Nancy Fraser (2019, p. 11), these messages thus evoke a 'progressive neoliberal' logic in which capitalist ideology is wrapped in the discourse of 'feminism, antiracism, multiculturalism, environmentalism, and LGBTQ+ rights'.

In this way, as analyzed below, these advertisements seek to disarm target publics – and undermine their agency – by playing to their humanistic impulses in order to 'sell' them on a global-capitalist ideal that is under increasing fire from numerous quarters (Stiglitz 2017). Yet, as discussed in the concluding section, while such campaigns appear to be 'successful' to a meaningful extent, their effects can only be *partial* rather than *totalizing*. Naturally, audiences – including, but not limited to, activists and social media users – may understand and respond to them in either unintended or even oppositional ways. To illustrate this delicate balancing act between promoting 'progressive' values and regulatory futility, I investigate three emblematic cases of transnational corporations that promulgate aesthetically and rhetorically appealing advertisements with a 'global' twist: Emirates Airlines, HSBC, and Brazilian bank Itaú. By interrogating their public discourses, this chapter demonstrates how powerful actors attempt to construct global (or regional-global) imaginaries and neoliberal visions of citizenship in the minds of consumers.

In this regard, what makes corporate advertisements a particularly compelling site of inquiry is both the extent to which they are regularly consumed by mass and elite audiences around the world, as well as the role they play, as pop-culture artifacts, in shaping received wisdom. In the present case, as I argue, the ambition of these advertisements is to demonstrate the *inevitability* of capitalism's global march: that is, that any attempt to regulate global capitalism's inexorable spread or their own profit-seeking activities is doomed to fail. In turn, as I briefly explore in the concluding section, this critical analysis of corporate globalizing discourses speaks directly to important political debates concerning citizenship and belonging, agency in globalization, the feasibility of state regulation of global capitalism, and the construction of alternative global imaginaries/orders.

'Citizens of the world': corporate imaginaries and the formation of global subjects

Business advertising – including commercials, promotional posters, and websites – is replete with assertions of global identities, both for corporations and potential clients. In essence, what is being asserted is a bifurcated form of citizenship in which ideal, 'global' citizens such as corporations and business elites are able to breeze past immigration checkpoints while others (that is, 'global non-citizens'), in practice, encounter increasing restrictions on their mobility. Crucially, elite members of the former group, as analyzed below, 'seek to re-make the world after their own image by postulating such a "global citizen" as the fitting identity for any fully integrated member of that order' (Chapman, Ruiz-Chapman and Eglin 2018, p. 145).

In this sense, as Debra D. Chapman, Tania Ruiz-Chapman, and Peter Eglin (2018) argue, 'global citizenship' often functions, in practice, as little more than 'neoliberal propaganda'. In celebrating globality (but only, in reality, for some), such rhetoric 'erases the material inequities of access to legal and social citizenship' (p. 154). This is not an oversight. Per the ruminations of 'globalist' neoliberal thinkers, the form of global citizenship that is being promoted revolves not around social justice or addressing inequality, but rather the inalienable 'rights' of those of sufficient means to move capital across borders and acquire property wherever they see fit (Slobodian 2018). Focusing on its deployment in higher-education contexts such as 'global studies' programs, Chapman, Ruiz-Chapman and Eglin (2018, p. 148) further suggest that, 'What [this neoliberal framing of global citizenship] does *not* do ... is educate young people about their actual place in the neoliberal world order of accumulation by dispossession, managed, supervised and protected by imperialist Northern states, above all the United States'. In turn, as exemplified by the below advertisements, it helps to sustain that same order. In this way, global citizenship – and, we might say, the global imaginary more broadly – becomes 'a concept steeped in Northern privilege implicating and implicated in neo-colonial relationships with the global South' (Chapman, Ruiz-Chapman and Eglin 2018, p. 148; see also Kamola 2019).

In turn, the purpose of this chapter is to understand *how* these 'global' citizen-corporations sell consumers on their would-be globality, to discover *how* capitalist elites 'project images of themselves as citizens of the world as well as of their places of birth' (Sklair 2016, p. 332), to explore these advertisements' effects on audiences, and to interrogate the political calculations behind these representations. Regarding the latter point, capitalist elites are naturally driven to flaunt, and even exaggerate, their global credentials as part of a 'self-conscious propaganda campaign' because doing so is in their material self-interest (Beder 2005, p. 116). In short, adopting and promoting their own 'flexible citizenship' function 'as strategies to accumulate capital and power' (Ong 1999, p. 6). This is the case because the actions of what Saskia Sassen (2007, p. 187) refers to as 'free-floating cosmopolitan classes with no national attachments or needs' would be significantly harder to regulate than those of their nationally oriented and rooted counterparts. Indeed, existing regulatory regimes, which are primarily centered on *national* laws and means of enforcement, are ill-equipped to constrain truly *global* actors (Rodrik 2012). Further, these global discourses feed into the public image – also beneficial for elites – that we live in the real-world equivalent of an ideal-type capitalist fantasyland, that is, a corporate utopia in which meaningful regulation of global capitalism's 'inevitable' spread appears unthinkable and impossible, and thus is not worth attempting.

Yet here, an important caveat is in order. The fact that capital does often seem to operate 'without borders' due to the insufficiency of both national and global regulatory frameworks does not automatically imply that these advertisements are literally 'correct' in asserting the globality of corporate structures or the impossibility of regulation (Harrington 2016). Instead, as suggested in the conclusion, the real problems are state capture by powerful interests, along with a lack of both political will and counter-imaginaries that are able to challenge the cultural-ideological hegemony of 'corporate globalization' or global citizenship, as defined in corporate-friendly terms (Juris 2008). The point of the present analysis, then, is to illuminate the material incentives that motivate advertisers to celebrate their (and their customers') globality, and, more importantly, to demonstrate *how* they construct global (capitalist) imaginaries and citizenships among and for audiences. Additionally, this chapter adds to our understanding of what Manuel Castells (2010, p. 442) refers to as 'the space of flows' around which 'society is constructed' – which includes not only 'capital', 'information', and 'organizational interaction', but also 'images, sounds, and symbols'. The circulation of corporate advertisements comprises an especially important (cultural) flow, as it aids in the production of a global imaginary that furthers the rule of capital.

Advertisements, like other forms of 'low data', are particularly salient in the construction of 'commonsense' imaginaries and cultural understandings among audiences (Caso and Hamilton 2015; McFall 2004). Jutta Weldes frames the issue well, noting that,

If we are asking why this neoliberal discourse makes sense – what renders this vision of globalization seemingly self-evident – we need to look at the broader cultural resources, the cultural image bank, that provide the tropes and narratives out of which it is constructed.

In other words, and more broadly, 'popular culture helps to create and sustain the conditions for contemporary world politics' (2015, pp. 230–4). It does so by reaching mass audiences around the world – not just elites, but also 'middling groups' (in societies from both the global North and South) with growing acquisitive power, or at least aspirations for such – and incorporating them symbolically 'as participants in global consumer culture and modernity' (Dávila 2016, p. 10). And, in turn, reconstituting them as global 'credit-card citizens': that is, debt-saddled, depoliticized, and alienated subjects whose rights, self-image, and perceived worth are increasingly dependent upon their ability to make purchases in accordance with global standards of consumption (Moulián 2014).

Corporate case studies

This section proffers case studies of three corporations' globalizing discourses, focusing on particularly emblematic and evocatively 'global' advertisements from their respective campaigns. To uncover how they seek to 'make' meanings for audiences, I conduct a discursive analysis of their words, images, and representations as they relate to 'the global' (Neumann 2008). This chapter thus follows an interpretive approach, both by 'taking [corporate] language seriously' and focusing on 'the centrality of meaning in human life' (Yanow and Schwartz-Shea 2015, p. xiv; see also Funk 2019). I pay particular attention to nuances, subtleties, and contextual clues that shed light on how these advertisements, as meaning-imbued cultural artifacts, attempt to construct global imaginaries that simultaneously appeal to and allure audiences, on one hand, and promote (inevitable) capitalist globalization and a corporate-friendly version of global citizenship, on the other.

Specifically, this section interrogates: (1) Emirates Airlines' bountiful production of evocatively cosmopolitan, lush, and visually alluring posters, which invoke connectivity, cultural exchange, and our would-be shrinking world; (2) the banking giant HSBC's more workmanlike advertisements, staples in global jet bridges, many of which stress capitalist globalization's inexorable spread; and (3) the Brazilian megabank Itaú's 'I Am a Global Latin American' campaign. The latter deploys regional cultural icons to convince potential Latin American customers that it is *the bank* through which they can 'go global', to show potential extra-regional customers that Itaú is a natural bridge that will allow their foreign capital to further 'globalize' Latin America's economic relations, and to construct a globalized, Latin American citizenship.

The above advertising campaigns are of particular interest for two reasons. First, as the specific advertisements chosen for analysis demonstrate, these corporations have invested especially heavily in the cultivation of global images. This includes the construction of a neoliberal-friendly version of global citizenship. One would expect no less from institutions whose lifeblood is global connectivity, and whose very activities – that is, facilitating commercial, financial, and travel flows – provide critical infrastructure that makes contemporary capitalist globalization 'possible' in the first place. In turn, their 'global' advertising campaigns have put them on the radar of numerous scholars of globalization as well as media observers. Second, as evidenced by an abundance of online commentary, their advertisements have elicited significant attention from audiences, who have expressed recurring interest in their aesthetic qualities and overall campaigns. While most advertising efforts seemingly pass largely unnoticed, Internet commentators have written a relatively large body of (generally fawning) blog posts, and compiled numerous image repositories, related to Emirates Airlines, HSBC, and Itaú. In sum, these cases demonstrate how corporations in different sectors – aviation and finance – and with heterogeneous but overlapping consumer audiences – such as air travelers, magazine readers, and English-language Internet users – pursue related strategies to construct similar global imaginaries and citizenships. These very industries, as suggested above, are not only essential to capitalist globalization. They are also central to how both scholarly and lay audiences *imagine* capitalist globalization and 'increased mobility' (Steger 2008, pp. 11, 181–2, 247).

Drawing from Weldes (2015 pp. 230–1), I understand corporate discourses as 'capital in the ubiquitous battle over meaning', through which ideologically charged and self-interested global imaginaries become 'common sense' by 'constitut[ing] the world as we know it'. Further, this analysis takes as its starting point that, in the present case, 'it is the economic processes in which cultural production is embedded that shape visual imagery' (Rose 2001, p. 20). As David Harvey (1990, p. 287) suggests, 'advertising and media images … have come to play a very much more integrative role in cultural practices and now assume a much greater importance in the growth dynamics of capitalism'. Accordingly, to understand contemporary capitalism, we must analyze how these discourses intermingle with and indeed reconstitute cultures to promote corporate self-interest. Thus, this chapter analyzes polyvalent meanings as powerful corporations seek to convey them, with a significant degree of success, to media consumers. While 'recipients' may of course develop unintended or oppositional understandings of and in response to (fractured) corporate discourses, this section focuses primarily on the agency of corporate actors. Indeed, Jon Bohland (2013, p. 102) correctly stresses the importance of 'reveal[ing] what the ideal reading of texts is as intended by their authors, even if we concede that the audience does not always receive them'. This 'ideal reading', as noted, is multifaceted and operates at distinct levels as it attempts to seduce audiences. The concluding section, in turn, briefly considers audience agency and the possibility – and necessity – of constructing more inclusive global counter-imaginaries and citizenships.

Emirates Airlines: 'Tomorrow thinks borders are so yesterday'

Only thirty years after its founding, the Dubai-based and state-owned Emirates Airlines has joined the ranks of the world's largest carriers by flying 'the fanciest product on the biggest planes on the longest routes'. Its meteoric rise has paralleled – and contributed to – that of Dubai, which in a few short decades rose from obscurity as a dusty port city and emirate to become a powerhouse of global capitalism and connectivity, a 'neutral ground' – peopled largely by non-citizens – 'on which to play, work, and cut deals'. And one with 'a top-notch airline to bring the world to its door' (Campbell 2017; see also Kanna 2011). As I peruse

Figure 11.5 Emirates, the airline of the 'global ruling class'.
Source: Campbell, 2017 (viewed 23 September 2017).

media-conscious Emirates' website, I am greeted by former *Friends* actress Jennifer Aniston. The commercial for which she was paid a reported $5 million depicts her moral outrage upon discovering that not all airlines match Emirates' amenities, which include showers and a cocktail bar.[3] Little wonder then that a recent cover of *Bloomberg Businessweek* – a source not prone to Marxist hyperbole – refers to Emirates as the airline of a particular kind of global citizen, that is, 'the global ruling class'.

Emirates is also a prolific producer of magazine and poster advertisements, the most telling of which for present purposes features the slogan, 'Tomorrow thinks borders are so yesterday'. It forms part of an ongoing print, digital, and television international advertising campaign – entitled 'Hello Tomorrow' – that was launched in 2012 to mark the airline's 'evolution from a travel brand to a global lifestyle brand'.[4] The background image displays child or adolescent skateboarders – including a hijab-wearing girl – gliding down a mostly barren street. It evokes gender equality and, perhaps more controversially (and subversively/politically charged) from a global North perspective, the full participation of visibly practicing Muslims in a cultural activity (skateboarding) that is constitutive of a middle-class, white, and suburban version of 'Americana'. It is the 'Springfield' of *Simpsons* lore, but with desert-like surroundings and olive-skinned bodies from what Samuel Huntington (1993) – and many fellow travelers – malign as the 'West's' great 'Other', the Islamic 'civilization'.

What explains this forthright statement of borderless creed? Why does Emirates pay to disseminate this message of global citizenship and what *Bloomberg* refers to as 'sunny globalism' (Campbell 2017)? Moreover, how does this idea resonate with audiences?

Figure 11.6 Children skateboarding in Emirates ad.
Source: https://khatijaliaqat.wordpress.com/2016/05/21/taglines-of-emirates-airline-unknown/ (viewed 15 January 2017).

Emirates, like all airlines, navigates a world order defined by national, not global, citizenship. That is, one in which *national* documents – passports and visas – of course determine who can enter a given country or take one of its flights. A borderless world in which 'everybody travels' (Lisle 2006) is thus an appealing utopia for a business that profits from increasing global connectivity. In turn, the centrality of 'tomorrow' to this particular advertisement and overall campaign suggests an inevitable trend in this direction. Though Emirates – with its massive Dubai hub – is a particularly evangelistic espouser of this ambition, it is shared broadly within the industry. Witness the statement by the International Air Transport Association CEO, French businessman Alexandre de Juniac, whose organization represents some 265 airlines. During the chaos that followed the Trump administration's January 2017 executive order on travel, immigration, and refugee policy – panned by critics as a 'Muslim ban' – he argued at the U.S. Chamber of Commerce's Aviation Summit that, 'We are deeply concerned with recent developments that point to a future of restricted borders and protectionism' (Jansen 2017).

Emirates seeks to concretize this ideal of a borderless world, to be populated by globally mobile citizens, through aggressive campaigning for the neoliberalization and deregulation of global commercial air travel. What Emirates desires, specifically, is 'true international competition and open skies'[5] – the latter of which, not coincidentally, is the name of its inflight magazine.[6] As noted by company president Tim Clark, 'we are a product of the multilateralism, the liberalization of trade'. He goes on to assert that despite Brexit, the world is not 'going back to the '30s', and the global-capitalist order 'will prevail' (Campbell 2017) – inevitably so, it seems.[7] The airline's global (and 'progressive neoliberal') spirit filters down to hiring practices, with the 'Cultural Diversity' section of Emirates' website observing that, 'our employee diversity of over 160 nationalities is our unique strength as a global organization'.[8] The immediate aim, as stated in their advertisements' fine print, is to encourage customers to 'Fly Emirates to 6 Continents'. But the larger political project is to tear down state-based obstacles to the circulation of people (that is, the 'ideal' kind of non-citizens), goods, capital, and indeed airlines, which would buttress fast-growing Emirates' efforts to cement Dubai's status as a – or *the* – global 'aviation hub'.[9] Notably, this would represent the supplanting of traditionally dominant Western nodes such as New York, Paris, London, Frankfurt, and Amsterdam.

Hence the international advertising campaign directed not merely at the 'global ruling class' – first-class passengers who enjoy private suites, a 'shower spa', 'the world's first moisturizing sleepwear for the skies', and 'exclusive … amenity kits' designed by a 'luxury Italian brand' ('fine leather' for men and 'sophisticated satin' for 'ladies').[10] But also another category of would-be global citizens: that is, (English-speaking) 'middling groups' from both the North and South who sit in the back of the plane. Indeed, some of Emirates' double-decker jets feature economy class-only configurations (Campbell 2017). In this vein of increasing connectivity for paying global citizen-customers, Dubai International Airport 'has been designed as a massive machine to facilitate [passenger] movements, a polished-stone fulcrum between Dar es Salaam and Guangzhou, Dallas and Dhaka' (Campbell 2017). It handles more international traffic than *any other airport*, much of it, as suggested, connecting faraway South–South and North–South city pairs. Gone are the days when North–North traffic, connected through Northern hubs, dominated global aviation. In turn, its successor airport is to dramatically enhance Dubai's status as node of all aviation nodes. With capacity for 220 million passengers, '[i]ts ambitions are consonant with its name: Dubai World Central' (Campbell 2017). It is in this rhetorical (and self-interested) sense that, to borrow from another Emirates ad, 'Dubai re-imagines the world'[11] – both for itself and its passengers.

HSBC: promoting (capitalist) globalization at an airport near you

Second is the case of HSBC, born in the great entrepôt of Hong Kong and currently based in London. Now one of the world's largest financial institutions, HSBC 'was established in 1865 to finance trade between Europe and Asia'.[12] A baldly phrased website heading reads, 'we are different', since from the beginning, 'we brought together different countries and cultures, as we still do today'.[13] Largely missing from this official history is direct acknowledgement that HSBC – originally incorporated as the Hongkong and Shanghai Banking Corporation – was founded as a 'colonial bank' under British rule before transforming itself into an 'imperial bank' that 'spread itself all over the regions under British influence' (Bonin 2016, p. 178). According to company strategy, 'Our aim is to be acknowledged as the world's leading international bank'. Accordingly, HSBC maintains 'an international network of around 6,100 offices in 72 countries and territories',[14] with a global cast of shareholders from 131 'countries and territories'.[15] Having previously declared itself through a global marketing campaign as 'the world's local bank', financial pressures have caused HSBC to reduce retail operations and focus instead on 'global banking and markets and commercial banking' (Farrell 2011).

In recent years, dating at least as far back as the 'world's local bank' days, HSBC has sought to 'bring [its] global network to life and demonstrate the power of international connections' by placing poster advertisements in jet bridges the world over. The altruistically framed purpose of this 'global brand campaign' is 'to encourage people' – English-speaking travelers – 'to think about where they are going in life and, by doing so, demonstrate our support to help them along their way'.[16] According to the trade publication *Adweek*, HSBC 'pioneered jet bridge advertising'. Subsequent to placing its first such advertisement at London Heathrow Airport in 2001, its campaigns have spread to dozens of airports worldwide (Bachman 2010). At one point, HSBC controlled *every* jet bridge in Tokyo's Narita International Airport.[17]

Typical are ads with trivia-style yet politically suggestive observations – 'Only 4% of U.S. films are made by women, compared to 25% in Iran'; 'Five times more people are learning English in China, than there are people in England'; 'Holland makes more exporting soy sauce than Japan'[18] – followed by clarion calls for weary travelers to 'find' or 'see' the world's potential (for further examples, see Best and Paterson 2010). Such 'provocative' references to Iran, Iranian women, and China in particular represent a nod to the rise of the postcolonial 'Other'.

Other slogans evince clearer normative assumptions about the evolving world order, with prodding implications about how audiences can join the (profitable) action. They read: 'In the future, South-South trade will be norm not novelty'

Figure 11.7 HSBC on 'emerging markets'.

Source: www.foresightinhindsight.com/article/show/3043 (viewed 2 April 2017).

'Progressive neoliberal' citizens 225

(accompanied by the message: 'There's a new world emerging'); 'In the future, new trade routes will reshape the world economy' (accompanied by the more imploring message: 'There's a new world emerging. Be part of it.'); 'In the future, even the smallest business will be multinational' (featuring the same accompanying message); and, 'In the future, there will be no markets left waiting to emerge' (accompanying message: 'HSBC's international network can help you discover new markets wherever they emerge next').[19]

In other words, according to this utopian vision, corporate globalization is creating a flat world by erasing traditional North–South distinctions (Robinson 2008). And, as suggested by recurring references to an 'emerging' and 'future' global reality, which *will* culminate when *all* businesses, 'markets', and geographical spaces have been fully integrated into the global capitalist system, we are to understand that its spread is inevitable and cannot be impeded or regulated. In such a world, even the neighborhood lemonade stand – as pictured in Figure 11.8, with prices in three different currencies – *will* have globalized accordingly. *Everyone*, including would-be capitalists with no capital to their names, can, should, and will participate by becoming global citizen-consumers. This includes passengers who are willing to pause and reflect on HSBC's aphoristic slogans, through which they may imbibe precisely the heightened global awareness that will be necessary to stay ahead of the business curve in 'tomorrow's' increasingly borderless capitalist landscape.

Indeed, business opportunities know no boundaries, whether geographical, racial, economic, citizenship-based, or otherwise. Hence the reminder, as another advertisement puts it, that 'Over 138 million people work outside their country of birth'.[20] Given that you as the audience are on your way to and/or from a flight at a global aviation hub, the implication is that neither should your own profit-seeking activities know any limitations. Again, in an increasingly nativist 'Western' world, such observations – especially about the mobility of *workers* – take on a 'subversive' quality vis-à-vis prevailing trends of xenophobia and parochialism.

For many audiences, and perhaps particularly those from traditionally excluded postcolonial societies, this is an appealing message. After all, there is a big capitalist world out there, and passengers who adopt a proper global mindset and

Figure 11.8 HSBC's lemonade stand.
Source: http://mustardpost.com/hsbc-airport-ads/ (viewed 30 March 2017).

break free from 'antiquated', place-based concerns, as well as 'imagined communities' that are limited by national citizenship, will be well situated to reap substantial material rewards. Since thriving in that world requires navigating the 'confusion' and 'frustration' that may accompany cross-cultural engagement – as portrayed in another commercial – HSBC provides, for a price, the 'solution' for the would-be global citizen-entrepreneur, as it 'will be there to help guide us through such foreign places' (Fitch 2015, p. 31). Hence the slogan, 'At HSBC we never underestimate the importance of local knowledge'.

Capturing this local–global duality, as Best and Paterson (2010, p. 4) argue vis-à-vis HSBC's advertising campaigns,

> the cultural character of contemporary political economy is decidedly global, both in that there are a set of shared meanings across the globe which enable similar marketing strategies to operate everywhere (even while those strategies highlight cultural difference as a particular marketing ploy) and that specific management cultures become globalized through the strategies of a firm like HSBC.

Evoking the world's cultural heterogeneity – or those aspects that have withstood the universalizing tendencies of capitalist globalization (Chibber 2013), the very process that is advanced, ironically, by these advertisements – is thus a money-making strategy. HSBC pursues it by selling cross-cultural expertise as 'the heavy artillery' that allows capital, as Marx and Engels (1888, p. 477) put it, to 'batter down all Chinese walls' that prevent further accumulation. Thus, as Veronika Koller (2007, p. 129) argues, 'HSBC seems to have recognised the *zeitgeist* in times of glocalisation' – the simultaneous valuation of the universal and particular – 'by metaphorically constructing itself both as a sophisticated cosmopolitan and as a friendly next-door neighbour'.

The recent rise of the exclusivist, jingoist, and highly reactionary, global far-right has, if anything, made HSBC's brand of 'progressive neoliberalism' even more palatable for consumers. Especially notable is its recent and United Kingdom-focused 'Together We Thrive' advertising campaign, the first commercial for which – titled, rather forthrightly, 'Global Citizen' – began airing in December 2017. Though the company denies that it is taking sides in the Brexit debate, a headline from the business press captures the presumed intent: 'HSBC shares internationalist vision for Brexit Britain with "Global Citizen" campaign'.[21] Tellingly, it was reportedly designed to overcome the perception that the bank was only interested in a particular kind of global citizen – that is, 'the international elite or the wealthy'.[22] It is perhaps no coincidence that the self-described 'HSBC UK Global Citizen TV ad' was narrated by the British actor Richard Ayoade, who himself evokes Britain's 'global', cosmopolitan, and multicultural milieu, as he was born to a Norwegian mother and Nigerian father. He begins the minute-long advertisement by recounting the highly globalized nature of everyday Britons' quotidian lives, from consuming Costa Rican coffee and Japanese cars to cheering

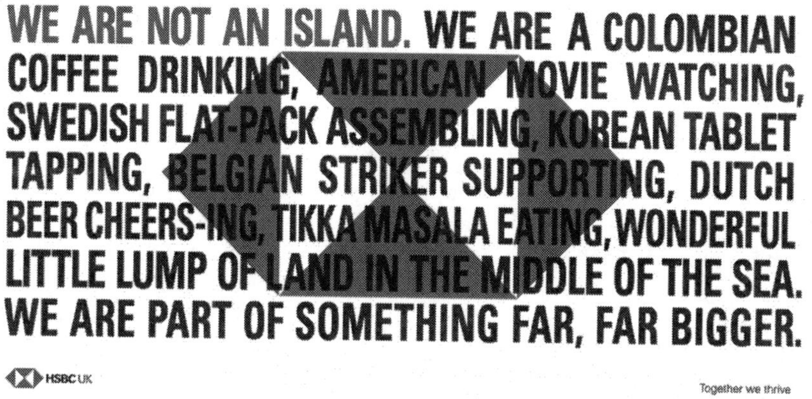

'Progressive neoliberal' citizens 227

> WE ARE NOT AN ISLAND. WE ARE A COLOMBIAN COFFEE DRINKING, AMERICAN MOVIE WATCHING, SWEDISH FLAT-PACK ASSEMBLING, KOREAN TABLET TAPPING, BELGIAN STRIKER SUPPORTING, DUTCH BEER CHEERS-ING, TIKKA MASALA EATING, WONDERFUL LITTLE LUMP OF LAND IN THE MIDDLE OF THE SEA. WE ARE PART OF SOMETHING FAR, FAR BIGGER.
>
> HSBC UK   Together we thrive

Figure 11.9 HSBC's UK 'Global Citizen' print ad.
Source: www.thedrum.com/news/2019/01/03/hsbc-continues-its-together-we-thrive-pledge-with-we-are-not-island-campaign (viewed 7 November 2019).

on Brazilians, Argentines, and Chileans in the Premier League, struggling to assemble Swedish flat-pack furniture, and 'watch[ing] American movies on Korean tablets'. He concludes with the dramatic observation that: 'We live on a wonderful little lump of land in the middle of the sea. But we are not an island. We are part of something far, far bigger'. While Ayoade speaks, he inserts the United Kingdom piece into a world map puzzle.[23]

As if it were not already clear that capitalist globalization is what is being invoked, other figures associated with the campaign note that 'We believe that the people, communities and businesses in the UK thrive most when connected and open' and that 'many of the things that make us quintessentially British are the things that make us inescapably international'. The latter speaker, who is the creative director at the London office of HSBC's ad agency, continues by making transparent the link between this particular construction of global citizenship and a broader discourse about global capitalism: 'And who better to point that out than the bank that's been connecting the world through trade for over 152 years'.[24]

Itaú: cultivating 'Global Latin Americans'

Also discursively navigating between the local, regional, and global is the São Paulo-based Itaú, which declares itself a 'Global Latin American bank'.[25] While its operations date back to 1924, its current incarnation – Itaú Unibanco Holding – is the product of a 2008 merger that 'gave rise to one of the most important conglomerates in the Southern Hemisphere' and 'created a corporation with a market capitalization that ranks it among [the world's] largest financial institutions'.[26] Itaú's operations encompass nearly two dozen countries and territories, ranging from South America, the United States, and Western Europe, to China, the Bahamas, and the United Arab Emirates. With thousands of branches within Brazil,[27] it claims the mantle as 'the leading choice for Latin American Corporate & Investment banking' (in its promotional materials, 'Latin American' is highlighted in orange, the official company color). Elsewhere, Itaú calls itself 'a Brazilian bank with global reach'[28] that 'goes wherever the clients are'.[29]

Itaú's digital presence evinces a predilection for corporate clichés. 'We are the bank that invests the most in people'.[30] 'We want everyone at [Itaú] to be able to think and act like an owner'.[31] 'The secret of life is not in the minutes that pass, it's in the moments that remain'. This textbox, along with an accompanying image of a smiling, smartphone-wielding, middle-aged woman snuggling with her black Labrador, occupied nearly the entire homepage.[32] The link transported me to the bank's now-defunct 'Moments that Count' domain, where visitors were invited to view two ninety-second inspirational videos in which mostly white, upper-middle-class interlocutors extolled the virtues of family time and living in the present.

A more profound message which deals directly with global citizenship emerges from Itaú's well-known, English-language 'I Am a Global Latin American' international advertising campaign, which was launched in 2011 to great fanfare but no longer appears to be active (Robertson 2015, p. 13; Hellinger 2015 p. 480). Notably, the responsible advertising agency bills itself as a 'global brand' that 'has no boundaries'.[33] It intended for this series of full-page magazine spreads (placed in publications such as *The Economist*) and online videos to promote 'international awareness' of Itaú by inviting 'well-known personalities to present the bank that is Brazilian, but also Latin American and global'.[34] It featured haute Latin American cultural and sporting elites from rarefied realms including polo, modeling, ballet, and wine-tasting – as well as, per Figures 11.10 and 11.11, the visual arts (respectively, the actress Alice Braga and photographer Vik Muniz, both Brazilian). These 'personalities' all appear to be light-skinned, thus conjuring for foreigners (and local, English-speaking elites) an unrepresentative 'white' version of Brazilian society. Such racial exclusions reflect the longstanding 'tendency to associate whiteness with economic development and progress' (Legg 2015, p. 220).

In these advertisements, orange text is maintained for the bold heading, 'I AM A ... LATIN AMERICAN,' with 'GLOBAL' inserted in white.[35] Audiences can thus perceive that Latin American-ness is able to both stand alone as a regional identity and exist within a broader 'global' (capitalist) context and form of citizenship. Accordingly, Itaú's interpretive horizons are simultaneously globally interconnected and regional. And when expressed in written language, they are in *English*, the international business language, not the Portuguese (or Spanish) that a locally rooted consciousness would suggest. As also witnessed vis-à-vis HSBC, this local–global balancing act is itself reflective of the 'tension between cultural homogenization and cultural heterogenization' that defines globalizing processes (Appadurai 1990, p. 295).

In his accompanying remarks, Muniz observes that, 'My goal is to create art that's as fascinating as Latin America, my continent'. He goes on: 'I'm a global Latin American. And Itaú is the global Latin American bank'. Others note that:

'Progressive neoliberal' citizens 229

Figure 11.10 Itaú 'global Latin American' ad 1.
Source: https://africaagency.wordpress.com/tag/global/ (viewed 11 January 2017).

Figure 11.11 Itaú 'global Latin American' ad 2.
Source: https://africaagency.wordpress.com/tag/global/ (viewed 11 January 2017).

'I play the leading role in my own life. And that's the kind of growing recognition Latin America is experiencing on the global stage'; 'my continent is already changing the whole world'; and, 'Just like my continent, I've struggled hard to earn my place in the world and to become an agent of change'.[36] Throughout this campaign, there is thus a recurring motif in which particular and typically privileged individuals serve as metonymic stand-ins for the rhetorical construction of a dynamic, rising Latin American region populated by regional–global citizens (Needell 2015). Also invoked here through these business-friendly, individualistic accounts is Colin Gordon's Foucault-inspired formulation that neoliberalized citizenship involves treating 'one's life as the enterprise of oneself' (as quoted in Chapman, Ruiz-Chapman and Eglin 2018, p. 146).

Itaú's story is perhaps less straightforward than Emirates' borderless utopia or HSBC's not-so-subtle exhortation that we summon our entrepreneurial spirit as global citizen-consumers and join the emerging and profitable flat-world global capitalist reality. That the Latin American regional context is built into Itaú's campaign suggests that 'place' still matters in global political economy, but perhaps only in the sense that not all places have traditionally 'enjoyed' the same degree of integration into the global capitalist system. If the above-cited cultural elites wish to celebrate that they have broken out from the postcolonial periphery to make waves in the core, then so too is Itaú asserting its pride of place as not merely *a*, but *the* 'global Latin American bank'. That is, notwithstanding the region's late entry into capitalist modernity – as the story goes – Latin America's elites, capitalist and otherwise, can compete with anyone's. Latin Americans, too, can take pictures that appear in Parisian art galleries, act in films that captivate audiences from Miami to Milan, and operate a vast international banking network that greases the wheels of global commerce, exchange, and financial flows.

As the Itaú advertisement, in Figure 11.12, frames the issue, 'The world powers changed. Itaú changes with them'. Next to this text stand three smiling young boys, whose respective phenotypes and the larger context surrounding 'emerging powers' (and the BRICS grouping) suggest they represent Brazil, China, and India (naturally, the Brazilian – who is noticeably less white than Itaú's standard actors and models – is holding the soccer ball). Capitalist globalization, we are to understand, is not a game to be played (or won) exclusively by the North.

How, then, to understand this assertion of me-too-ness?

Itaú's message can be read as nationalist/regionalist, political-economic pride in Brazil, Latin America, and the global South: as formerly colonized peoples and places from Washington's 'backyard' pulling themselves up by their bootstraps, becoming 'makers' instead of 'takers' in the global economy and asserting their belonging as proper global citizens (Funk 2015a). It is again a mildly subversive message, though not one that subverts the system itself. What it does, instead, is critique the notion that only Northerners can be capitalism's 'winners' (Funk 2013). More mundanely, Itaú suggests that Latin America is part of a global (capitalist) story. And that the path for Latin Americans to become global citizens,

Figure 11.12 Itaú 'world powers' ad.
Source: http://prcb.espm.br/2011/o-mundo-muda (viewed 13 January 2017).

or for extra-regional actors to engage economically with the region, goes through them. If Latin America is your point of departure or destination, Itaú is your bank.

Yet beyond Itaú's narrow business concerns, the larger narrative is familiar: there is an objectively globalizing capitalist world that is inevitably compressing time, citizenship, and space – hinted at through the fact that even a traditionally 'peripheral' region like Latin America has become an evangelist for global capitalism. Moreover, it is a world in which you can be an 'agent of change', *no matter your provenance*, whether it be in the core or periphery, First or Third World, or global North or South. Globalization is for *you*. It promotes a true universal form of citizenship to which all may aspire.

The world has thus changed indeed. And while we may celebrate Latin America's growing protagonism within it, what we are toasting, per Itaú's vision, is less the rise of a long-suffering region than the triumphalism of a totalizing, global, capitalist model and globally oriented, capitalist elite, in Latin America and beyond, that is inexorably remaking the world – from North to South – in its image (Robinson 2008; Sklair 2001).

Summary and analysis

It is unsurprising that Emirates, HSBC, Itaú, and other corporations would invest in the diffusion of global or regional–global presentations of self – and of customers, current or potential – for reasons unrelated to any sort of 'real', felt globality (Funk 2015b). Instead, naturally, they project such an identity, and globalized form of citizenship, to reap material benefits (that is, profits). As Aihwa Ong (1999, p. 6; emphasis added) notes, 'in their quest to accumulate capital and social prestige in the global arena, subjects *emphasize*, and are regulated by, practices favoring flexibility, mobility, and repositioning in relation to markets, governments, and cultural regimes'.

In turn, how do these corporate globalizing discourses 'work', and what is their intended effect? As I argue, global elites deploy advertisements not only to challenge regulatory efforts (and the body politic) to 'catch them if they can' as they conjure 'spaces where the production of profit can evade or minimize contestation' (Appel 2012, p. 698). They also suggest that we live in an inevitably globalizing and 'frictionless' world in which they *cannot* be caught or contained (Appel 2012, p. 706). Regulation, in other words, is now 'futile' (Chang 2009, p. 97). As Dani Rodrik argues, business elites (and economists) have advanced a 'hyper-globalization agenda' that asserts corporate rights over states' abilities to promote social welfare (Pearlstein 2011). Again, one way in which this business-friendly agenda – a deep-seated aversion to certain kinds of regulations – is pursued is through corporate advertising that stresses the global credentials of their own institutions and capitalist elites more generally, along with the inexorability of capitalism's global spread (Beder 2005). Accordingly, corporate discourses promoting globality, and 'tomorrow's' borderless utopia, are a political performance by capitalist entities to promote their own profit-seeking interests (Ho 2005). They are a rhetorical form of 'heavy artillery' to 'batter down all walls' – regulatory, ideational, and otherwise – that prevent further capital accumulation. Yet, as explored below, the present analysis/deconstruction of these seemingly hegemonic, corporate discourses also brings to the fore 'fissures' that allow for the contemplation of regulatory efforts and alternative global imaginaries (Ho 2005). As well as, potentially, less exclusionary forms of global citizenship.

Conclusions

In deconstructing recurring global imaginaries in corporate advertisements and analyzing the ways in which such discourses function as key sites in the production of 'commonsense' understandings, this chapter links the propagation of global imaginaries with the corporate quest for profit. Contrary to contemporary ethno-nationalist surges in the United States, Europe, and elsewhere, these discourses suggest humanity is crossing national, racial, religious, cultural, geographic, gender, and citizenship-based boundaries to create a new and more fully integrated global society. Accordingly, these advertisements construct 'global' subjects. Such global imaginaries evoke harmonious cross-cultural contact, *Condé Nast*-style cosmopolitan consumption patterns (in food, music, film, and so on),[37] and universal human rights, values, citizenship, and belonging. Indeed, to the degree that such advertisements are 'successful', it is in part due to their ability to tap into existing (pleasing) mental frameworks among (some) audiences. They also 'succeed' as pop-culture artifacts that captivate viewers through suggestive (and, at times, 'subversive') sloganeering and seductive visual displays that undermine traditional North–South dichotomies.

Yet corporations have little incentive to reinforce consumers' budding globality without an accompanying ideological and profit-seeking project: that is, not merely acquiring customers, but also positing a globalized (capitalist) world that is so globalized that it is borderless. The imagined corporate globalization of their conjuring is a capitalist paradise in which capitalist elites have no unwanted material or ideational attachments to the state and the regulation of flows of goods, services, capital, and (certain classes and categories of) people is unthinkable and impossible. More fundamentally, this chapter both asserts the underlying importance of pop-culture representations in constructing such imaginaries and interrogates *how* corporate globalizing discourses function as 'devices' vis-à-vis audiences.

To conclude briefly, where does this analysis leave us regarding contemporary political debates relating to agency in globalization and the ability of popular forces to end state capture by economic elites (Robinson 2014), the power of national governments to regulate global capitalism (Chang 2009), and the imagining, as well as construction, of alternative globalizations based on truly inclusionary forms of cross-border citizenship (Evans 2008; King 2016)?

As argued, this borderless imaginary exists more in corporate advertisements than in a material world defined by passport controls at airports, wall-building, and the militarization of borders (Brown 2010), and *national* governments that function as lenders (and spenders) of last resort during (global) economic crises. Indeed, state actors can choose – especially in the case of North America and Europe – to circumscribe the activities of even heavily 'globalized' corporations such as Facebook. Accordingly, regulation – whether for good or ill – *is possible* (Rodrik 2012). As is another world order, or form of citizenship, entirely. In other words, since we do not live in Thomas Friedman's 'flat world', then contrary to Margaret Thatcher's (in)famous assertion, there *are* alternatives, provided that there is sufficient political will to pursue them. These range from the 'global Trumpist' (Blyth 2016) mix of xenophobia and white identity politics to more inclusive forms of people-first globalization. Considering how to engage in meaningful forms of global governance, as well as imagining other possible worlds and citizenships, are thus imperatives for our time, and within the public's collective power to contemplate (Acharya 2016). They are doubtlessly *difficult* tasks, but not the *near-impossible* ones that would confront us if borders had truly become 'so yesterday' and sovereignty had devolved completely to capital (Brown 2010; Hardt and Negri 2000). Whatever its utopian desires, a would-be global capitalist class that still has 'national attachments' and 'needs', and that must navigate a world order in which state-based authority structures matter, will be easier to regulate, or even potentially unseat.

Contrary, then, to still-prominent discourses of inevitability, teleology, and the 'end of history', the global capitalist utopia of a borderless economy is thus not a fait accompli. Rather, it is an ideological project advanced through corporate advertisements and other means. Indeed, contrary to these deterministic messages, global capitalism, and particularly of the neoliberal 'variety', are not naturally occurring systems, but instead have 'political origins'. Accordingly, through critically analyzing discursive efforts to 'sell' these ideas to audiences, and by constructing counter-imaginaries, we may come to the realization that these seemingly timeless structures can also be 'politically reversed' (Schwartz 2014, p. 519; see also Polanyi 2001). Beyond the present scholarly exercise, numerous other agents – including activists and social media users – are well suited to this task. That is to say, the 'body' of global capitalism is much more 'open, porous, seeping, and dripping' – and thus vulnerable to variegated responses and audience agency – than its corporate promoters seek to portray (Maurer 2000, p. 672). As Karen Ho (2005, pp. 68, 83, 86) observes, beyond the veneer of 'totalizing' and 'triumphalist discourses of global capitalism', there are opportunities to expose it as 'partial, incomplete, high-pressured, and ephemeral'. And, in turn, to construct a truly cosmopolitan world order in which cross-border solidarity is the norm, and that is based on a form of global citizenship that is free of class-based or other exclusions. Returning to Marx and Engels (1888, p. 488), 'The working [people] have no country. We cannot take from them what they have not got'.

Notes

1 This chapter is a modified, reframed, and updated version of an article that was previously published as: Funk, K 2018, 'Between freedom and futility: on the political uses of corporate globalizing discourses', *Journal of Cultural Economy*, vol. 11, no. 6, pp. 565–90. It is reprinted here with permission from Taylor & Francis Ltd, www.tandfonline.com.
2 This term is derived from Michael Billig's (1995, p. 6) well-known concept of 'banal nationalism'. The latter refers to 'the ideological habits which enable the established nations of the West to be reproduced', as these practices are deeply embedded in 'everyday life'.
3 See www.youtube.com/watch?v=kwYr4LAIUjk (viewed 17 January 2016).
4 See https://worldairlinenews.com/2012/04/09/emirates-launches-its-hello-tomorrow-ad-campaign/ (viewed 28 January 2018).
5 See www.emirates.com/english/about/int-and-gov-affairs/international-and-government-affairs-new.aspx (viewed 17 January 2016). Perhaps ironically (but fully in line with neoliberal practice, if not theory), Emirates and other Middle Eastern airlines have repeatedly been accused of benefiting from 'massive government subsidies' (see www.openandfairskies.com/ [viewed 31 January 2017]). The above *Bloomberg* cover cheekily refers to two of Emirates' competitive advantages: 'no unions' and 'no shareholders'.
6 See www.emirates.com/ro/english/open-skies/issue/2866682/january-2016 (viewed 17 January 2016).
7 Though he adds the caveat: 'Maybe I'm just being a little bit naive, overoptimistic'.

8   See www.emiratesgroupcareers.com/english/about/cultural_diversity.aspx (viewed 17 January 2016).
9   See www.emirates.com/english/about/the_emirates_story.aspx (viewed 17 January 2016).
10 See www.emirates.com/us/english/flying/cabin_features/first_class/first_class.aspx (viewed 17 March 2017).
11 See http://adsoftheworld.com/media/print/emirates_burj?size=original (viewed 17 January 2016).
12 See www.hsbc.com/about-hsbc/company-history (viewed 17 January 2016).
13 See www.hsbc.com/citizenship/diversity-and-inclusion (viewed 17 January 2016).
14 See www.hsbc.com/about-hsbc (viewed 17 January 2016).
15 See www.hsbc.com/about-hsbc/our-purpose?WT.ac=HGHQ_Ah_h1.2_On (viewed 17 January 2016).
16 See www.hsbc.com/about-hsbc/advertising (viewed 17 January 2016).
17 See http://sparksheet.com/banking-on-airports-qa-with-hsbcs-global-advertising-head/ (viewed 28 January 2018).
18 See these and other slogans at http://blog.rev.com/articles/culture/hsbc-airport-ads-share-remarkable-insight-to-our-world/ (viewed 17 January 2016).
19 The advertisements can be viewed at http://mustardpost.com/hsbc-airport-ads/ (viewed 17 January 2016).
20 See http://blog.rev.com/articles/culture/hsbc-airport-ads-share-remarkable-insight-to-our-world/ (viewed 17 January 2016).
21 See www.campaignlive.co.uk/article/hsbc-shares-internationalist-vision-brexit-britain-global-citizen-campaign/1453460 (viewed 17 October 2019).
22 See www.marketingweek.com/together-we-thrive-hsbc-nailed-it-not-gone-far-enough/ (viewed 17 October 2019).
23 See https://youtu.be/KJ3uwPHUV9w (viewed 17 October 2019).
24 See www.thedrum.com/news/2019/01/03/hsbc-continues-its-together-we-thrive-pledge-with-we-are-not-island-campaign (viewed 17 October 2019).
25 See www.itau.com/ (viewed 17 January 2016).
26 See www.itau.com.br/itaubba-en/about-itau-bba/who-we-are/itau-unibanco-holding (viewed 11 January 2017).
27 See www.itauunibanco.com.br/relatoriodesustentabilidade/ra/10.htm (viewed 11 January 2017).
28 See www.itau.com.br/itaubba-en (viewed 11 January 2017).
29 See www.itau.com.br/itaubba-en/our-business/wholesale-bank (viewed 11 January 2017).
30 See www.itau.com.br/sobre/quem-somos/visao/ (viewed 11 January 2017).
31 See www.itau.com.br/itaubba-en/about-itau-bba/who-we-are/our-purpose (viewed 11 January 2017).
32 See www.itau.com.br/ (viewed 11 January 2017).
33 See https://africaagency.wordpress.com/ (viewed 12 January 2017).
34 See https://africaagency.wordpress.com/tag/global/ (viewed 12 January 2017).
35 The same slogan appears on Itaú-branded notebooks. See www.pmaise.com.br/portfolio/peca/caderneta-i-am-a-global-latin-american (viewed 12 January 2017).
36 See https://africaagency.wordpress.com/tag/global/ (viewed 12 January 2017).
37 Note *Condé Nast Traveler*'s suggested hashtag, '#AtHomeInTheWorld'. See www.condenast.com/brands/conde-nast-traveler/ (viewed 15 January 2017). The magazine declares itself 'the global citizen's bible and muse'.

References

Acharya, A (ed.) 2016, *Why govern? Rethinking demand and progress in global governance*, Cambridge University Press, Cambridge.

Anderson, B 2006, *Imagined communities: reflections on the origin and spread of nationalism*, Verso, New York.

Appadurai, A 1990, 'Disjuncture and difference in the global cultural economy', *Theory, Culture & Society*, vol. 7, pp. 295–310.

Appel, H 2012, 'Offshore work: oil, modularity, and the how of capitalism in Equatorial Guinea', *American Ethnologist*, vol. 39, pp. 692–709.

Bachman, K 2010, 'HSBC campaign arrives at L.A. Airport', *Adweek*, 20 January, viewed 28 January 2018, www.adweek.com/brand-marketing/hsbc-campaign-arrives-la-airport-106961/.

Beck, U 2002, 'The cosmopolitan society and its enemies', *Theory, Culture & Society*, vol. 19, pp. 17–44.

Beder, S 2005, 'Corporate propaganda and global capitalism: selling free enterprise?' in M Lacy and P Wilkin, (eds), *Global politics in the information age*, 116–30, Manchester University Press, Manchester, UK.

Best, J and Paterson, M (eds) 2010, *Cultural political economy*, Routledge, New York.

Billig, M 1995, *Banal nationalism* Sage, London.

Blyth, M 2016, 'Global Trumpism: why Trump's victory was 30 years in the making and why it won't stop here', *Foreign Affairs*, 15 November.

Bohland, J 2013, '"And they have a plan": critical reflections on *Battlestar Galactica* and the hyperreal genocide', in N Kiersey and I Neumann (eds), *Battlestar Galactica and international relations*, 98–118, Routledge, New York.

Bonin, H 2016, 'Concluding remarks: colonial banking, imperial banking, overseas banking, imperialist banking: convergences, osmoses and differentiation', in H Bonin and N Valério (eds), *Colonial and imperial banking history*, 174–82, Routledge, New York.

Brown, W 2010, *Walled states, waning sovereignty*, Zone Books, Brooklyn, NY.

Campbell, M 2017, 'Is Emirates Airline running out of sky?' *Bloomberg Businessweek*, 5 January, viewed 23 September 2017, www.bloomberg.com/news/features/2017-01-05/is-emirates-airline-running-out-of-sky.

Caso, F and Hamilton, C (eds) 2015, *Popular culture and world politics: theories, methods, pedagogies*, E-International Relations, Bristol, UK.

Castells, M 2010, *The rise of the network society*, 2nd edn, Wiley-Blackwell, Malden, MA.

Chandra, U 2013, 'The case for a postcolonial approach to the study of politics', *New Political Science*, vol. 35, pp. 479–91.

Chang, H 2009, *Bad samaritans: the myth of free trade and the secret history of capitalism*, Bloomsbury Press, New York.

Chapman, DD, Ruiz-Chapman, T and Eglin, P 2018, 'Global citizenship as neoliberal propaganda: a political-economic and postcolonial critique', *Alternate Routes: A Journal of Critical Social Research*, vol. 29, pp. 142–66.

Chibber, V 2013, *Postcolonial theory and the specter of capital*, Verso, Brooklyn, NY.

Dávila, A 2016, *El mall: the spatial and class politics of shopping malls in Latin America*, University of California Press, Oakland, CA.

Evans, P 2008, Is an alternative globalization possible? *Politics & Society*, vol. 36, no. 2, pp. 271–305.

Farrell, S 2011, 'Gulliver moves HSBC away from "world's local bank" tag in review', *Independent*, 11 May, viewed 23 September 2017, www.independent.co.uk/news/business/news/gulliver-moves-hsbc-away-from-worlds-local-bank-tag-in-review-2282646.html.
Fitch, M 2015, *Global tangos: travels in the transnational imaginary*, Bucknell University Press, Lanham, MD.
Fraser, N 2019, *The old is dying and the new cannot be born: from progressive neoliberalism to Trump and beyond*, Verso, New York.
Friedman, T 2005, *The world is flat: a brief history of the twenty-first century*, Farrar, Straus & Giroux, New York.
Fukuyama, F 1992, *The end of history and the last man*, Free Press, New York.
Funk, K 2013, 'The political economy of South America's global South relations: states, transnational capital, and social movements', *Latin Americanist*, vol. 57, no. 1, pp. 3–20.
Funk, K 2015a, 'U.S.–Latin American relations after September 11, 2001: between change and continuity', in I Ness and Z Cope (eds), *The Palgrave encyclopedia of imperialism and anti-imperialism*, 454–62, Palgrave Macmillan, New York.
Funk, K 2015b, 'The global South is dead, long live the global South! The intersectionality of social and geographic hierarchies in global capitalism', *New Political Science*, vol. 37, pp. 582–603.
Funk, K 2019, 'Making interpretivism visible: reflections after a decade of the Methods Café', *PS: Political Science & Politics*, vol. 52, pp. 465–9.
García Canclini, N 2014, *Imagined globalization*, Duke University Press, Durham, NC.
Hardt, M and Negri, A 2000, *Empire*, Harvard University Press, Cambridge, MA.
Harrington, B 2016, *Capital without borders: wealth managers and the one percent*, Harvard University Press, Cambridge, MA.
Harvey, D 1990, *The condition of postmodernity: an enquiry into the origins of cultural change*, Blackwell, Malden, MA.
Hellinger, D 2015, *Comparative politics of Latin America: democracy at last?* 2nd edn, Routledge, New York.
Ho, K 2005, 'Situating global capitalisms: a view from Wall Street investment banks', *Cultural Anthropology*, vol. 20, pp. 68–96.
Huntington, S 1993, 'The clash of civilizations?' *Foreign Affairs*, vol. 72, no. 3, pp. 22–3, 25–32, 39–41, 49.
Jansen, B 2017, 'Airline group urges Trump to keep borders open', *USA Today*, 2 March, viewed 23 September 2017, www.usatoday.com/story/travel/flights/todayinthesky/2017/03/02/airline-group-urges-trump-keep-borders-open/98644448/.
Juris, J 2008, *Networking futures: the movements against corporate globalization*, Duke University Press, Durham, NC.
Kamola, I 2019, *Making the world global: U.S. universities and the production of the global imaginary*, Duke University Press, Durham, NC.
Kanna, A 2011, *Dubai, the city as corporation*, University of Minnesota Press, Minneapolis.
King, N 2016, *No borders: the politics of immigration control and resistance*, Zed Books, London.
Koller, V 2007, '"The world's local bank": glocalisation as a strategy in corporate branding discourse', *Social Semiotics*, vol. 17, pp. 111–31.
Legg, B 2015, 'The bicultural sex symbol: Sônia Braga in Brazilian and North American popular culture', in S Albuquerque and K Bishop-Sanchez (eds), *Performing Brazil: essays on culture, identity, and the performing arts*, 202–23, University of Wisconsin Press, Madison.

Lisle, D 2006, *The global politics of contemporary travel writing*, Cambridge University Press, New York.
Marx, K and Engels, F 1888, 'Manifesto of the Communist Party', in R Tucker (ed.), *The Marx-Engels reader*, 2nd edn, 469–500, WW Norton, New York, original work published 1848.
McFall, L 2004, *Advertising: a cultural economy*, Sage, London.
Maurer, B 2000, 'A fish story: rethinking globalization on Virgin Gorda, British Virgin Islands', *American Ethnologist*, vol. 27, pp. 670–701.
Meena, K 2016, 'Border theory and globalization: perspectives from the South', *International Studies*, vol. 50, no. 1–2, pp. 1–15.
Moulián, T 2014, 'The credit-card citizen', in EQ Hutchison, TM Klubock, NB Milanich and P Winn (eds), *The Chile reader: culture, politics, history*, 547–52, Duke University Press, Durham, NC.
Needell, J (ed.) 2015, *Emergent Brazil: key perspectives on a new global power*, University Press of Florida, Gainesville.
Neumann, I 2008, 'Discourse analysis', in A Klotz and D Prakash (eds), *Qualitative methods in international relations: a pluralist guide*, 61–77, Palgrave Macmillan, New York.
Ong, A 1999, *Flexible citizenship: the cultural logics of transnationality*, Duke University Press, Durham, NC.
Pearlstein, S 2011, 'Dani Rodrik's "The globalization paradox"', *Washington Post*, 13 March, viewed 23 September 2017, www.washingtonpost.com/wpdyn/content/article/2011/03/11/AR2011031106730.html.
Polanyi, K 2001, *The great transformation: the political and economic origins of our time*, 2nd edn, Beacon Press, Boston, MA.
Prashad, V 2007, *The darker nations: a people's history of the Third World*, New Press, New York.
Robertson, J 2015, *Localizing global finance: the rise of Western-style private equity in China*, Palgrave Macmillan, New York.
Robinson, W 2008, *Latin America and global capitalism: a critical globalization perspective*, Johns Hopkins University Press, Baltimore, MD.
Robinson, W 2014, *Global capitalism and the crisis of humanity*, Cambridge University Press, New York.
Rodrik, D 2012, *The globalization paradox: democracy and the future of the world economy*, WW Norton, New York.
Rose, G 2001, *Visual methodologies: an introduction to the interpretation of visual materials*, Sage, London.
Sassen, S 2007, *A sociology of globalization*, WW Norton, New York.
Schwartz, J 2014, 'Resisting the exploitation of contingent faculty labor in the neoliberal university: the challenge of building solidarity between tenured and non-tenured faculty', *New Political Science*, vol. 36, pp. 504–22.
Sklair, L 2001, *The transnational capitalist class*, Blackwell, Malden, MA.
Sklair, L 2016, 'The transnational capitalist class, social movements, and alternatives to capitalist globalization', *International Critical Thought*, vol. 6, pp. 329–41.
Slobodian, Q 2018, *Globalists: the end of empire and the birth of neoliberalism*, Harvard University Press, Cambridge, MA.
Smith, N 2005, 'Neo-critical geography, or, the flat pluralist world of business class', *Antipode*, vol. 37, pp. 887–99.

Sparke, M 2007, 'Everywhere but always somewhere: critical geographies of the global South', *Global South*, vol. 1, no. 1–2, pp. 117–26.
Steger, M 2008, *The rise of the global imaginary: political ideologies from the French revolution to the global war on terror*, Oxford University Press, New York.
Stiglitz, J 2017, *Globalization and its discontents revisited: anti-globalization in the era of Trump*, WW Norton, New York.
Tsing, A 2000, 'The global situation', *Cultural Anthropology*, vol. 15, pp. 327–60.
Weldes, J 2015, 'High politics and low data: globalization discourses and popular culture', in D Yanow and P Schwartz-Shea (eds), *Interpretation and method: empirical research methods and the interpretive turn*, 2nd edn, 228–38, Routledge, New York.
Yanow, D and Schwartz-Shea, P (eds) 2015, *Interpretation and method: empirical research methods and the interpretive turn*, 2nd edn, Routledge, New York.

Chapter 12

The empire of 'global civil society'

Corporations, NGOs, and international development

Kyle Bailey

Introduction

Beginning in the 1980s, discourses of 'global citizenship' and 'global civil society' have played a central role in the proliferation of global neoliberalism. Far from denoting a purely 'economic' process, neoliberal practices and ideas about global citizenship have contributed to securing capitalist class hegemony across a wide variety of civil, corporate, intellectual, and policy domains, including national governments, multinational corporations (MNCs) and their business organizations, nongovernmental organizations (NGOs), international and United Nations (UN) agencies, trade unions, and universities (Sinha 2005).

In the sphere of international development, neoliberal global citizenship initiatives – beginning in the 1980s but intensifying through the 1990s and into the twenty-first century – have seen MNCs and their business associations link arms with mainstream NGOs in mobilizing around a growing range and variety of 'voluntary' corporate social responsibility (CSR) and sustainable development initiatives. Advanced under rubrics such as 'corporate citizenship' and 'partnership', these initiatives include codes of conduct; environmental stewardship, certification, and labelling schemes; occupational health and safety measures; 'stakeholder dialogues' with UN agencies and selected civil society organizations; increased support for community development projects; and 'triple bottom line' reporting on corporate financial, social, and environmental performance, to name but a few.

The basic claim of this chapter is that this panoply of global citizenship, CSR, and sustainable development initiatives functions to legitimate and reproduce the exploitative capitalist system – and the globalized order of uneven and unequal international development it generates and sustains – by endowing nominally 'private' and 'economic' entities such as MNCs with a sense of 'civic' identity and 'public' purpose. In this way, corporations can represent the inequality, exploitation, and domination at the heart of neoliberal globalization as economically 'long term', socially 'responsible', and ecologically 'sustainable'. Consequently, their claim to act as 'good' corporate citizens within many states both strengthens the material differentiation between the economic and the political constitutive of capitalist social relations whilst simultaneously blurring the discursive boundary between the public and private spheres.

The argument is threefold, drawing together the economic, political, and ideological implications of global citizenship discourse and practice for the maintenance of capitalist hegemony across the interlocking domains of state, economy, and civil society.

In the realm of *ideology*, discourses of global citizenship validate the central neoliberal axiom of the 'retreat of the state' in the face of a globalizing capitalist economy. In addition to privileging 'voluntary' civic action over mandatory state regulation as the quasi-spontaneous and seemingly 'natural' response to addressing the world's most pressing problems, such discourses simultaneously depoliticize the juridico-legal rights conferred upon MNCs by capitalist states in the name of facilitating the ongoing exploitation of labour by capital and corporate transgressions against nature and society.

In the sphere of *politics*, neoliberal global citizenship denotes a hegemonic practice of intellectual and moral leadership through which ruling classes and their cadres of organic intellectuals seek to elicit the active consent of subordinate classes by inculcating hegemonic values conducive to systemic stability, the rejection and/or co-optation of 'radical' alternatives, and the disorganization and marginalization of resistance from below (cf. Gramsci 1971; Jessop 1982; Carnoy 1984; Barrow 1993).

Finally, by naturalizing capitalist social relations under the guise of an abstract liberal ideal of formal equality between free and independent citizens, the discourse of global citizenship facilitates the expanded reproduction of neoliberal *economic* hegemony, perpetuating class exploitation and domination on a world scale within a privatized 'economic' sphere that appears separate from the state and society and subject to its own quasi-natural laws persisting independently of human volition and political decision-making.

'Global citizenship' as capitalist ideology

Whereas under feudalism, tributary surplus extraction was premised on direct state intervention in the sphere of production and the right to engage in such extraction was tied to the performance of larger 'public' purposes and 'social' duties, under capitalism there is a differentiation of economic and political spheres and the domains of state, economy, and society appear as separate entities governed by their own immutable and quasi-natural laws (Wood 1995; Rosenberg 1994). In other words, capitalist ownership and control over the means of production is not dependent upon the fulfilment of overarching social or political goals, but only on hard 'economic' calculation, accumulation for its own stake, and the constant revolutionizing of productive forces.

Yet, capital is not a 'thing', but rather a social relation of exploitation between capital and labour. Relations between social classes transcend narrow institutional divides between states and markets and the apparent 'separation' between the economic and the political is itself a historical product of capitalist social relations. The totality of these relations therefore cannot be divided a priori in accordance with the bourgeois conceptual triplet of autonomous economic, political, and social spheres. Rather, the lines of symbolic difference which constitute these and other categories must themselves be socially constructed, both materially and discursively, and therefore be subject to possible transformation based on variations in the balance of social, political, and class forces.

In other words, practices, institutions, and demands presently articulated as 'economic' may in the past have been thought of as 'social', 'political', 'cultural', etc., and may in the future likewise be reconfigured once again as the conditions of their symbolization are consciously or unconsciously transformed. Most crucially, important political issues related to the control of the production process, the appropriation of the labour of others, the allocation of resources and human capabilities appear in capitalist society as their opposite – i.e. as immutable 'laws of nature'.

From a Marxist perspective informed by historical materialism, the discourse of 'global citizenship' in contemporary capitalism can be understood as internalizing some of the fundamental tensions, antagonisms, and contradictions of the capitalist mode of production in its neoliberal phase of development.

An enduring insight of Marx's critical theory is to pinpoint the essential contradiction between the use-value and exchange-value moments of the commodity form in and through which value is crystallized as the alienated form of wealth produced by social labour under capitalism (Postone 1993; Saad-Filho 2003; Foster, Clark and York 2011). The purchase of commodities as use values presupposes the abundant natural and social wealth of the commons, which exists in constant tension with the socially induced scarcity of ongoing primitive accumulation and enclosure, the endless privatized accumulation of market-mediated monetary value, and the exploitation of labour by capital without which commodities would not be produced. Insofar as under capitalism wealth is only counted as value, the domination of use value by exchange value entails the systematic distortion, devaluation, and destruction of the former by the latter.

The 'soulful corporations' of contemporary global capitalism may claim to be benevolent 'global citizens' who privilege the long-term creation of use values for stakeholders over the competitive maximization of exchange value for shareholders. Likewise, they may trumpet their sense of social purpose by advocating causes from poverty reduction to the promotion of democracy, human rights, women's empowerment, and the environment. However, this formal championing of the progressive cause of use value as the basis for a kinder, gentler, and more inclusive capitalism is nonetheless belied by the real domination of exchange value under capitalist social relations.

As Soederberg (2006, p. 62) clarifies, an underlying premise of the mainstream understanding of the corporation as a 'moral person' or 'soulful corporation' is that

> because the modern corporation is marked by the separation between owners and managers ... it may move beyond mere goals of profit-maximization

towards non-economic interests, such as a robust and humane corporate culture, community and environmental responsibility, global business acumen, maximising customer satisfaction, and so forth.

However, this portrayal of MNCs as moral agents is inherently contradictory:

> [MNCs] must live up to their image as caring, responsible, and fair legal entities. The compulsion to do so is driven purely by economic factors, however. A corporation's reputation is not just a moral issue; it is a valuable asset in its own right, which can affect financial performance and provide a source of competitive advantage. It also can be lost overnight [...] the image of a soulful corporation and the desire to strive towards profit-maximization, even in the face of crisis, come into conflict.
>
> (ibid., pp. 62–4)

Rather than its triumph, the real history of capitalist expansion is that of the tendential alienation and obliteration of use value through the widening and deepening of the logic of profit-oriented and market-mediated exchange value effected by the progressive commodification of nature and society.

The contradiction between the 'civic' identity of MNCs as 'soulful' entities motivated by a sense of 'public' purpose and the real economic compulsion that drives them is further reflected in the tensions plaguing corporate discourses on 'sustainable development'. A *sustainable* environment implies definite limits on the capitalist market and accumulation for its own sake – less capitalism, not more – whereas ongoing capitalist *development* necessitates the commodification, financialization, and privatization of nature – more capitalism, not less. The domination of use value by exchange value entails that what is typically presented as an effort to 'embed' capitalist value relations in nature ends up embedding nature in capitalist value relations in ways that extend, rather than challenge, the mass production–mass consumption logic at the heart of (post-)Fordist flexible and transnational accumulation. Since only large-scale and vertically integrated capitalist MNCs engaged in unsustainable production and consumption accumulate enough 'waste' to make its recovery profitable, it becomes possible to understand why their CEOs have emerged as some of the most ardent advocates of sustainability. In this way, discourses of 'sustainable development' fail to adequately address the symptoms of capitalism's worsening ecological crisis while nonetheless further entrenching, and distracting from, their underlying systemic causes.

Despite the growing attempts of MNCs to portray their forays into 'global citizenship' and 'sustainable development' as an innovative form of profit-oriented economic rationality encompassing a long-term ethical commitment to nature ('eco-efficiency') and society ('social capital'/'shared value') (Porter and Kramer 2011), the relative scarcity of 'win–win' scenarios rather points to an overarching political and ideological project. The latter is concerned to buttress and maintain capitalist hegemony, absorb and co-opt certain short-term demands advocated by labour and social movements, and thus marginalize more radical and long-term counter-hegemonic alternatives (Levy 1997; Murphy and Bendell 1999; Utting 2005).

The actuality of global citizenship, CSR, and sustainable development discourses as moments of a political and ideological project intended to legitimate and reproduce neoliberal globalization underscores the central role played by capitalist states in mediating, depoliticizing, and neutralizing class conflict as a condition for securing their own reproduction. In this regard, the bourgeois ideological discourse of citizenship functions to naturalize inequality and exploitation in the guise of liberty and equality – i.e. as equal exchanges between free and instrumentally rational individuals who are likewise free and equal citizens of an overarching political community. As Jessop (2008, p. 417) points out, under capitalism 'economic agents' freedom to engage in exchange (belied by the factory despotism within the labour process) is matched by the freedom of individual citizens to determine public policy (belied by the state's subordination to the logic of capital)'.

Likewise, the formal freedom and equality of 'global citizens' to determine the direction of 'globalization' is belied by the reality of grossly uneven and unequal development on a world scale. Far from one competing interest group among many advancing their interests across neutral and diverse government institutions, MNCs form the fundamental vector of capital accumulation in the world economy. Insofar as the capacity of states to govern economic activity remains structurally dependent upon their expanded profitability and growth, an unequal structure of representation will prevail which renders state institutions more open to capitalist influences than to other social forces (Jessop 1990).

Yet, far from being passive victims of external market forces beyond their control, the relationship between globalization and states is an internal one. For, as Ryner (2007, p. 9) points out, 'in advanced capitalism, social reproduction is so fundamentally dependent on state intervention that any transnationalisation is dependent on state action for that purpose'. Consequently, transformations in international capitalism associated with the transition from Keynesianism to neoliberalism do not entail the 'retreat of the state', but rather the *restructuring* of its form and functions in accordance with the reproduction requirements of the US-led, post-Fordist global economy (Barrow 2005).

In other words, states are the primary authors of globalization, but globalization entails a transformation in the nature of the capitalist state, which, despite retaining its national form, is nonetheless required to respond to the strategic dilemma of how to internalize and reproduce a more complex set of class relations associated with networks of multinational production, labour, and finance within its territory (Bieler and Morton 2004, p. 92; Panitch 1994, 2000).

By assuming that global citizenship, CSR, and sustainable development strategies emerge on a level playing field bringing together a plurality of state and non-state actors from various local, national, regional, and global spaces, mainstream theories of 'global governance' (Rosenau 1992) reveal themselves as ahistorical and pluralist apologies for neoliberal globalization which function both to obscure the capitalist nature of the state within the context of class conflicts over global capital accumulation and neoliberal restructuring, and to naturalize the growing structural power of MNCs over labour, nature, and society across the North and the South (Soederberg 2006, p. 55).

The corporation as moral agent: ideologies of global corporate citizenship from monopoly capitalism to the postwar order

The notion of the capitalist corporation as a moral agent which undergirds contemporary neoliberal discourses of CSR and global citizenship has a lineage dating to nineteenth century corporate giants such as Carnegie, Rockefeller, and Ford – the so-called 'Foundations of the American Century' (Parmar 2015) – as well as Lever, Boots, and Cadbury in the UK. More specifically, it is rooted in an assumed separation of ownership and control of means of production in large, private, joint-stock companies.

Expressing the general tendency of capital to socialize its operations by concentrating and centralizing them into ever fewer and larger organizational units, the rise of monopoly capitalism between 1870 and 1914 gave rise to a small number of giant capitalist corporations. As the socialization and interpenetration of capital advanced through mergers and amalgamations of scores of family businesses, the scale and complexity of the technical division of labour increased, resulting in the tendential displacement of the 'robber baron', 'free market', and 'minimal state' characteristic of liberal capitalism by a more managed and organized form concerned to reduce organizational uncertainty through the long-term planning, standardization, and regulation permitted by non-market forms of authoritative allocation and greater extra-economic control over market forces.

This turn to monopoly capitalism also saw the gradual replacement of autocratic and paternalistic owner-entrepreneurs by a professional-managerial cadre that controlled far more capital than it owned and was more bureaucratic and consultative. By virtue of its extra-economic role in mediating between capital and labour – controlling and disciplining the latter on behalf of the former – and maintaining social cohesion, this managerial stratum came to be delegated a degree of autonomy from capital to pursue its own distinct technocratic and meritocratic agendas (Poulantzas 1978; Wright 1978; van der Pijl 1998).

At a time of widespread working-class disillusionment with capitalism and the growing popularity of an alternative European socialist vision of worker-run factory councils and democratic planning of production, the 'new liberalism' of the professional-managerial cadre articulated a vision of 'progressive capitalism' rooted in the idea that class antagonisms could be resolved *within* capitalism via the greater labour productivity, income redistribution, and consumerism enabled by intensive production organization and progressive social policy. While this vision of 'progressive capitalism' was advanced in the United States under President Roosevelt's New Deal during the 1930s, it fell by the wayside in Europe, which descended into the interimperialist barbarism of the Thirty Years' Crisis (1914–1945) (Rupert 1990; Anievas 2014).

Following the resuscitation of 'progressive capitalism' by the 'new collectivism' supposedly embodied in postwar European welfare capitalism and the renewed growth of the large corporation, the period from 1945 until 1979 saw the further development of market-displacing tendencies curtailing the 'excesses' of liberal capitalism. Widely interpreted as 'embedding' the capitalist market in socially beneficial constraints upon market exchange, the ideology of corporate citizenship received expression in the managerialist ideology that professional managers were the harbingers of a new social (but far from socialist) ethic of responsible capitalism. The institutional autonomy accorded to the large private corporation by virtue of its characteristic separation of ownership and control supposedly insulated professional managers from the financial demands of profit-maximizing shareholders, thus freeing them to pursue profits and growth subject to extra-market social values and interests that were altogether more 'modern', less 'selfish', and even 'soulful' (Scott 1997; Galbraith 1967; Rostow 1960; Lipset 1960; Bell 1973; Shonfield 1965; Kaysen 1957).

Insofar as managers aspired towards 'good' labour relations (rather than seeking to lay off workers at the first sign of difficulty) and sought to avoid 'externalizing' the social costs of capitalist production onto communities and the environment, the political and ideological implication of managerialism was that society was not anymore meaningfully 'capitalist' and divided onto antagonistic social classes (Miliband 1969; Albo 2005). No longer propelled by the imperatives of capital accumulation and class domination, the postwar 'mixed economy' of the 1950s and 1960s was instead the expression of an industrial society comprising large, joint-stock companies controlled by technocratic managers and a neutral, pluralist state that provided a level playing field for political competition amongst societal groups (and in which business was just one competing interest group amongst a plurality of others).

An ideology of class compromise functioning to legitimate the reconstituted form of bourgeois hegemony in postwar capitalism, the ideology of managerialism having superseded capitalist imperatives and ended class divisions thus denied the centrality of capital accumulation and class domination to all stages of capitalist development (Baran and Sweezy 1966; Mandel 1975; Aglietta 1979; Miliband 1969; Carnoy 1984; Albo 2005). In particular, the teleological 'markets versus hierarchies' framework undergirding managerialism, which, following Weber, emphasized the gradual displacement of liberal by managerial capitalism as part of a transition to increasingly impersonal organization, overlooked how labour, land, and money in postwar capitalism continued to be bought and sold on the market as factors of production, while state regulation reinforced, rather than challenged, the centrality of market exchange. As Lacher (1999, pp. 344–5) highlights the partial 'decommodification' of labour in the welfare state was linked to (and even presupposed) a widening and deepening of commodity relations which took place under the umbrella of the regime of embedded liberalism. Taken together, these seemingly contradictory processes can best be grasped by conceptualising welfare capitalism as the continuation of the dialectic of laissez-faire and protectionism, which has characterised capitalism from the start.

It follows that 'this reorganisation of social purpose never challenged the ultimate basis of the market as a disembedded institution itself: the commodification of human labour' (ibid.). Indeed, this dialectic of liberalization and protectionism mediated by state regulation actually further reinforced the centrality of the capitalist market to social life, while the cumulative incorporation of the short-term 'reformist' interests of dominated classes within the state apparatus placed limits on the extent of capitalist competition and internationalization – limits which, by the 1970s, had contributed to a structural crisis of accumulation necessitating a political response from capital (Lacher 2007; Dale 2010; Bailey 2016).

The aborted challenge to global corporate citizenship: from postwar crisis to neoliberal restructuring

During the 1970s, the crisis of the postwar order brought with it a significant challenge to the ideology of corporate citizenship. In the core capitalist states, the onset of 'stagflation' – rising unemployment *and* inflation – disrupted the long-run viability of class compromises and distributional bargains centred on the incorporation of working classes within national power blocs through economistic trade unionism, full employment in Fordist mass production industries, and the mass consumerism facilitated by the Keynesian welfare state. Across Europe, a series of prolonged and bitter industrial disputes combined with a radicalized social-democratic legislative agenda reflecting the popular pressure exerted on states by labour and social movements.

As the Vietnam War contributed to a crisis of hegemony which called into serious question the legitimacy of the West's relationship with the Third World, the growing strength of national liberation movements in the periphery, as manifested in the adoption of import substitution industrialization (ISI) policies, threatened to prevent the recovery of profits and shift the balance of class forces against capital.

This shifting balance of forces within states crystallized in the UN General Assembly, where the creation of the UN Conference on Trade and Development (UNCTAD) in 1964 codified demands for a 'New International Economic Order' (NIEO) based on fairer terms of trade and more liberal terms for financing development. Along similar lines, the UN Centre on Transnational Corporations (UNCTC) established in 1974 formulated a binding Code of Conduct for MNCs which was sceptical of the idea of corporate managers as self-regulating moral agents and went beyond the voluntary corporate responsibility guidelines favoured by the US and G7 backed International Monetary Fund (IMF) and World Bank and embodied in the Organisation for Economic Co-operation and Development's pre-emptive 1976 *Declaration on International Investment and Multinational Enterprises* (Soederberg 2006, pp. 61–2; Feld 1980).

Representing a clear challenge to the dominant imperialist logic of managing North–South relations, this counter-hegemonic strategy valorizing the centrality of state intervention in promoting economic development threatened to impose greatly increased mandatory government regulation of the economic activities of big business. Nevertheless, far from being a zero-sum game, the tensions *between* Western-based MNCs and Third World states manifested during the 1970s stagflation crisis and the struggle for the NIEO and UNCTC Code were primarily concerned with which interests would benefit from the internalization of foreign capital *within* peripheral social formations: foreign investors and firms demanding the restructuring of domestic social relations and institutions or peasants, workers, and national capitalists long protected from foreign competition by state-sponsored subsidization and ISI (Soederberg 2006, p. 67). Primarily concerned to reassert dominance over workers and peasants by instigating passive revolutions on national terms, the NIEO and UNCTC Code therefore represented

> the attempt to serve and protect ruling class interests in the South, during an intensified crisis of capitalism, by forming a pact between Third World states and foreign capitalists ... The Code sought to achieve more wriggle-room for the ruling classes of the Third World with regard to TNCs, while depoliticizing conflict in their societies by displacing the locus of struggle to the international realm: the UNCTAD.
>
> (ibid., p. 65)

Against the backdrop of the burgeoning environmental movement in the global North, the 1970s stagflation crisis also formed the backdrop for a revised neocolonial accommodation between Western and Third World ruling classes regarding the relationship between environment and development. Many G77 leaders regarded environmental regulation as a neocolonial impediment to development defined in national economic terms rather than as an inherent part of it, arguing that since the G7 countries accumulated vast wealth without much consideration of environmental degradation and caused most of the environmental damage, they should pay the costs for environment protection. Intended to mediate this political clash of ideas between Third World states favouring national economic growth and core capitalist states' Malthusian concerns regarding the 'conservation' of natural resources, the UN Conference on the Human Environment (UNCHE) held in Stockholm in 1972 under the leadership of UNCHE Secretary-General Maurice Strong proposed the integration of environment and development through the seemingly holistic notion of 'ecodevelopment'. Resembling the ideas put forward by the Club of Rome in its influential 1972 report on *The Limits to Growth* and underpinning the creation of the UN Environment Programme (UNEP), the concept 'ecodevelopment' would thereafter serve as the foundation upon which the 'sustainable development' dialogue would be built (Weiss et al. 2007).

Neoliberalism's 'human face': 'global citizenship' and 'sustainable development' in the long 1990s

As neoliberalism underwent a 'Third Way' rebalancing and consolidation during the 'long 1990s' (1992–2007), global citizenship, CSR, and sustainable development initiatives became associated with the project to put a 'human face' on neoliberal capitalist globalization.

Following the demise of the Soviet Union, neoliberal ideologues declared the 'end of history' (Fukuyama 1992), 'globalization' became the intellectual and cultural zeitgeist of the era, and there occurred a second wave of institutional restructuring in the capitalist world system designed to 'lock in' the neoliberal economic reforms of the 1980s. Despite proclamations of sweeping structural change associated with the 'retreat of the state', US economic decline, a growing 'European challenge' to American hegemony, and the 'rise of the BRICs' (Brazil, Russia, India, China, and South Africa), the US state nonetheless played the leading role in 'constitutionalizing' free trade through the creation of the North American Free Trade Agreement and the World Trade Organization (WTO).

While these architectural reforms might have appeared to infringe upon US national sovereignty, they actively strengthened the US state's capacity to promote the realization of capitalist globalization, while also transforming the institutional context within which big business operated and facilitating the further development of MNCs along lines pioneered in the US. In this way, a resurgent 'stateless' Anglo-American capitalism fuelled by an advanced technology boom seemingly triumphed over Northern European and Japanese state-managed capitalisms mired in economic malaise, propelling the deepening structural subordination of European to American capitalism and growing US–China/emerging markets integration (Panitch and Gindin 2012; Cafruny and Ryner 2007; Kiely 2015, 2016).

The way in which corporations portray themselves as contributing to the resolution of 'public' problems also came to reflect the capitalist imperatives of finance-led accumulation and shareholder-value maximization. Faced with a growing 'anti-globalization' backlash from labour and social movements, capitalist states sought to address big business' growing legitimacy deficit by articulating a vision of neoliberal globalization with a 'human face' capable of renewing the perception of MNCs as moral agents acting in the general interest of society.

In practice, this entailed the selective incorporation of MNCs, NGOs, and public agencies within flexible and networked forms of multi-stakeholder 'global governance' congruent with the reproduction requirements of the post-Fordist global economy, with the aim of organizing them into social forces capable of assuming greater responsibility for reproducing and legitimizing neoliberal capitalist globalization.

The closure of UNCTC in 1993 marked the final nail in the coffin of the project to formulate a binding Code of Conduct to regulate multinational business investment, clearing the way for 'voluntary' codes of behaviour. Struggling to retain its legitimacy in a 'post-Westphalian' world where private capital flows far outstripped development aid, the UN called for 'global partnerships for sustainable development' with all sectors of civil society in the run-up to the 1992 Rio Earth Summit. With the Cold War officially over, this expanded notion of 'sustainable development' as entailing an ethical commitment to nature and society in addition to national economic growth provided a renewed Malthusian justification for Western foreign policy interests and a global system of market-based inequality as the only means of forestalling global resource depletion and the 'tragedy of the commons' (Ross 1998).

In contrast to traditional CSR and philanthropy, which target areas outside the corporate core, ongoing finance-led restructuring under the aegis of 'global governance' saw the growing integration of multi-stakeholder CSR and sustainability initiatives into the core operations of MNCs (Pruegl 2019). Intended to augment the core capabilities of particular firms, integrated CSR remains grounded in the 'practical realities' of big business. The less autonomy CSR initiatives acquire from the core operations, the better. These efforts are subsequently communicated by highlighting the integration into MNC business activities of the three principles of 'sustainable development' – the so-called 'triple bottom line' of environmental integrity, social equity, and economic prosperity (Elkington 1997).

As part of this movement to incorporate social and environmental concerns into global neoliberalism on a market-led, 'voluntary' basis, a high-profile group of MNCs moved beyond defensive posturing and 'greenwash', narrowly conceived, to actively shape the CSR reform agenda 'from above'. Among them were industrial giants such as BP, Dow Chemical, Dupont, Ford, IKEA, Migros, Rio Tinto, Shell, Tata, Toyota, and Unilever, as well as banks, institutional investors, accountancy and auditing firms, and credit rating agencies engaged in 'socially responsible' investing, reporting, and certification (Utting 2005).

Seeking more legitimate ties with governments, NGOs, trade unions, universities, and UN agencies, business organizations such as the World Economic Forum (WEF), the International Chamber of Commerce (ICC), and the World Business Council for Sustainable Development (WBCSD) likewise cultivated notions of 'corporate citizenship', 'stakeholder value', and 'partnership' as the basis for rebranding themselves, no longer as private 'merchants', but as major 'public' international organizations and 'civic' NGOs.

Having repelled the challenge of the NIEO and UNCTC Code of Conduct amidst the 1970s stagflation crisis and been empowered by the neoliberal turn to structural adjustment programmes in the subsequent decade, the ICC began a process of institutional renewal under the chairmanship of Helmut Maucher, the then CEO of Nestlé and chair of the European Roundtable of Industrialists (ERT).

Maucher sought to address the ICC's legitimacy deficit by collaborating with the WEF – the so-called 'International Organization for Public–Private

Cooperation' – to cultivate a new identity for itself as a major public international organization (Kelly 2001, 2005; Hocking and Kelly 2002). A crucial step in this process was its rebranding as the 'World Business Organization' and the recruitment of Maria Livanos Cattaui – who had spent 19 years at the WEF, rising to become Managing Director with overall responsibility for the annual Davos meeting – as the new ICC Secretary-General (Kelly 2005, p. 263).

Against the backdrop of Kofi Annan's 'quiet revolution' in line with longstanding US demands for administrative reform and greater cooperation with the IMF and World Bank, the ICC also sought a new 'partnership' with the UN. Announced at the 1999 WEF meeting in Davos by Annan – who is described by Anderson (2007) as the 'academically dim son of a manager for Unilever in colonial Ghana' – the UN Global Compact remains the world's largest voluntary CSR initiative. Pitched as a 'coalition to make globalization work for all', it claims to 'embed' corporate behaviour in voluntary principles drawn from the Universal Declaration of Human Rights, the International Labour Organization's Declaration on Fundamental Principles and Rights at Work, and the UN Conference on Environment and Development's (UNCED) Rio Declaration. In a 2001 interview with the *International Herald Tribune*, Cattaui lauded the virtues of the kind of corporate self-regulation represented by the Compact over the state interventionist approach of the UNCTC Code of Conduct:

> The compact is – or should be – open-ended, free from 'command and control.' It can be a catalyst for good corporate citizenship and the spread of good business practices. It appeals to the competitive instincts of the market and will encourage companies always to raise their sights and go one better in upholding its principles. It mobilizes the virtues of private enterprise in fulfilment of the UN's goals.
>
> (as cited in Soederberg 2006, p. 89)

A top-down political strategy intended to 'bluewash' corporate reputations and depoliticize/co-opt counterhegemonic struggles in the burgeoning anti-globalization movement, the Compact functioned to legitimate dominant ideas by denying the structural role of capitalist states in reproducing neoliberal globalization and shifting responsibility on to 'voluntary' initiatives emanating from 'global civil society' (ibid., pp. 92–3). In this way, big business found in Annan 'a valuable supportive voice advocating the benefits of free trade and arguing that issues such as human rights and the environment should not be loaded on to the WTO system' (Hocking and Kelly 2002, p. 210; see also Sagafi-nejad and Dunning 2008).

In an era where NGO-driven consumer politics threatened to damage corporate profits, the Business Council for Sustainable Development (BCSD) aimed to transcend the discourse of 'business versus the environment' by re-envisioning big business as an environmental NGO. Formed to influence the 1992 Rio Earth Summit process when UNCED Secretary-General Maurice Strong asked Swiss industrialist Stephan Schmidheiny to be his special adviser on business and environment, the BCSD merged with the ICC's World Industry Council for the Environment (WICE) in January 1995 to form the WBCSD – the world's 'pre-eminent business voice on sustainable development' advocating for 'win–win' public–private and business–NGO partnerships.

As highlighted in the WBCSD's 1997 document *The Value of Membership*: 'Five years ago, it is unlikely that NGOs in particular would have forged links with a business organization like ours' (as cited in Najam 1999, p. 68). Indeed, in a 1998 speech WBCSD President Björn Stigson explained that 'the world since UNCED has changed in that environmental discussions are no longer bi-polar (governments and NGOs) but are now tri-polar, between governments, business and civil society' (as cited in ibid., p. 68).

Other, related initiatives to forge new linkages between business and environmental groups include the Global Reporting Initiative (GRI) founded in 1997 by the Coalition for Environmentally Responsible Economies (CERES) and the Prince of Wales's Business Leaders Forum set up in 1990 (Soederberg 2006, p. 83). Disillusioned with the inability of capitalist states to curb environmental destruction after Rio, NGOs seized the apparent 'opportunities' afforded by neoliberal globalization and the 'retreat of the state' by embracing market-based, voluntary strategies for regulating corporate behaviour (Murphy and Bendell 1999).

The neocolonialist World Wildlife Fund (WWF) led the way constructing multi-stakeholder global partnerships for sustainable development, including the Forest Stewardship Council (FSC) launched with the DIY/home improvement chain B&Q in 1993, the Marine Stewardship Council (MSC) co-founded as a joint venture with Unilever in 1996, the Roundtable on Sustainable Palm Oil (RSPO) established with Swiss retailer Migros in 2003, and the Roundtable for Responsible Soy (RTRS) set up with another Swiss retailer – Coop – in 2004 (Schwarzenbach 2011; Huismann 2014).

The FSC was founded in response to protests against ongoing primitive accumulation, tropical deforestation, and the violent repression of indigenous peoples, trade unions, and NGOs (including the murder of the Xapuri Rural Workers Union leader, Chico Mendes) by cattle ranchers, loggers, and rubber barons in Brazil's Amazon rainforest (Murphy and Bendell 1999; Auld 2014).

Modelled after the FSC, the MSC was set up as a reaction to overfishing following the collapse of the Grand Banks cod fishery in Canada in 1992, which saw 35,000 fishers and plant workers from over 400 coastal communities lose their jobs (Constance and Bonanno 2000; Ward and Phillips 2008; Auld 2014; Wijen and Chiroleu-Assouline 2019).

Rooted in the growing rift in the social metabolism between humanity and nature inaugurated by capitalism's separation of the direct producers from their land, these and other 'global partnerships for sustainable development' assume that the systematic undervaluation of nature within capitalist social relations can be resolved by a corporate-led, market-based strategy of internalizing externalities through the ongoing commodification, privatization, and financialization of nature and the global commons.

Surpassing mere co-optation by big business, this strategic shift reflected the growing corporatization of NGO activism, blurring the boundary between NGOs and MNCs in a similar way to the emergence of 'activist companies' such as the Body Shop (INCITE! 2017). More fundamentally, it presupposed the broad shift from 'producer' to 'consumer' politics inaugurated by the Reagan–Thatcher counter-revolution's smashing of the labour movement (Gallas 2015). Whereas producer politics expressed the collective power and organization of the working class, the advent of consumer politics marked its effective decomposition, disorganization, and atomization.

Conclusion: revaluing capitalism for the long term?

In the wake of the 2007–08 Financial Crisis and Great Recession that kicked off in the United States before spreading to the Eurozone (Panitch and Gindin 2012; Foster and Magdoff 2009; Konings 2010; Lapavitsas et al. 2012), the mainstream debate has not focused on the choice between socialism or barbarism, but rather on 'reinventing capitalism' (Porter and Kramer 2011; Barton and Wiseman 2014; Mazzucato 2019; Mayer 2019).

Fearing that neoliberal globalization's intensifying legitimation crisis will lead the growing masses 'left behind' by economic stagnation, social inequality, and environmental injustice to 'scapegoat' the capitalist system by embracing the 'totalitarianism' of the radical left or extreme right, a leading fraction of the capitalist class has cohered around a hegemonic project of economically 'long-term', socially 'inclusive', and ecologically 'sustainable' capitalism as the apparent solution to the system's multidimensional and overdetermined organic crisis (Bailey 2019).

Economically 'long term' means empowering 'non-financial' corporate executives and their managerial cadres against 'the capitalist threat to capitalism' posed by financial short-termism; socially 'inclusive' means responsibility to multiple stakeholders, rather than just to shareholders; and ecologically 'sustainable' means a 'Green New Deal' for global neoliberalism.

Perhaps the most articulate spokesperson for this fraction of capital is Paul Polman, who championed a supposedly long-term, multistakeholder, and inclusive form of capitalism while CEO of Unilever from 2009 to 2019, representative of big business on the UN High Level Panel which devised the Sustainable Development Goals in 2012, Chair of the WBCSD from 2012–2017, and, since 2018, as Chair of the ICC and Vice-Chair of the UN Global Compact. Polman is also a leading member of two influential business groups promoting 'long-term capitalism' (the Coalition for Inclusive Capitalism and Focusing Capital on the Long-Term) and the chair of Richard Branson's B Team (a group of 27 'visionary' leaders and CEOs united around the slogan of 'People, Planet, Profit'). The B Team and WBCSD are driving forces behind the We Mean Business coalition, a front group also made up of Business for Social Responsibility, Carbon Disclosure Project, CERES, the Climate Group, and the Prince of Wales's Corporate Leaders' Group which was launched one week before the New York People's Climate March in 2014 and calls upon world leaders to ratify the 2015 UN Paris Agreement.

More recently, in January 2019, Larry Fink, the CEO of BlackRock (the world's largest investment management fund) argued that 'every business needs a purpose ... Purpose is not the sole pursuit of profits but the animating force for achieving them'. In August 2019, the US Business Roundtable issued a statement redefining the purpose of a corporation as promoting 'an economy that serves all Americans' rather than just shareholders. In September 2019, the *Financial Times* published its 'Capitalism. Time for a Reset' front cover, arguing that '[t]he long-term health of free enterprise capitalism will depend on delivering profit with purpose' (as cited in Mayer 2019, p. 15). And, in January 2020, the WEF's Annual Meeting in Davos focused on stakeholder capitalism and the Paris agreement alongside publishing a universal 'ESG scorecard' to update its 1973 'Davos Manifesto'.

In an era of renewed class conflict marked by growing support for as-yet-ambiguous socialist alternatives, this new 'progressive capitalism' is seen by the ruling class as the last, best hope for restoring confidence in the system. Appealing to societal fairness and responsibility rather than economic acquisitiveness and aspiration, it aims to redefine neoliberalism as a progressive, dynamic force for reform in response to its own crisis – a nostalgic 'technocratic populism' that mobilizes the masses behind the CEOs, managers, and 'experts' who apparently know best.

However, this increased centrality of 'inclusive capitalism' within the big bourgeoisie is belied by heightened political polarization and the waning of neoliberal 'centrist' hegemony. Faced with a populist 'other' ranging from 'Trump and Brexit' to the popular but as-yet-ill-defined 'socialism' of Corbyn and Sanders, the ruling class faces the strategic dilemma of how to unify a capitalist power bloc and disorganize subordinate classes on the terrain of the state. On the one hand, the free-market conservative right represented by US President Donald Trump, UK Prime Minister Boris Johnson, and Brazilian President Jair Bolsonaro remains steadfastly committed to the economic rule of capital yet opposes the shift away from shareholder primacy and expanded fiscal-investment role for the state implied by 'inclusive capitalism'. On the other hand, the 'socialism' of Corbyn and Sanders accepts the broad contours of this shift but only at the cost of a broader challenge to capitalist power premised on inclusive ownership, income redistribution, progressive taxation, and nationalization. In the absence of a reliable political instrument capable of advancing the cause of 'moderate' reform, it is currently unclear whether 'inclusive capitalism' will be able to function according to its official mandate of inculcating hegemonic values during a period of organic crisis and instability in capitalism.

Nevertheless, big business's strategy of blurring the boundary between the public and private spheres retains the potential to divide the left by pre-empting, co-opting, and neutralizing demands for more radical transformation advocated by labour and social movements. By muddying the waters, it hinders the identification of real solutions and obscures the stark choice between capitalism and socialism facing humanity. If the left today is to advance beyond 'Third Way' social democracy's embrace of an increasingly predatory, exclusionary, and ecocidal form of financialized global capitalism, it therefore cannot settle for global capitalism with a 'human face', but must pose genuine, worker-centred, socialist alternatives – a dual social and ecological revolution that fundamentally transforms the exploitative capitalist system which generates these inequalities, degradations, and oppressions in the first place.

References

Aglietta, M 1979, *A theory of capitalist regulation: the US experience*, Verso, London.

Albo, G 2005, 'Contesting the "new capitalism"', in D Coates (ed.), *Varieties of capitalism, varieties of approaches*, 63–82, Palgrave Macmillan, Basingstoke, UK.

Anderson, P 2007, 'Our man', *London Review of Books*, vol. 29, no. 9, pp. 9–12.

Anievas, A 2014, *Capital, the state, and war: class conflict and geopolitics in the thirty years' crisis, 1914–1945*, University of Michigan Press, Ann Arbor.

Auld, G 2014, *Constructing private governance: the rise and evolution of forest, coffee, and fisheries certification*, Yale University Press, New Haven, CT.

Bailey, K 2016, 'Book review: from the great transformation to the great financialization: on Karl Polanyi and other essays, edited by Kari Polanyi Levitt', *Journal of International Development*, vol. 28, no. 1, pp. 156–8.

Bailey, K 2019, 'Revaluing capitalism for the long-term?', *Bullet*, web blog post, 11 November, viewed 20 November, https://socialistproject.ca/2019/11/revaluing-capitalism-for-the-long-term/.

Baran, PA and Sweezy, PM 1966, *Monopoly capital: an essay on the American economic and social order*, Monthly Review Press, New York.

Barrow, CW 1993, *Critical theories of the state: Marxist, neo-Marxist, post-Marxist*, University of Wisconsin Press, Madison.

Barrow, CW 2005, 'The return of the state: globalization, state theory, and the new imperialism', *New Political Science*, vol. 27, no. 2, pp. 123–45.

Barton, D and Wiseman, M 2014, 'Focusing capital on the long term', *Harvard Business Review*, January–February, pp. 44–51.

Bell, D 1973, *The coming of post-industrial society: a venture in social forecasting*, Basic Books, New York.

Bieler, A and Morton, AD 2004, 'A critical theory route to hegemony, world order and historical change: neo-Gramscian perspectives in international relations', *Capital & Class*, vol. 28, no. 1, pp. 85–113.

Cafruny, AW and Ryner, M 2007, *Europe at bay: in the shadow of US hegemony*, Lynne Rienner, London.

Carnoy, M 1984, *The state and political theory*, Princeton University Press, Princeton, NJ.

Constance, D and Bonanno, A 2000, 'Regulating the global fisheries: the World Wildlife Fund, Unilever, and the Marine Stewardship Council', *Agriculture and Human Values*, vol. 17, pp. 125–39.

Dale, G 2010, *Karl Polanyi: the limits of the market*, Polity Press, Cambridge, UK.

Elkington, J 1997, *Cannibals with forks: the triple bottom line of 21st century business*, Capstone, Oxford, UK.

Feld, WJ 1980, *Multinational corporations and UN politics: the quest for codes of conduct*, Pergamon Press, New York.

Foster, JB and Magdoff, F 2009, *The great financial crisis: causes and consequences*, Monthly Review Press, New York.

Foster, JB, Clark, B and York, R 2011, *The ecological rift: capitalism's war on the earth*, Monthly Review Press, New York.

Fukuyama, F 1992, *The end of history and the last man*, Penguin Books, London.

Galbraith, JK 1967, *The new industrial state*, Hamish Hamilton, London.

Gallas, A 2015, *The Thatcherite offensive: a neo-Poulantzasian analysis*, Brill, Leiden, Netherlands.

Gramsci, A 1971, *Selections from the prison notebooks*, eds and trans. Q Hoare and G Nowell Smith, International Publishers, New York.

Hocking, B and Kelly, D 2002, 'Doing the business? The International Chamber of Commerce, the United Nations, and the Global Compact', in AF Cooper, J English and R Thakur (eds), *Enhancing global governance: towards a new diplomacy?* 203–28, United Nations University, Tokyo, Japan.

Huismann, W 2014, *Panda leaks: the dark side of the WWF*, Nordbook, Keminmaa, Finland.

INCITE! Women of Color Against Violence 2017, *The revolution will not be funded: beyond the non-profit industrial complex*, South End Press, Cambridge, MA.

Jessop, B 1982, *The capitalist state: Marxist theories and methods*, Oxford University Press, Oxford, UK.

Jessop, B 1990, *State theory: putting the capitalist state in its place*, Polity Press, Cambridge, UK.

Jessop, B 2008, 'States, state power, and state theory', in J Bidet and S Kouvelakis (eds), *Critical companion to contemporary Marxism*, Brill, Leiden, Netherlands.

Kaysen, C 1957, 'The social significance of the modern corporation', *American Economic Review*, vol. 47, no. 2, pp. 311–19.

Kelly, D 2001, 'The business of diplomacy: the International Chamber of Commerce meets the United Nations', CSGR Working Paper No. 74/01, Centre for the Study of Globalisation and Regionalisation, Warwick, UK.

Kelly, D 2005, 'The International Chamber of Commerce', *New Political Economy*, vol. 10, no. 2, pp. 260–71.

Kiely, R 2015, *The BRICs, US 'decline' and global transformations*, Palgrave Macmillan, Basingstoke, UK.

Kiely, R 2016, *The rise and fall of emerging powers: globalisation, US power and the global north–south divide*, Palgrave Macmillan, Basingstoke, UK.

Konings, M 2010, *The great credit crash*, Verso, London.

Lacher, H 1999, 'Embedded liberalism, disembedded markets: reconceptualising the Pax Americana', *New Political Economy*, vol. 4, no. 3, pp. 343–60.

Lacher, H 2007, 'The slight transformation: contesting the legacy of Karl Polanyi', in A Buğra and K Ağartan (eds), *Reading Karl Polanyi for the twenty-first century: market economy as a political project*, 49–64, Palgrave Macmillan, Basingstoke, UK.

Lapavitsas, C, Kaltenbrunner, A, Labrinidis, G, Lindo, D, Meadway, J, Michell, J, Painceira, JP, Pires, E, Powell, J, Stenfors, A, Teles, N and Vatikiotis, L 2012, *Crisis in the Eurozone*, Verso, London.

Levy, D 1997, 'Environmental management as political sustainability', *Organization & Environment*, vol. 10, no. 2, pp. 126–47.

Lipset, SM 1960, *Political man: the social bases of politics*, Doubleday, New York.

Mandel, E 1975, *Late capitalism*, New Left Books, London.
Mayer, C 2019, 'Principles for purposeful business: how to deliver the framework for the future of the corporation: an agenda for business in the 2020s and beyond', British Academy Future of the Corporation Programme, London.
Mazzucato, M 2019, 'How to create a more purposeful capitalism', *World Economic Forum Annual Meeting*, web blog post, 15 January, viewed 20 November 2019, www.weforum.org/agenda/2019/01/purposeful-capitalism-economics-mariana-mazzucato/.
Miliband, R 1969, *The state in capitalist society*, Basic Books, New York.
Murphy, D and Bendell, J 1999, 'Partners in time? Business, NGOs and sustainable development', Discussion Paper No. 109, UNRISD, Geneva.
Najam, A 1999, 'World Business Council for Sustainable Development: the greening of business or a greenwash?' in HO Bergesen, G Parmann and OB Thommessen (eds), *Yearbook of international co-operation on environment and development 1999/2000*, 65–77, Routledge, London.
Panitch, L 1994, 'Globalization and the state', in R Miliband and L Panitch (eds), *The socialist register 1994: between globalism and nationalism*, 60–93, Merlin Press, London.
Panitch, L 2000, 'The new imperial state', *New Left Review*, vol. 2, March–April, pp. 5–20.
Panitch, L and Gindin, S 2012, *The making of global capitalism: the political economy of American empire*, Verso, London.
Parmar, I 2015, *Foundations of the American century: the Ford, Carnegie, and Rockefeller Foundations in the rise of American power*, Columbia University Press, New York.
Porter, ME and Kramer, MR 2011, 'Creating shared value', *Harvard Business Review*, January–February, pp. 62–77.
Postone, M 1993, *Time, labor, and social domination: a reinterpretation of Marx's critical theory*, Cambridge University Press, Cambridge, UK.
Poulantzas, N 1978, *Political power and social classes*, Verso, London.
Pruegl, E 2019, 'Feminism washing: are multinationals really empowering women?' *Conversation*, web blog post, 3 September, viewed 20 November 2019, https://theconversation.com/feminism-washing-are-multinationals-really-empowering-women-120353.
Rosenau, J 1992, 'Governance, order, and change in world politics', in J Rosenau and E Cziempel (eds), *Governance without government: order and change in world politics*, 1–29, Cambridge University Press, Cambridge, UK.
Rosenberg, J 1994, *The empire of civil society: a critique of the realist theory of international relations*, Verso, London.
Ross, E 1998, *The Malthus factor: poverty, politics and population in capitalist development*, Zed Books, London.
Rostow, WW 1960, *The stages of economic growth: a non-communist manifesto*, Cambridge University Press, Cambridge, UK.
Rupert, M 1990, 'Producing hegemony: state/society relations and the politics of productivity in the United States', *International Studies Quarterly*, vol. 34, no. 4, pp. 427–56.
Ryner, M 2007, 'US power and the crisis of social democracy in Europe's second project of integration', *Capital & Class*, vol. 31, no. 3, pp. 7–26.
Saad-Filho, A 2003, 'Value, capital and exploitation', in A Saad-Filho (ed.), *Anti-capitalism: a Marxist introduction*, 27–41, Pluto Press, London.
Sagafi-nejad, T and Dunning, JH 2008, *The UN and transnational corporations: from code of conduct to global compact*, Indiana University Press, Bloomington.
Schwarzenbach, A 2011, *Saving the world's wildlife: WWF – the first 50 years*, Profile Books, London.

Scott, J 1997, *Corporate business and capitalist classes*, Oxford University Press, Oxford, UK.

Shonfield, A 1965, *Modern capitalism*, Oxford University Press, New York.

Sinha, S 2005, 'Neoliberalism and civil society: project and possibilities', in A Saad-Filho and D Johnston (eds), *Neoliberalism: a critical reader*, 163–9, Pluto Press, London.

Soederberg, S 2006, *Global governance in question: empire, class and the new common sense in managing north–south relations*, Pluto Press, London.

Utting, P 2005, 'Corporate responsibility and the movement of business', *Development in Practice*, vol. 15, no. 3/4, pp. 375–88.

van der Pijl, K 1998, *Transnational classes and international relations*, Routledge, London.

Ward, T and Phillips, B (eds) 2008, *Seafood ecolabelling: principles and practice*, Blackwell, Oxford, UK.

Weiss, TG, Forsythe, DP, Coate, RA, and Pease, K-K 2007, *The United Nations and changing world politics*, 5th edn, Westview Press, Boulder, CO.

Wijen, F and Chiroleu-Assouline, M 2019, 'Controversy over voluntary environmental standards: a socioeconomic analysis of the Marine Stewardship Council', *Organization & Environment*, vol. 32, no. 2, pp. 98–124.

Wood, EM 1995, *Democracy against capitalism: renewing historical materialism*, Verso, London.

Wright, EO 1978, 'Intellectuals and the working class', *Insurgent Sociologist*, vol. 8, no. 1, pp. 5–18.

Index

ableism 13, 69
Abraham, J 12, 14, 194–208
accumulation by dispossession 11, 68, 83, 101, 216
Addams, J 25, 27–8, 39n33
advertising 112, 219, 223; business 216; campaigns 218–19, 221–2, 226, 228; corporate 233
Afghanistan 7, 177, 184, 186
Aga Khan 185, 186–8, 189, 191n6
Aga Khan Development Network 183
Aga Khan Foundation Canada (AKFC) 4, 92, 176, 183, 185, 189
Akula, V 204, 205
Alldred, P and Fox, NJ 120–1
'American dream' 51, 54, 73, 75, 77
American School Peace League 28, 36, 38
Andreotti, V 5, 108, 155–8, 165, 166, 177
Anthropocene 7, 9
Appiah, KA 175–6, 178, 188
Ashoka 201
Asian restaurant industry 11, 64, 65, 66, 71, 72, 73, 76, 79n1
Australia 8, 107, 119, 137, 138, 149n5
Avaaz 4

benevolence 26, 83, 100, 101, 173, 175–83; global citizen 12, 243
Bailey, K 12, 14, 241–59
Biccum, A 14, 16n4, 84, 93, 129–52, 155, 191n8
bio (-)politics 15, 38n14, 60n2
border (s) 7, 43, 45, 46, 47–9, 55, 58, 63, 75, 168, 216, 217, 220, 221, 222, 234; barriers/fences/walls 49–52; Cartesian 57; citizenship, cross- 234; of citizenship 63, 64; control 54, 60n2; immanent 63, 64, 65–70, 72, 78; programs, cross- 105; racial 47; solidarity, cross- 235; struggles 69, 70, 79; US-Mexican 11, 45, 49–54
borderless: capitalist landscape 225; creed 214, 221; economy 215, 235; fanaticism 16n6; imaginary 234; utopia 231, 233; world 211, 215, 222, 234; world order 214
Boochani, B 8
Braidotti, R 108, 112, 120, 121
Brexit 194, 200, 222, 226, 255
Bridges that Unite 176, 183–9
Brown, W 130, 132, 133, 142, 143

Canada 102n2, 107, 109, 138, 149n5, 175–8, 183–91, 253; government of 58, 84, 184; multicultural 176; peacekeeper mythology 185; *see also* universities
Canadian International Development Agency (CIDA) 89
capitalism 5, 7, 13, 26, 27, 53, 101, 132, 137, 197, 203, 214, 219, 231, 233, 242, 244, 245, 247, 249, 250, 253, 254–6; corporate/global/monopoly/neoliberal/ NGCC 5, 7–10, 24, 45, 63–80, 149n9, 154, 155, 198, 215, 216, 217, 220, 227, 228, 231, 232, 234, 235, 243, 246–8, 256; hegemony 5, 241, 242, 244; 'inclusive' 243, 254, 255; as mode of production 101, 243; 'progressive' 246–7, 255; state 242, 245, 248, 249, 250, 252, 253; sustainable 254; welfare 247, 248; world order/system 23, 47, 222, 241, 250; *see also* class (es); globalization; ideology; imperialism; modernity
Carleton University 4, 102n4, 102n10
Cartesian subject 45–62; *see also* border (s)

cartography 48
Chapman, DD 3, 5, 12, 14, 15, 15n1, 59n1, 63, 68–9, 79, 83–104, 108, 109, 195, 216–17
Cheng, W 66, 67, 76
Centre for Global Citizens 148n6
Citigroup 3, 12
'citizenly contributions' 65, 71, 76–7, 78
citizenship: corporeal 63–80; digital 87; global (neoliberal) 64, 66, 69, 70, 78; green 70; imperial 13; liberal 63, 66, 68–70, 78; nonexistent 71; studies 14, 15, 16n3, 120, 154; technologies of 60n2; universal 13, 67, 68; world 32, 35, 100; *see also* corporate citizen (ship); global citizenship education
class (es) 57, 63, 65, 66, 67, 72, 74, 76, 78, 79n2, 149n9, 190, 234, 235, 242, 243, 245, 247, 248; capitalist 74, 234, 241, 254; communities, working- 200; conflict 245, 246, 255; consuming 215; co-ordinator 13; cosmopolitan 217; exploitable 48; exploiting 57; lower- 78; middle- 66, 201, 221; privileged yet parochial 28; ruling 10, 28, 242, 249, 255; subordinate 242, 255; upper-middle- 228; working 66, 246, 248, 254; *see also* global ruling class
Colombia 9, 106, 113–19
colonial (ism) 10, 11, 25, 47, 48, 63, 111, 113, 130, 136–7, 156, 175–6, 180, 185, 186, 188, 189, 197, 223, 252; anti- 37, 137, 141; neo- 10, 49, 83, 96, 216, 249, 253; post- 3, 5, 10, 15n1, 15n3, 45, 47, 141, 155, 157, 188, 224, 225, 231; *see also* ideology; 'Other'; postcolonial sentimentalism; rac (ial)(ist/m)
coloniality 47
corporate citizen (ship) 12, 246–50; global 12; good 46, 241, 252
corporate global imaginaries 211–40
corporate social responsibility (CSR) 10, 12, 202, 241, 245, 246, 250, 251, 252
corporation (s) 11, 46, 49, 52, 84, 97–8, 101, 202; global 9; as a moral agent 246–8; multinational 6, 14, 209–59; (neoliberal) capitalist 12, 246; Power 97; soulful 243–4; trans-national 14, 49, 52–3, 83, 209–59; *see also* United States
cosmopolitanism 154, 155, 168, 175–6, 178, 185–6, 189, 190; banal 214
Costa, F 14, 139, 153–72

critical discourse analysis (CDA) 10, 106
critical global citizen (ship) 118, 157–8, 166–8

Dagger, R 135–6
death zones 45, 55–7
deconstruction (ist) 15, 118, 119, 233
deportation 50, 51, 56, 57–9
Descartes, R 47–8
detention 8, 50, 57–9, 60n2
deterrence theory 50–1, 55
deterritorialization 49, 119
development-security nexus 133, 144
disability 32, 55, 57, 63
Dower, N 99–100, 175
Drayton, W 200–2
DuBois, WEB 37
Duffield, M 132–3

'ecodevelopment' 249–50
ecological crisis 9, 244
education 6, 8, 14, 15n2, 22–42, 83–104, 153, 157, 159–69, 183, 184, 196, 201, 204, 216; development (DE) 137, 138, 149n5, 159, 176, 183, 190; for Global Citizenship 4, 28, 106, 107, 163, 164; international 13, 22, 24, 28, 31–7, 83, 86, 93, 96; Preventing Violent Extremism through (PVE-E) 129, 130, 134, 136–40, 143, 144, 145, 147; 2030 Agenda 107, 141; *see also* global citizenship education; Global Education First Initiative (GEFI); Global Education Governance (GEG)
Eglin, P 3–21, 68, 79, 108, 195, 216–17
Emirates Airlines 211, 215, 218–20
empire 8, 136, 197, 198; British 149n3; *see also* global civil society; imperialism; United States
European Union (EU) 111, 113, 137, 154, 169n2
exclusionary logic 106, 118
Experiment in International Living 33, 35, 36, 37, 38

Falk, R 16n9
Fassin, D 179, 181, 183, 190
Foster, C 178
Foster, JB 5, 6, 8, 9, 10, 11
Foucault, M 10, 11, 12, 38n14, 55–6, 131, 155, 231
Freire, P 108, 113, 115, 117, 119–20, 168–9
Funk, K 12, 14, 211–40

gender 63, 66, 69, 93, 112–13, 139, 149n9, 163, 164, 181, 184, 190, 221, 233
Giroux, H 99
Global Citizen 4, 46–7
global citizenship education (GCE) 5, 10, 14, 83, 100, 101, 105–26, 129–52, 158, 163–5, 176; in Canada 85, 88, 89, 93–4; in Colombia 113–18; critical 5, 106, 109; not neoliberal 142; socio-emotional dimension of 129, 164; in the United Kingdom 111–13; in the United States 22–42, 109–11; *see also* critical global citizenship; Education for Global Citizenship
global citizenship experience 119
Global Citizenship Foundation 140
global citizenship studies 14, 16n3
global civil society 144; empire of 241–59
Global Compact 14, 252, 254
global competence 24, 168; from the perspective of the OECD 159–67
global economy 5, 9, 65, 96, 166, 231; post-Fordist 199, 245, 250
Global Education First Initiative (GEFI) 139, 146–7, 164
Global Education Governance (GEG) 129–31, 138–9, 144–5
global governance 5, 15, 130–4, 144, 234, 245, 250, 251
global imaginaries *see* corporate global imaginaries
global mindedness 161, 166
global non-citizen (ship) 10, 11, 13, 43–80, 216
global philanthropy 5, 10
global ruling class 220, 221, 222
global studies 3, 15n3, 85, 93, 102n5, 105, 109, 216; WLU programme 90, 97
global subject 216–18
globalization 5, 7, 11, 13, 24, 25, 91, 94, 106, 114, 194, 214, 215–16, 218, 219, 232, 234, 252; agenda, hyper- 233; alternative 234; capitalist 155, 218–19, 223–7, 231, 250; corporate 215, 217, 225, 234; movement, anti- 9, 250, 252; neoliberal 64, 99, 241, 245–6, 250, 252, 253, 254
Golovátina-Mora, P 3, 14, 105–26, 149n8
Gombay, N 56
'Green New Deal' 254
Gullion, JS 105–26

Hacking, I 56
Harper, S 105–26
Harvey, D 9, 11, 47, 68, 101, 219
heteronormativity 13
HSBC 215, 218, 219, 223–7, 228, 231, 232
humanitarianism 179, 180, 187

ideology: capitalist 215, 242–6; of corporate citizenship 247, 248; of global citizenship 46, 101; managerialist 247; Marxist concept of 10; postcolonial 11, 130; *see also* neoliberal (ism)
immigrants 22, 27–8, 186, 215; Asian/Latinx/Mexican 63–74; fears/parties/sentiment, anti- 7, 25, 31, 67; (restaurant) workers 71–9; *see also* migrants
imperialism 5, 10, 12, 13, 24, 34, 47, 48, 69, 107, 110, 130, 136, 176, 188, 247, 249; capitalist 13; movements, anti- 114; *see also* United States
inclusion 24, 63, 64, 65, 66, 67, 68, 69, 71, 74, 75, 76, 116, 121, 130, 141, 234; affective 71, 72, 77, 78; differential 64, 65, 69, 78; exclusionary 68; psychosomatic 64, 70, 78; social 73
inequality 5–6, 10, 34, 100, 106, 132, 163, 179, 183, 215, 216, 241, 245, 251; carbon 7; economic 7, 34, 36, 46, 87, 101, 176; global 136; social 87, 114, 254; structural 184, 190; structures 106, 118–21
International Chamber of Commerce (ICC) 251–4
international policy influencers 153–72
internationalists 25–8, 31
Isin, E 63, 64; and Nyers 154
Itaú 215, 218, 219, 227–32

Jefferess, D 12, 14, 94, 175–93

Karatzogianni, A 105–26
Keynesian (ism) 245; consensus 197–8; welfare state 248
Ki-moon, B 3, 139, 149n6
knowledge/power 132, 134, 139
Krabill, R 110, 111

Larsen, MA 109, 118, 156, 158, 166
Latin America 25, 34, 36, 54, 89, 113, 114–15, 149n8, 218, 227–32
LGBTQ students 112–13; *see also* rights
Lee, CT 3, 11, 16n3, 63–80

Lewis, S 176–91
liberal (ism) 12, 13, 14, 69, 133, 248; democracy 154; new 246; state 11, 69; white racial 23–4, 36
'looping effect' 56–9

McMurtry, J 16n6
Mamdani, M 175, 189
Marx, K 38, 53, 135, 243; and Engels, F 10, 12, 226, 235
Marxist: analysis 10; hyperbole 221; perspective 243; theoretical framework 11; *see also* ideology; political economy
membershipping 120
Mexico 47, 48, 52–4, 66; Juárez 52–3; *see also* borders
Mezzadra, S and Neilson, B 63, 64, 69, 70, 78
microfinance (MFI) 183, 203–5
migrants 7, 69, 91, 113, 155, 158; Latinx 50, 56; as non-human 45–62; undocumented 45–62, 69
Mill, JS 117, 118, 121
Millennium Development Goals (MDGs) 130, 138
modernity 47, 110, 133, 176, 218; capitalist 231; signature of 176, 189–90
Mont Pelerin Society 198

North American Free Trade Agreement (NAFTA) 52–3, 250
neoliberal (ism) 11, 12, 13, 14, 23, 37, 53, 65, 97, 98, 108, 110, 113, 130, 131, 132, 137, 144, 198, 200, 222, 245, 250, 255; agenda 46; citizens, progressive 211–40; consensus 199; development paradigm 133; discourse 246; environment 166; global 241, 254; global citizen (ship) 24, 63, 64, 66, 68, 69, 70, 78, 96, 107, 219, 241, 242; governmentality 131–2, 139; hegemony 114, 242; 'human face' 250–4; ideology 131, 196, 242, 250; intervention 204; logic, progressive 215; multiculturalism 23; (political) economy 68, 83, 195, 196, 199, 205; practice 16n8, 235n5; propaganda 59, 216; restructuring 246, 248–50; state 11, 69, 200; universities 83, 84; world order 11, 13, 59, 83; *see also* capitalism; corporations; empire; global citizenship education; globalization; subjectivity
neo-republicanism 129–52
nomad and new materialist perspective 120

non-governmental organizations (NGOs) 12, 14, 15, 56, 129, 133, 136–9, 141, 142, 144, 153, 165, 241–59; Canadian 157, 187; international (INGOs) 12, 14

Organisation for Economic Co-operation and Development (OECD) 14, 138, 139, 153–72, 249
Operation Understanding 36, 37, 38
Orbinski, J 176–83, 185, 187, 188, 190, 191n2
'Other' 12, 48, 111, 161, 167, 221; populist 255; postcolonial 224; racialized 189; rights of the 165
Oxfam 4, 137, 149n4

patriarchy 13
Petit, P 135–6, 143
philanthropists 24, 25, 39n33, 46, 87
philanthropy 175–7, 251; discourse 63; entrepreneurial 10, 187; global 5, 10; organizations 14
Polanyi, K 130, 134, 138, 149n1; contradiction 134; double movement 16n4, 129, 130, 155
political economy 5, 15n3, 96, 130; analytic commentary 97–101; of corporate global imaginaries 211–40; of 'global monopoly-finance capitalism' 11; of human rights 15; Marxist 10; problem 46; structure 68; *see also* neoliberal (ism)
Ponte e Sousa, P 14, 139, 153–72
postcolonial sentimentalism 3; in the United States 109–11
post-structuralism 10, 11
poverty 4, 5, 6–7, 12, 46, 47, 51, 54, 94, 100, 132, 133, 157, 163, 176, 178, 179, 181, 184, 190; child 6; extreme 114; global 45, 100, 184; reduction 243; urban 194; world 100
power-knowledge 24, 132; *see also* knowledge/power
privatization 11, 46–7, 53, 68, 253; of nature 244
Program for International Students Assessment (PISA) 159, 160, 162, 166, 167

racializ (ed)(ation) 64, 68, 77, 78, 188; bodies 47; differential 66–7, 76; as not white 181, 186, 188–9, 191n7; settlers 48; violence 175; *see also* 'Other'

264 Index

rac (ial)(ist/m) 8, 10–11, 13, 23, 25, 26, 27, 28, 31, 33, 34, 36, 38, 55, 57, 63, 65, 66, 67, 72, 79n2, 113, 119, 121; Aryan 26; biological 36; colonial 176, 179, 190; discrimination 30; education, anti- 137; global citizenship, post- 176; justice 34, 37; logics 48; politics, post- 175–93; prejudice 33; supremacy 27; trope 109; *see also* borders; liberalism
Rancière, J 79n1
Razack, N 188
Razack, S 8, 51, 180, 185, 190
refugee (s) 7, 8, 158; policy 222; students 92
Regulation School *see* regulation: theory
regulation: mode of 195, 197–8; theory 195–6
rights 154–5, 164, 216, 218, 252; corporate 233; human 12, 14, 15, 16n5, 60n4, 94, 100, 107, 114, 139, 157, 163, 165, 190, 233, 243; juridico-legal 242; LGBTQ (+) 114, 215; non-existent 65, 71, 72, 76–8, 79n1; *see also* 'Other'; Universal Declaration of Human Rights
Ruiz-Chapman, T 3, 5, 45–62, 68, 79, 108, 195, 216–17
Rygiel, K 11, 58, 60n2

Said, E 10–11, 176
Sant, E and González Valencia, G 114–15
Schattle, H 5, 14, 16n7, 83
service (-)learning 96, 97, 110, 112; international 15, 83, 85, 98, 100, 109
sexual orientation 112
Simmons, T 105–26
Social Darwinism 26, 27
social entrepreneur (ship) 88, 140, 194–208; programmes at universities 12
social innovation 194, 196, 199, 202
social psychology 156
socialism 135, 199, 254, 255
socio-emotional: attitudes and competences 162, 166; development 166–7; skills 23, 24, 161; virtues 29
Soederberg, S 243, 252
Spencer, H 26–7
stateless persons 8, 59
subjectivity 64, 69, 117, 120, 143, 145, 162, 195; neoliberal 11–13, 131–6; at the US-Mexican border 45–62; *see also* Cartesian subject
sustainable development 45, 116, 139, 147, 148, 164, 165, 241, 244, 245, 250; and global citizenship 250–4; 2030 Agenda for 146, 159, 162, 169n3; World Business Council for (WBCSD) 251, 253, 254
Sustainable Development Goals (SDGs) 4, 10, 129, 130, 134, 138–9, 143, 145, 147, 160, 162, 163, 164, 166, 254
Swayam Krishi Sangham (SKS) 204–5

'Third Way' 199, 250, 255
'triple bottom line' 241, 251
Trump, D 7, 22–4, 37, 49, 50, 194, 222, 234, 255

United Kingdom (UK) 106, 107, 111–13, 119, 226, 227
United Nations (UN) 8, 11, 45, 89, 138, 139, 146, 153, 159, 241; *see also* UNCTAD; UNCTC; UNESCO
United Nations Centre on Transnational Corporations (UNCTC) 248, 249, 251, 252
United Nations Conference on Trade and Development (UNCTAD) 248, 249
United Nations Education, Scientific and Cultural Organization (UNESCO) 14, 107, 129, 137–48, 149n4, 149n7, 153–72
United States 10, 48, 58, 65–8, 75, 106, 107, 114, 119, 134, 135, 137, 227; corporations 9; ethnonationalist surges in 233; fiscal austerity in 199; imperialism 8, 83, 216; life expectancy 6; as metropole 48; neoliberal empire 22–42, 2007–8 Financial Crisis in 254; under President Roosevelt's New Deal 247; universities in 99; unlike Canada 186; and whiteness 48; *see also* borders; death zones; global citizenship education (GCE); postcolonial sentimentalism
Universal Declaration of Human Rights (UDHR) 6, 12, 163, 252
universities 3, 4, 5, 9, 12, 14, 29, 81–126, 198, 203, 241, 251; Canadian 83–104; in Colombia 113–19; *see also* neoliberal (ism)

value: exchange 243–4; use 243–4

Washington consensus 5; post- (PWC) 16n4, 130, 132, 134, 138
welfare state 54, 198; *see also* Keynesian (ism)

white subject 49, 69, 185, 190
whiteness 47, 48, 66–7, 68, 76–8, 178, 185–7, 189–90, 228; global citizenship as the spectacle and erasure of 179–83
Wittgenstein, L 10, 11
World Bank 46, 47, 133, 138, 153, 249, 252
World Trade Organization (WTO) 11, 250, 252
World Wildlife Fund 253
'world-mindedness' 10, 33, 34, 36; *see also* global mindedness

York University (YU) 4, 84, 92, 102n4, 102n8, 102n10
Young, M 200–2
Young Pioneers 34, 37
youth 130, 131, 133–4, 144, 146–8, 160, 162, 166, 167; American 28, 33, 34, 37; engagement 136–43; Engagement Initiative 129, 140; skills 159
Yunus, M 203

Zemach-Bersin, T 10, 13, 22–42, 83, 96